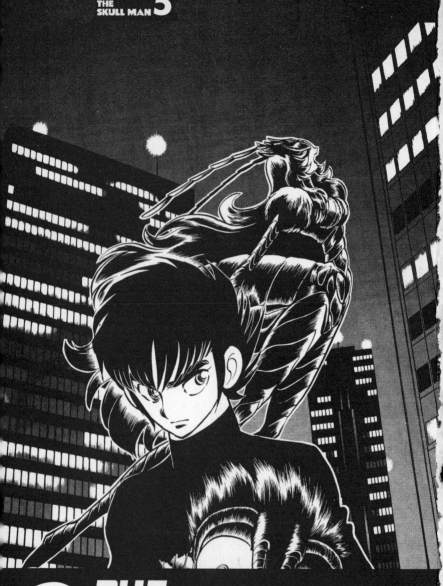

THE
SKULL MAN 5

THE
SKULL MAN

ALSO AVAILABLE FROM ☺TOKYOPOP®

MANGA

ACTION

ANGELIC LAYER*
CLAMP SCHOOL DETECTIVES* (April 2003)
DIGIMON (March 2003)
DUKLYON: CLAMP SCHOOL DEFENDERS* (September 2003)
GATEKEEPERS* (March 2003)
GTO*
HARLEM BEAT
INITIAL D*
ISLAND
JING: KING OF BANDITS* (June 2003)
JULINE
LUPIN III*
MONSTERS, INC.
PRIEST
RAVE*
REAL BOUT HIGH SCHOOL*
REBOUND* (April 2003)
SAMURAI DEEPER KYO* (June 2003)
SCRYED* (March 2003)
SHAOLIN SISTERS* (February 2003)
THE SKULL MAN*

FANTASY

CHRONICLES OF THE CURSED SWORD (July 2003)
DEMON DIARY (May 2003)
DRAGON HUNTER (June 2003)
DRAGON KNIGHTS*
KING OF HELL (June 2003)
PLANET LADDER*
RAGNAROK
REBIRTH (March 2003)
SHIRAHIME:TALES OF THE SNOW PRINCESS* (December 2003)
SORCERER HUNTERS
WISH*

CINE-MANGA™

AKIRA*
CARDCAPTORS
KIM POSSIBLE (March 2003)
LIZZIE McGUIRE (March 2003)
POWER RANGERS (May 2003)
SPY KIDS 2 (March 2003)

ANIME GUIDES

GUNDAM TECHNICAL MANUALS
COWBOY BEBOP
SAILOR MOON SCOUT GUIDES

ROMANCE

HAPPY MANIA* (April 2003)
I.N.V.U. (February 2003)
LOVE HINA*
KARE KANO*
KODOCHA*
MAN OF MANY FACES* (May 2003)
MARMALADE BOY*
MARS*
PARADISE KISS*
PEACH GIRL
UNDER A GLASS MOON (June 2003)

SCIENCE FICTION

CHOBITS*
CLOVER
COWBOY BEBOP*
COWBOY BEBOP: SHOOTING STAR* (June 2003)
G-GUNDAM*
GUNDAM WING
GUNDAM WING: ENDLESS WALTZ*
GUNDAM: THE LAST OUTPOST*
PARASYTE
REALITY CHECK (March 2003)

MAGICAL GIRLS

CARDCAPTOR SAKURA
CARDCAPTOR SAKURA: MASTER OF THE CLOW*
CORRECTOR YUI
MAGIC KNIGHT RAYEARTH* (August 2003)
MIRACLE GIRLS
SAILOR MOON
SAINT TAIL
TOKYO MEW MEW* (April 2003)

NOVELS

SAILOR MOON
SUSHI SQUAD (April 2003)

ART BOOKS

CARDCAPTOR SAKURA*
MAGIC KNIGHT RAYEARTH*

TOKYOPOP KIDS

STRAY SHEEP (September 2003)

THE SKULLMAN

Vol. 5

Written and Illustrated by
Kazuhiko Shimamoto

Created by
Shotaro Ishinomori

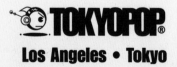
Los Angeles • Tokyo

English Adaptation - Fred Patten
Translator – Ray Yoshimoto
Retouch and Lettering – Max Porter
Cover Layout - Anna Kerbaum

Senior Editor – Luis Reyes
Production Manager – Mario M. Rodriguez
Art Director – Matt Alford
VP of Production – Ron Klamert
COO @ President - John Parker
Publisher – Stuart Levy

Email: editor@TOKYOPOP.com
Come visit us at www.TOKYOPOP.com

A 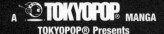 MANGA

TOKYOPOP® Presents
The Skull Man Vol. 5 by Kazuhiko Shimamoto Shotaro Ishinomori
TOKYOPOP® is a registered trademark of Mixx Entertainment, Inc.

ISBN: 1-931514-69-0
First TOKYOPOP® Printing: February 2003

10 9 8 7 6 5 4 3 2 1

Printed in the USA

The Story So Far...

Fearing that the genetic research being undertaken by his son and daughter-in-law posed a danger to humanity, Toratsuki Chisato murdered them and destroyed their lab, intending to raise their two children Ryusei and Maya in an environment free from the evils of that science. However Garo, a mutagenetic creature that became a childhood companion to the young Ryusei, rescued the frightened toddler from the attack. As a young man, Ryusei set out to avenge his parents' murder, an obsession that turned him into the kind of murderer he longed to destroy. Many innocent people died in the wake of his vengeance.

After years of searching, he catches up with the killer only to learn that it's his own grandfather. Toratsuki would rather he and his legacy perish than expose the world to the mysterious powers possessed by Ryusei and his sister, so he engineers a trap to kill all three of them. But the children lived and transcended to whatever state of being exists between mortality and divinity. Now, freed of crippling vengeance and guided by his pacifist sister, Ryusei Chisato, a.k.a. the Skull Man, has committed himself to protecting humanity. But his past may still haunt him.

Recently, armies of mutated humans have swarmed Tokyo in what appears to be a coordinated effort by a group called the Syndicate to subdue humankind. And the Skull Man may be the only one that stands in their way. However, his list of allies is growing - already his sister Maya and Garo man their secret compound high in the mountains; Maria, another supernatural being, has become disillusioned with the Syndicate and may join the Skull Man's ranks; and Detective Hioka, originally committed to bringing down the mass murderer the Skull Man, has begun to realize that there is a much bigger threat looming on the horizon. Among the Skull Man's adversaries: Rasputin, the leader of the Syndicate who may have links to Ryusei's parents; the Queen Wasp, the leader of a legion of female warriors currently experimenting with mind control serums; Mr. Goshiki, the boss of the Chameleon army; the Cobra Man, in charge of a brute squad of snake men; and Ayase Goro, the Scorpion... and Ryusei's former schoolmate.

The Skull Man

Vol. 5

Table of Contents

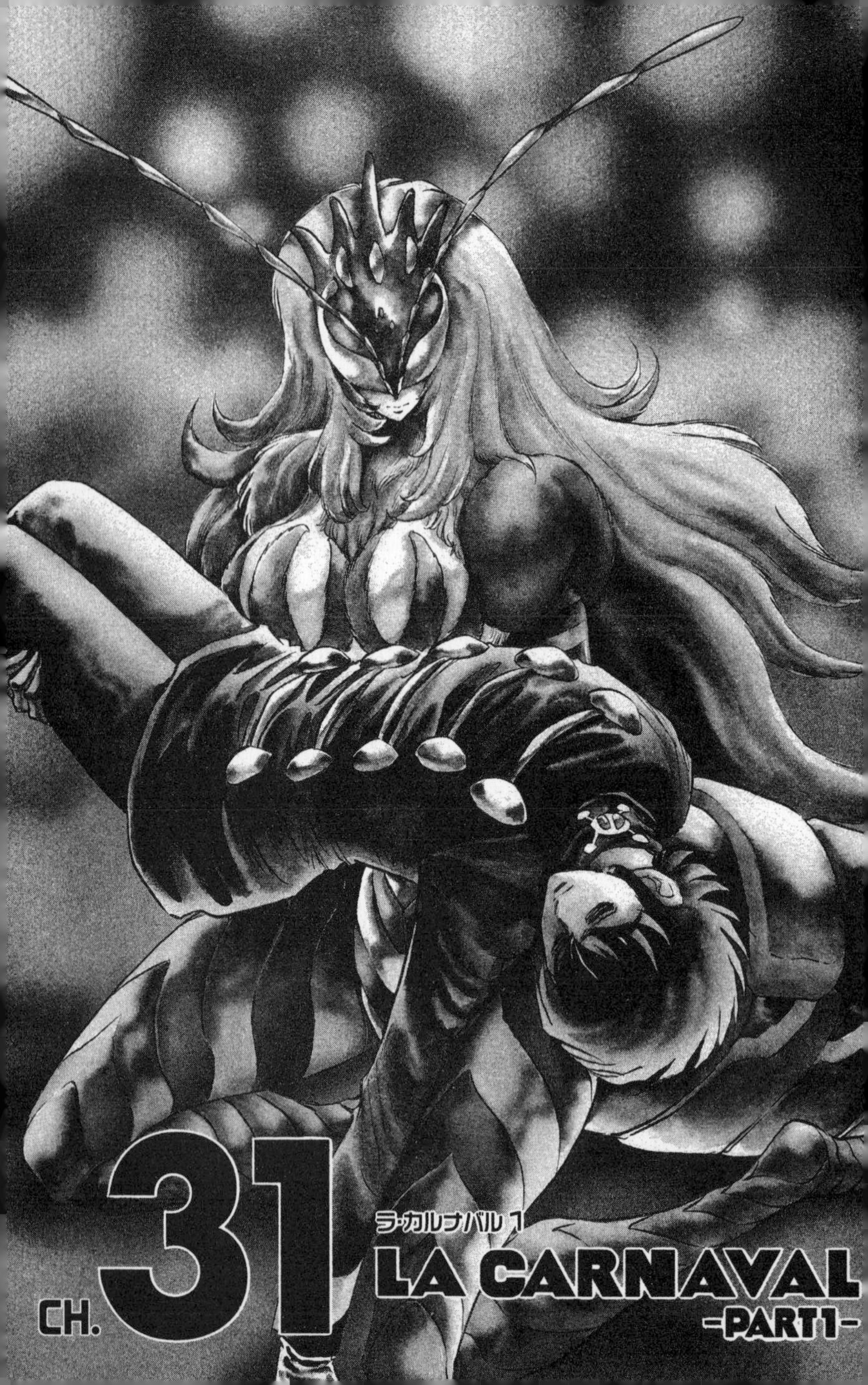
CH. 31
ラ·カルナバル 1
LA CARNAVAL
-PART 1-

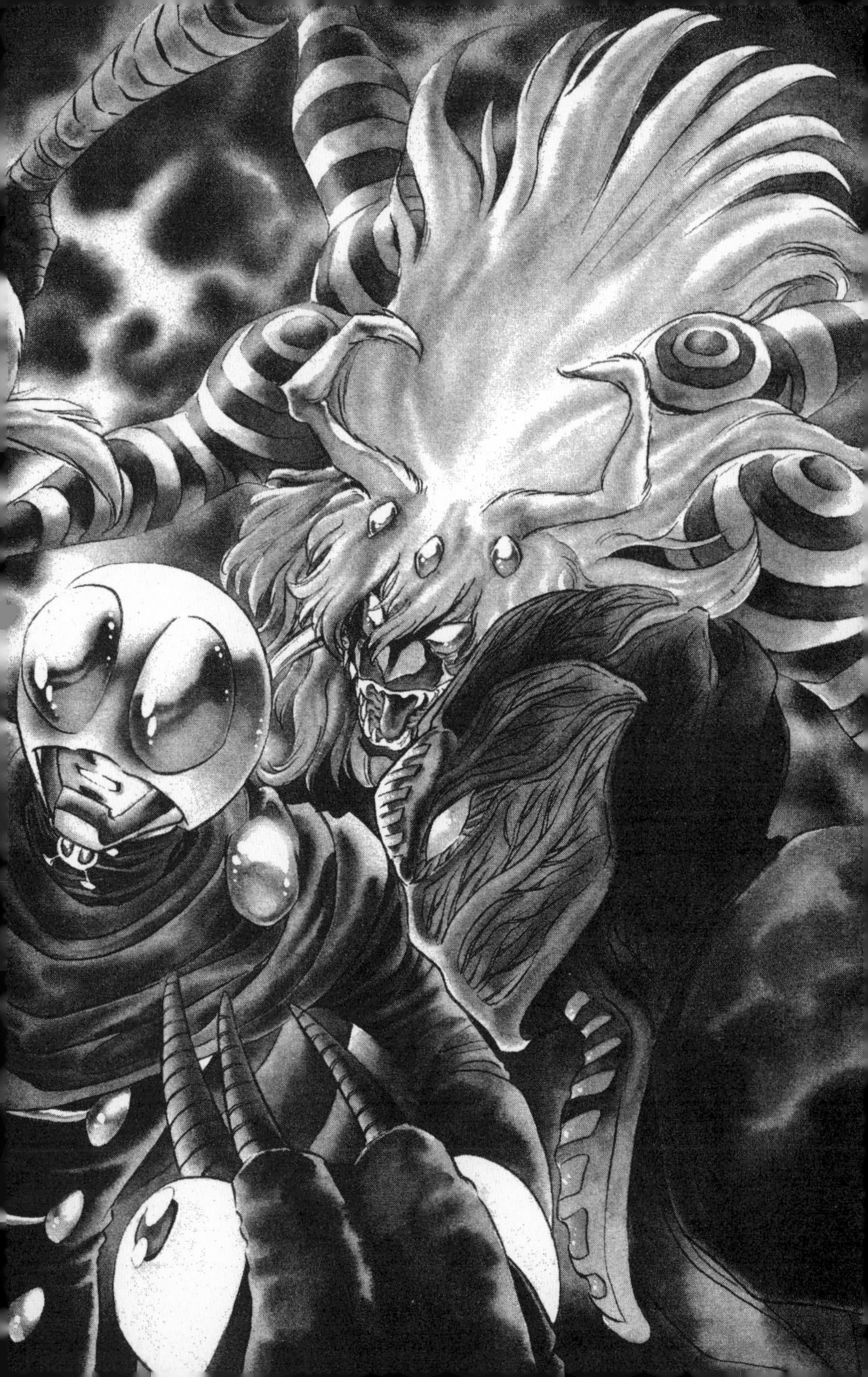

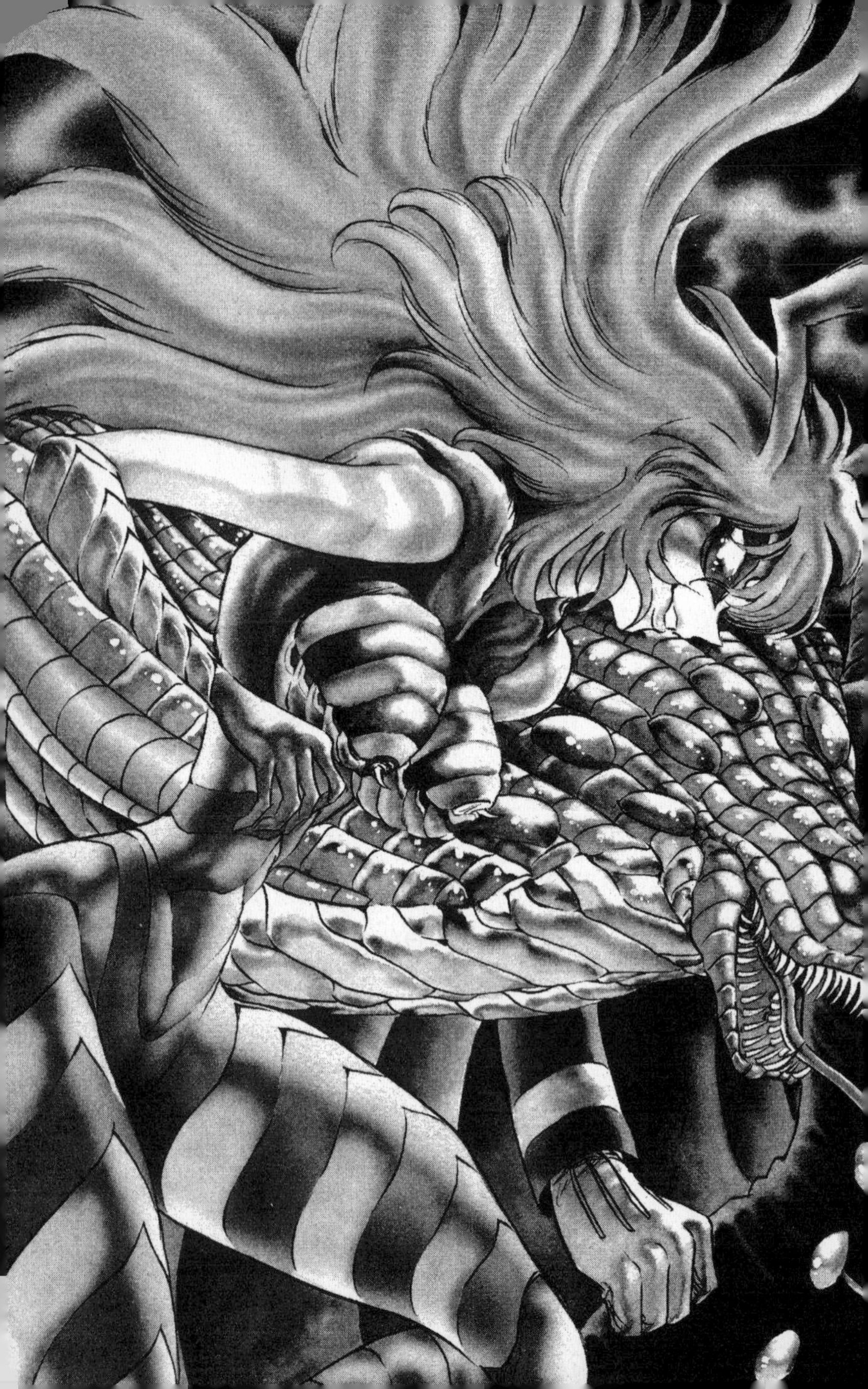

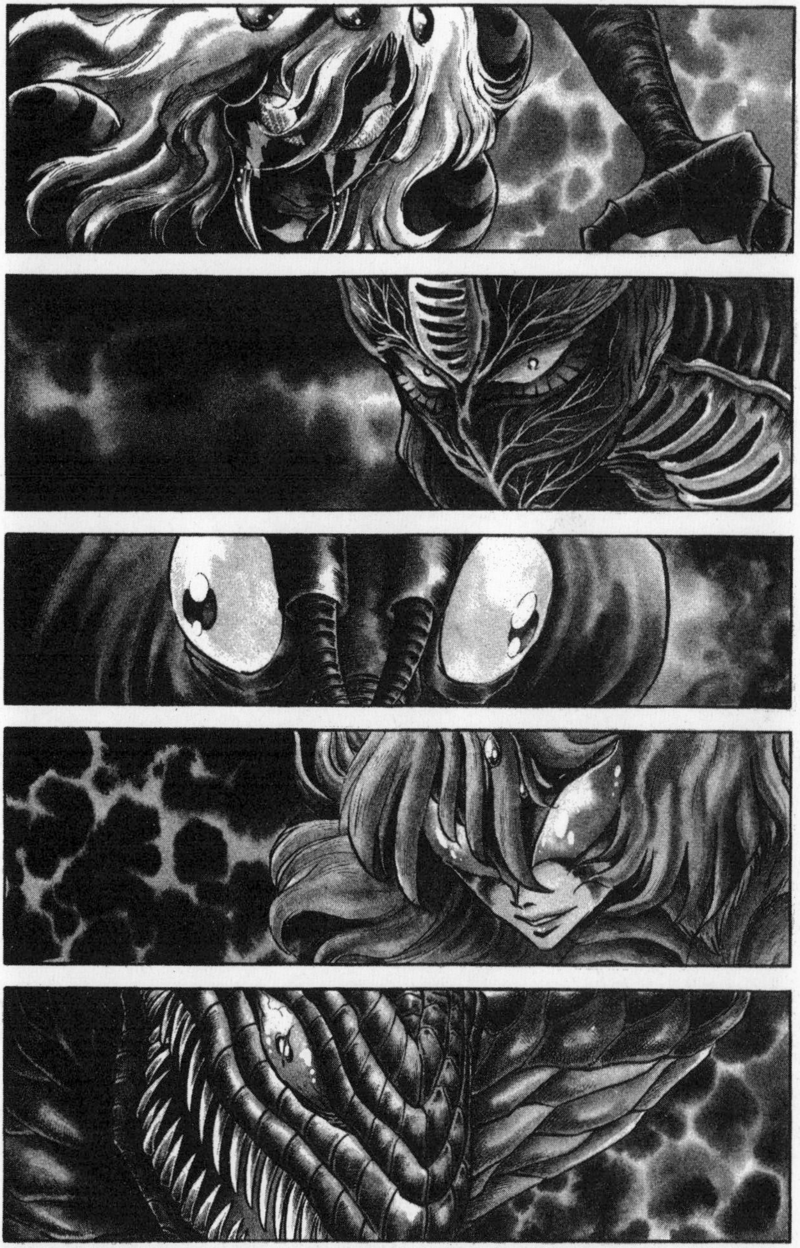

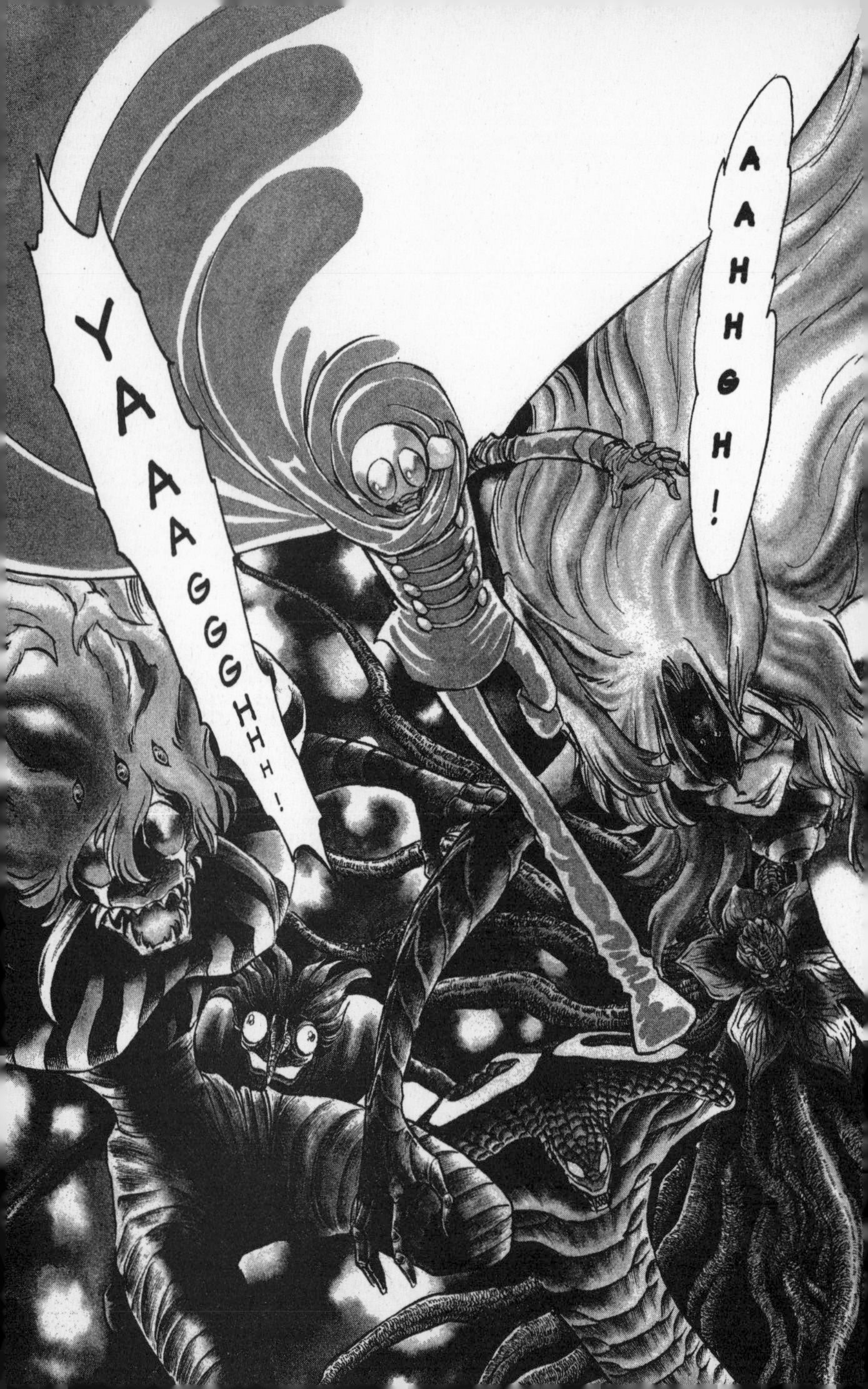
AAHHGH!
YAAAGGGHHH!

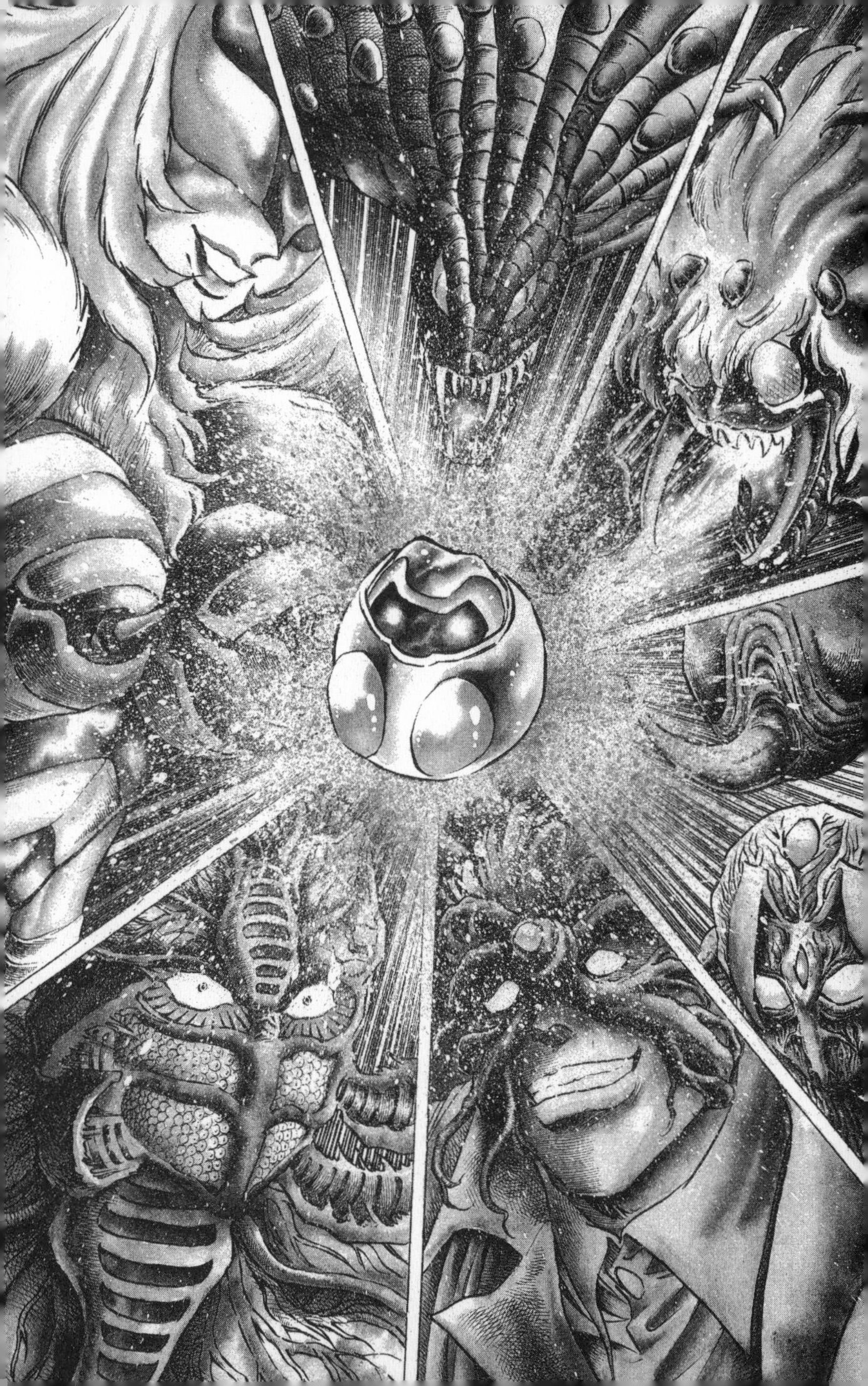

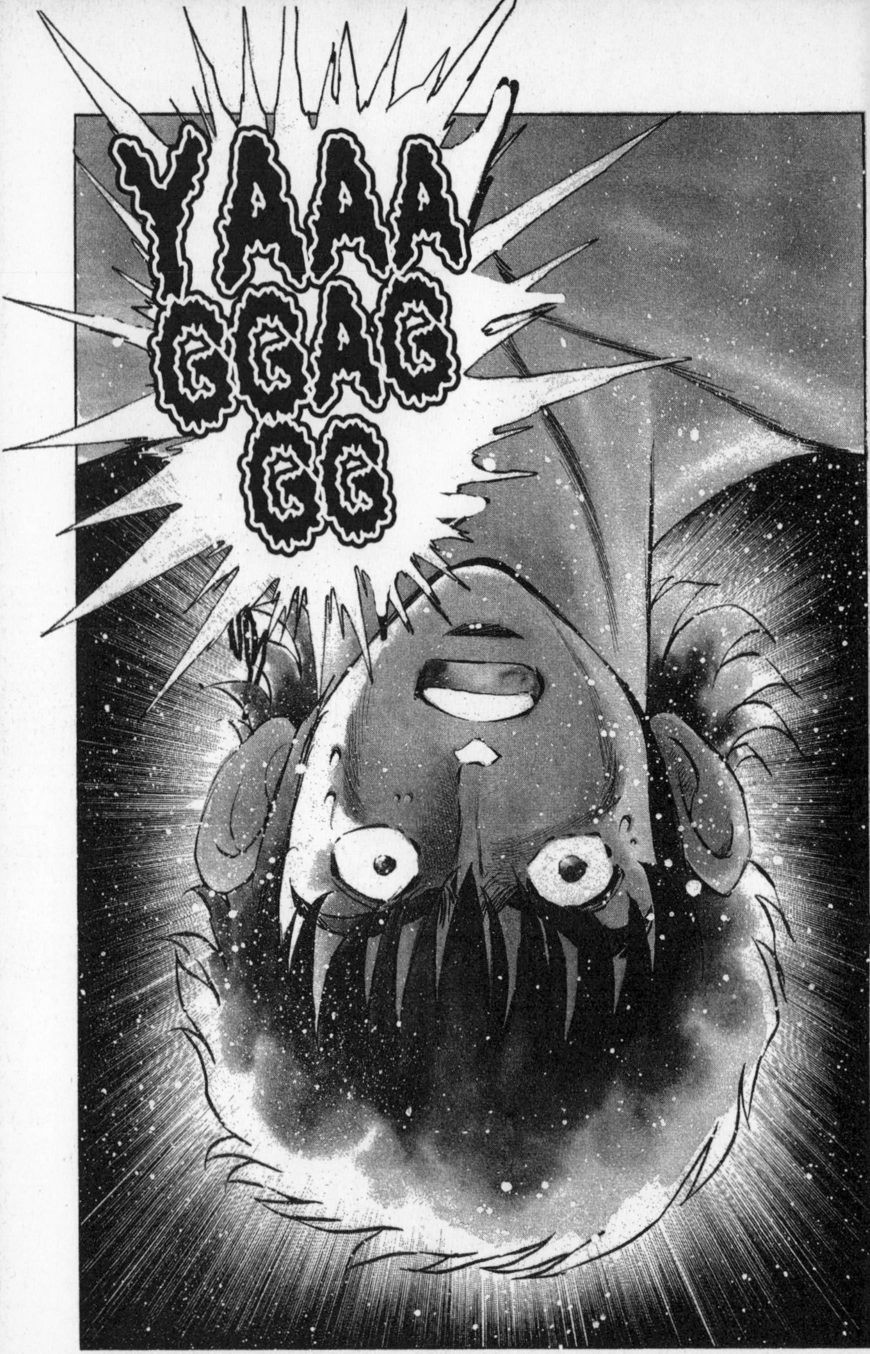
YAAA
GGAG
GG

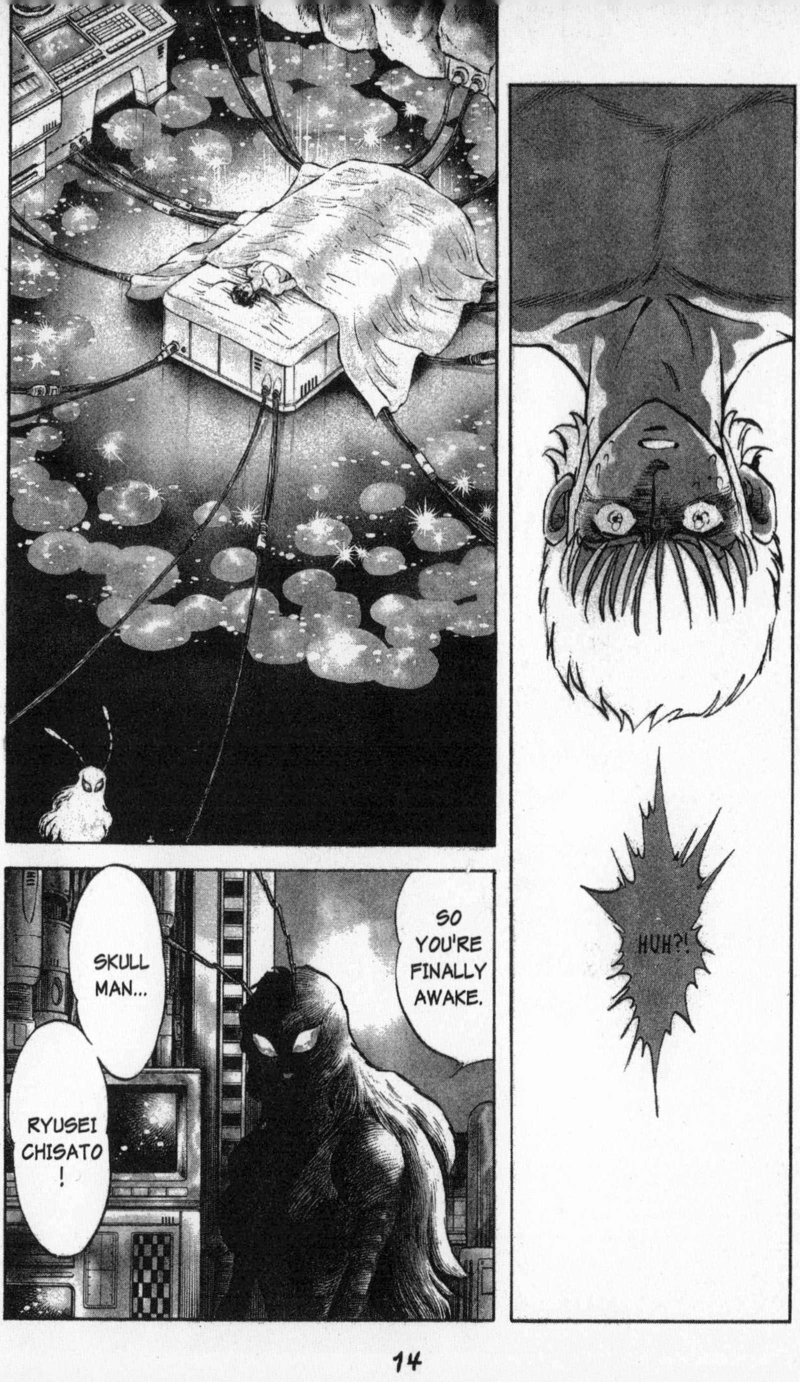
HUH?!
SO YOU'RE FINALLY AWAKE.
SKULL MAN...
RYUSEI CHISATO!

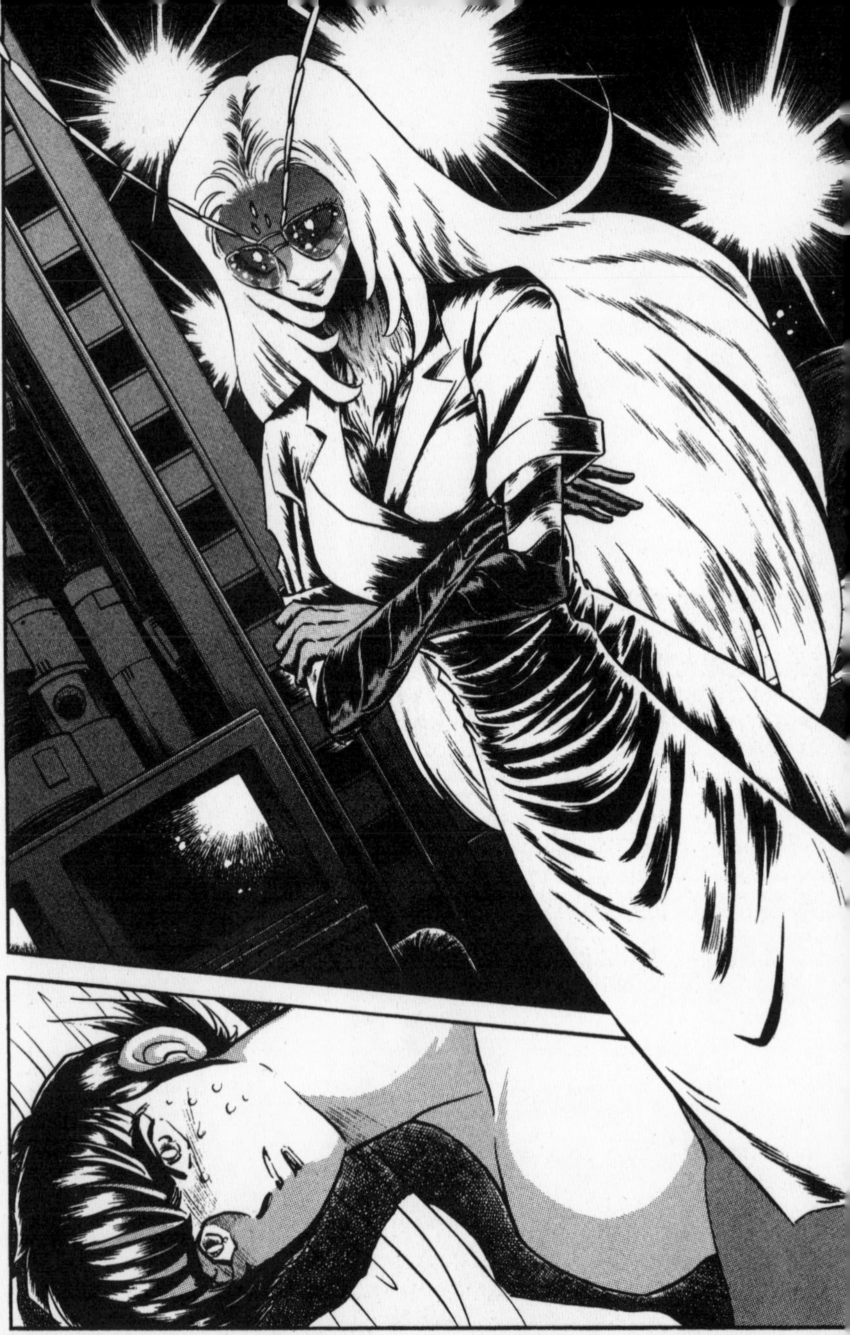

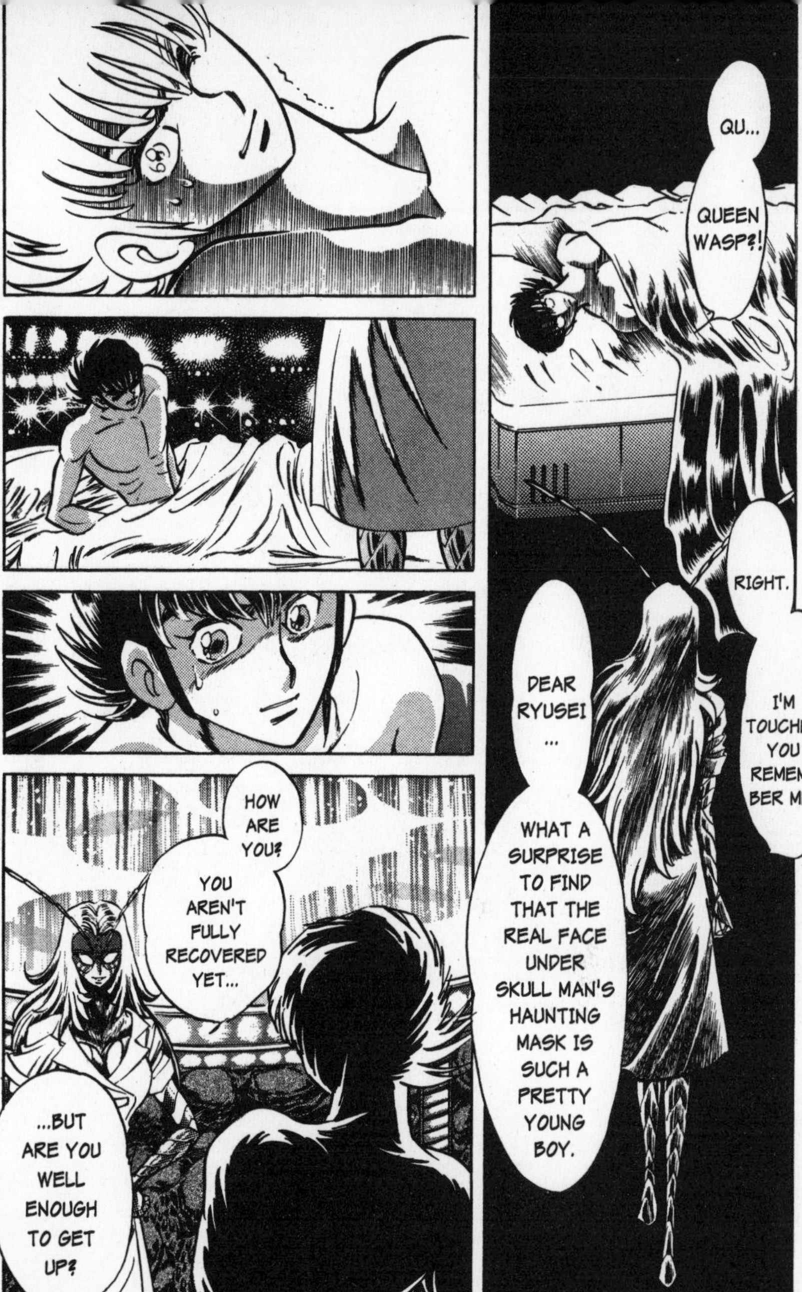
QU...
QUEEN WASP?!
RIGHT.
I'M TOUCHED YOU REMEMBER ME.
DEAR RYUSEI ...
WHAT A SURPRISE TO FIND THAT THE REAL FACE UNDER SKULL MAN'S HAUNTING MASK IS SUCH A PRETTY YOUNG BOY.
HOW ARE YOU?
YOU AREN'T FULLY RECOVERED YET...
...BUT ARE YOU WELL ENOUGH TO GET UP?

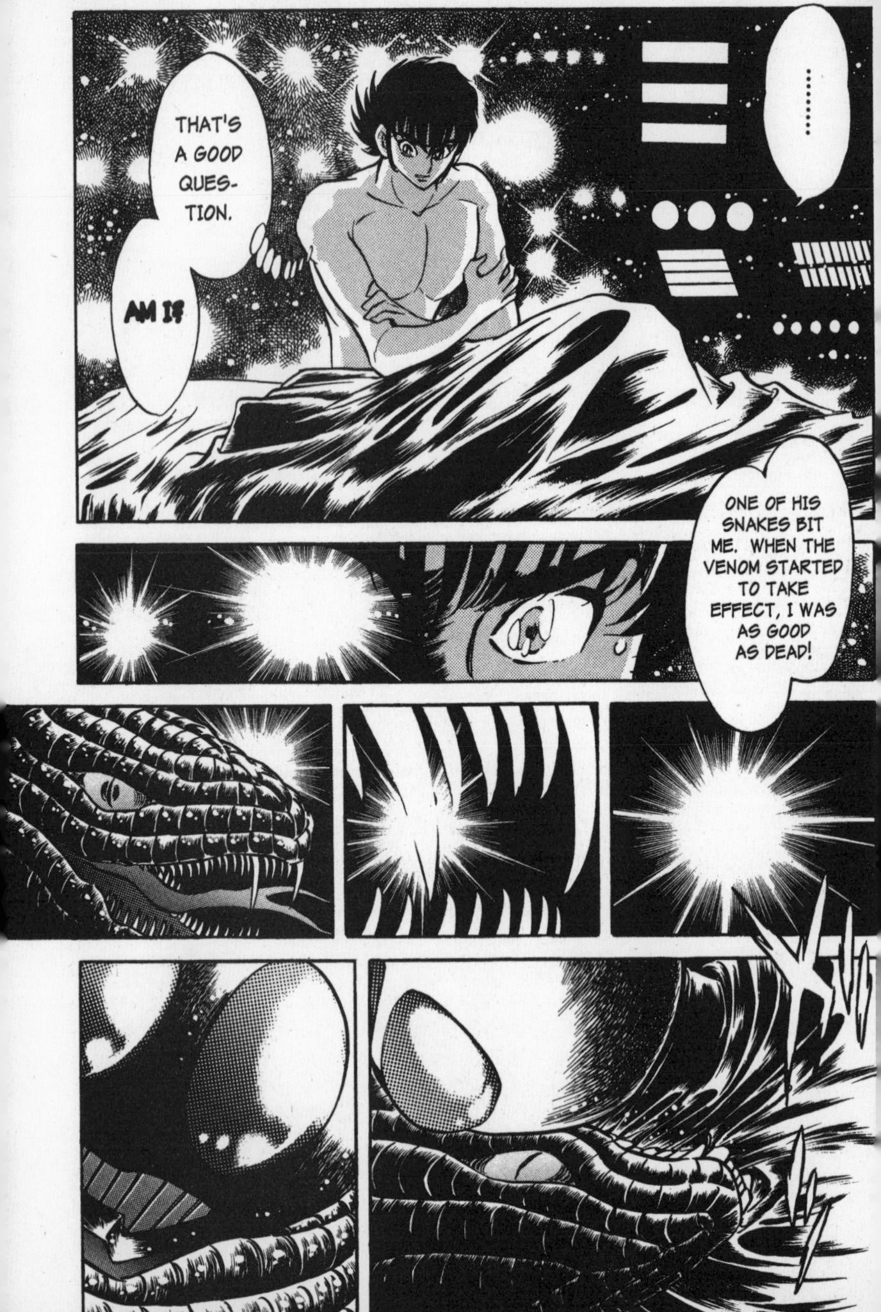
......
THAT'S A GOOD QUES-TION.
AM I?
ONE OF HIS SNAKES BIT ME. WHEN THE VENOM STARTED TO TAKE EFFECT, I WAS AS GOOD AS DEAD!

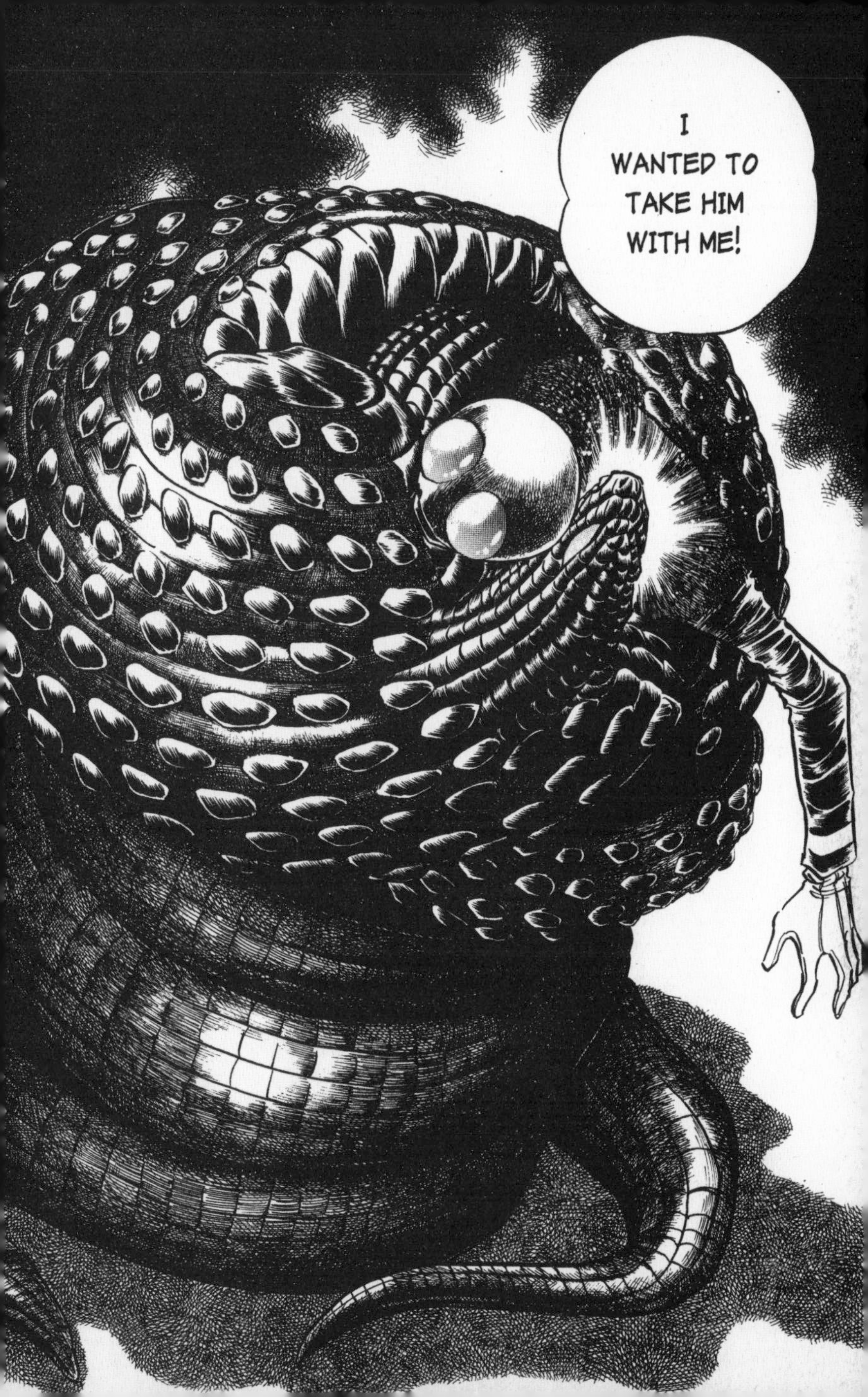
I WANTED TO TAKE HIM WITH ME!

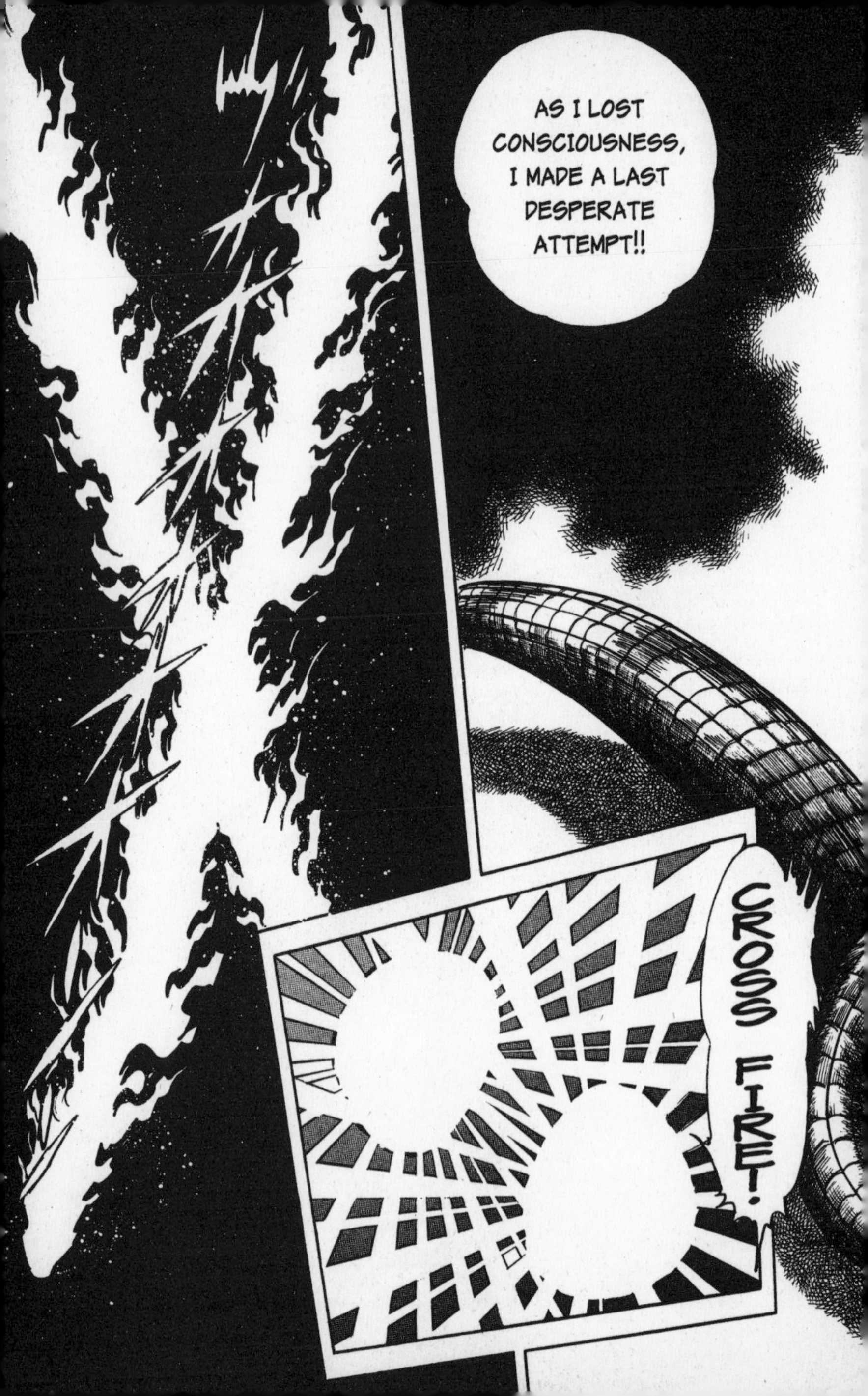
AS I LOST CONSCIOUSNESS, I MADE A LAST DESPERATE ATTEMPT!!
CROSS FIRE!

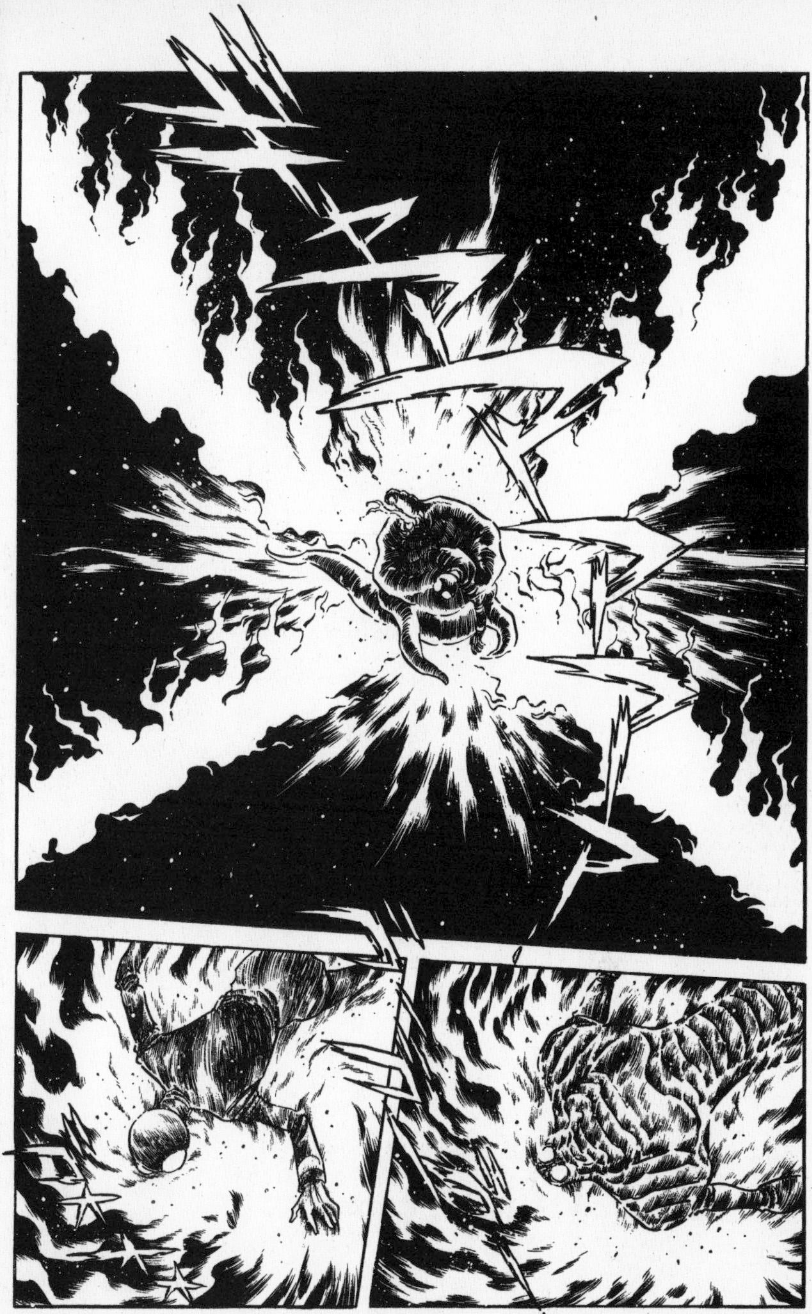

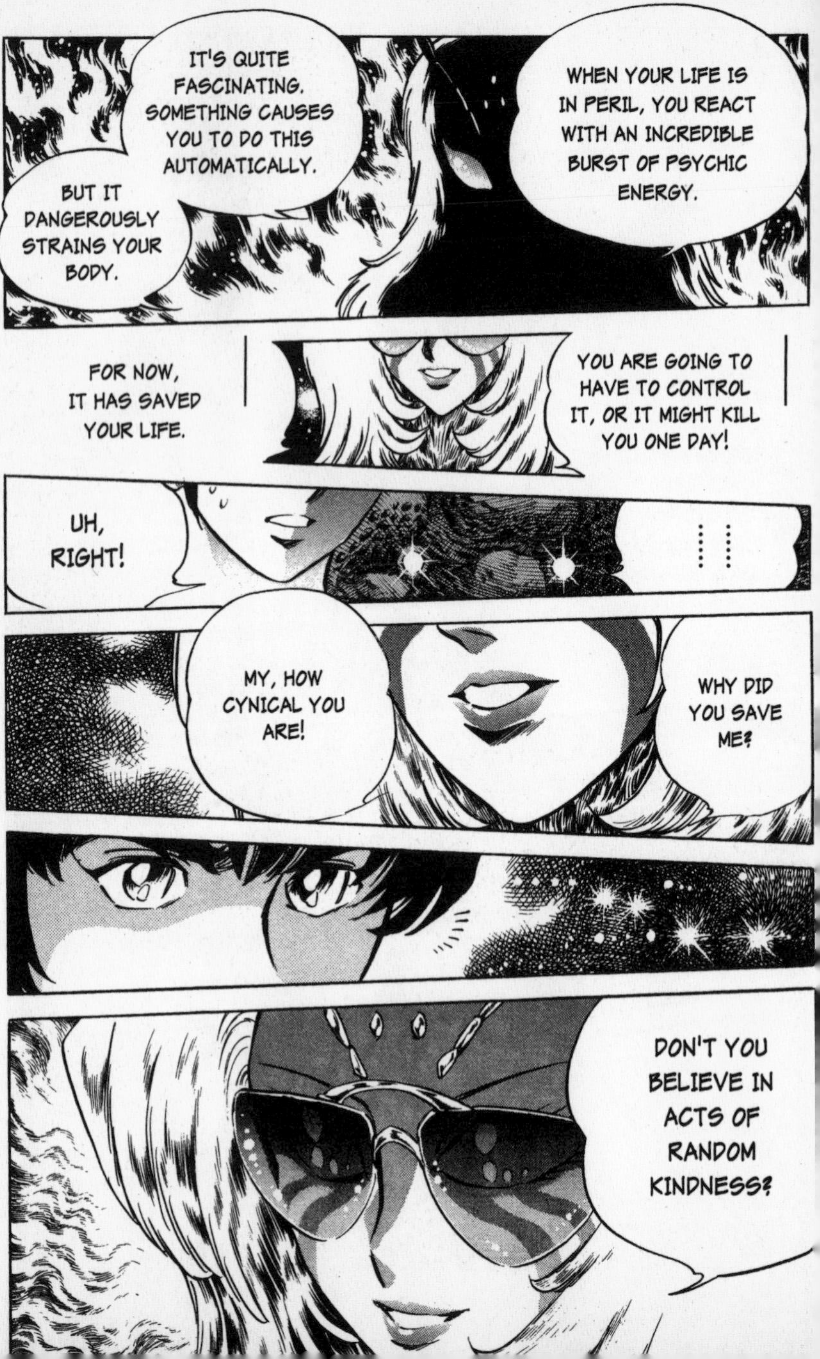
WHEN YOUR LIFE IS IN PERIL, YOU REACT WITH AN INCREDIBLE BURST OF PSYCHIC ENERGY.
IT'S QUITE FASCINATING. SOMETHING CAUSES YOU TO DO THIS AUTOMATICALLY.
BUT IT DANGEROUSLY STRAINS YOUR BODY.
YOU ARE GOING TO HAVE TO CONTROL IT, OR IT MIGHT KILL YOU ONE DAY!
FOR NOW, IT HAS SAVED YOUR LIFE.
......
UH, RIGHT!
WHY DID YOU SAVE ME?
MY, HOW CYNICAL YOU ARE!
DON'T YOU BELIEVE IN ACTS OF RANDOM KINDNESS?

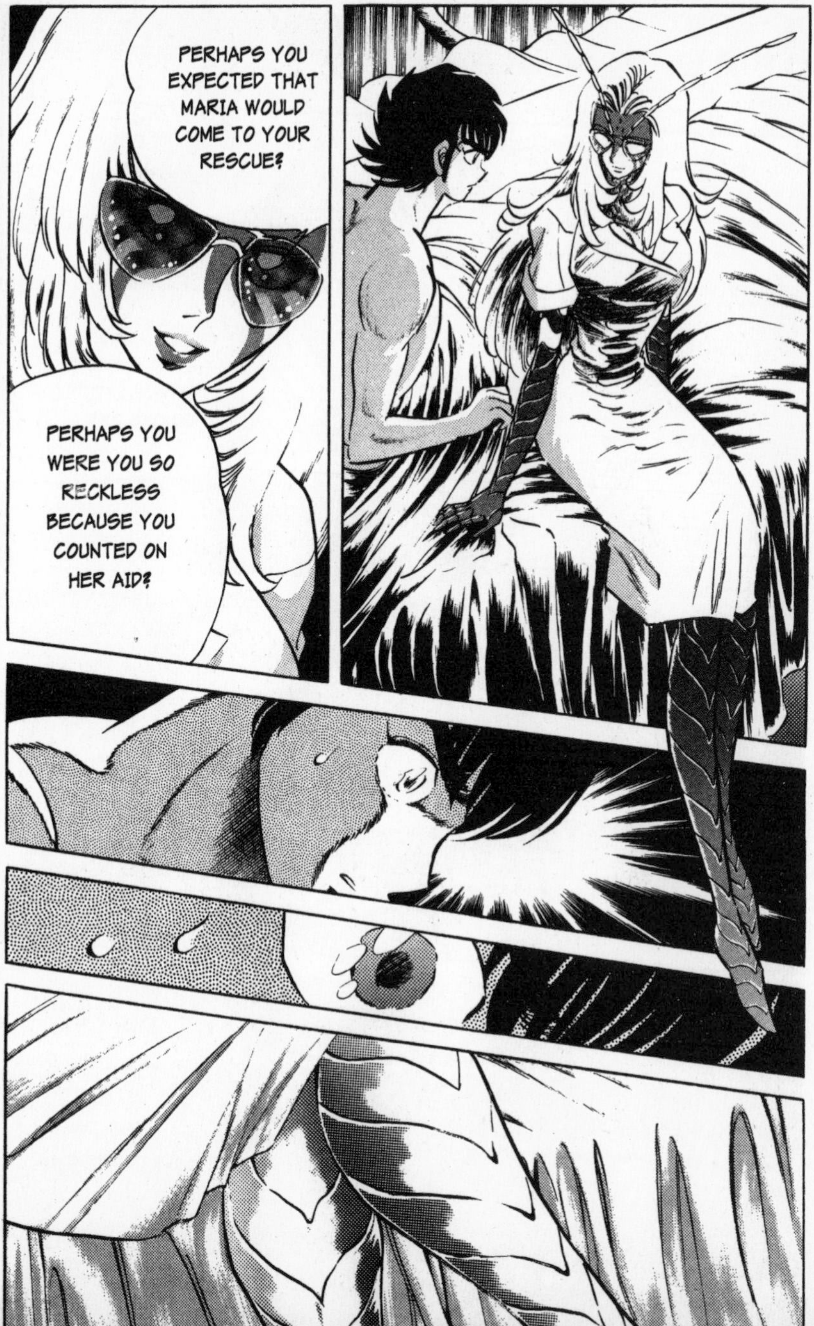
PERHAPS YOU EXPECTED THAT MARIA WOULD COME TO YOUR RESCUE?
PERHAPS YOU WERE YOU SO RECKLESS BECAUSE YOU COUNTED ON HER AID?

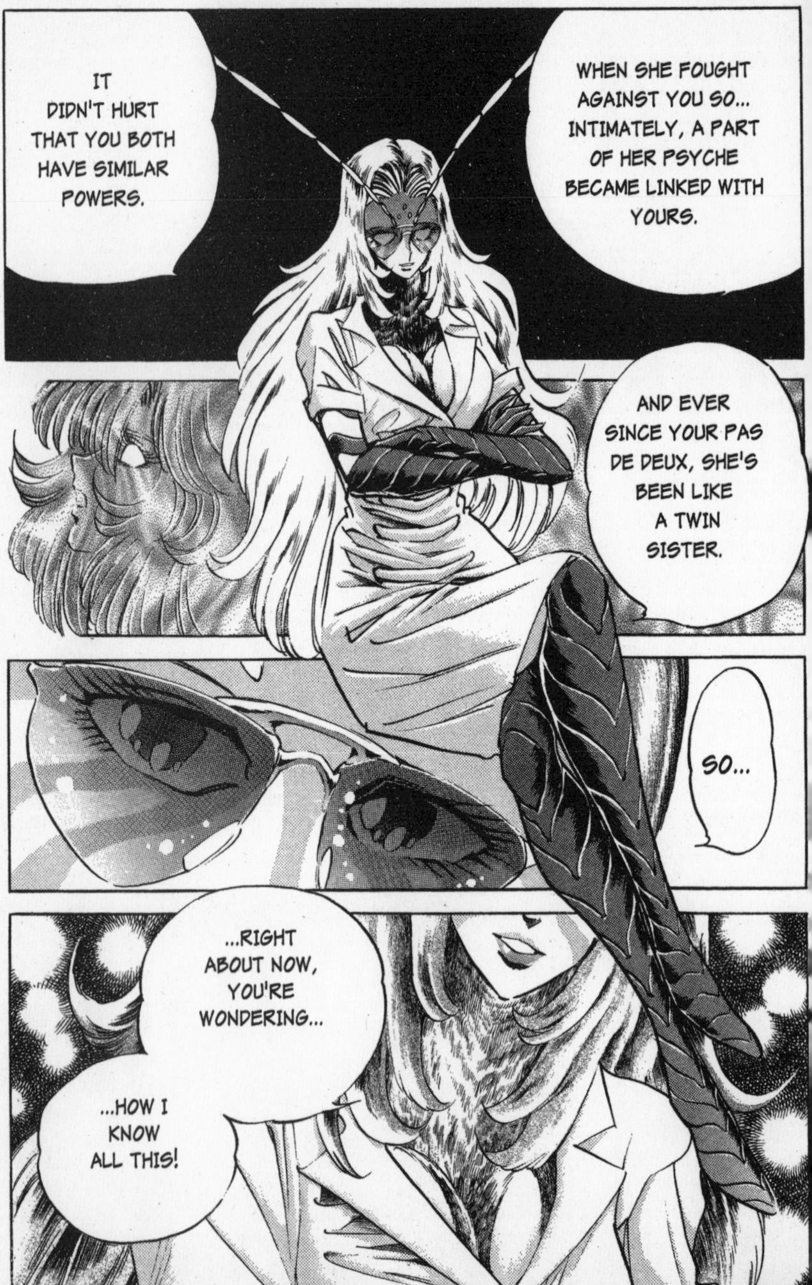
WHEN SHE FOUGHT AGAINST YOU SO... INTIMATELY, A PART OF HER PSYCHE BECAME LINKED WITH YOURS.
IT DIDN'T HURT THAT YOU BOTH HAVE SIMILAR POWERS.
AND EVER SINCE YOUR PAS DE DEUX, SHE'S BEEN LIKE A TWIN SISTER.
SO...
...RIGHT ABOUT NOW, YOU'RE WONDERING...
...HOW I KNOW ALL THIS!

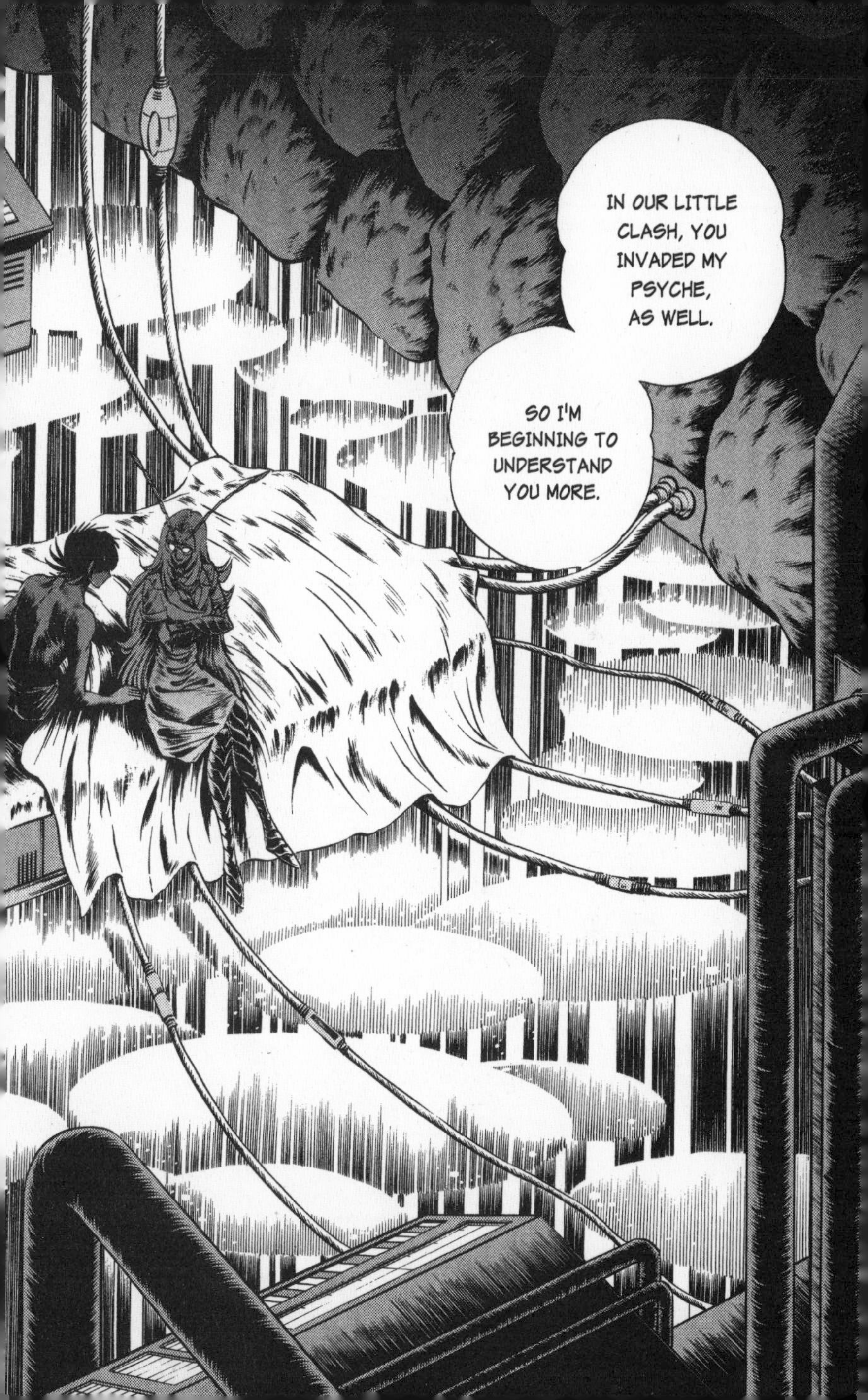
IN OUR LITTLE CLASH, YOU INVADED MY PSYCHE, AS WELL.
SO I'M BEGINNING TO UNDERSTAND YOU MORE.

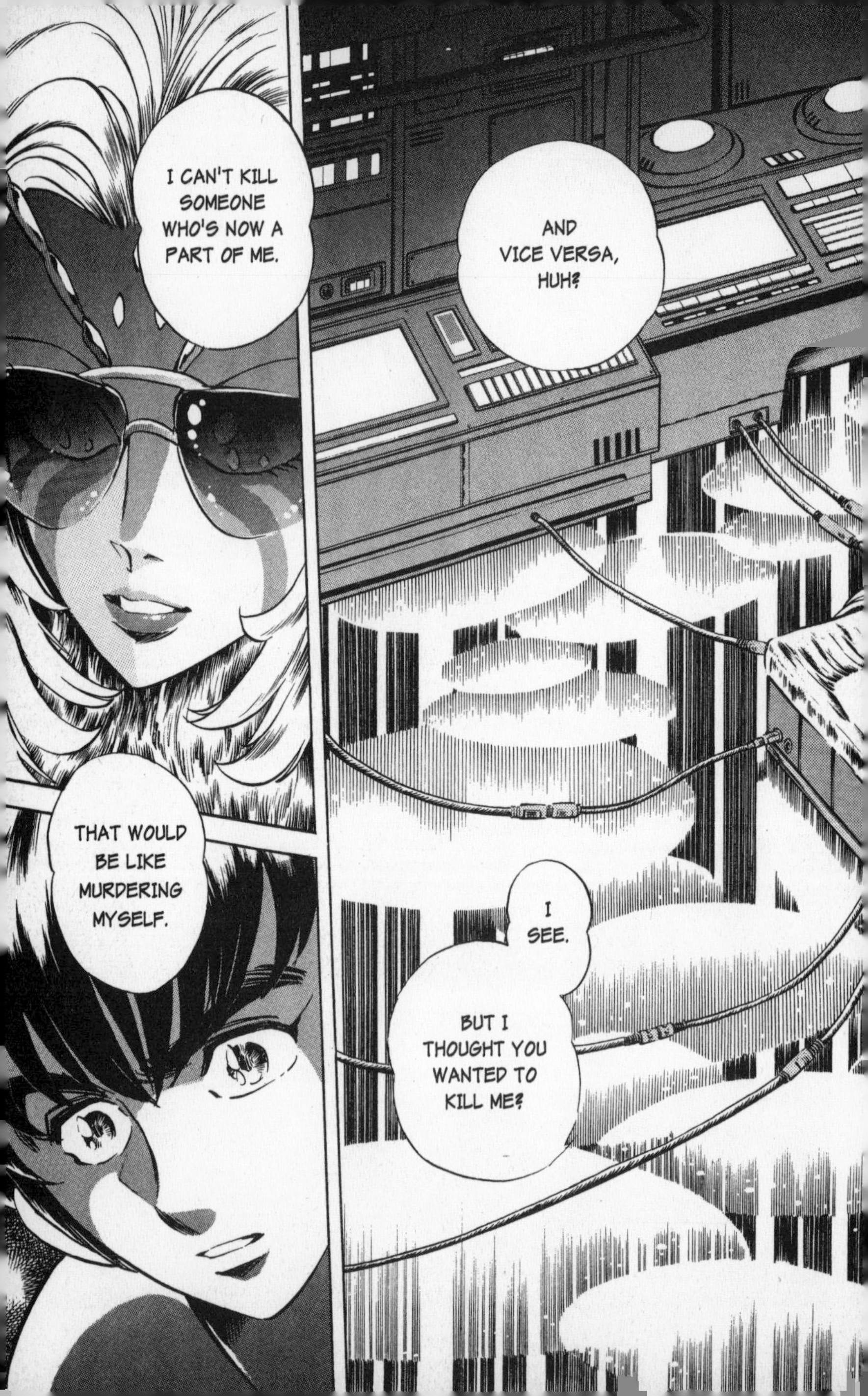
I CAN'T KILL SOMEONE WHO'S NOW A PART OF ME.
AND VICE VERSA, HUH?
THAT WOULD BE LIKE MURDERING MYSELF.
I SEE.
BUT I THOUGHT YOU WANTED TO KILL ME?

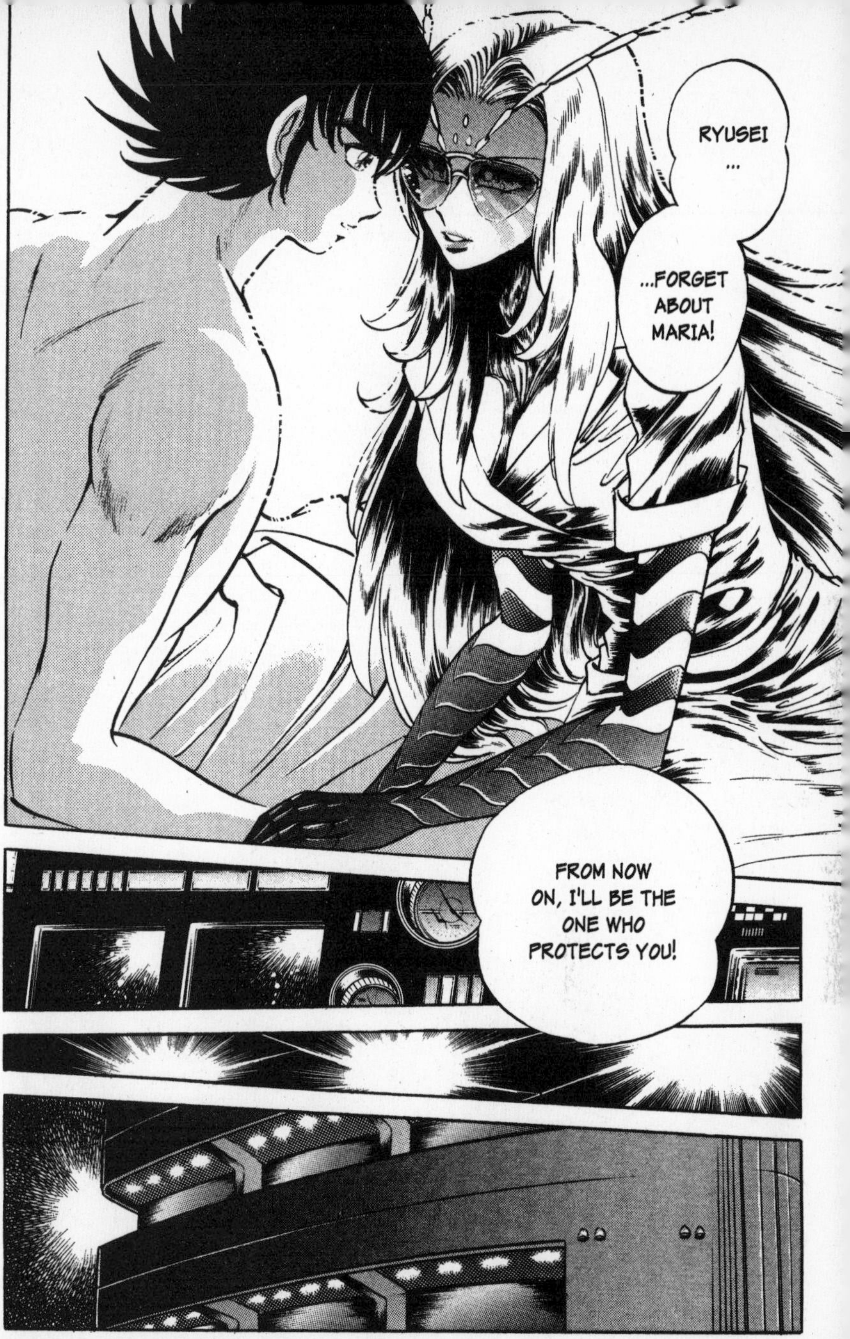
RYUSEI ...
...FORGET ABOUT MARIA!
FROM NOW ON, I'LL BE THE ONE WHO PROTECTS YOU!

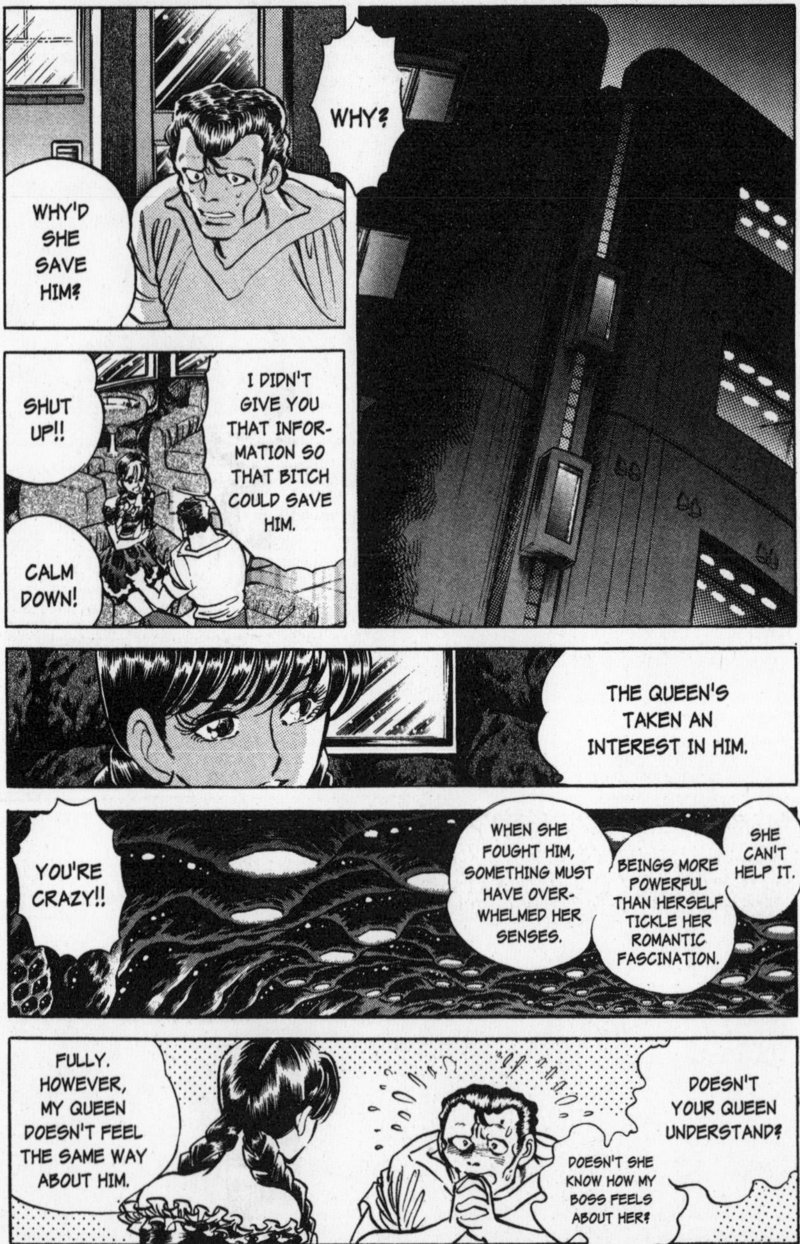
WHY?
WHY'D SHE SAVE HIM?
I DIDN'T GIVE YOU THAT INFORMATION SO THAT BITCH COULD SAVE HIM.
SHUT UP!!
CALM DOWN!
THE QUEEN'S TAKEN AN INTEREST IN HIM.
SHE CAN'T HELP IT.
BEINGS MORE POWERFUL THAN HERSELF TICKLE HER ROMANTIC FASCINATION.
WHEN SHE FOUGHT HIM, SOMETHING MUST HAVE OVERWHELMED HER SENSES.
YOU'RE CRAZY!!
DOESN'T YOUR QUEEN UNDERSTAND?
DOESN'T SHE KNOW HOW MY BOSS FEELS ABOUT HER?
FULLY. HOWEVER, MY QUEEN DOESN'T FEEL THE SAME WAY ABOUT HIM.

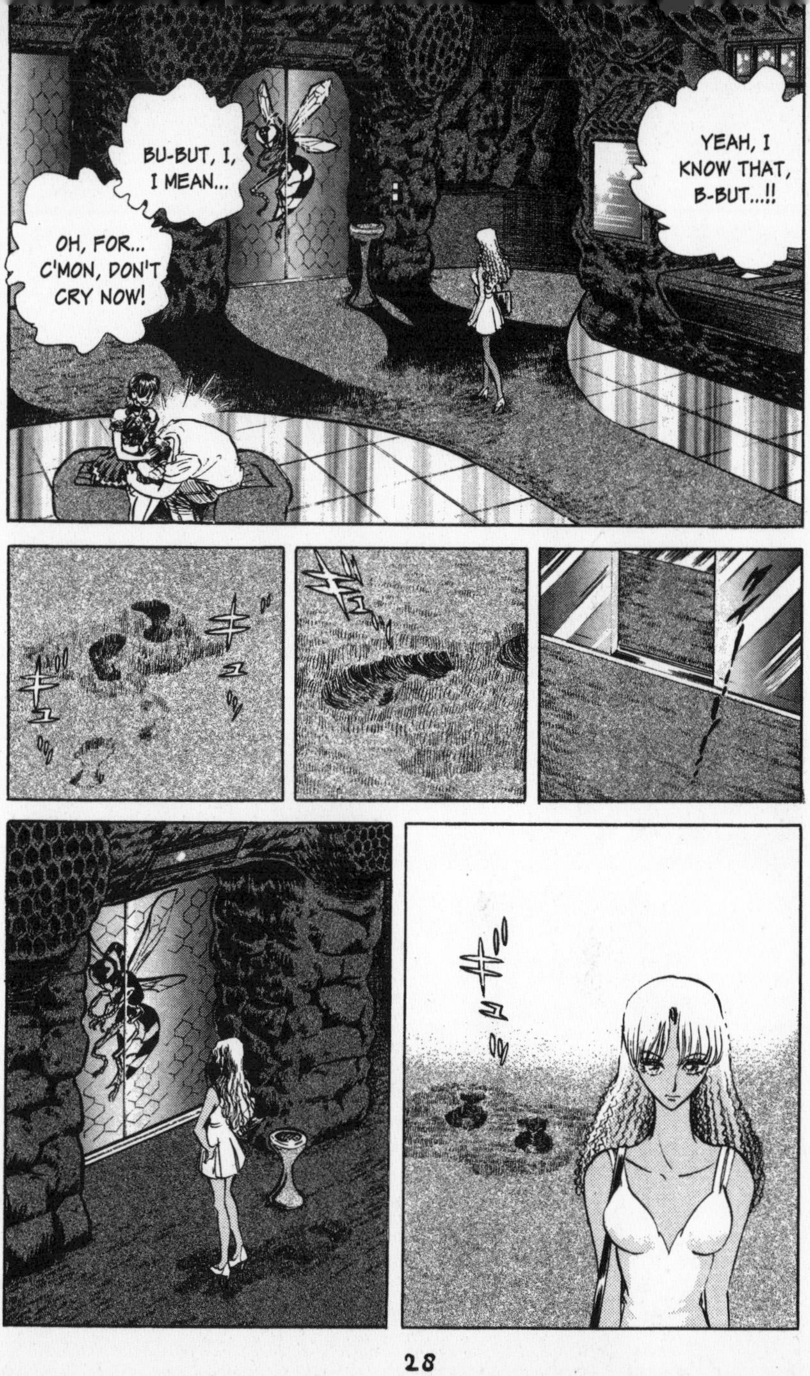
YEAH, I KNOW THAT, B-BUT...!!
BU-BUT, I, I MEAN...
OH, FOR... C'MON, DON'T CRY NOW!

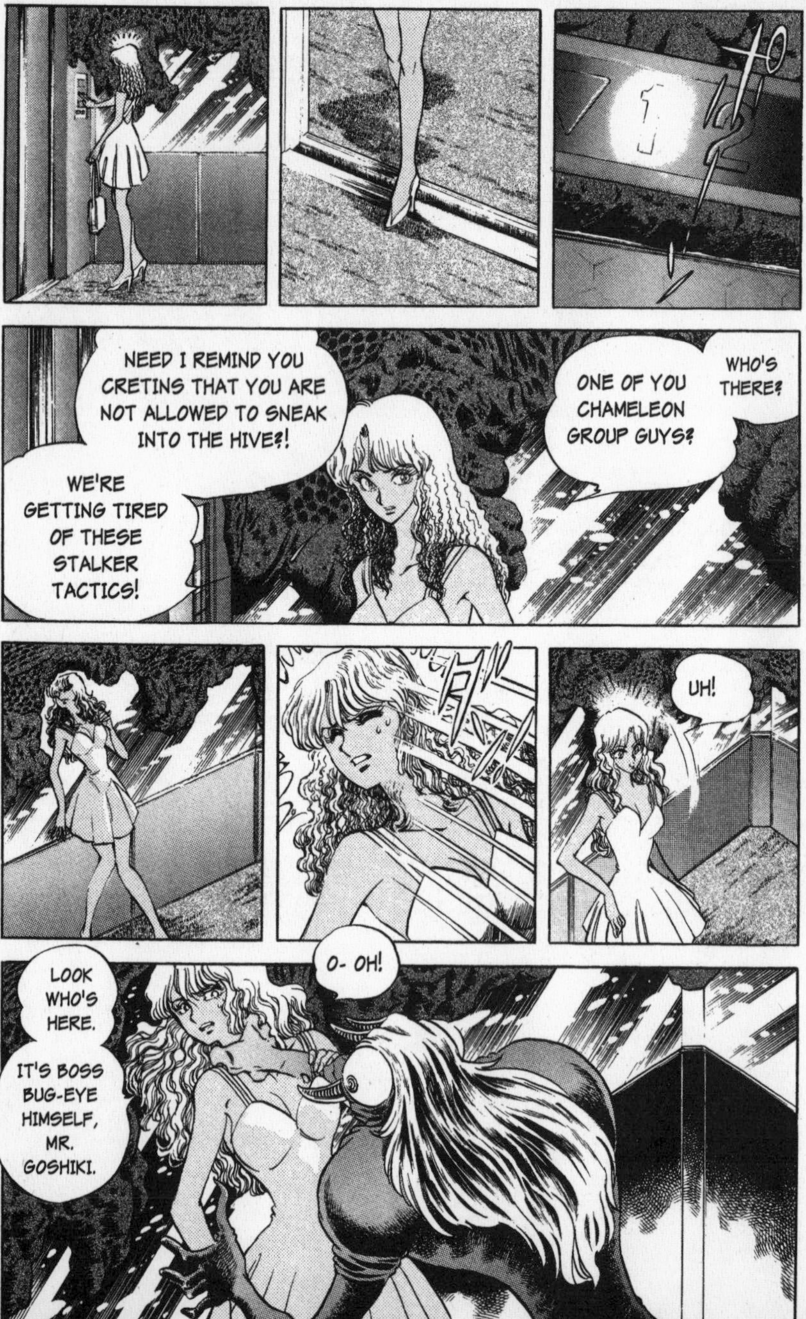
WHO'S THERE?
ONE OF YOU CHAMELEON GROUP GUYS?
NEED I REMIND YOU CRETINS THAT YOU ARE NOT ALLOWED TO SNEAK INTO THE HIVE?!
WE'RE GETTING TIRED OF THESE STALKER TACTICS!
UH!
O- OH!
LOOK WHO'S HERE.
IT'S BOSS BUG-EYE HIMSELF, MR. GOSHIKI.

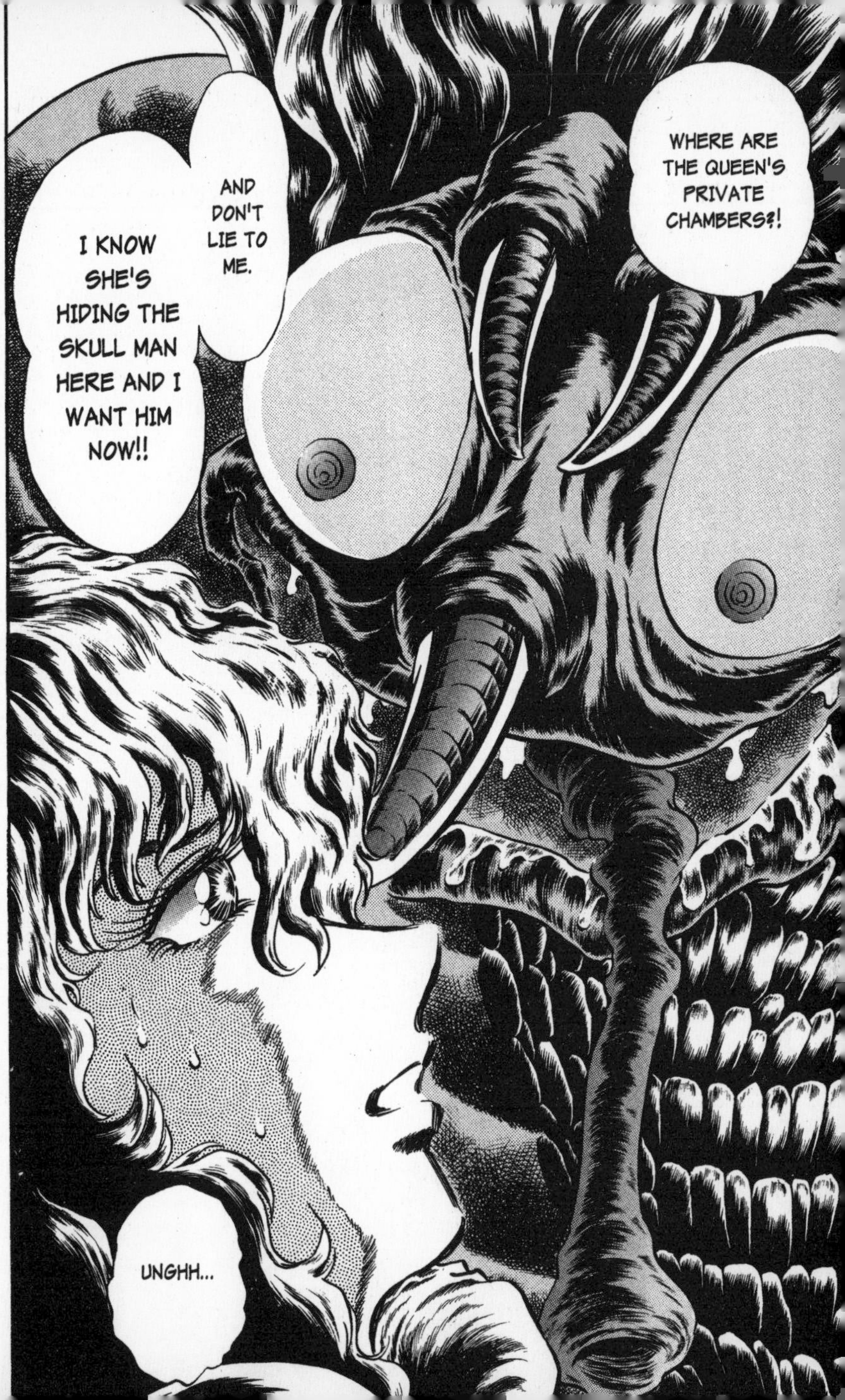
WHERE ARE THE QUEEN'S PRIVATE CHAMBERS?!
AND DON'T LIE TO ME.
I KNOW SHE'S HIDING THE SKULL MAN HERE AND I WANT HIM NOW!!
UNGHH...

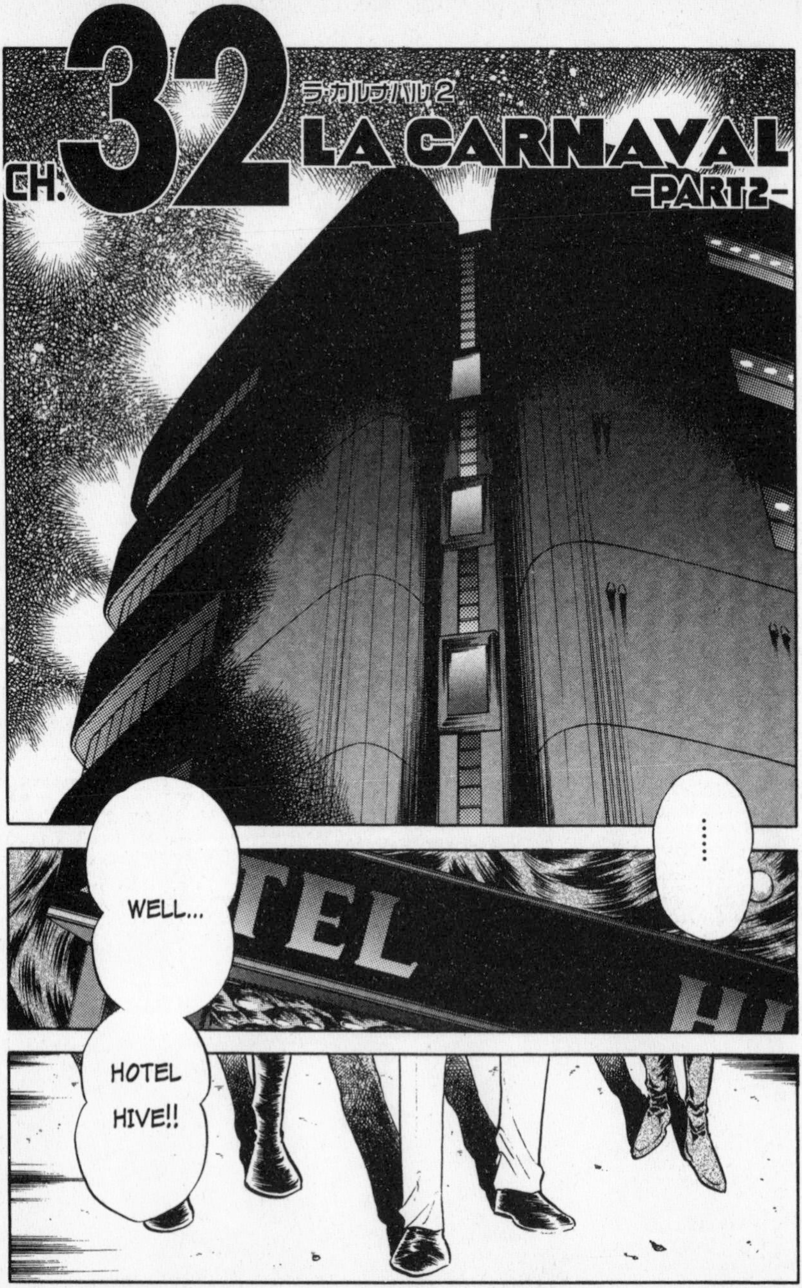
CH. 32
ラ・カルナバル 2
LA CARNAVAL
-PART 2-
......
WELL...
HOTEL HIVE!!

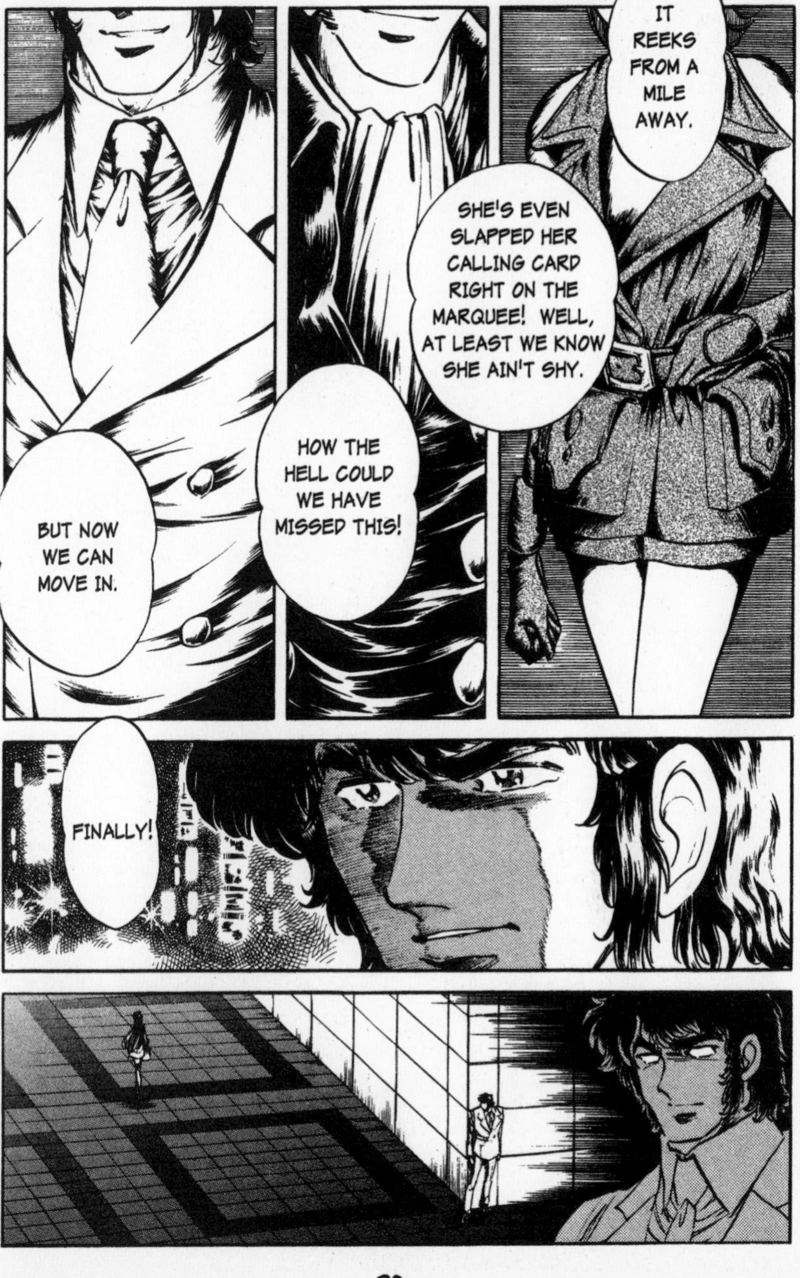
IT REEKS FROM A MILE AWAY.
SHE'S EVEN SLAPPED HER CALLING CARD RIGHT ON THE MARQUEE! WELL, AT LEAST WE KNOW SHE AIN'T SHY.
HOW THE HELL COULD WE HAVE MISSED THIS!
BUT NOW WE CAN MOVE IN.
FINALLY!

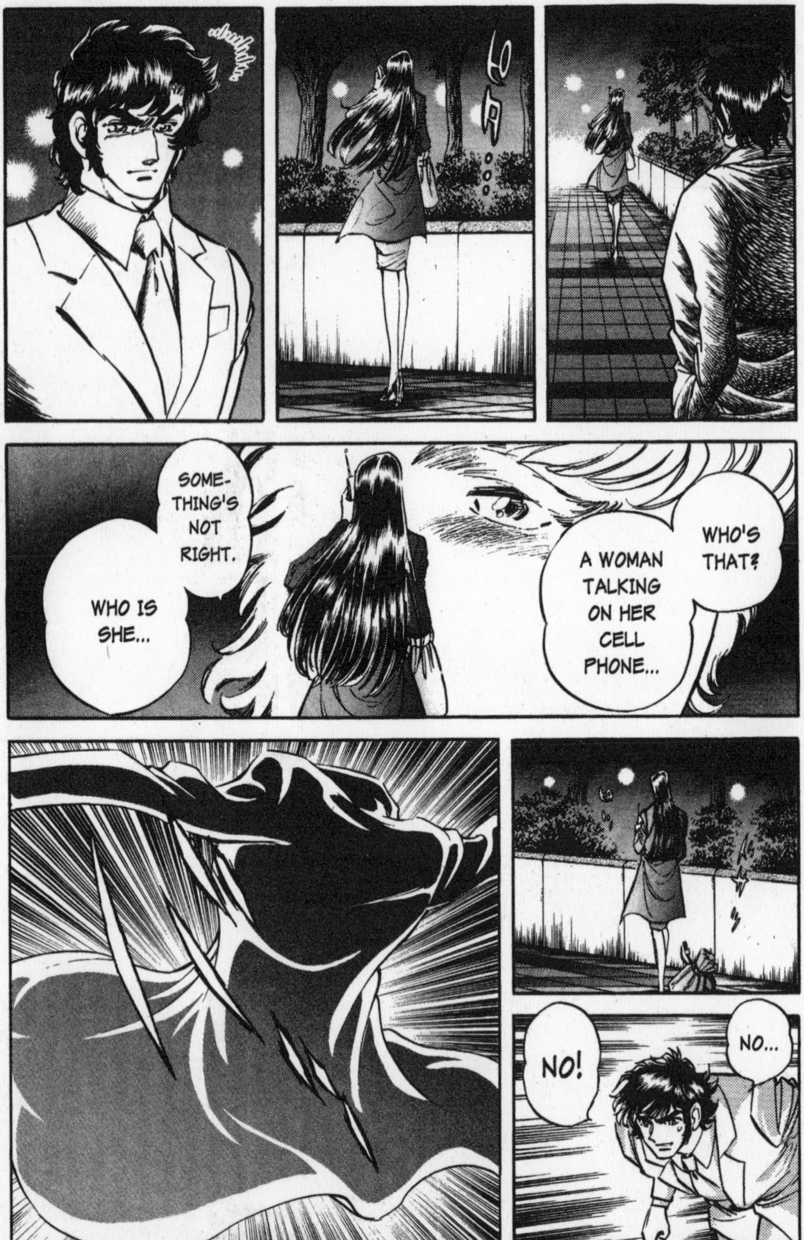
WHO'S THAT?
A WOMAN TALKING ON HER CELL PHONE...
SOME-THING'S NOT RIGHT.
WHO IS SHE...
NO...
NO!

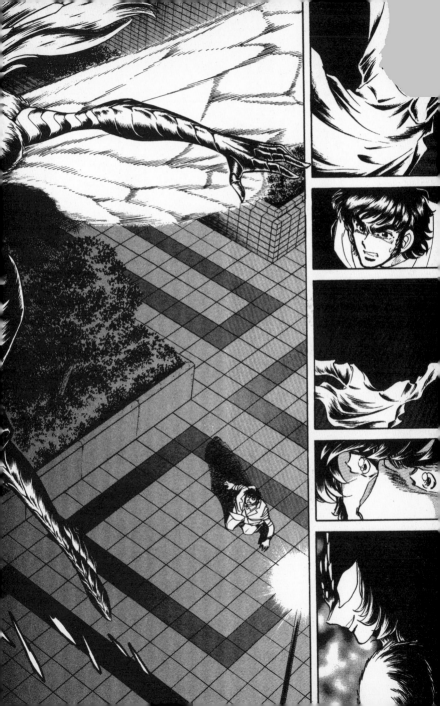

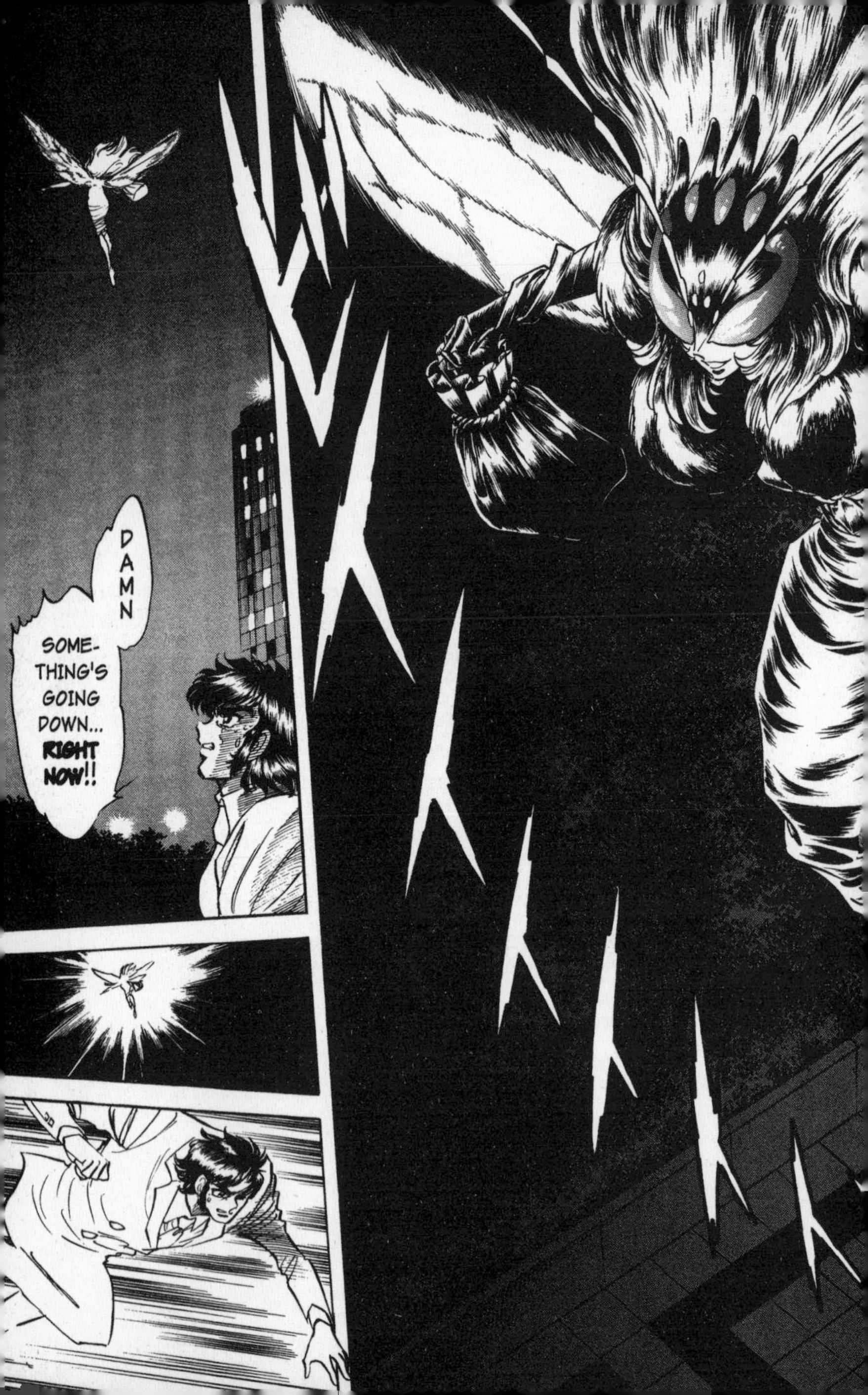
DAMN
SOME-THING'S GOING DOWN... **RIGHT NOW!!**

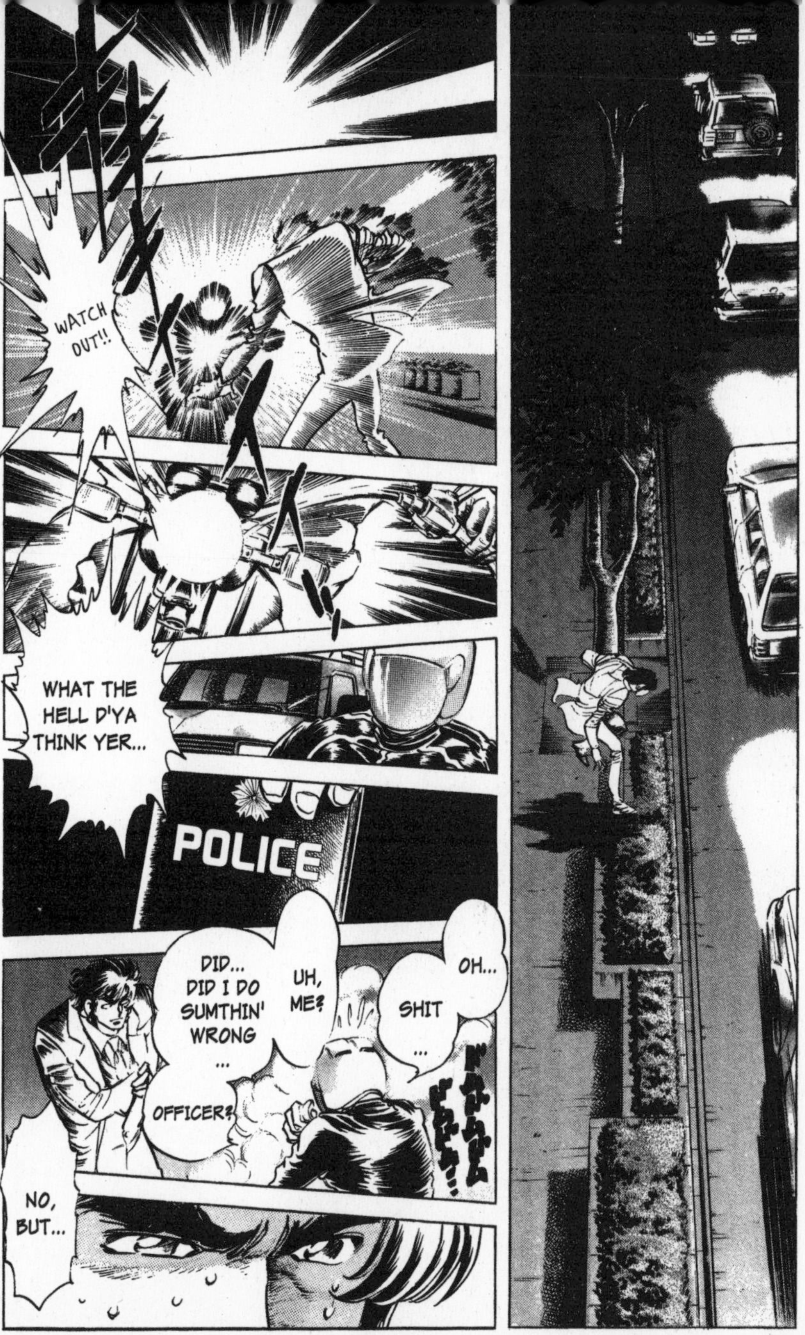
WATCH OUT!!
WHAT THE HELL D'YA THINK YER...
POLICE
OH... SHIT ...
UH, ME?
DID... DID I DO SUMTHIN' WRONG ... OFFICER?
NO, BUT...

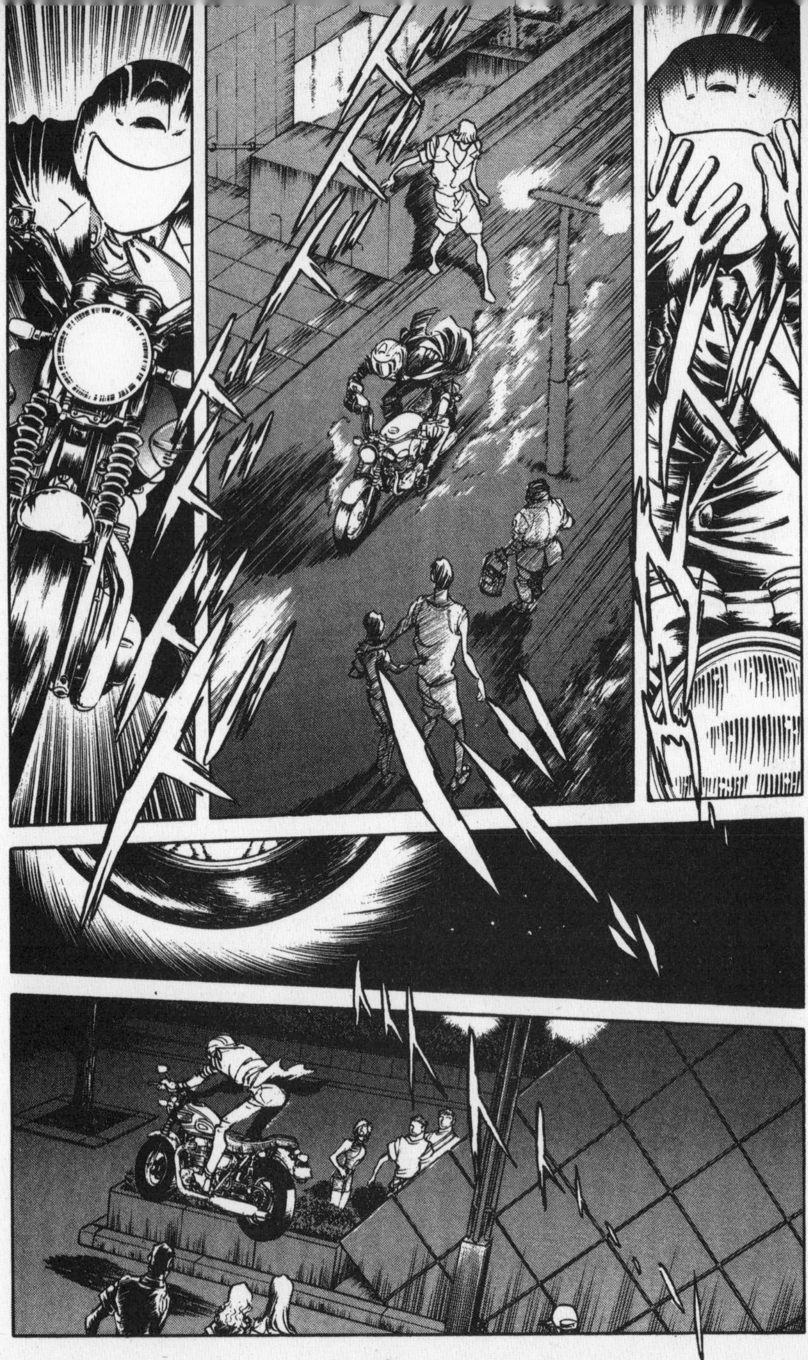

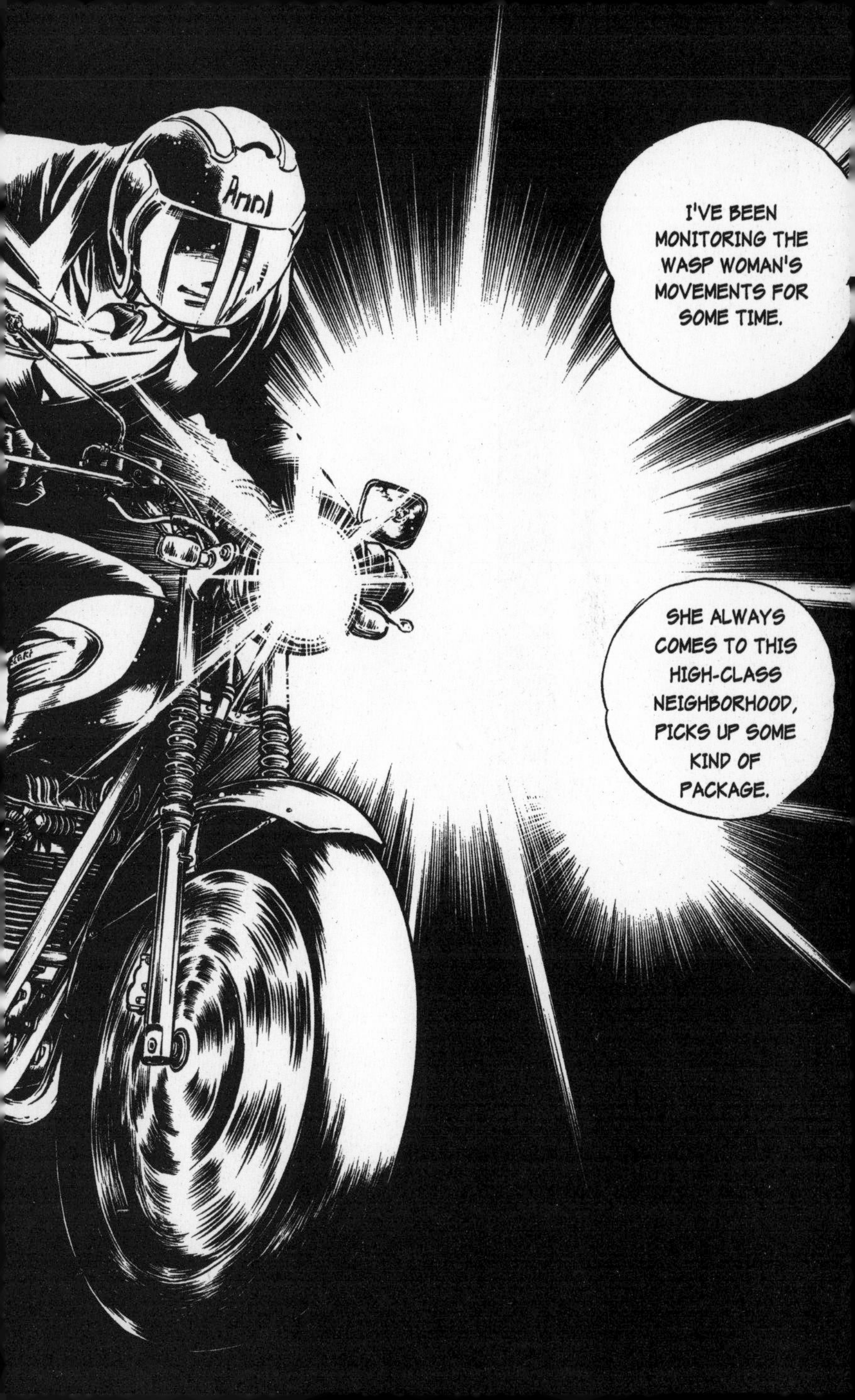
I'VE BEEN MONITORING THE WASP WOMAN'S MOVEMENTS FOR SOME TIME.
SHE ALWAYS COMES TO THIS HIGH-CLASS NEIGHBORHOOD, PICKS UP SOME KIND OF PACKAGE.

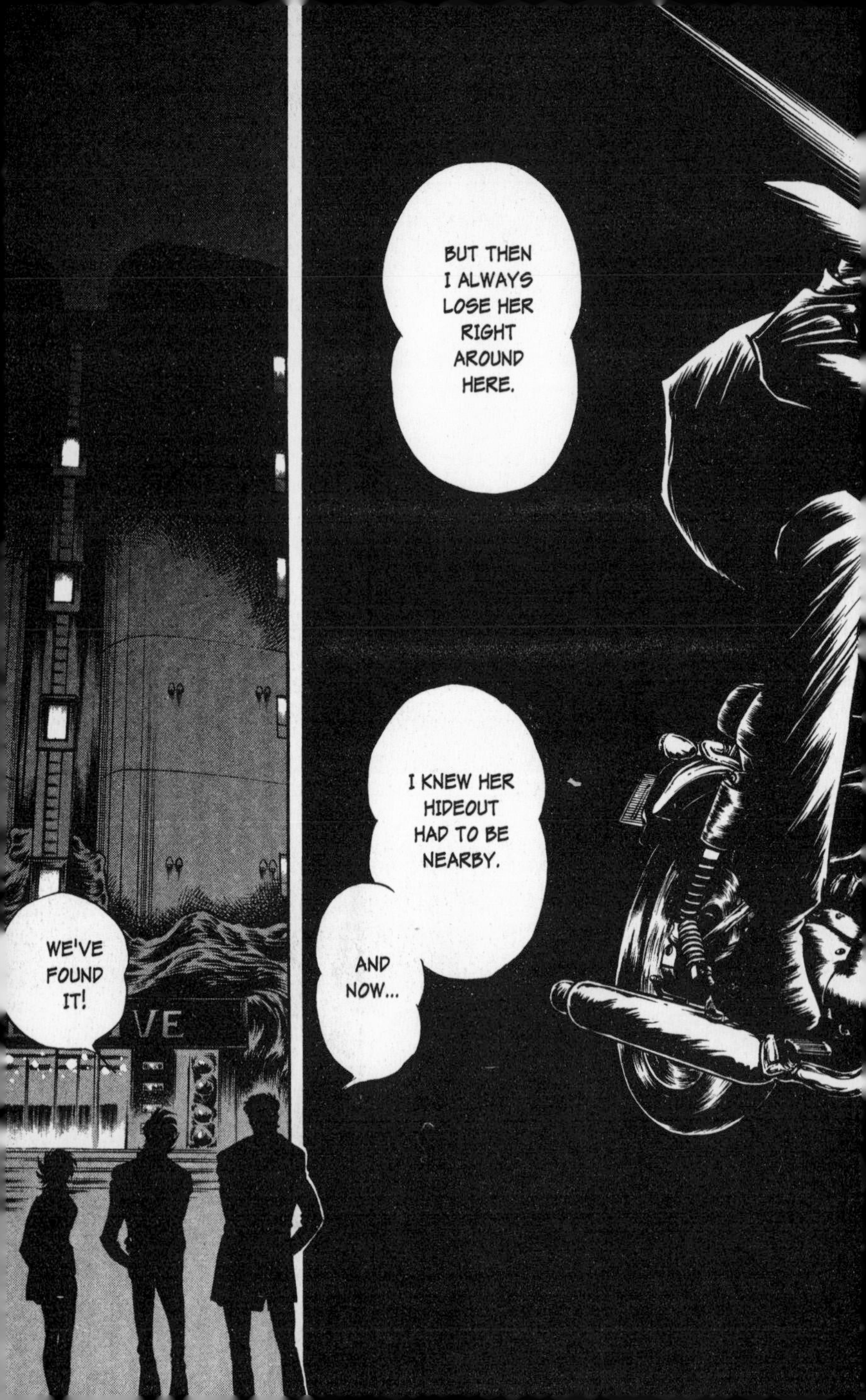
BUT THEN I ALWAYS LOSE HER RIGHT AROUND HERE.
I KNEW HER HIDEOUT HAD TO BE NEARBY.
AND NOW...
WE'VE FOUND IT!

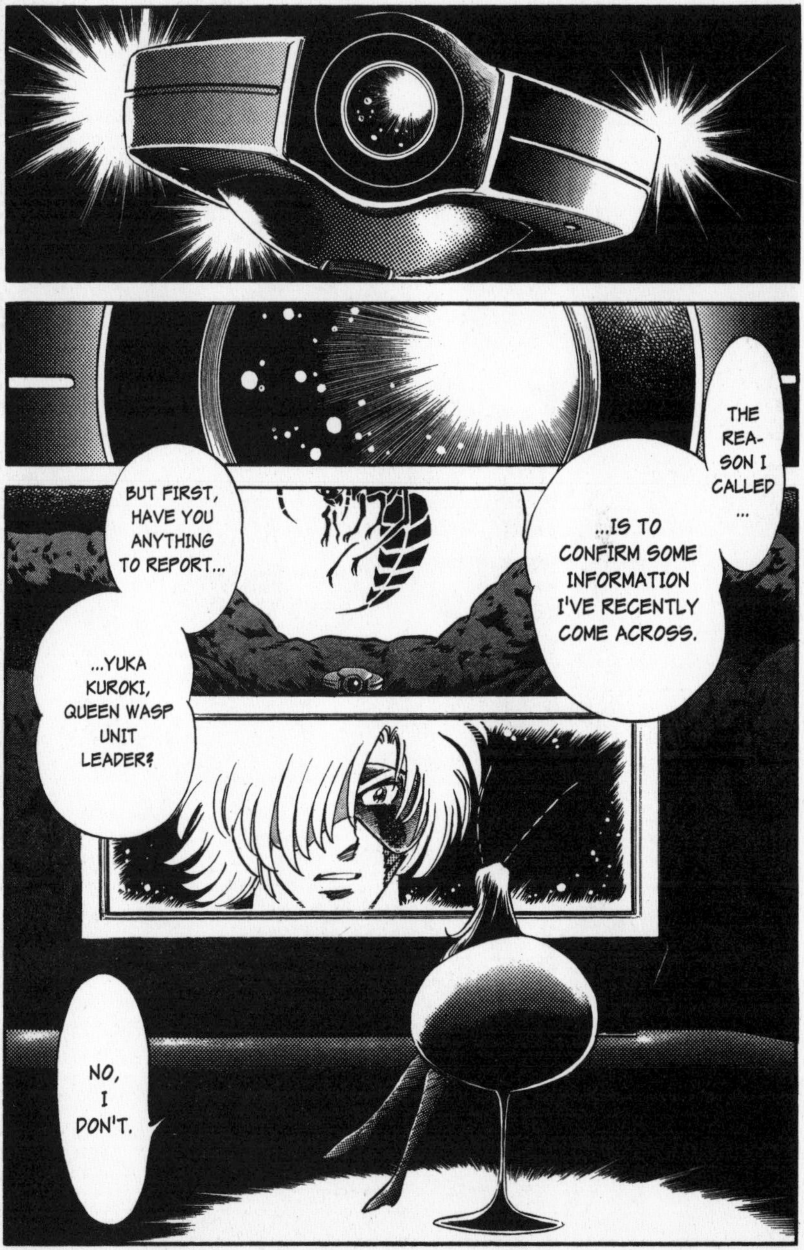
THE REA-SON I CALLED ...
...IS TO CONFIRM SOME INFORMATION I'VE RECENTLY COME ACROSS.
BUT FIRST, HAVE YOU ANYTHING TO REPORT...
...YUKA KUROKI, QUEEN WASP UNIT LEADER?
NO, I DON'T.

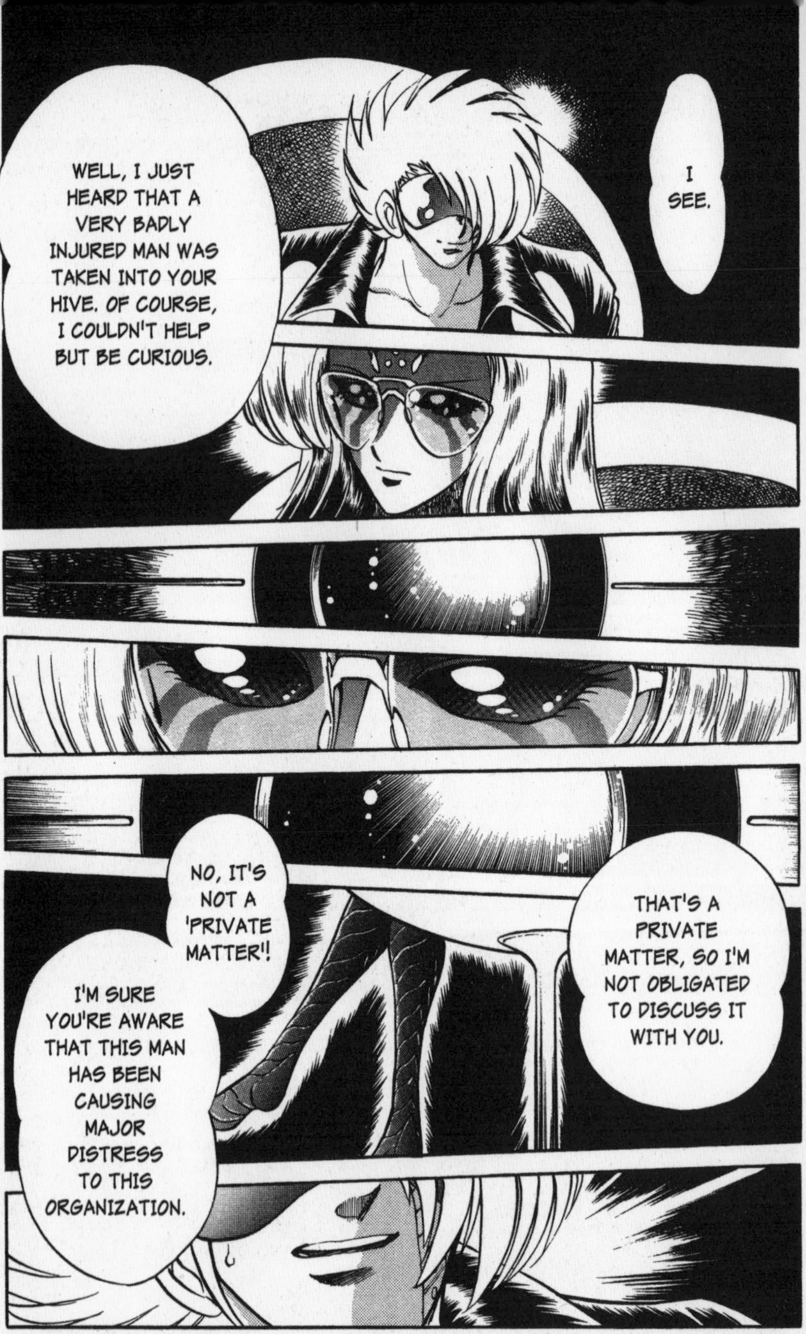
I SEE.
WELL, I JUST HEARD THAT A VERY BADLY INJURED MAN WAS TAKEN INTO YOUR HIVE. OF COURSE, I COULDN'T HELP BUT BE CURIOUS.
THAT'S A PRIVATE MATTER, SO I'M NOT OBLIGATED TO DISCUSS IT WITH YOU.
NO, IT'S NOT A 'PRIVATE MATTER'!
I'M SURE YOU'RE AWARE THAT THIS MAN HAS BEEN CAUSING MAJOR DISTRESS TO THIS ORGANIZATION.

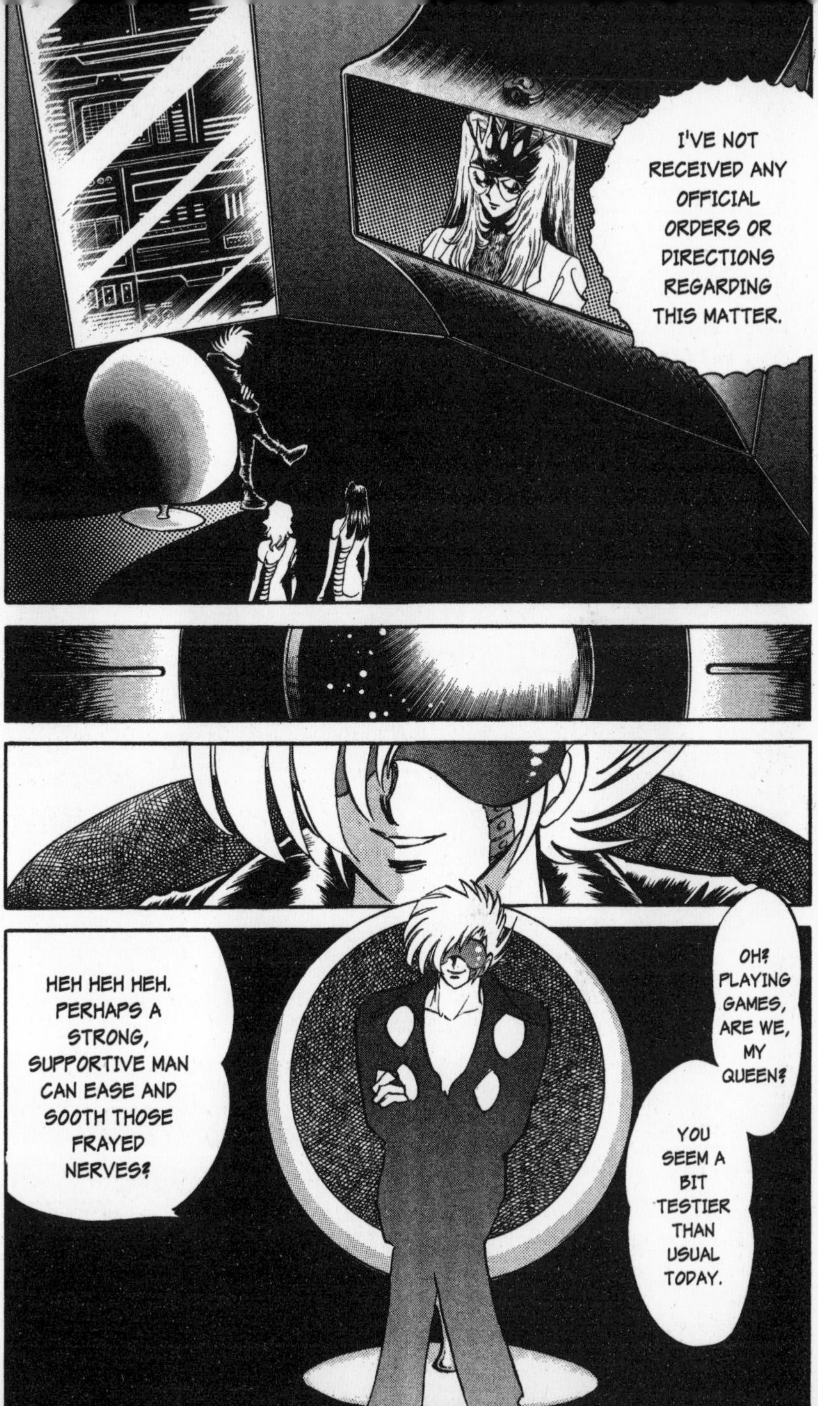
I'VE NOT RECEIVED ANY OFFICIAL ORDERS OR DIRECTIONS REGARDING THIS MATTER.
OH? PLAYING GAMES, ARE WE, MY QUEEN?
YOU SEEM A BIT TESTIER THAN USUAL TODAY.
HEH HEH HEH. PERHAPS A STRONG, SUPPORTIVE MAN CAN EASE AND SOOTH THOSE FRAYED NERVES?

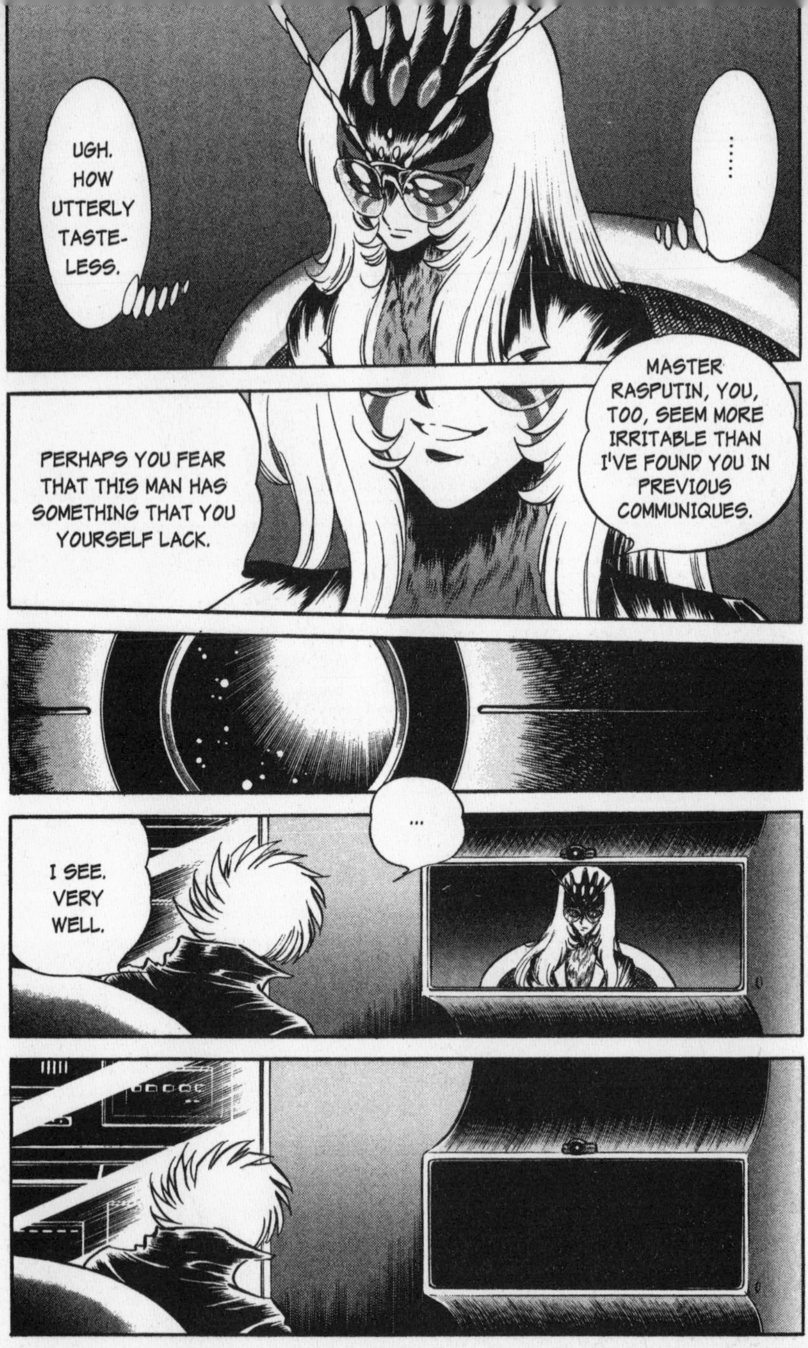
......
UGH. HOW UTTERLY TASTE-LESS.
MASTER RASPUTIN, YOU, TOO, SEEM MORE IRRITABLE THAN I'VE FOUND YOU IN PREVIOUS COMMUNIQUES.
PERHAPS YOU FEAR THAT THIS MAN HAS SOMETHING THAT YOU YOURSELF LACK.
...
I SEE. VERY WELL.

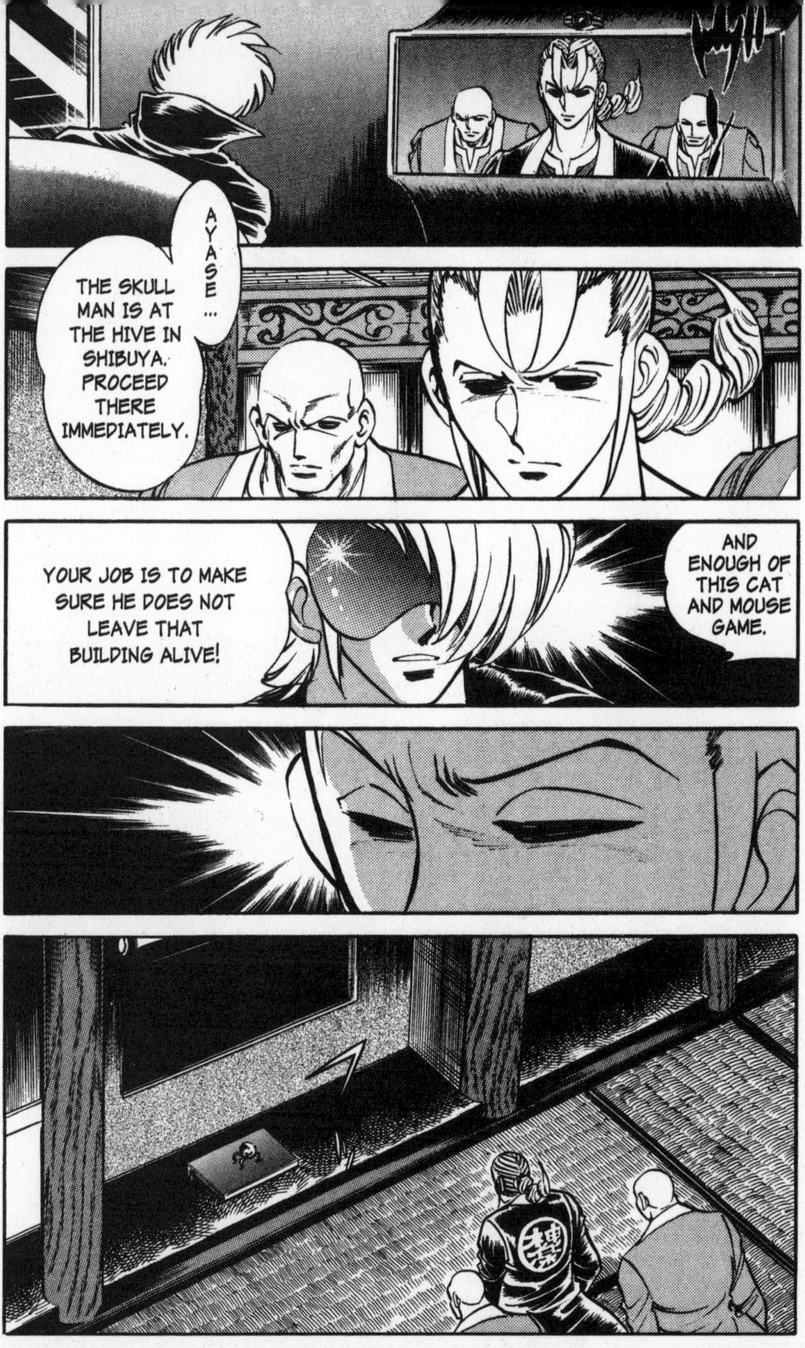

AYASE ...
THE SKULL MAN IS AT THE HIVE IN SHIBUYA. PROCEED THERE IMMEDIATELY.
AND ENOUGH OF THIS CAT AND MOUSE GAME.
YOUR JOB IS TO MAKE SURE HE DOES NOT LEAVE THAT BUILDING ALIVE!

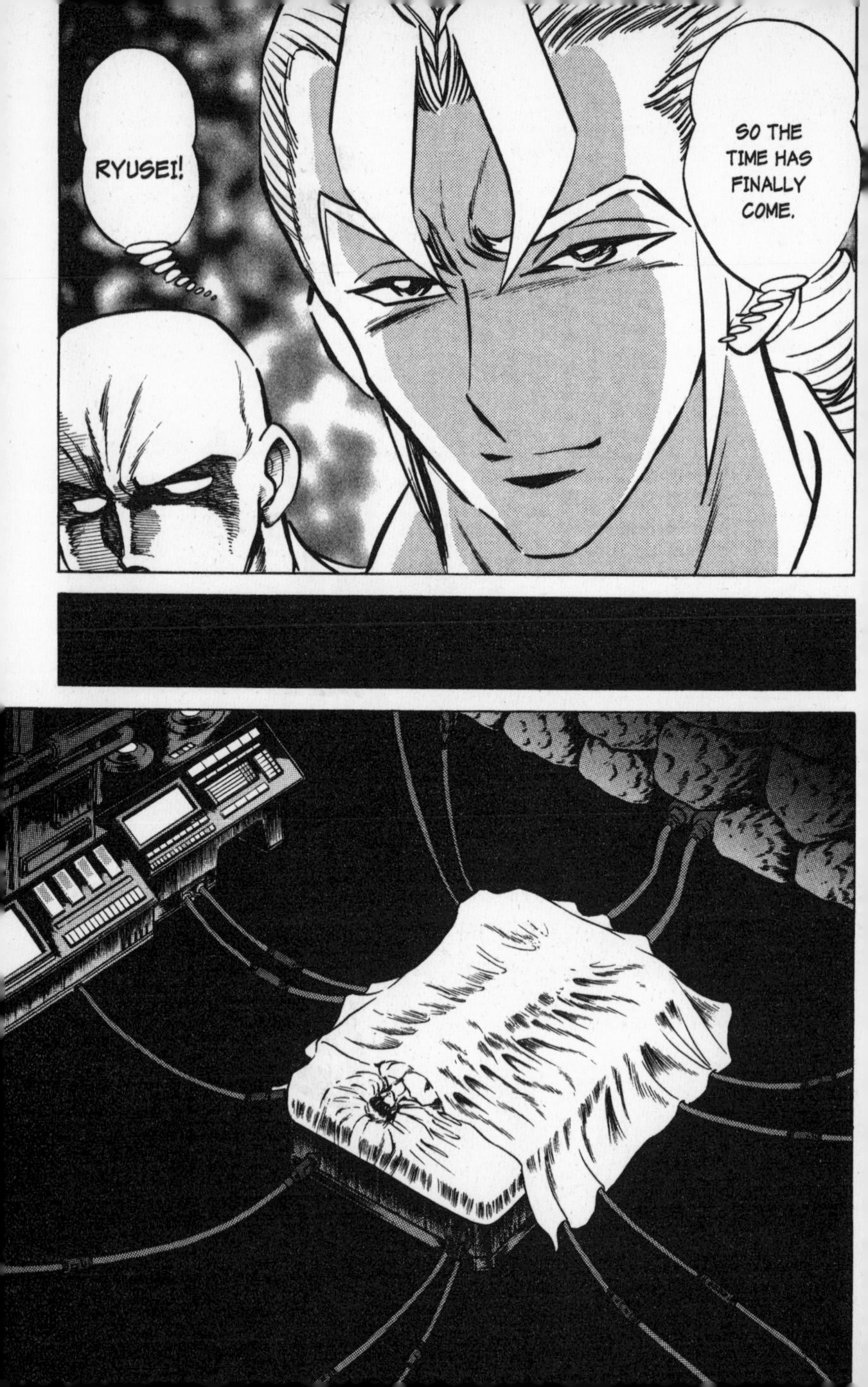
SO THE TIME HAS FINALLY COME.
RYUSEI!

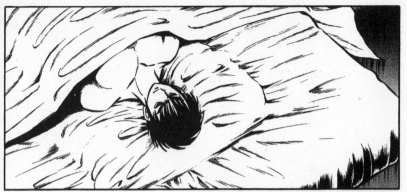

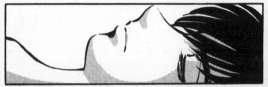

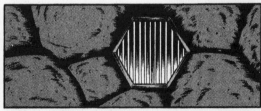

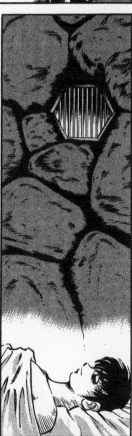

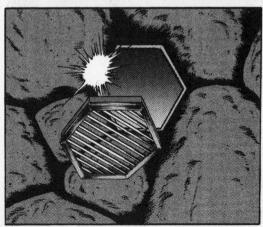

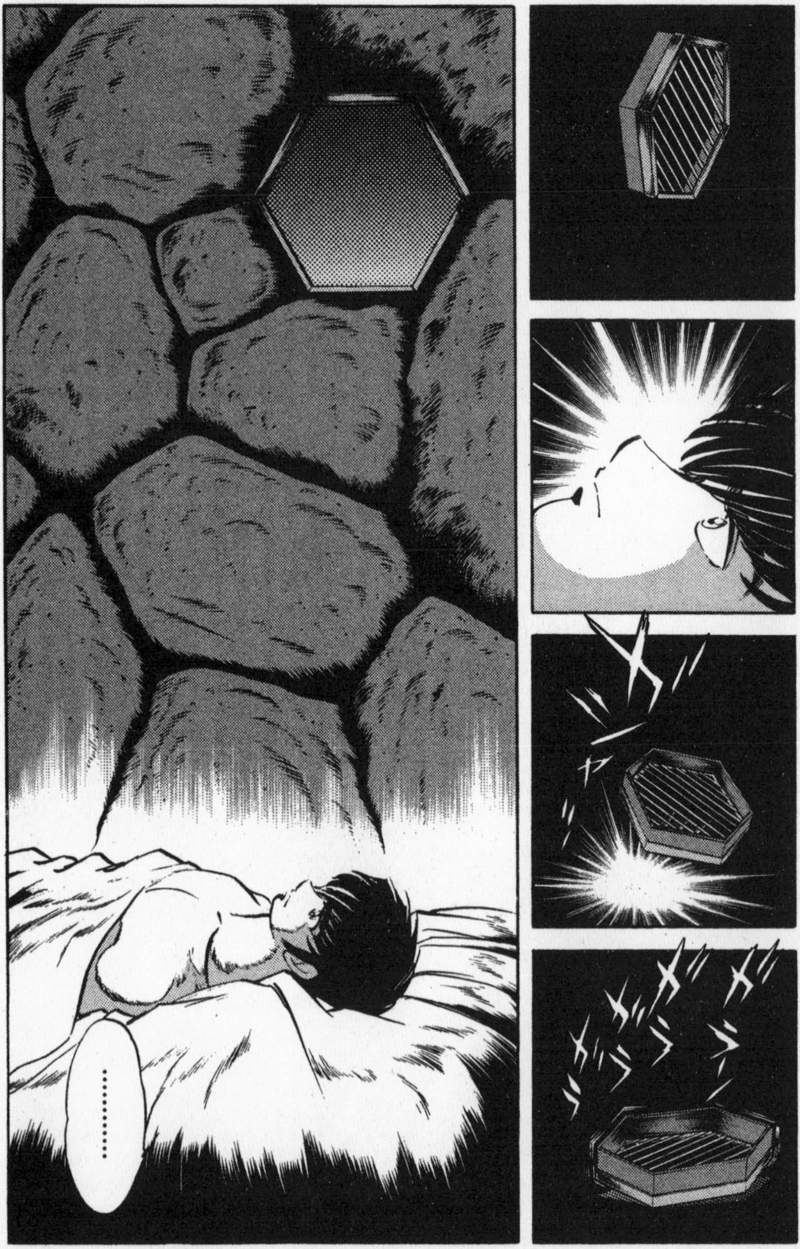
……

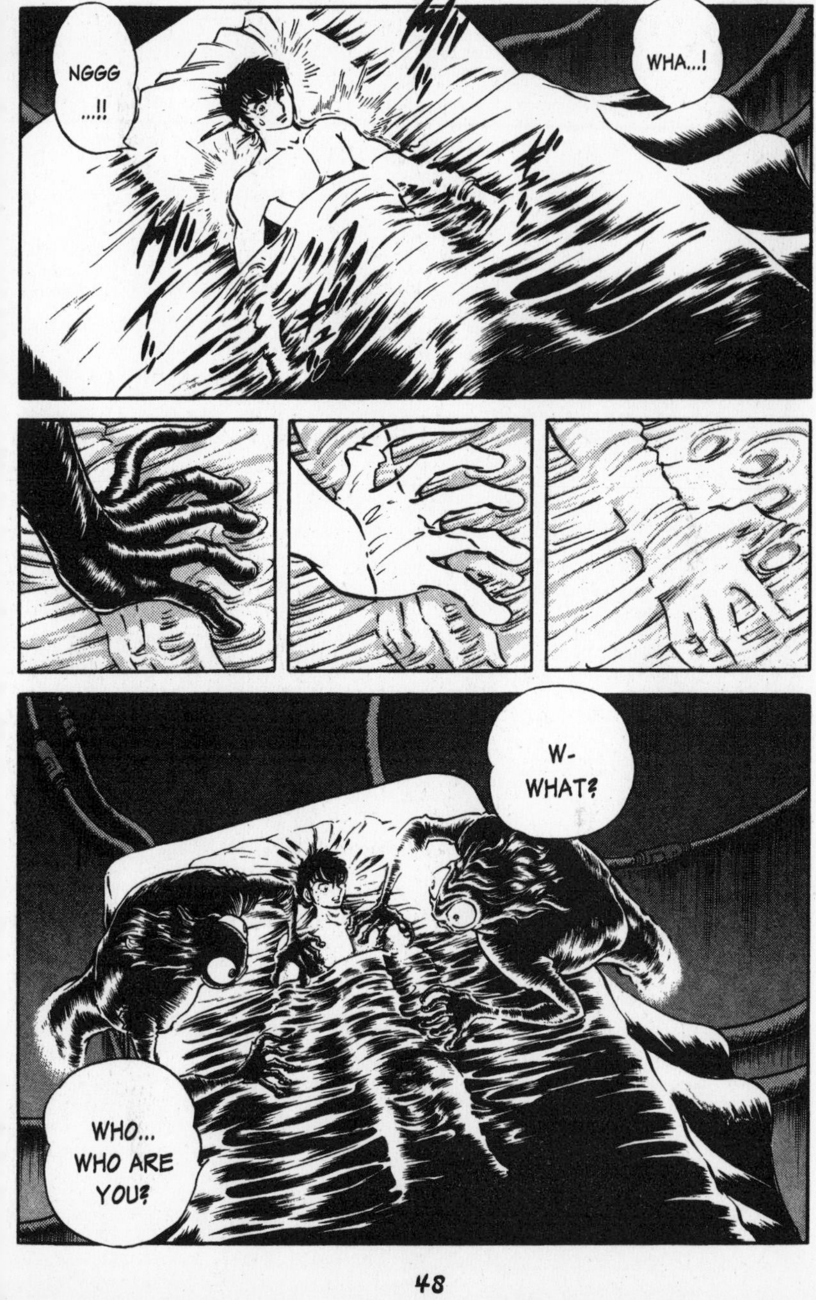
WHA...!
NGGG ...!!
W- WHAT?
WHO... WHO ARE YOU?

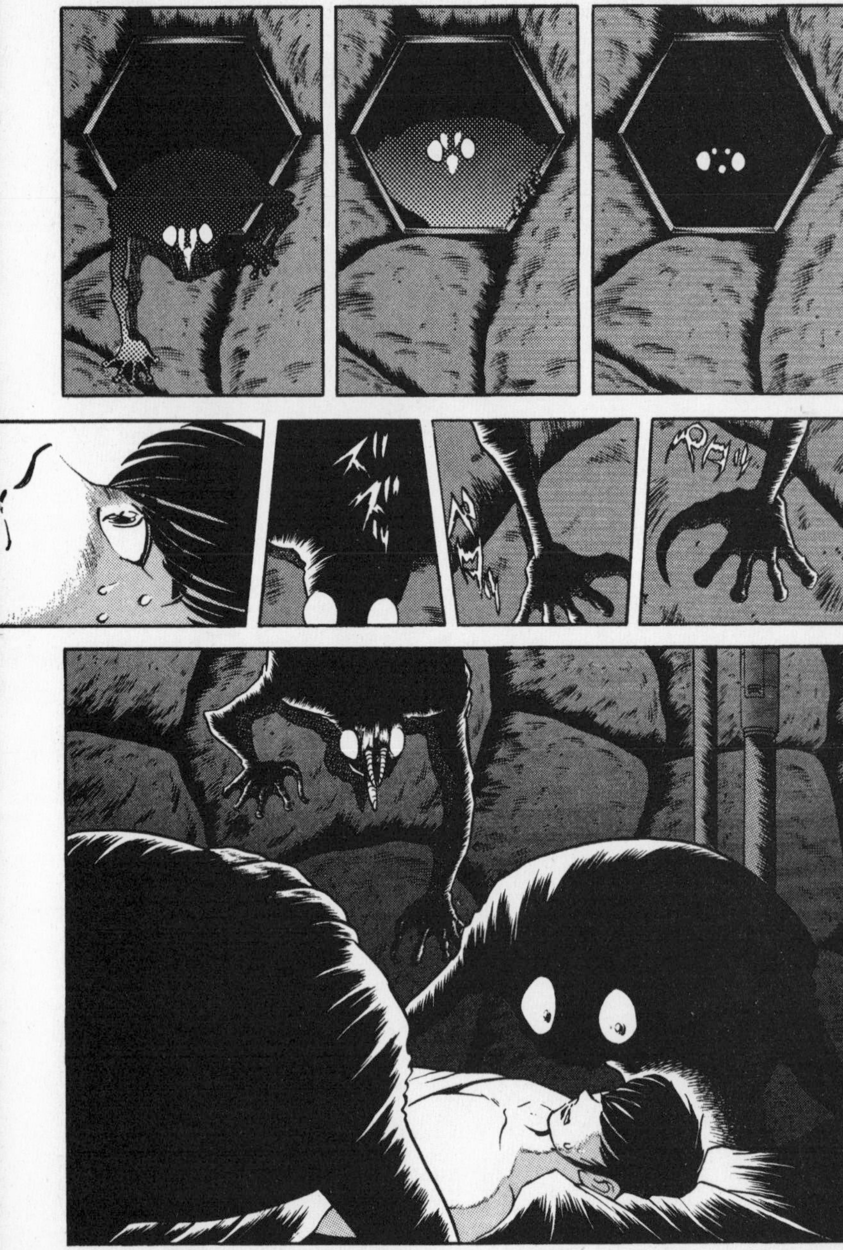
ペタッ
ズリ ズリ

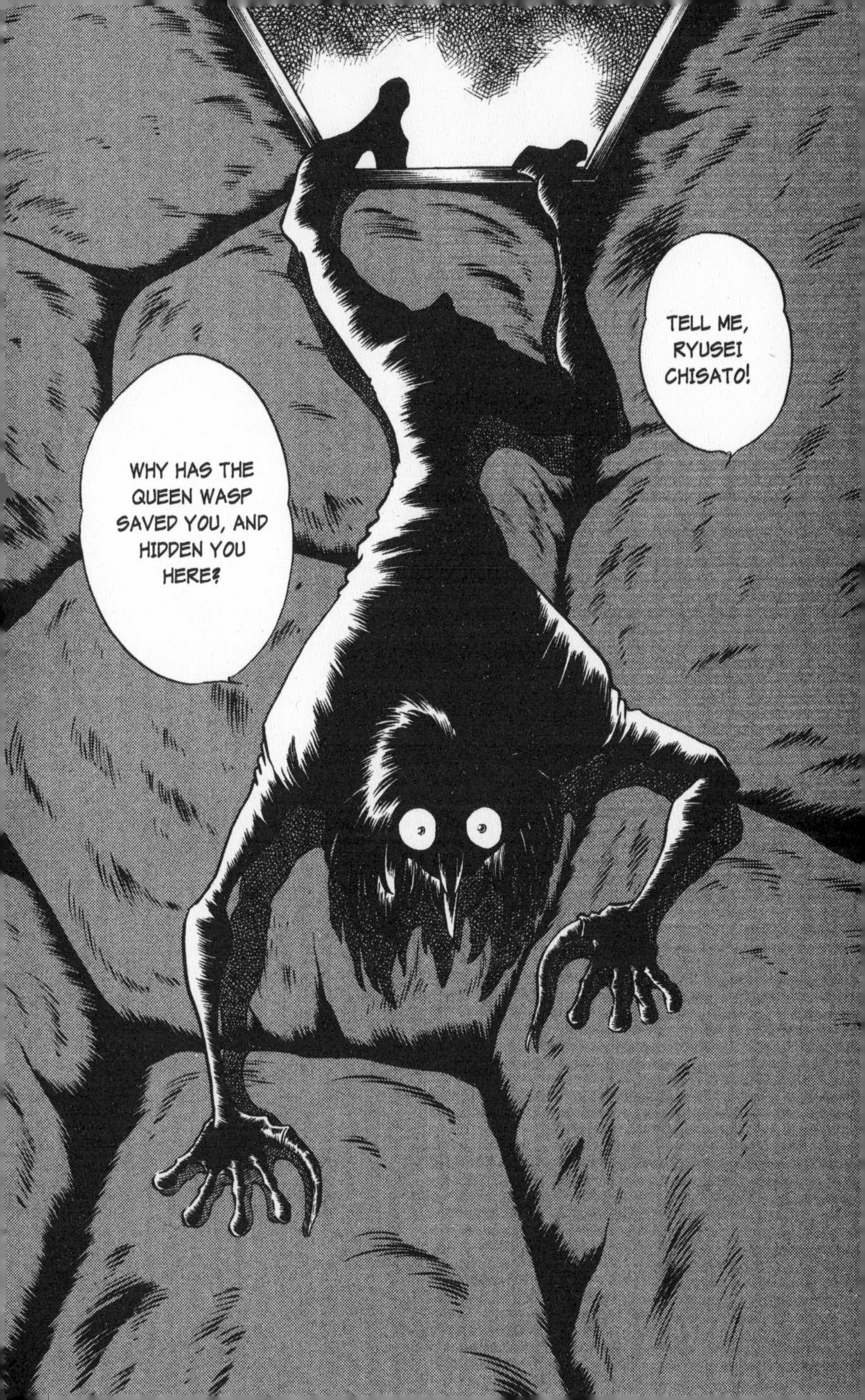
TELL ME, RYUSEI CHISATO!
WHY HAS THE QUEEN WASP SAVED YOU, AND HIDDEN YOU HERE?

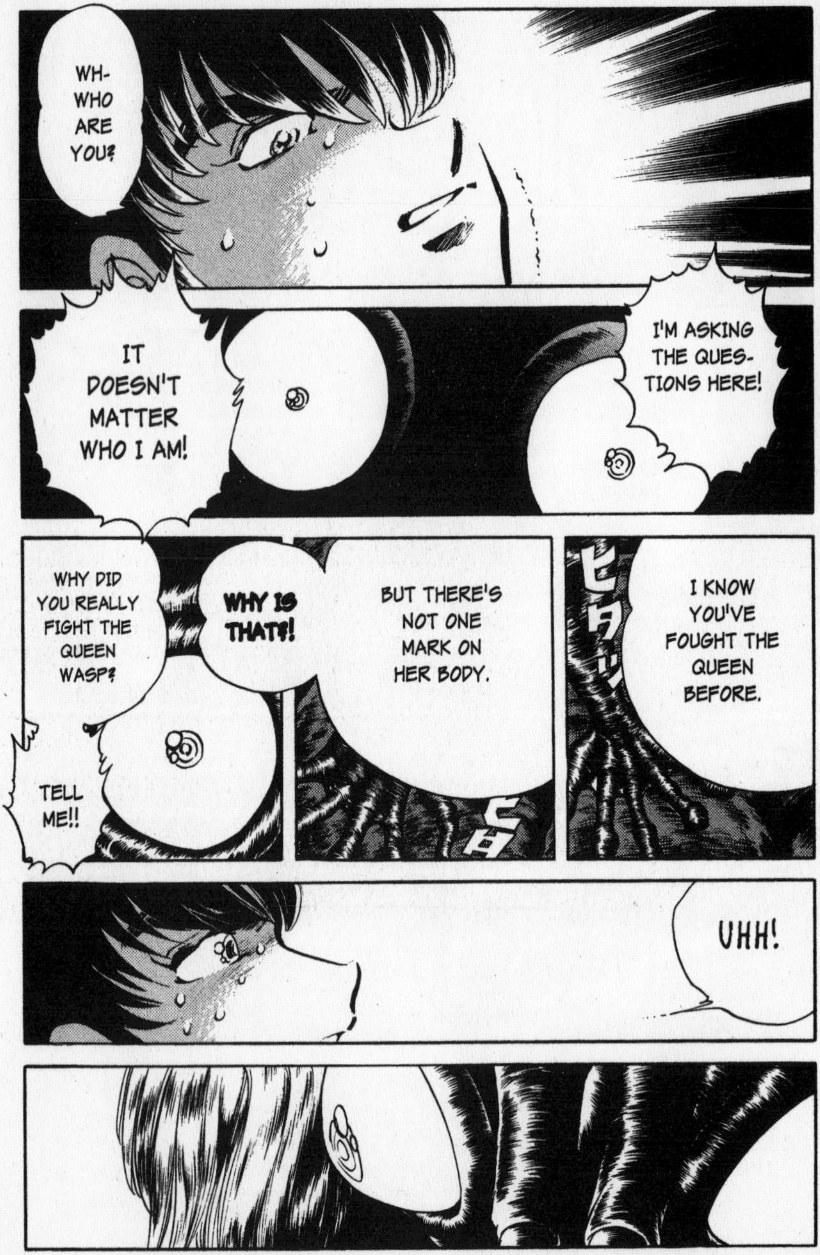
WH- WHO ARE YOU?
I'M ASKING THE QUES-TIONS HERE!
IT DOESN'T MATTER WHO I AM!
ヒタッ
I KNOW YOU'VE FOUGHT THE QUEEN BEFORE.
BUT THERE'S NOT ONE MARK ON HER BODY.
WHY IS THAT?!
WHY DID YOU REALLY FIGHT THE QUEEN WASP?
TELL ME!!
UHH!

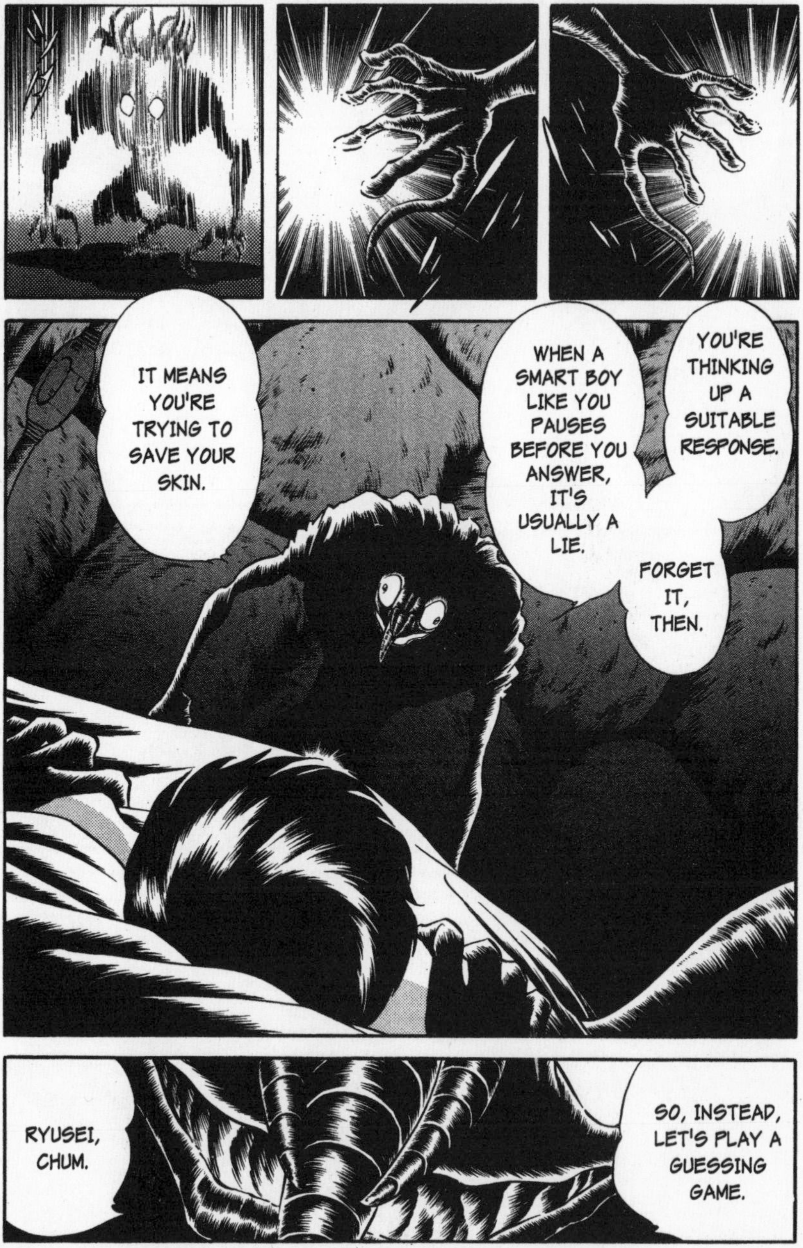
YOU'RE THINKING UP A SUITABLE RESPONSE.
WHEN A SMART BOY LIKE YOU PAUSES BEFORE YOU ANSWER, IT'S USUALLY A LIE.
IT MEANS YOU'RE TRYING TO SAVE YOUR SKIN.
FORGET IT, THEN.
SO, INSTEAD, LET'S PLAY A GUESSING GAME.
RYUSEI, CHUM.

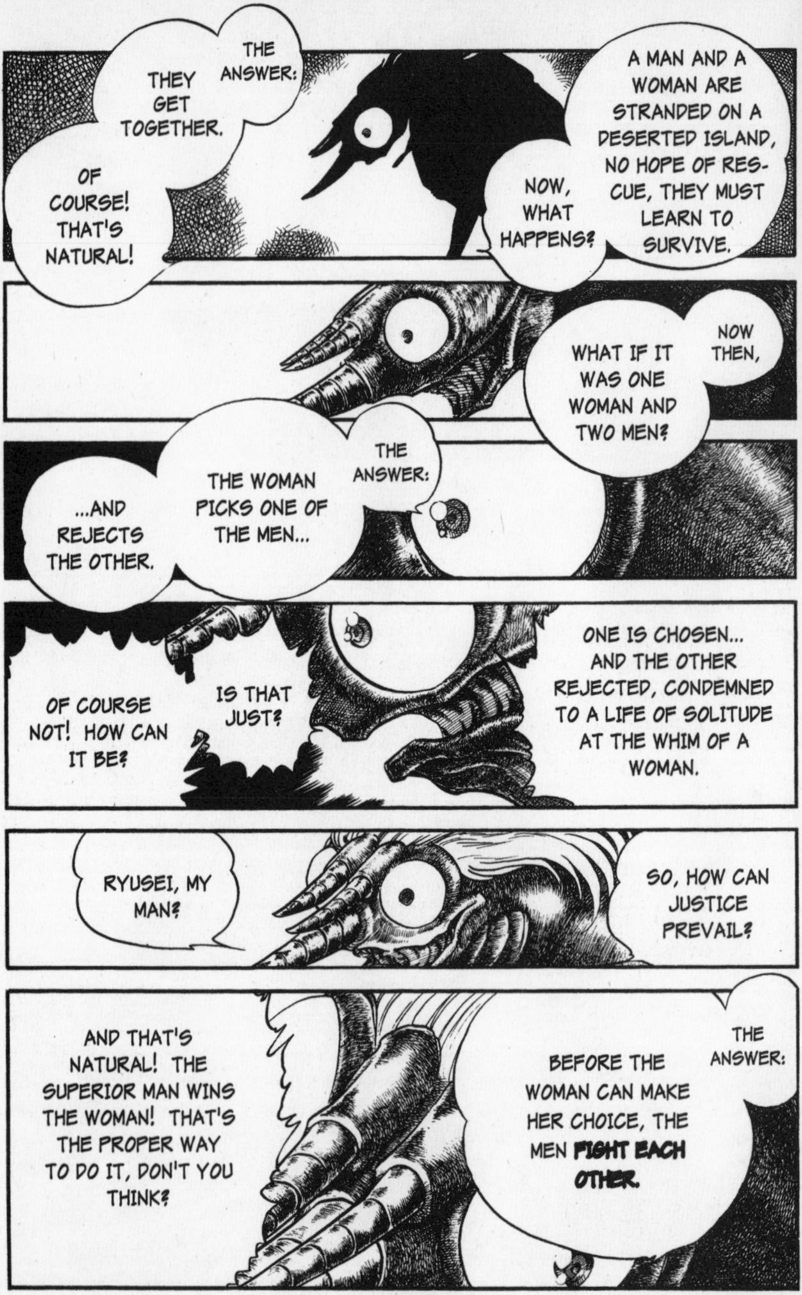
A MAN AND A WOMAN ARE STRANDED ON A DESERTED ISLAND, NO HOPE OF RES-CUE, THEY MUST LEARN TO SURVIVE.
NOW, WHAT HAPPENS?
THE ANSWER:
THEY GET TOGETHER.
OF COURSE! THAT'S NATURAL!
NOW THEN,
WHAT IF IT WAS ONE WOMAN AND TWO MEN?
THE ANSWER:
THE WOMAN PICKS ONE OF THE MEN...
...AND REJECTS THE OTHER.
ONE IS CHOSEN... AND THE OTHER REJECTED, CONDEMNED TO A LIFE OF SOLITUDE AT THE WHIM OF A WOMAN.
IS THAT JUST?
OF COURSE NOT! HOW CAN IT BE?
SO, HOW CAN JUSTICE PREVAIL?
RYUSEI, MY MAN?
THE ANSWER:
BEFORE THE WOMAN CAN MAKE HER CHOICE, THE MEN **FIGHT EACH OTHER.**
AND THAT'S NATURAL! THE SUPERIOR MAN WINS THE WOMAN! THAT'S THE PROPER WAY TO DO IT, DON'T YOU THINK?

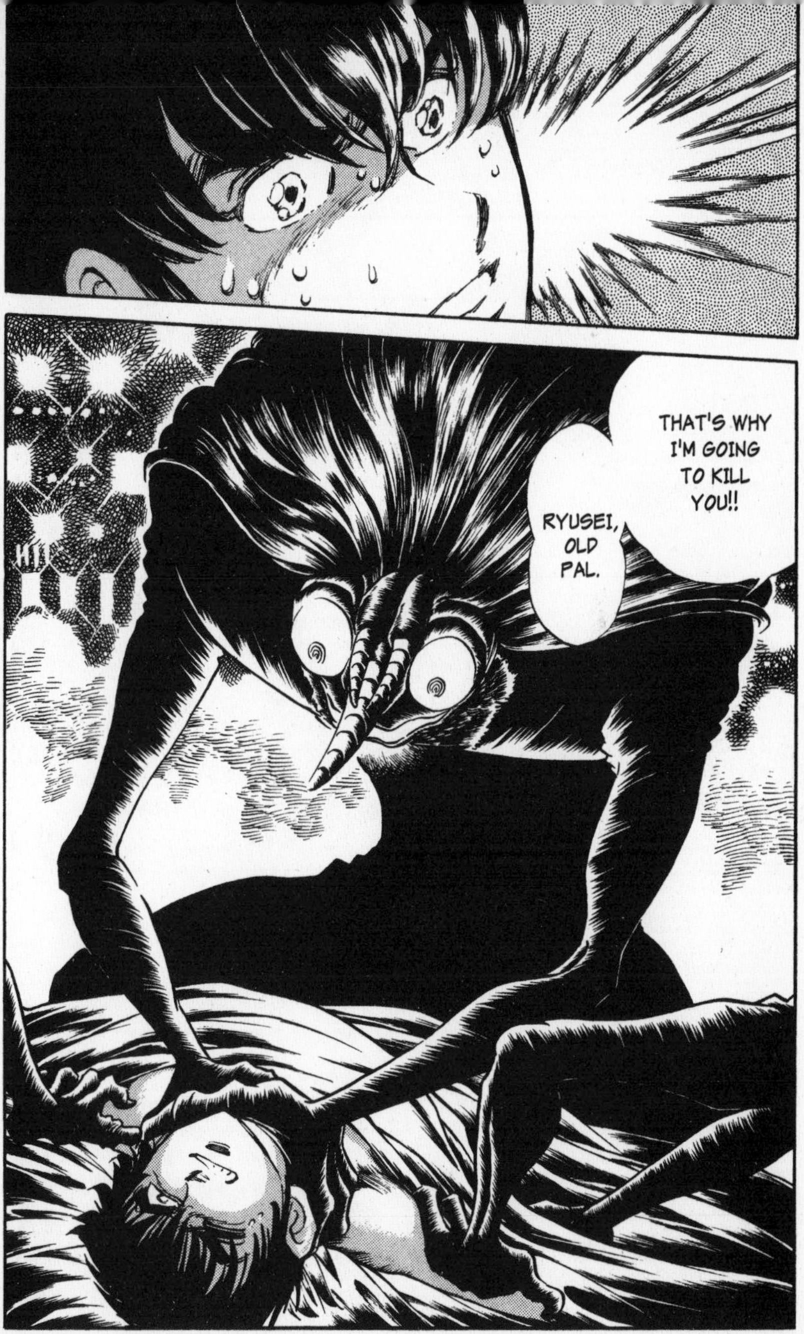
THAT'S WHY I'M GOING TO KILL YOU!!
RYUSEI, OLD PAL.

CH. 33 蜂女VSカメレオン男 THE QUEEN WASP VS THE CHAMELEON MAN

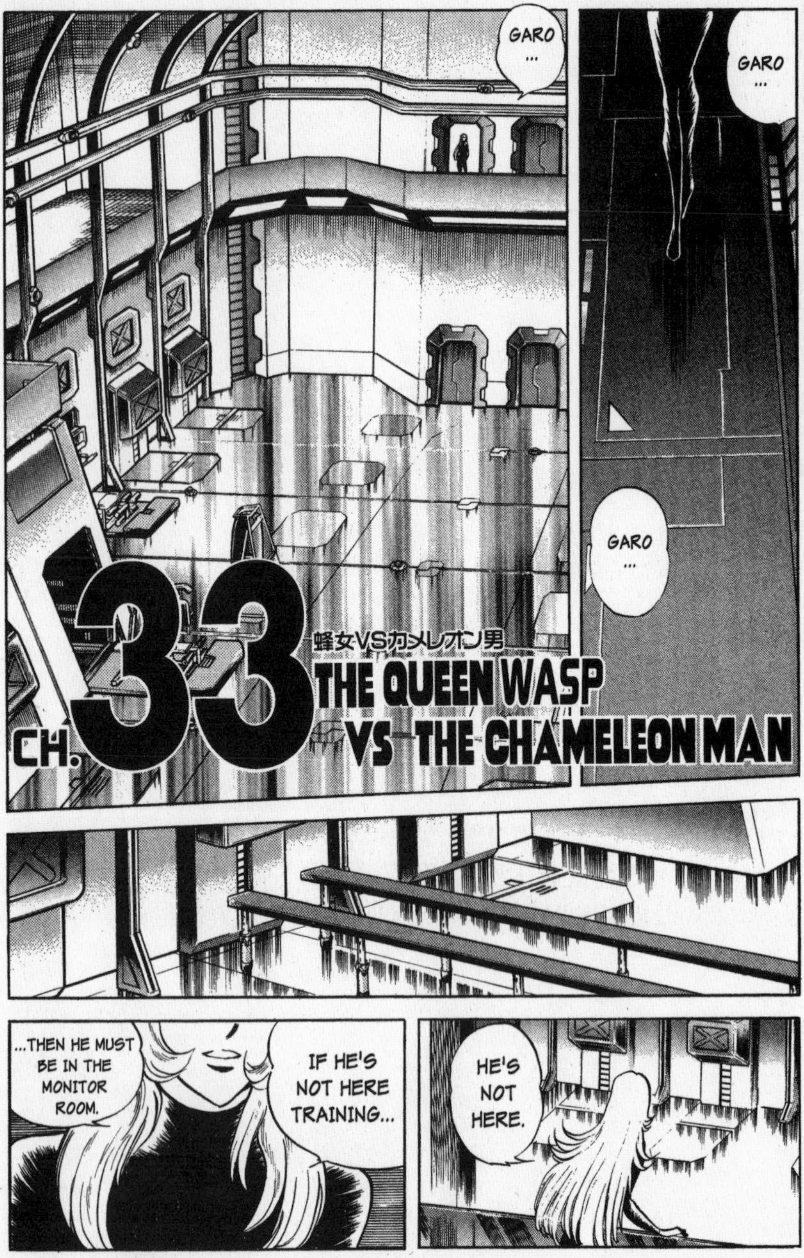
GARO ...
GARO ...
GARO ...
HE'S NOT HERE.
IF HE'S NOT HERE TRAINING...
...THEN HE MUST BE IN THE MONITOR ROOM.

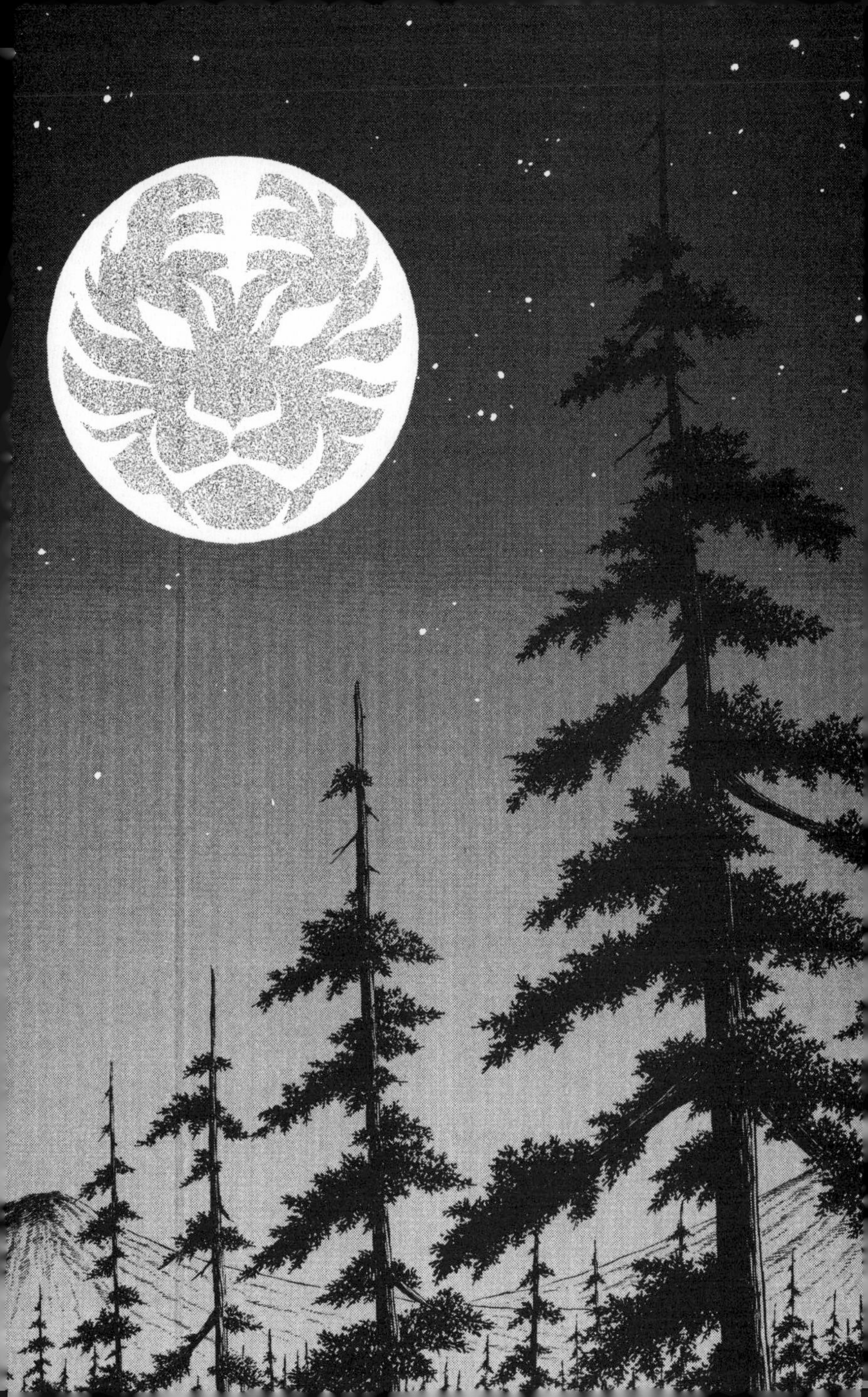

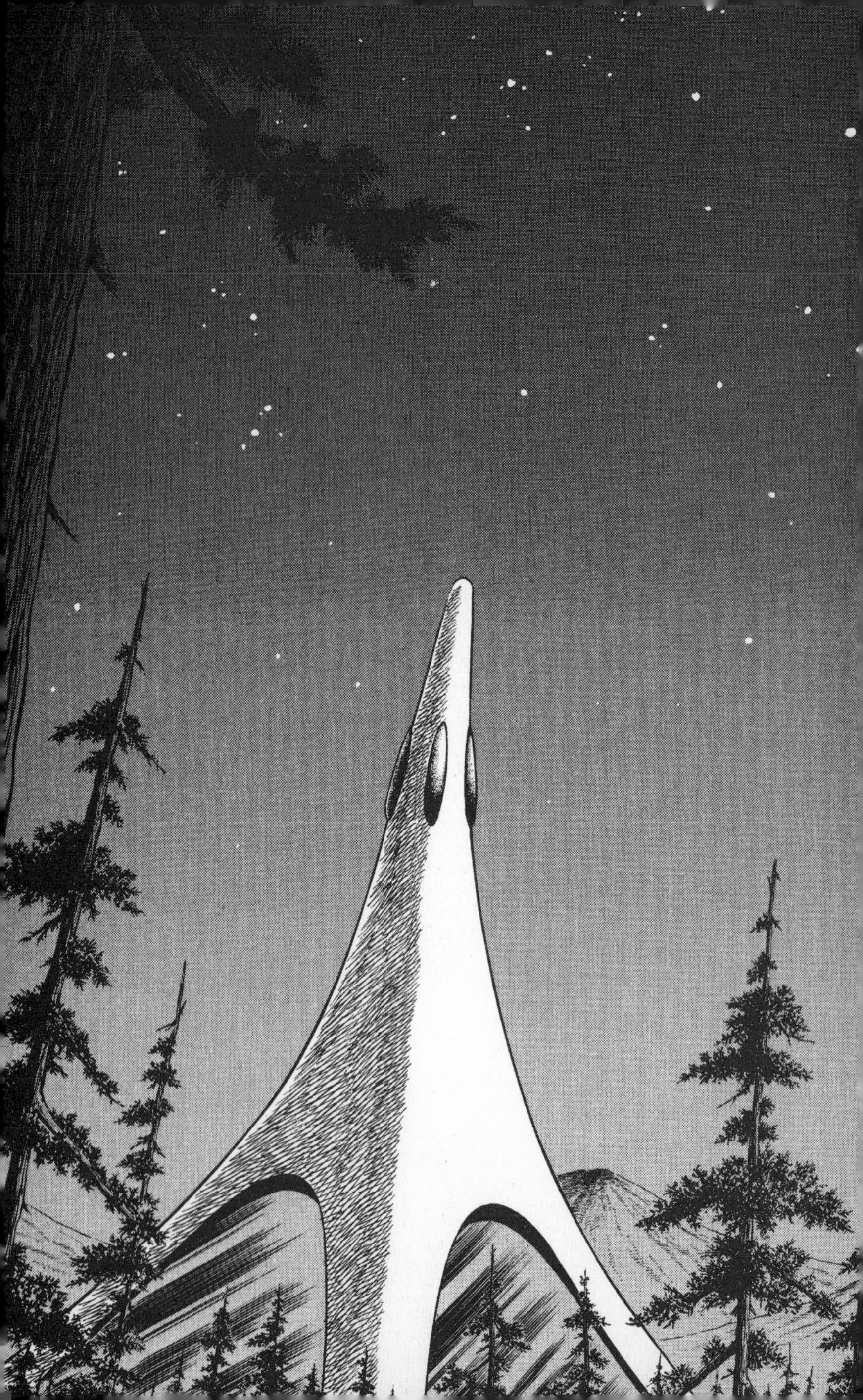

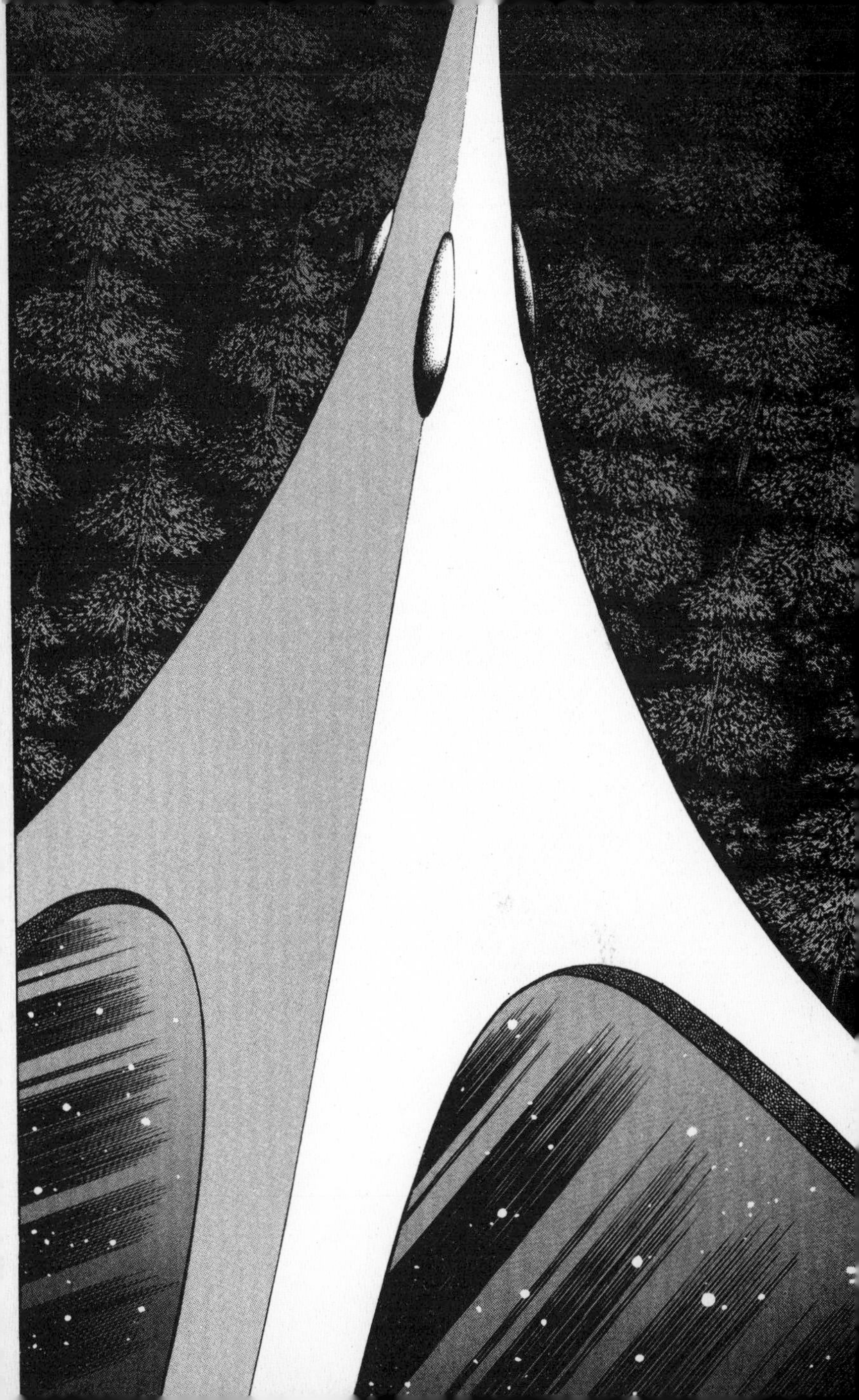

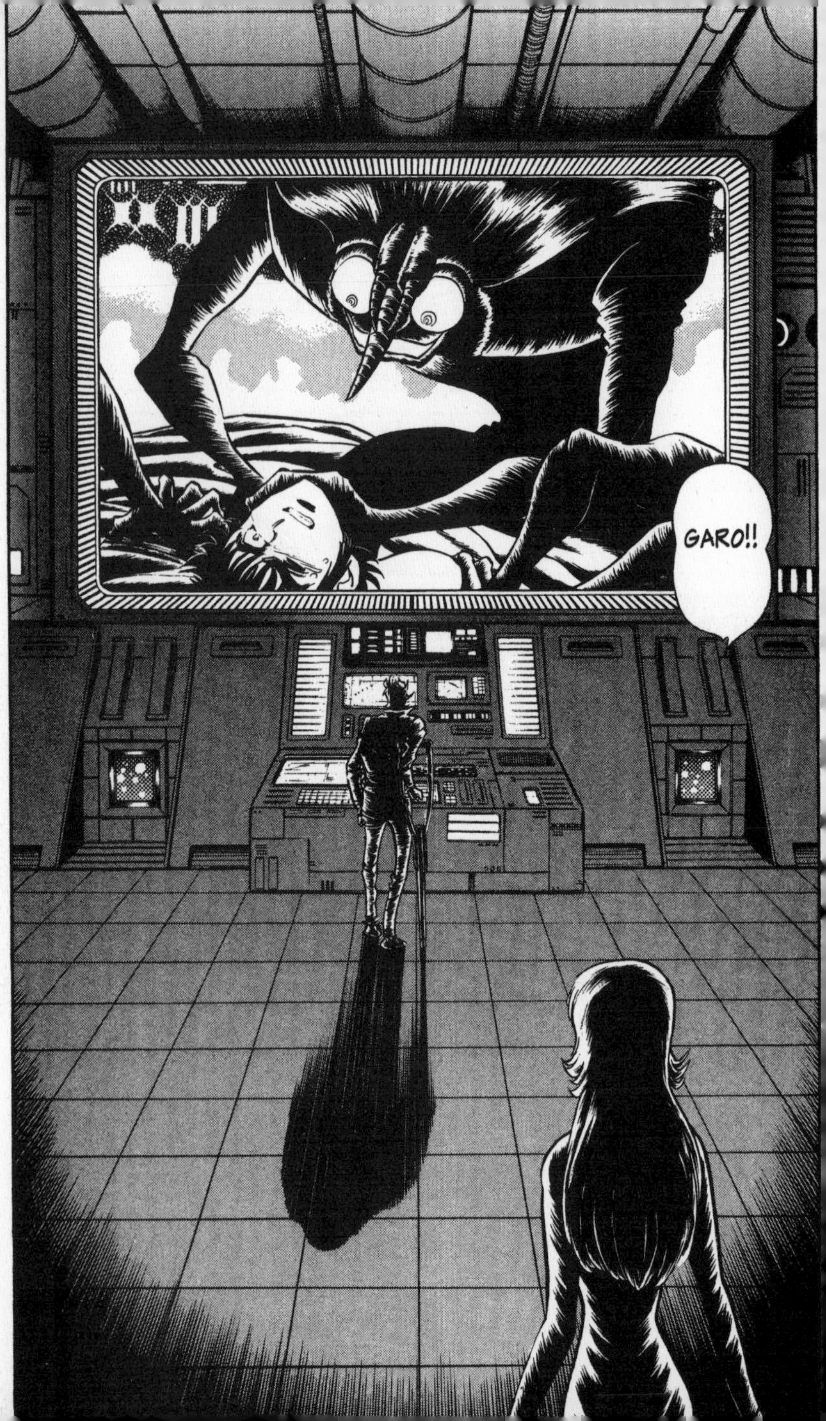
GARO!!

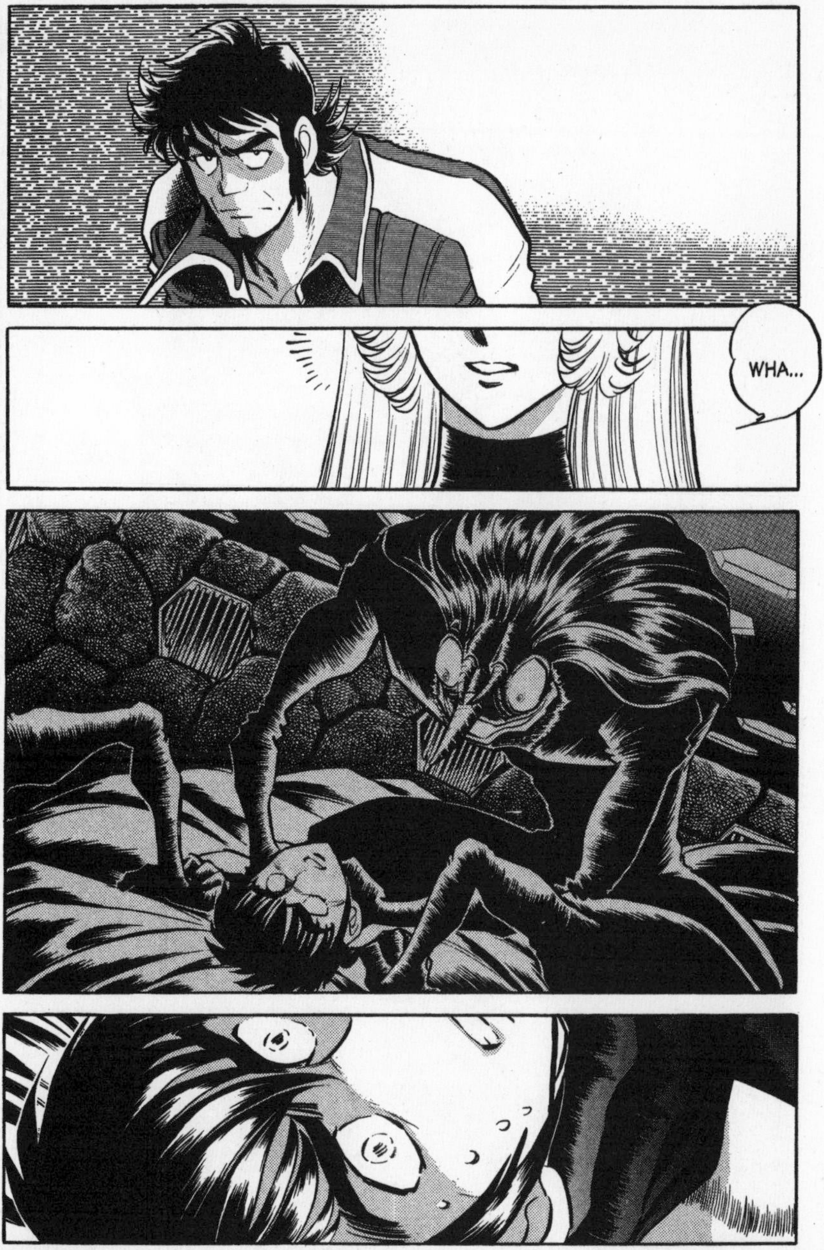
WHA...

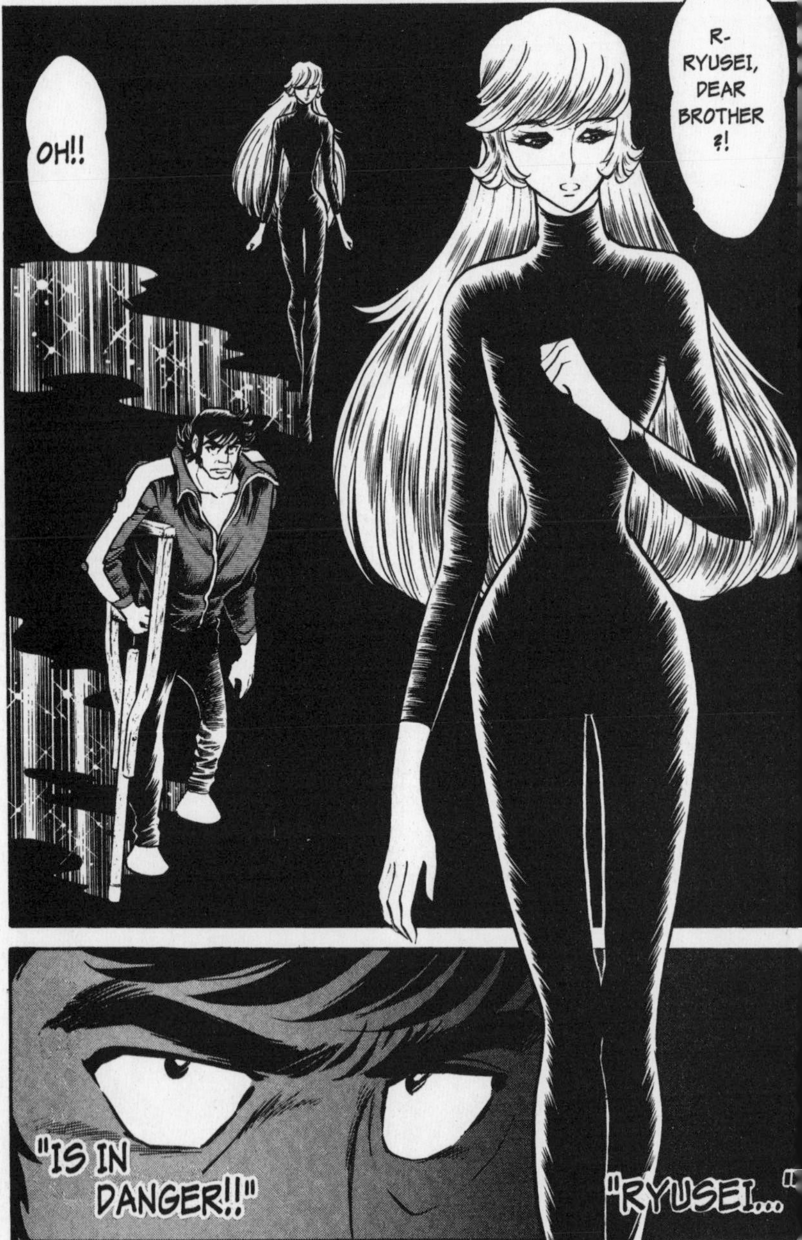
R-RYUSEI, DEAR BROTHER ?!
OH!!
"RYUSEI..."
"IS IN DANGER!!"

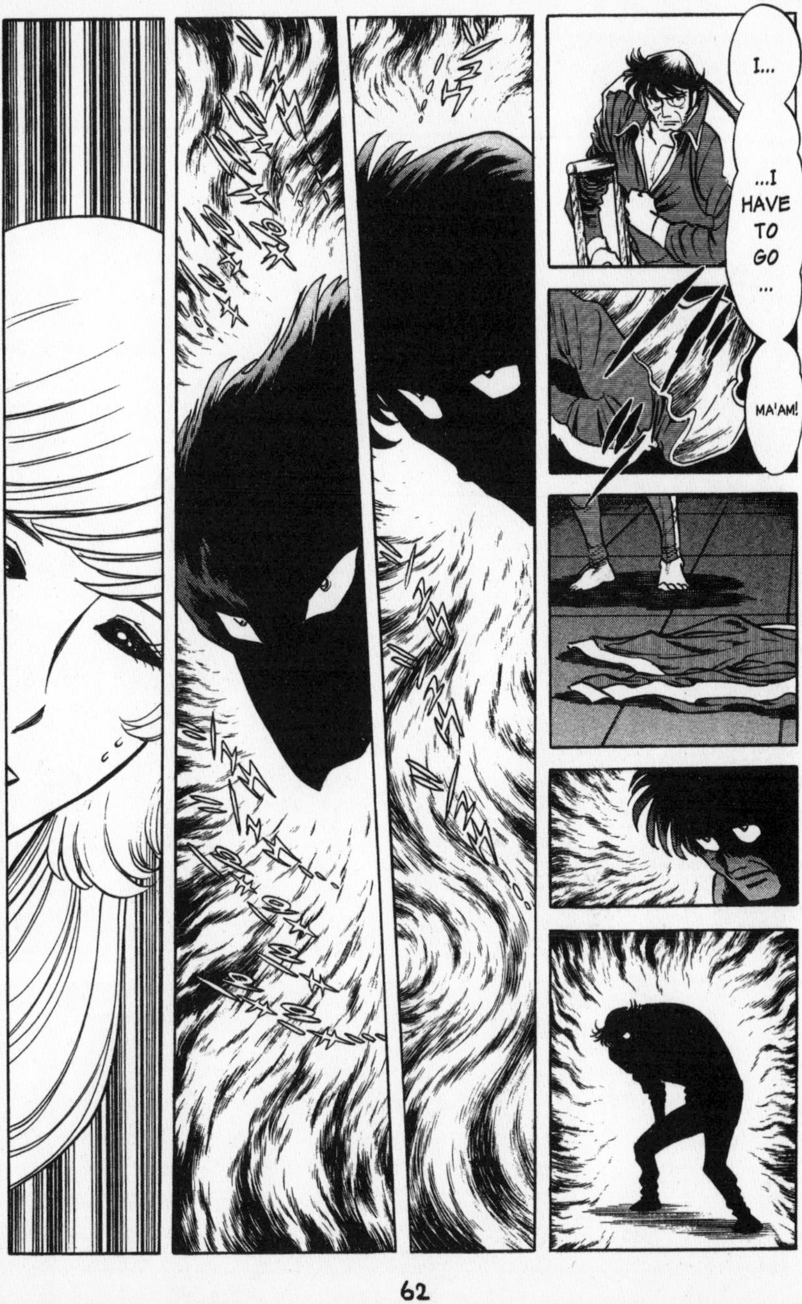
I...
...I HAVE TO GO ...
MA'AM!

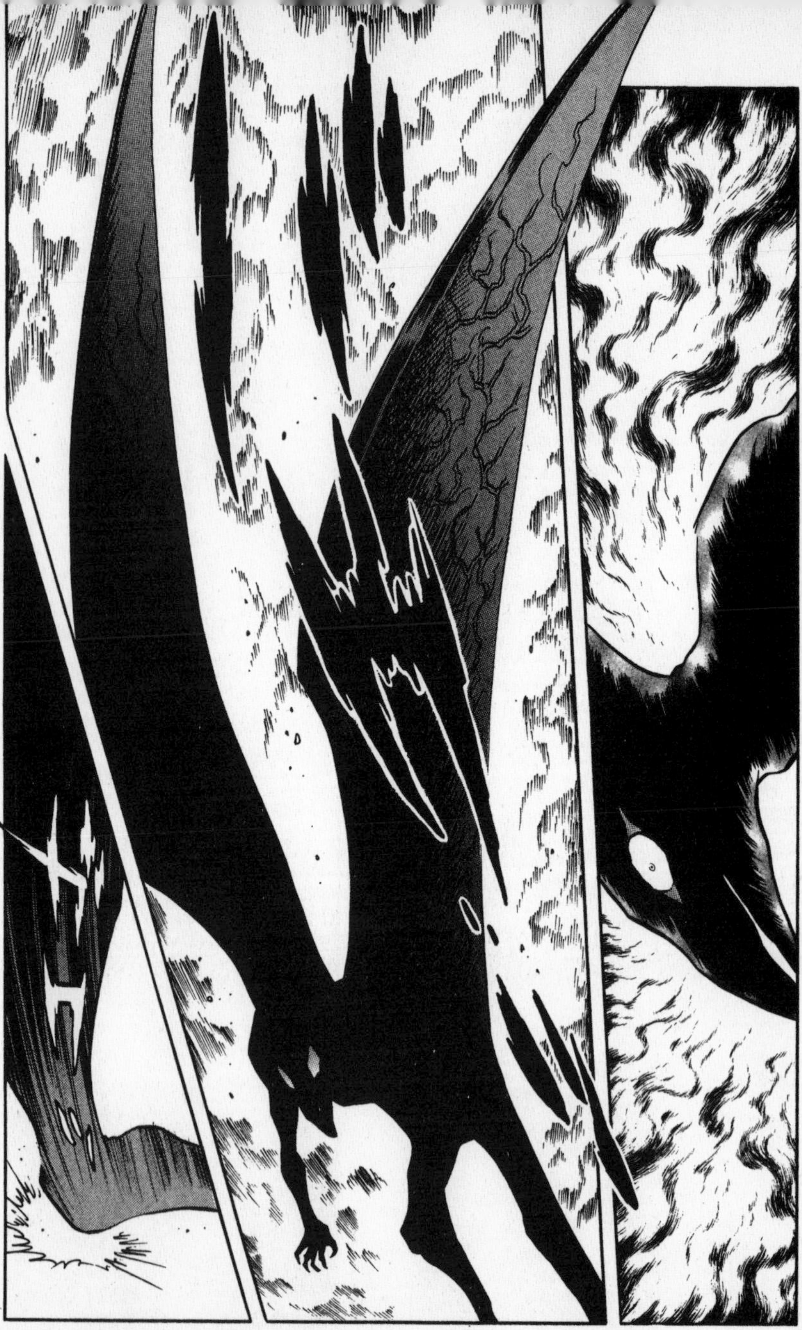

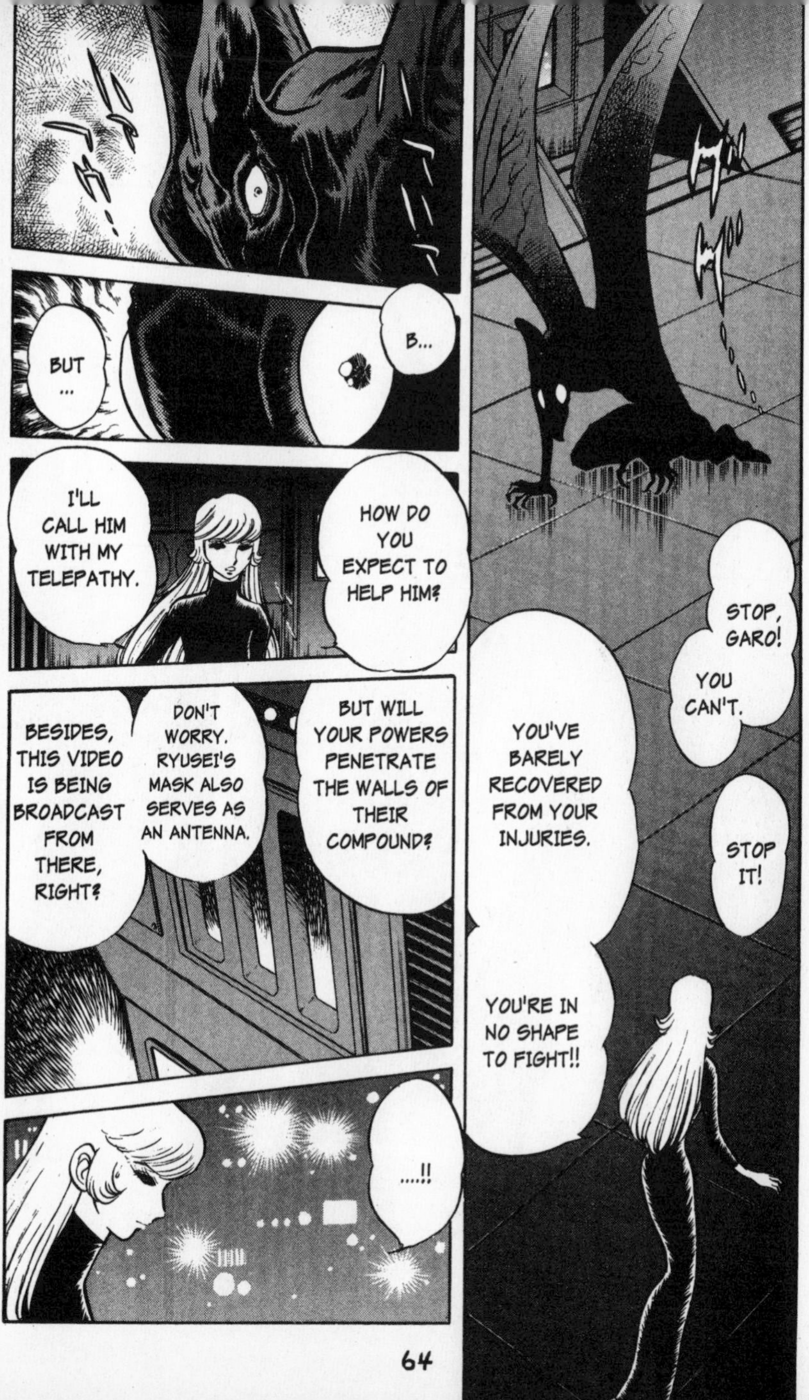
STOP, GARO!
YOU CAN'T.
STOP IT!
YOU'VE BARELY RECOVERED FROM YOUR INJURIES.
YOU'RE IN NO SHAPE TO FIGHT!!
B...
BUT ...
HOW DO YOU EXPECT TO HELP HIM?
I'LL CALL HIM WITH MY TELEPATHY.
BUT WILL YOUR POWERS PENETRATE THE WALLS OF THEIR COMPOUND?
DON'T WORRY. RYUSEI'S MASK ALSO SERVES AS AN ANTENNA.
BESIDES, THIS VIDEO IS BEING BROADCAST FROM THERE, RIGHT?
......!!

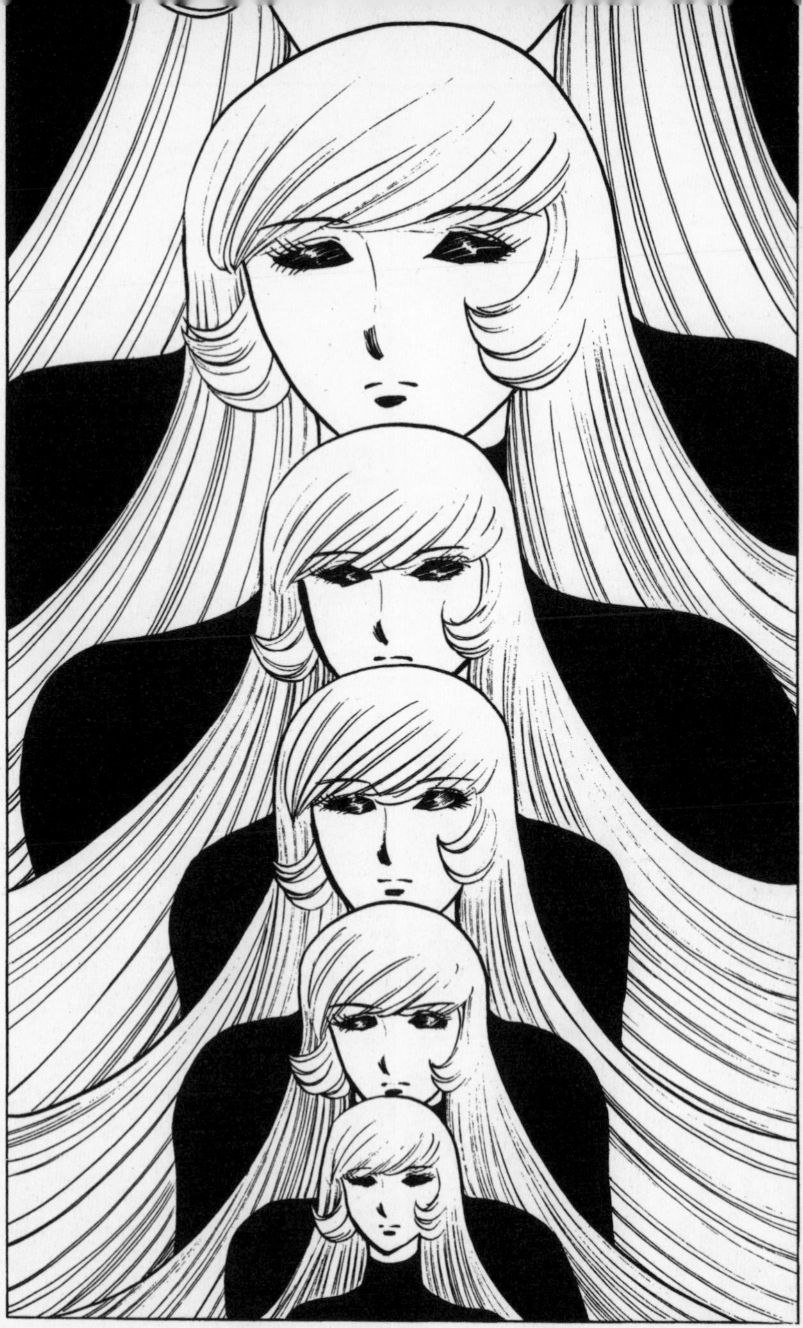

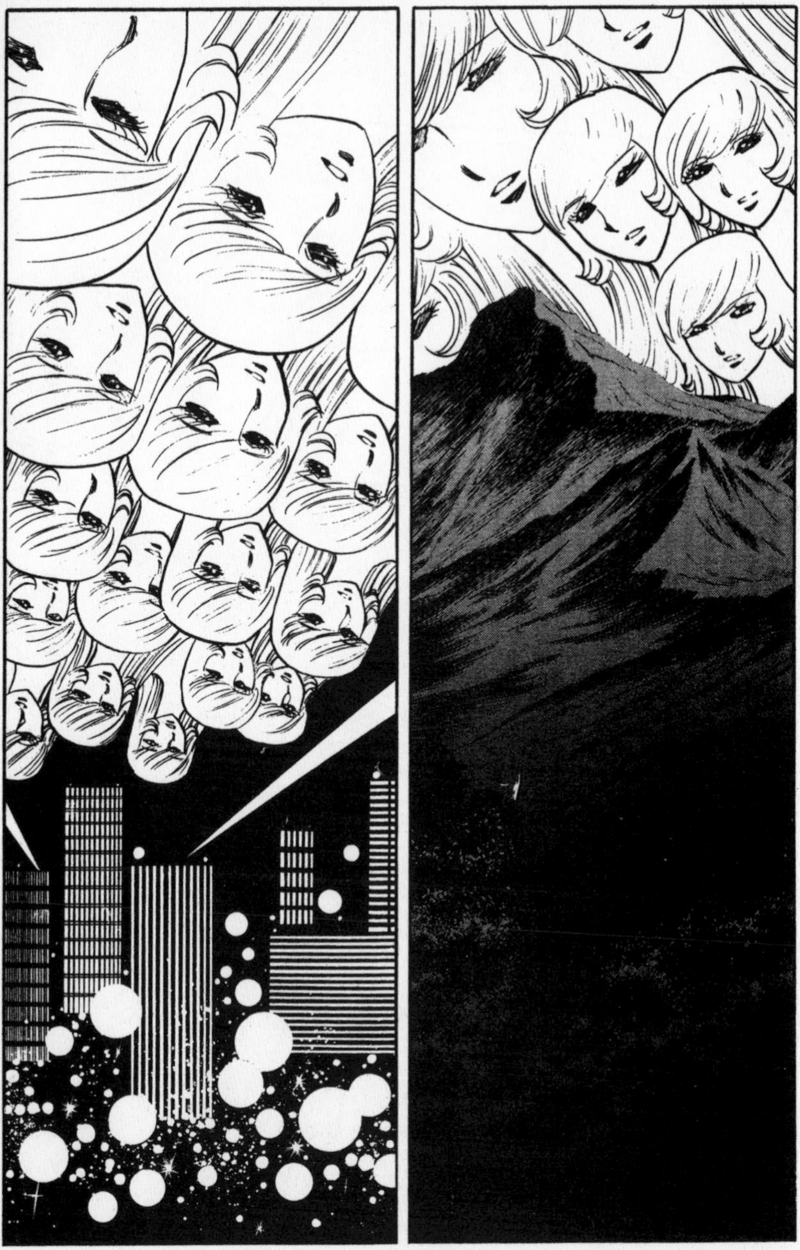

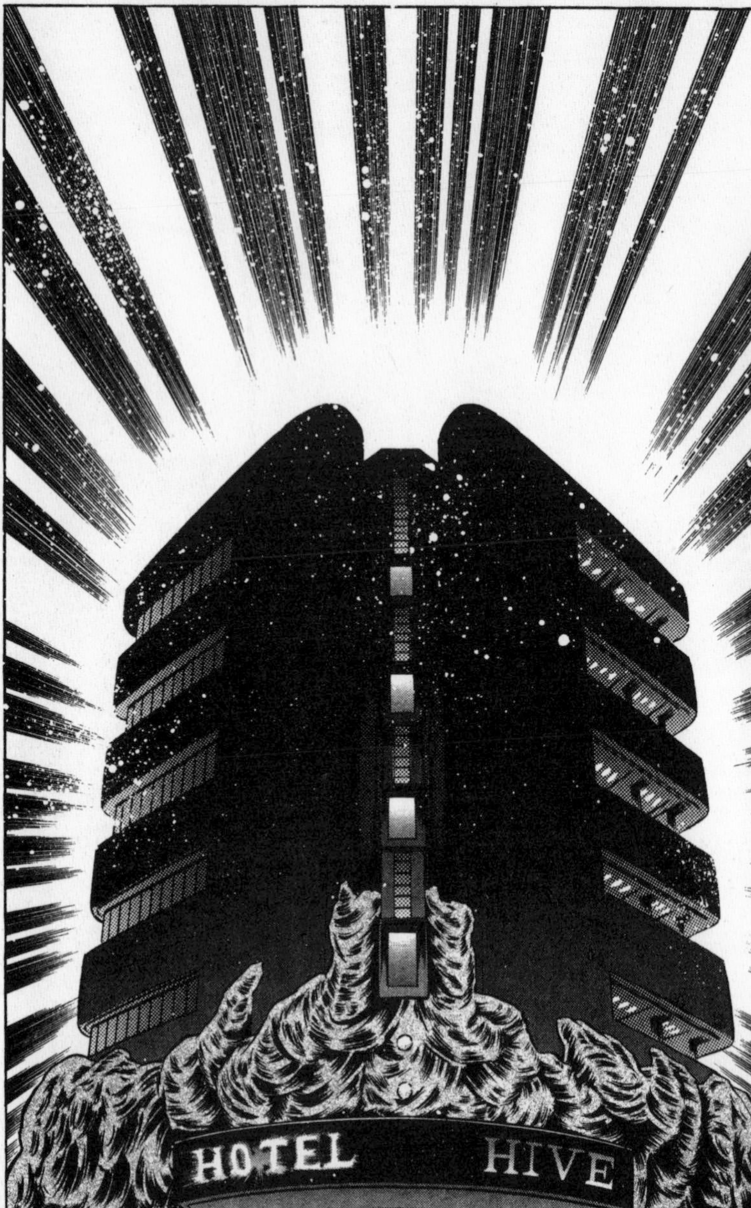
HOTEL HIVE

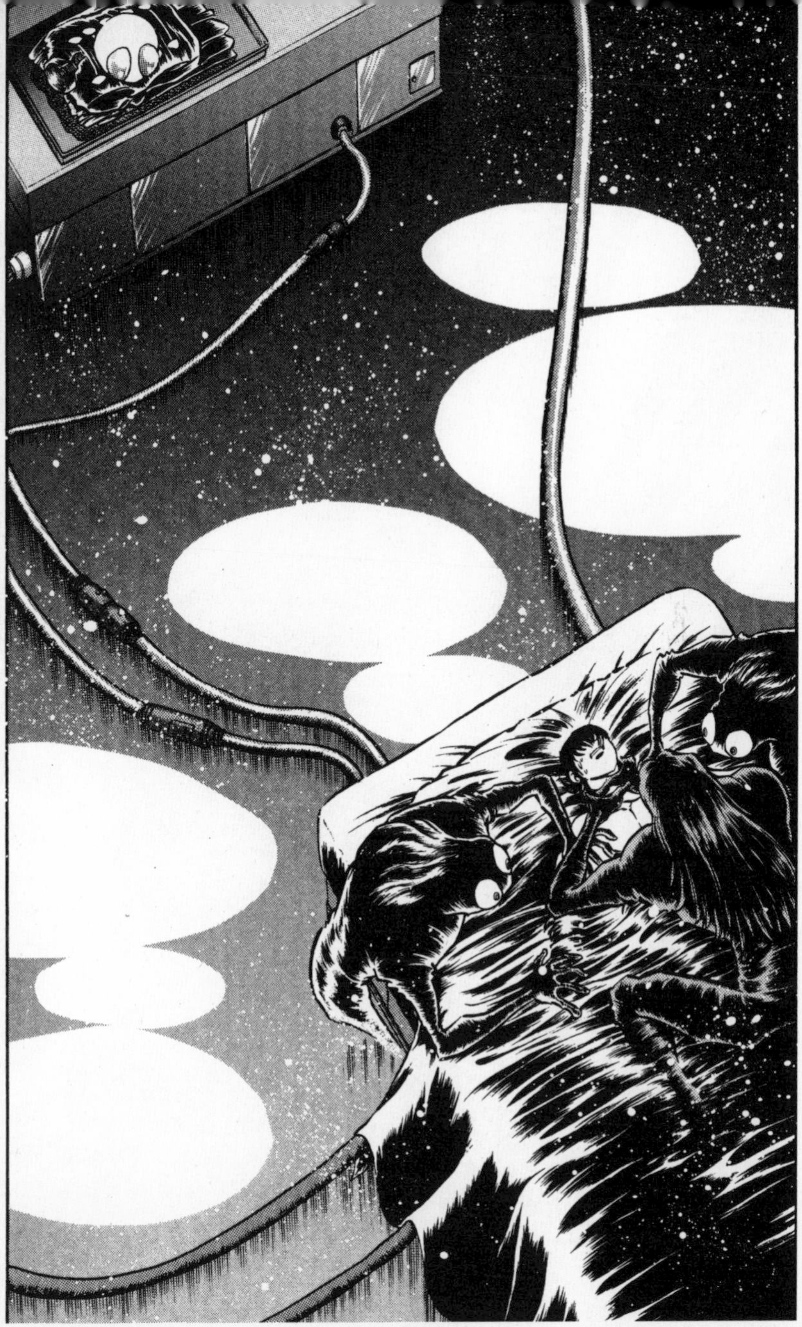

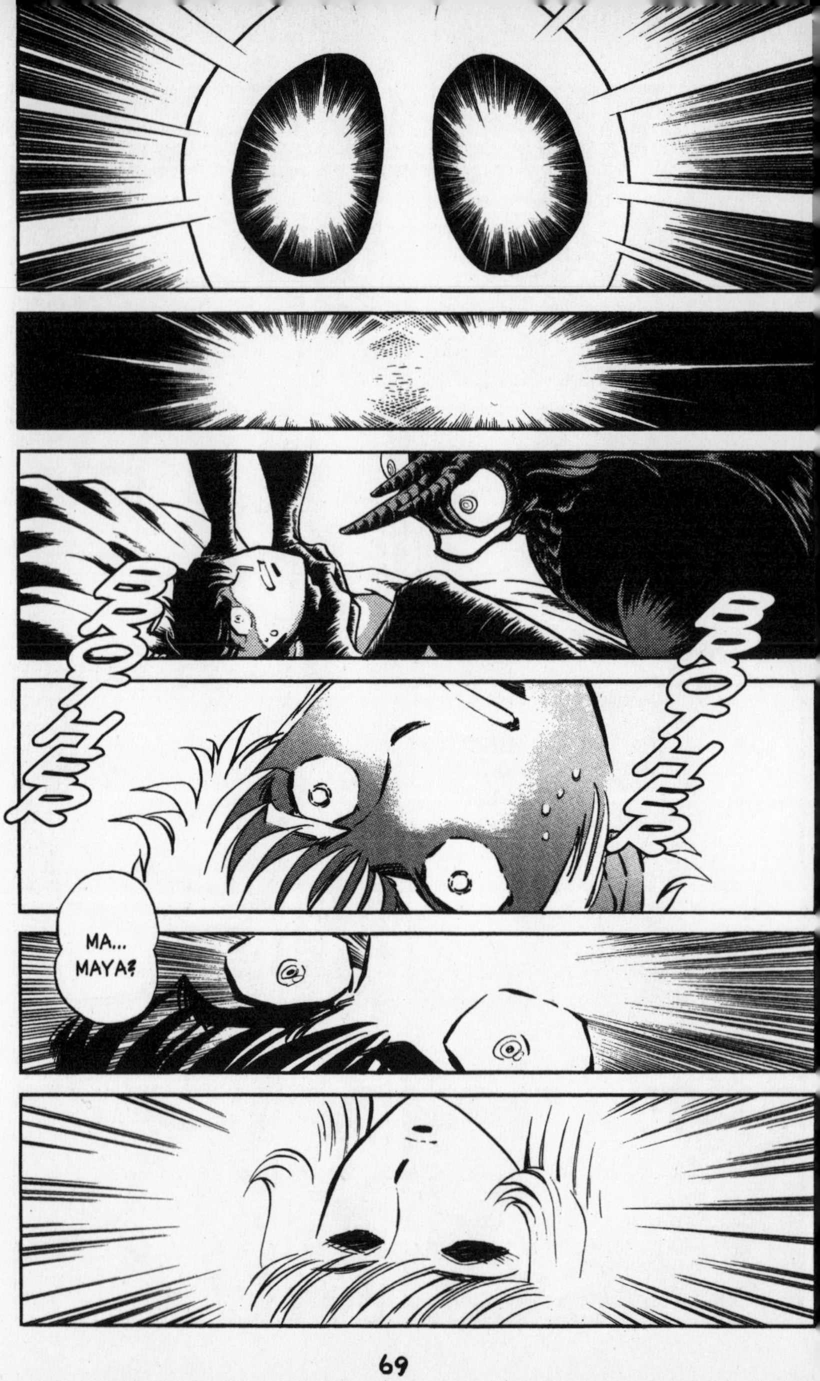
BROTHER
BROTHER
MA... MAYA?

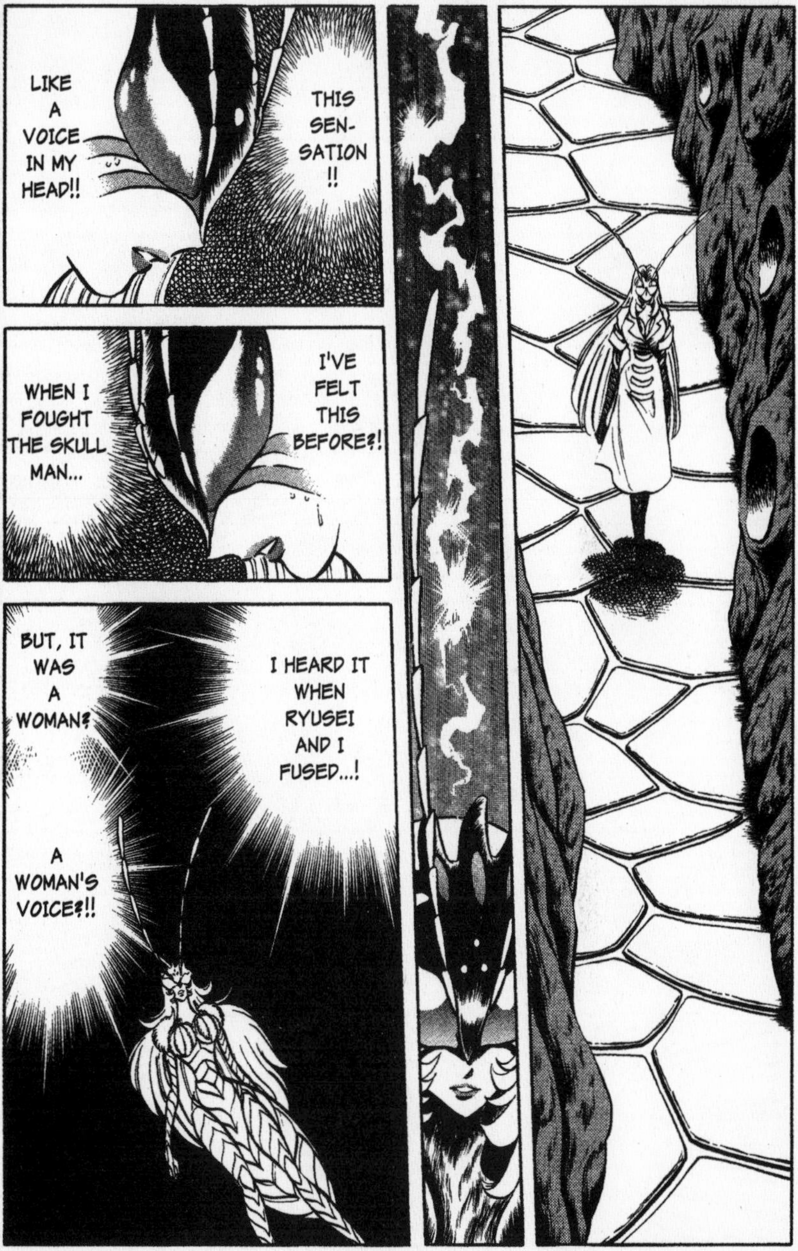
THIS SEN-SATION!!
LIKE A VOICE IN MY HEAD!!
I'VE FELT THIS BEFORE?!
WHEN I FOUGHT THE SKULL MAN...
I HEARD IT WHEN RYUSEI AND I FUSED...!
BUT, IT WAS A WOMAN?
A WOMAN'S VOICE?!!

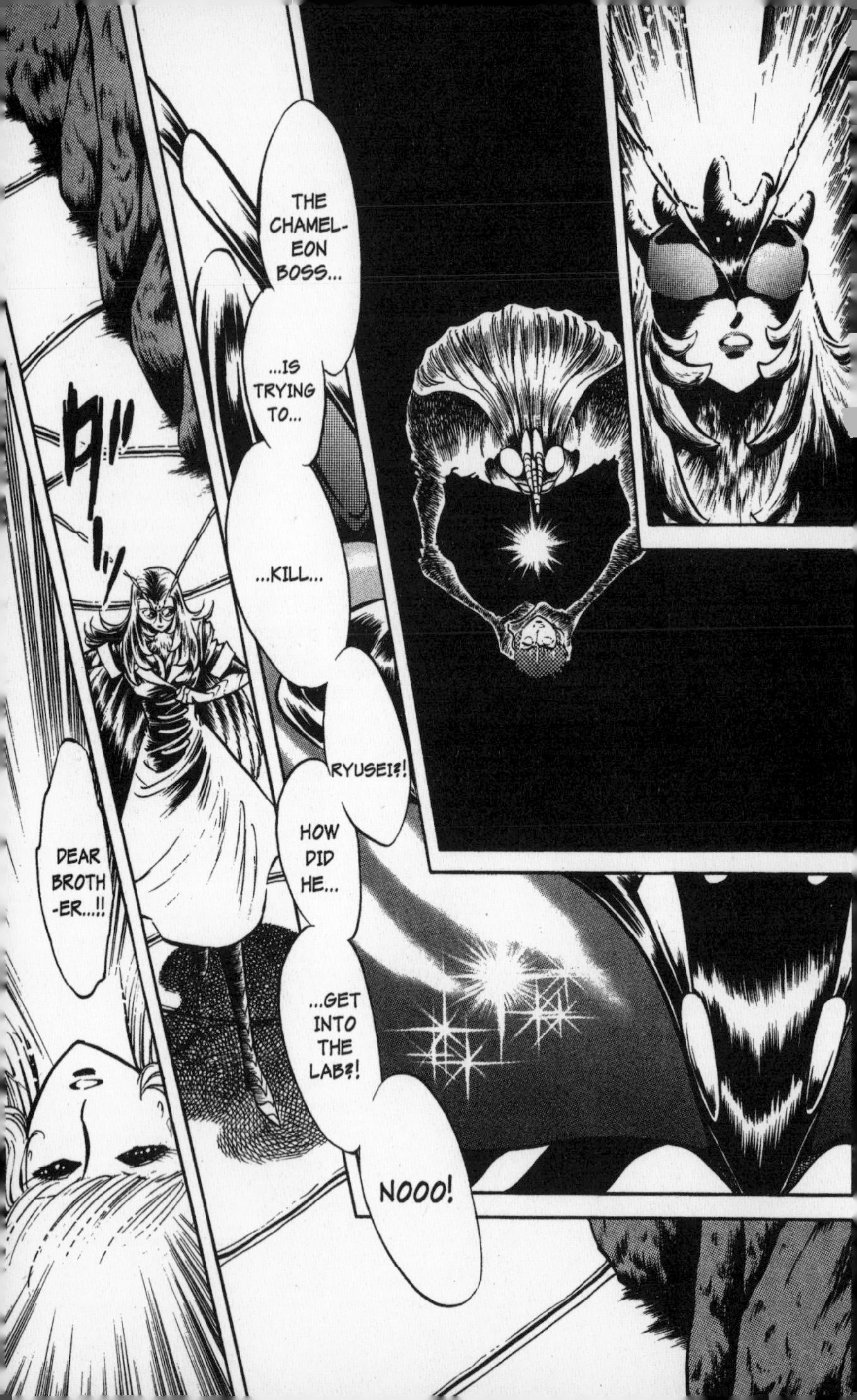
THE CHAMEL-EON BOSS...
...IS TRYING TO...
...KILL...
RYUSEI?!
HOW DID HE...
...GET INTO THE LAB?!
NOOO!
ダッ
DEAR BROTH-ER...!!

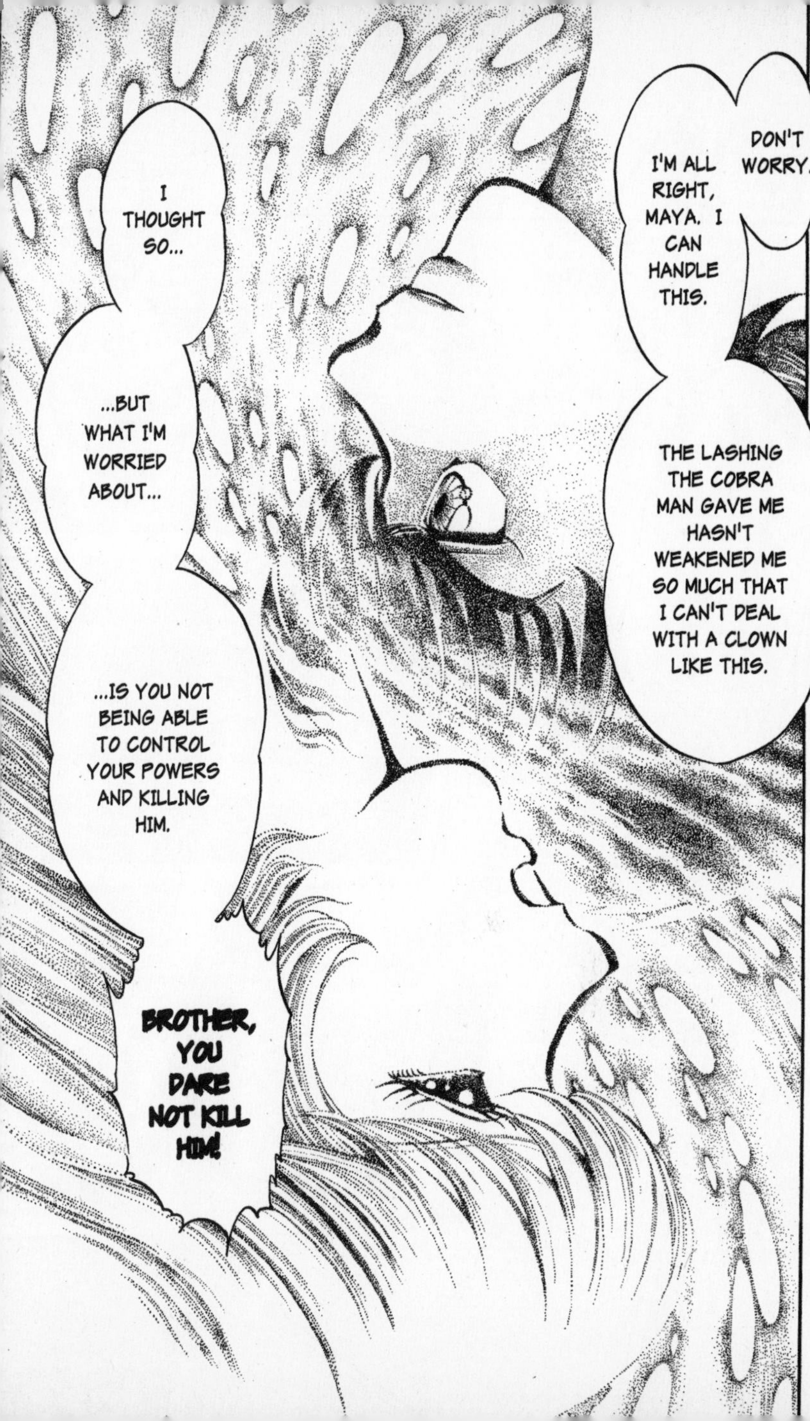
DON'T WORRY.
I'M ALL RIGHT, MAYA. I CAN HANDLE THIS.
THE LASHING THE COBRA MAN GAVE ME HASN'T WEAKENED ME SO MUCH THAT I CAN'T DEAL WITH A CLOWN LIKE THIS.
I THOUGHT SO...
...BUT WHAT I'M WORRIED ABOUT...
...IS YOU NOT BEING ABLE TO CONTROL YOUR POWERS AND KILLING HIM.
BROTHER, YOU DARE NOT KILL HIM!

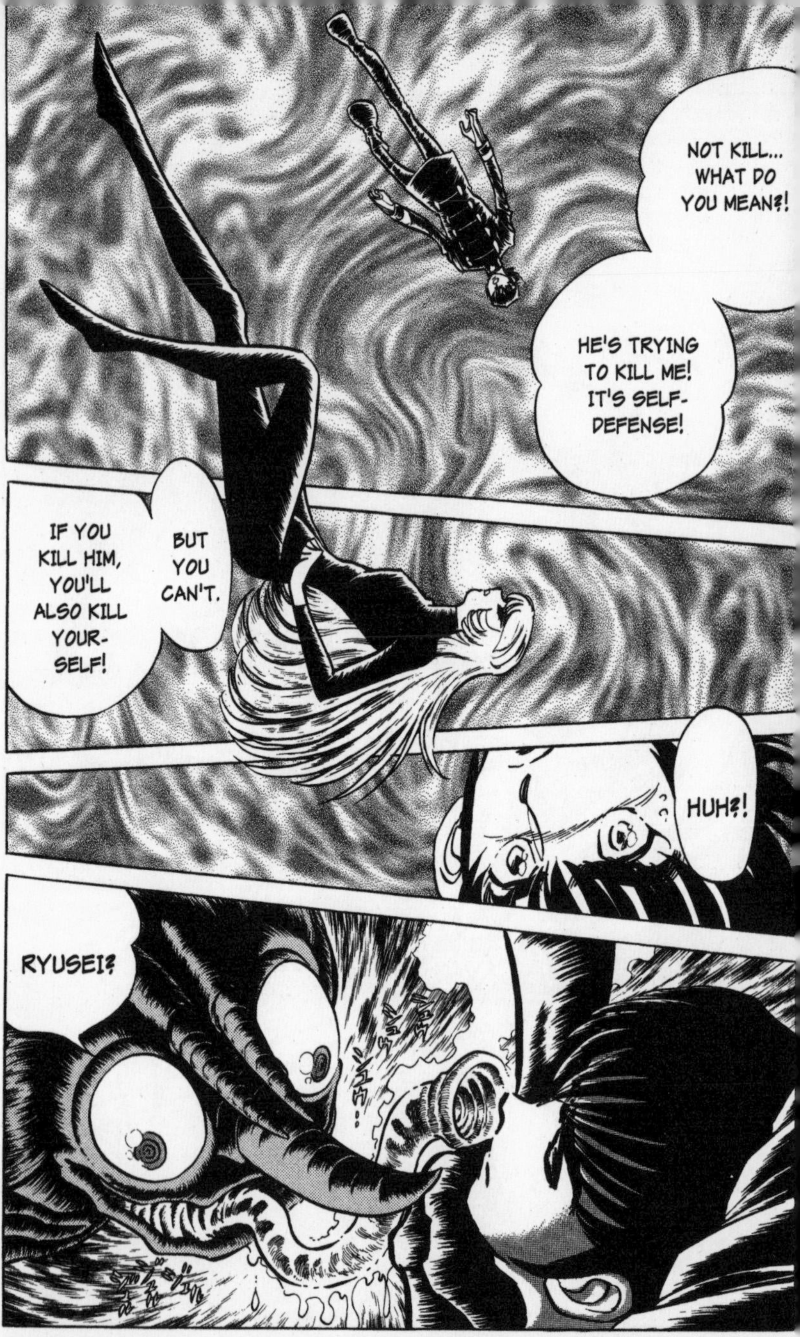
NOT KILL... WHAT DO YOU MEAN?!
HE'S TRYING TO KILL ME! IT'S SELF-DEFENSE!
BUT YOU CAN'T.
IF YOU KILL HIM, YOU'LL ALSO KILL YOUR-SELF!
HUH?!
RYUSEI?

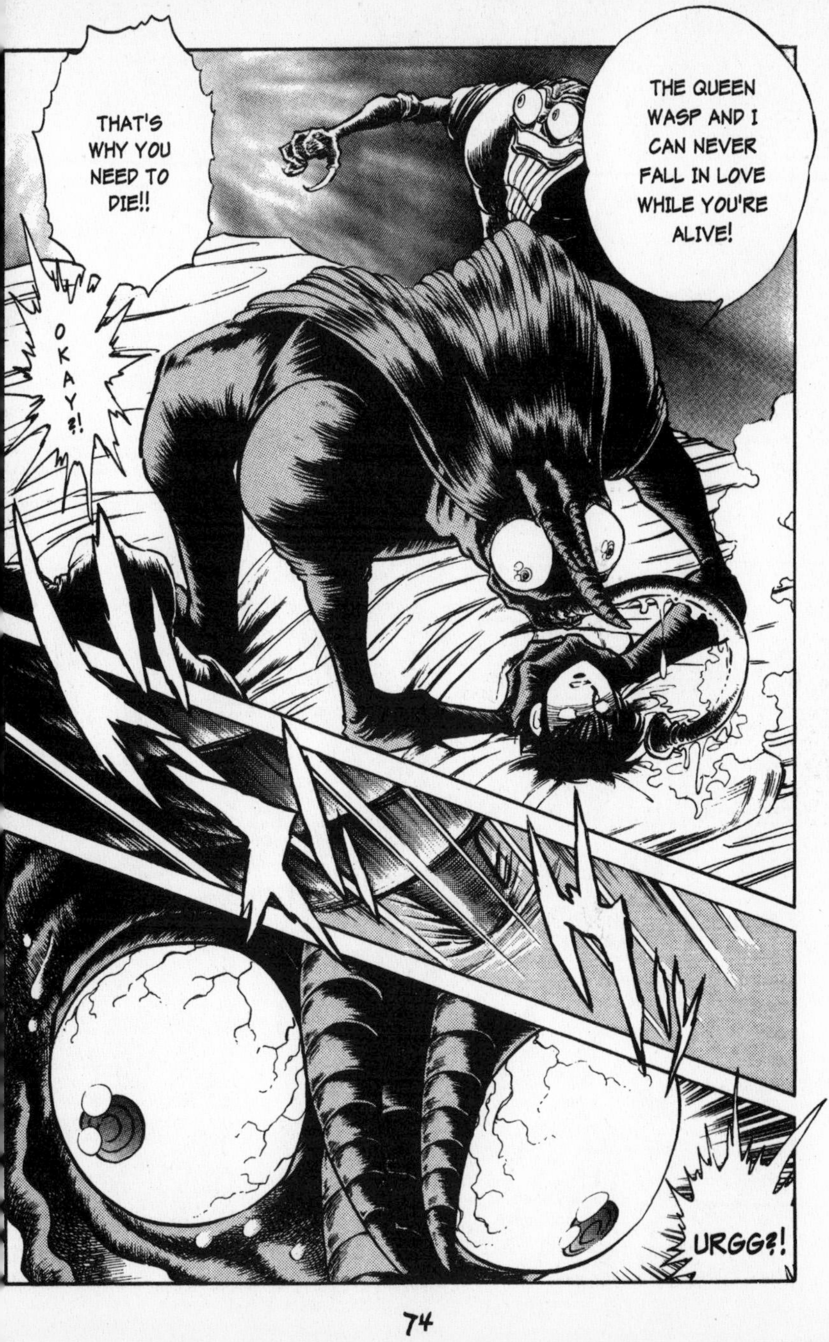
THE QUEEN WASP AND I CAN NEVER FALL IN LOVE WHILE YOU'RE ALIVE!
THAT'S WHY YOU NEED TO DIE!!
OKAY?!
URGG?!

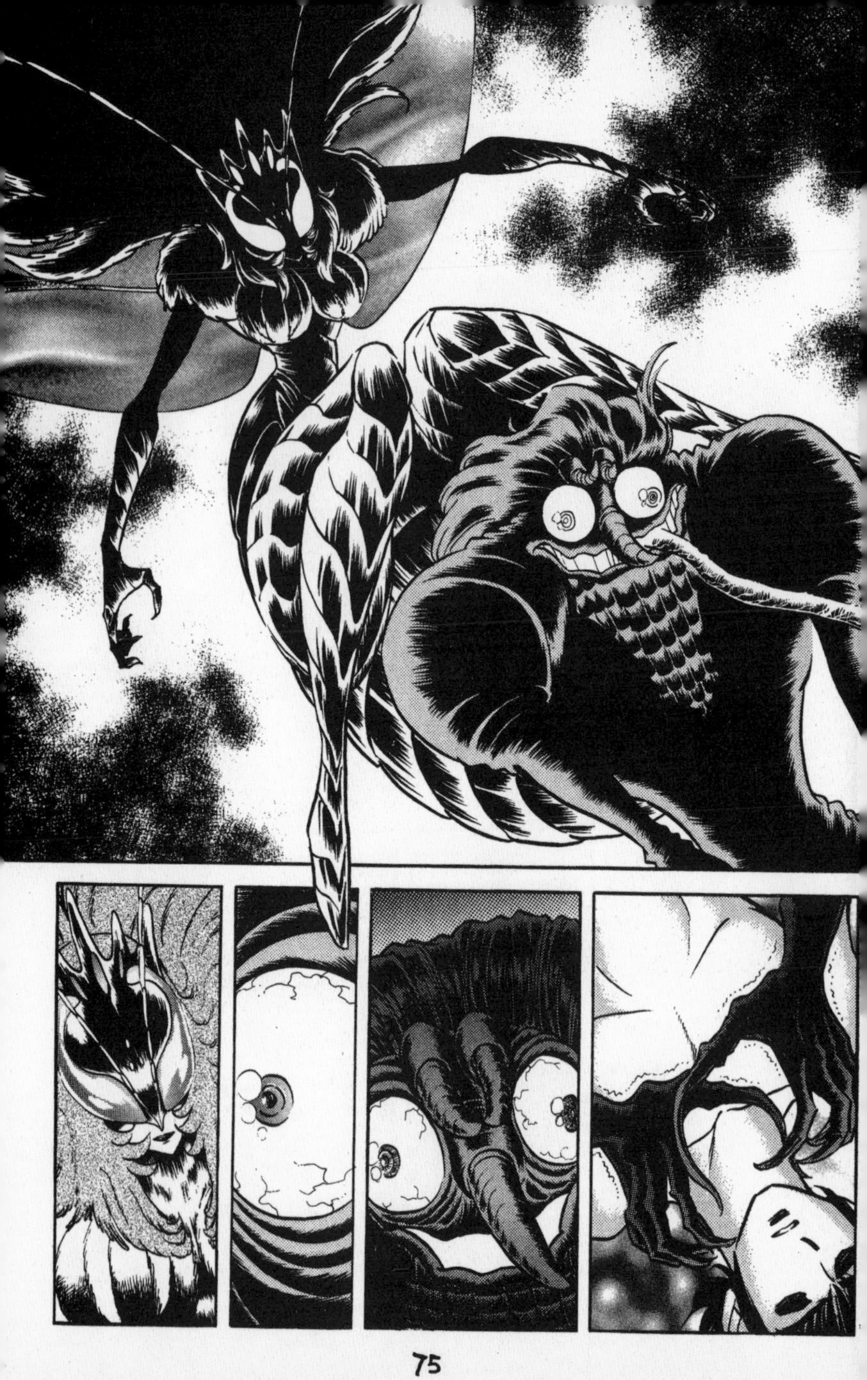

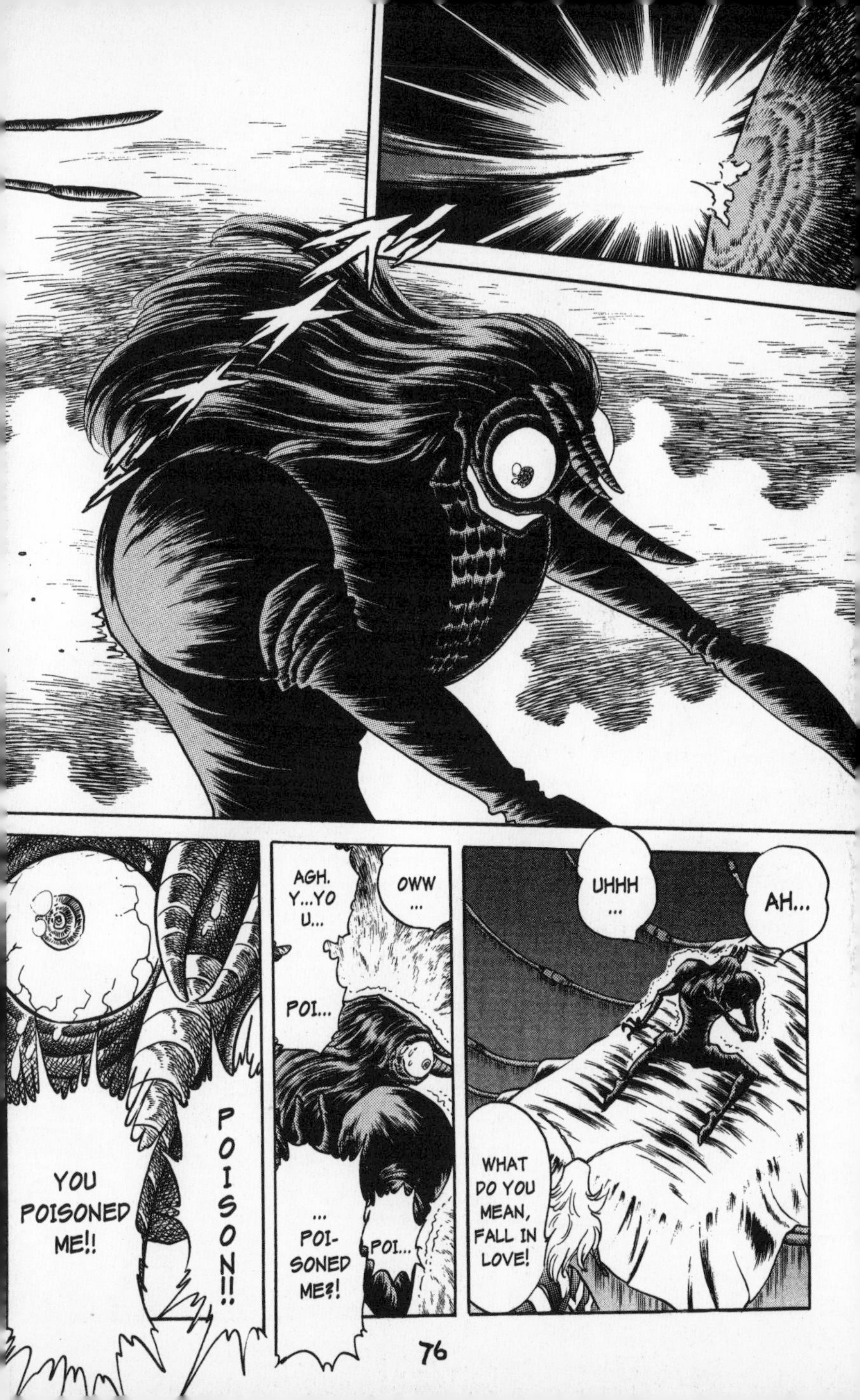
AH...
UHHH ...
WHAT DO YOU MEAN, FALL IN LOVE!
OWW ...
AGH. Y...YO U...
POI...
... POI- SONED ME?!
POI...
POISON!!
YOU POISONED ME!!

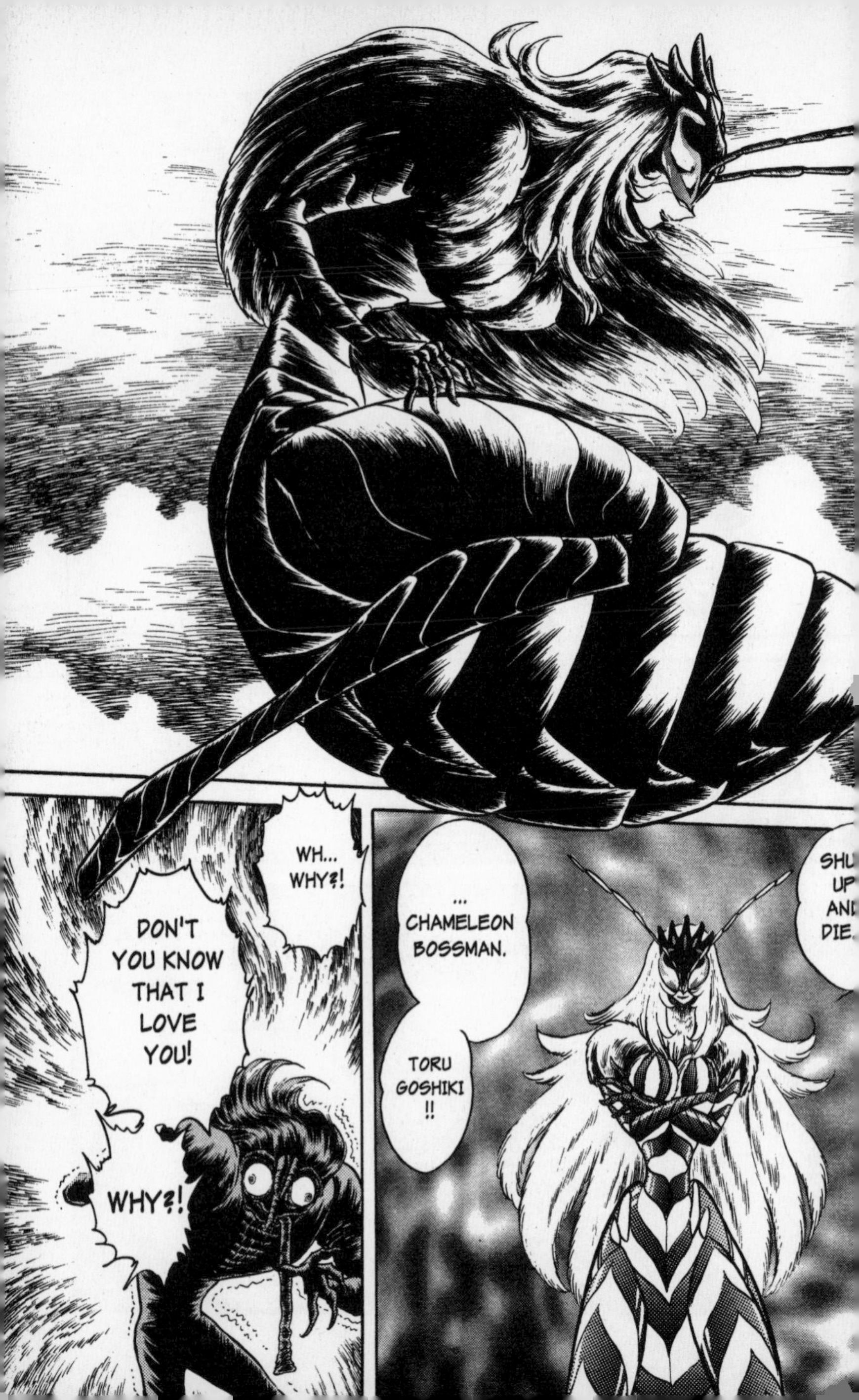
SHU UP AND DIE.
... CHAMELEON BOSSMAN.
TORU GOSHIKI !!
WH... WHY?!
DON'T YOU KNOW THAT I LOVE YOU!
WHY?!

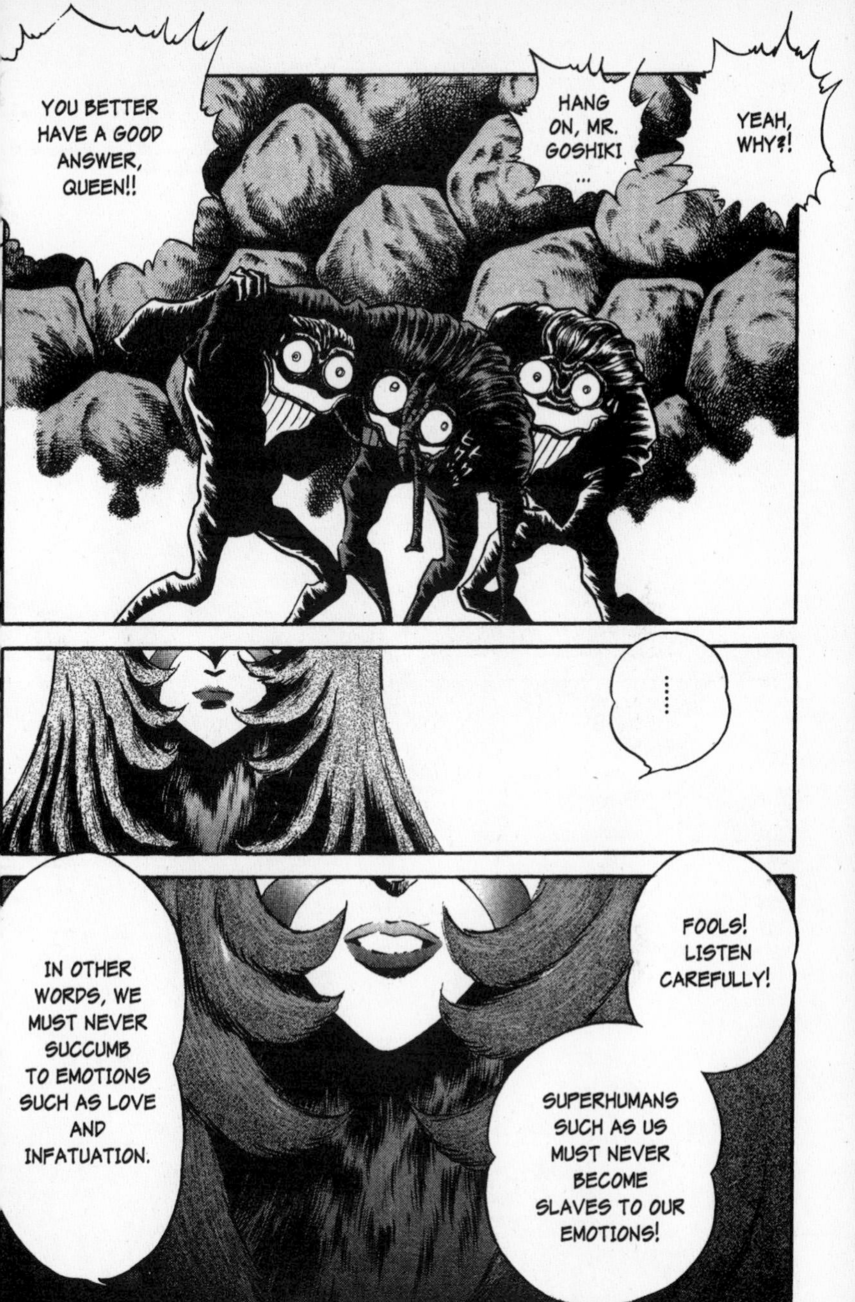
YEAH, WHY?!
HANG ON, MR. GOSHIKI ...
YOU BETTER HAVE A GOOD ANSWER, QUEEN!!
......
FOOLS! LISTEN CAREFULLY!
SUPERHUMANS SUCH AS US MUST NEVER BECOME SLAVES TO OUR EMOTIONS!
IN OTHER WORDS, WE MUST NEVER SUCCUMB TO EMOTIONS SUCH AS LOVE AND INFATUATION.

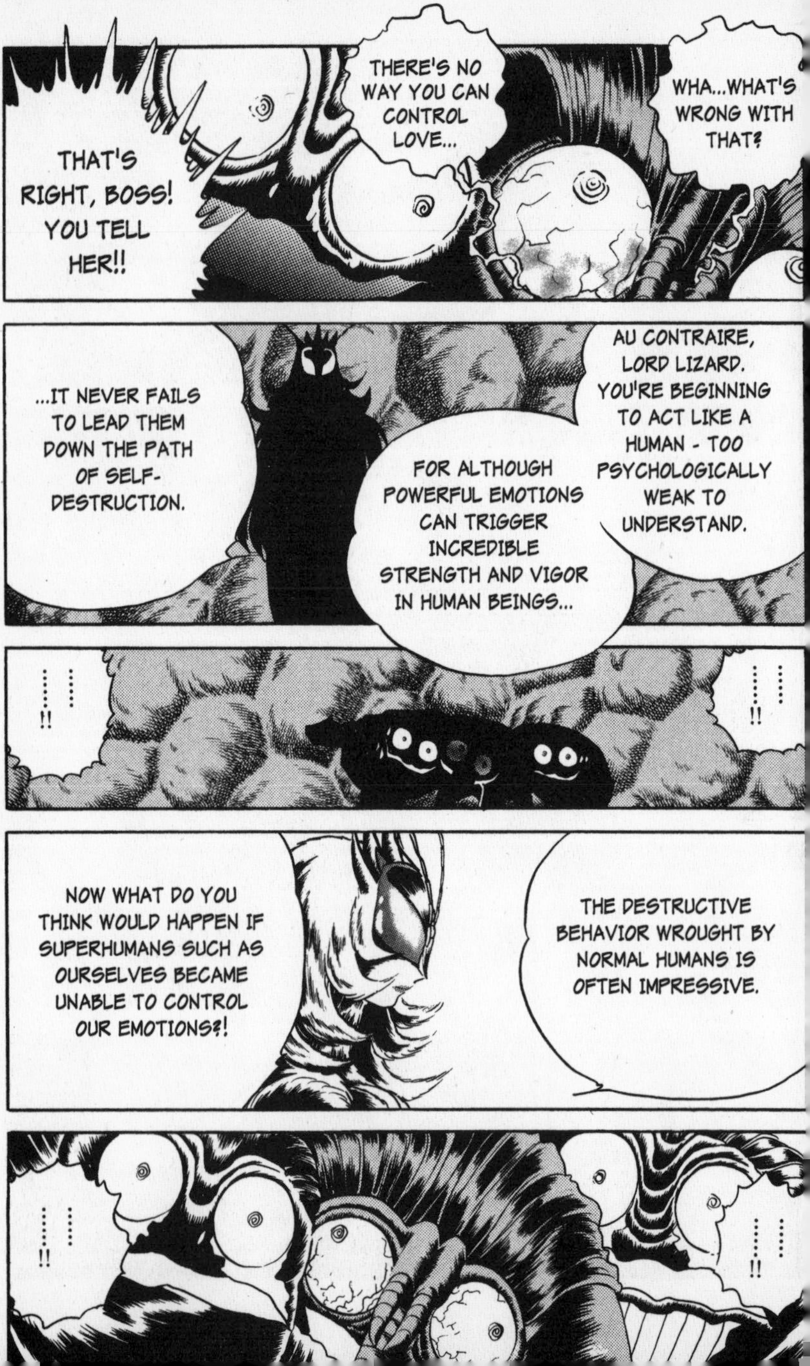
WHA...WHAT'S WRONG WITH THAT?
THERE'S NO WAY YOU CAN CONTROL LOVE...
THAT'S RIGHT, BOSS! YOU TELL HER!!
AU CONTRAIRE, LORD LIZARD. YOU'RE BEGINNING TO ACT LIKE A HUMAN - TOO PSYCHOLOGICALLY WEAK TO UNDERSTAND.
FOR ALTHOUGH POWERFUL EMOTIONS CAN TRIGGER INCREDIBLE STRENGTH AND VIGOR IN HUMAN BEINGS...
...IT NEVER FAILS TO LEAD THEM DOWN THE PATH OF SELF-DESTRUCTION.
......!!
......!!
THE DESTRUCTIVE BEHAVIOR WROUGHT BY NORMAL HUMANS IS OFTEN IMPRESSIVE.
NOW WHAT DO YOU THINK WOULD HAPPEN IF SUPERHUMANS SUCH AS OURSELVES BECAME UNABLE TO CONTROL OUR EMOTIONS?!
......!!
......!!

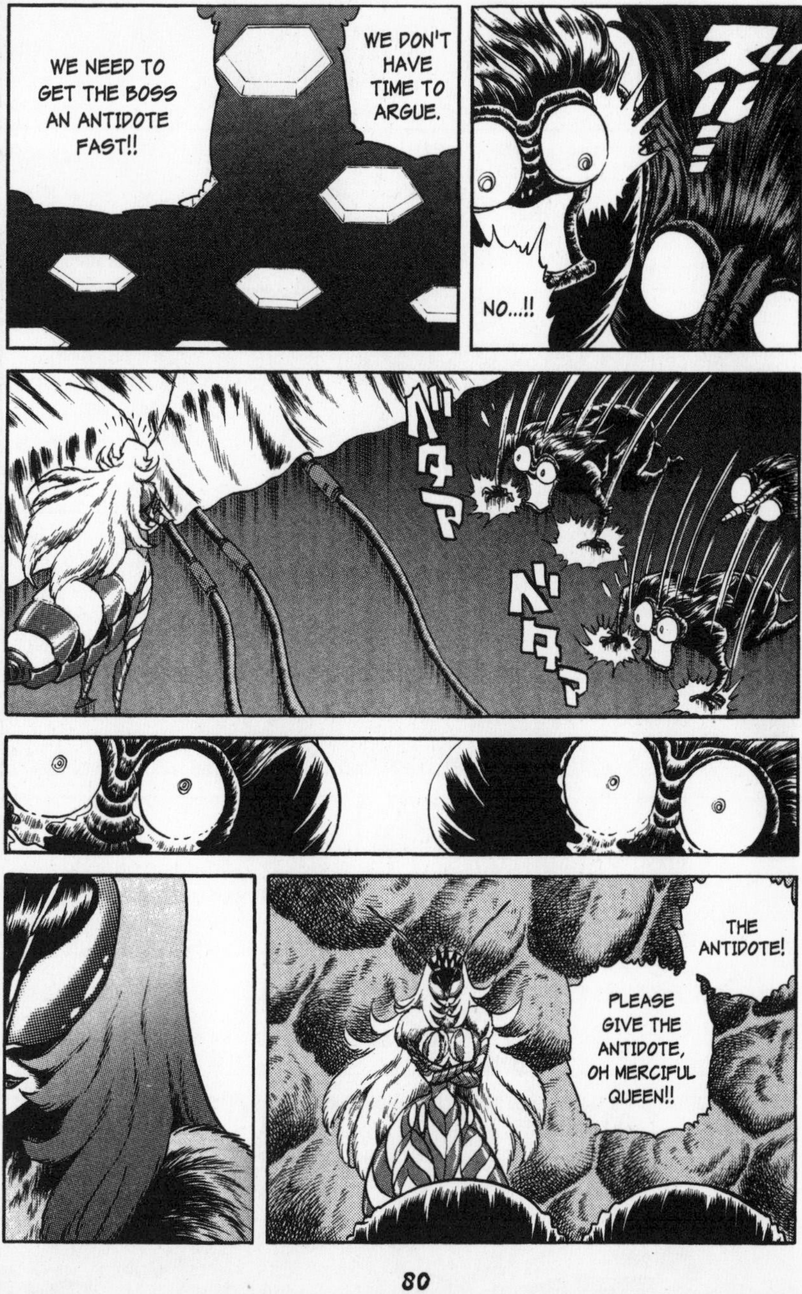
NO...!!
WE DON'T HAVE TIME TO ARGUE.
WE NEED TO GET THE BOSS AN ANTIDOTE FAST!!
THE ANTIDOTE!
PLEASE GIVE THE ANTIDOTE, OH MERCIFUL QUEEN!!

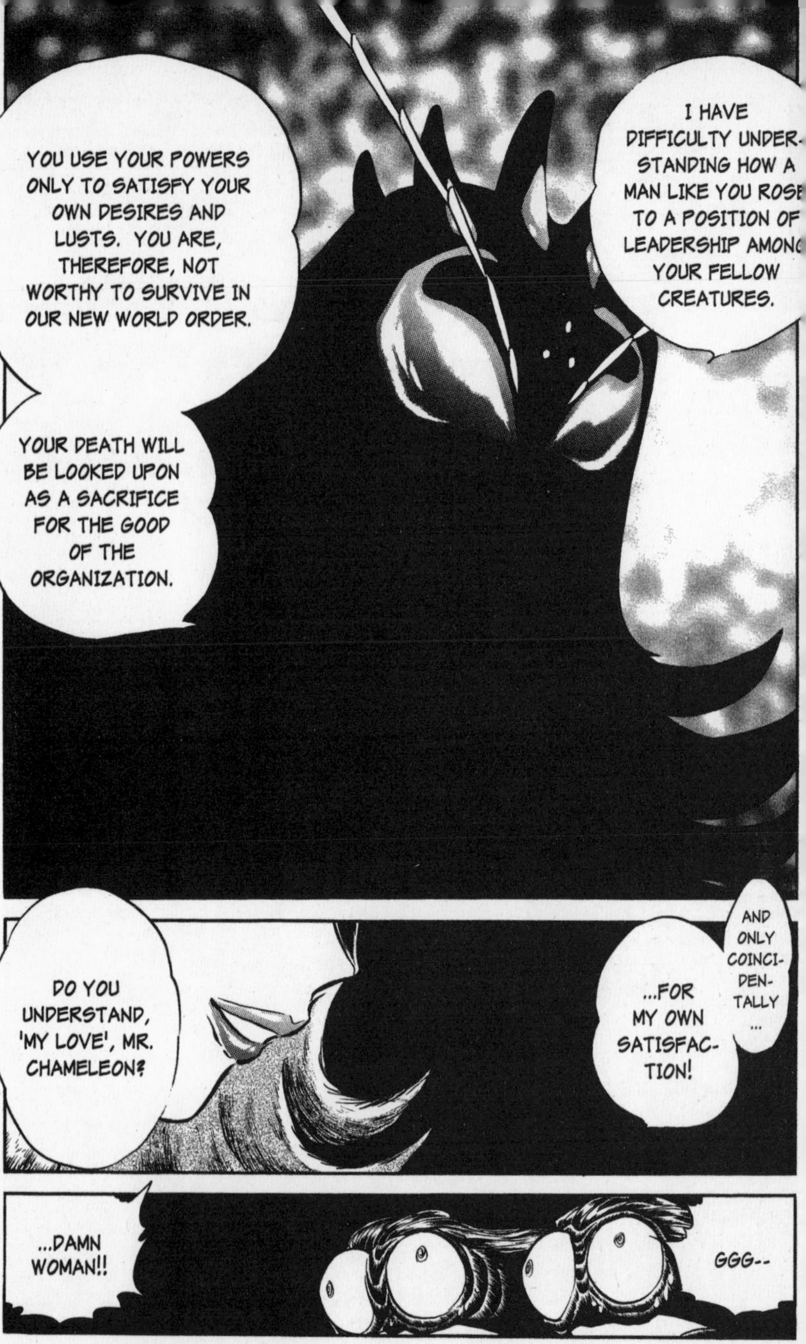

I HAVE DIFFICULTY UNDER-STANDING HOW A MAN LIKE YOU ROSE TO A POSITION OF LEADERSHIP AMONG YOUR FELLOW CREATURES.
YOU USE YOUR POWERS ONLY TO SATISFY YOUR OWN DESIRES AND LUSTS. YOU ARE, THEREFORE, NOT WORTHY TO SURVIVE IN OUR NEW WORLD ORDER.
YOUR DEATH WILL BE LOOKED UPON AS A SACRIFICE FOR THE GOOD OF THE ORGANIZATION.
AND ONLY COINCI-DEN-TALLY ...
...FOR MY OWN SATISFAC-TION!
DO YOU UNDERSTAND, 'MY LOVE', MR. CHAMELEON?
GGG--
...DAMN WOMAN!!

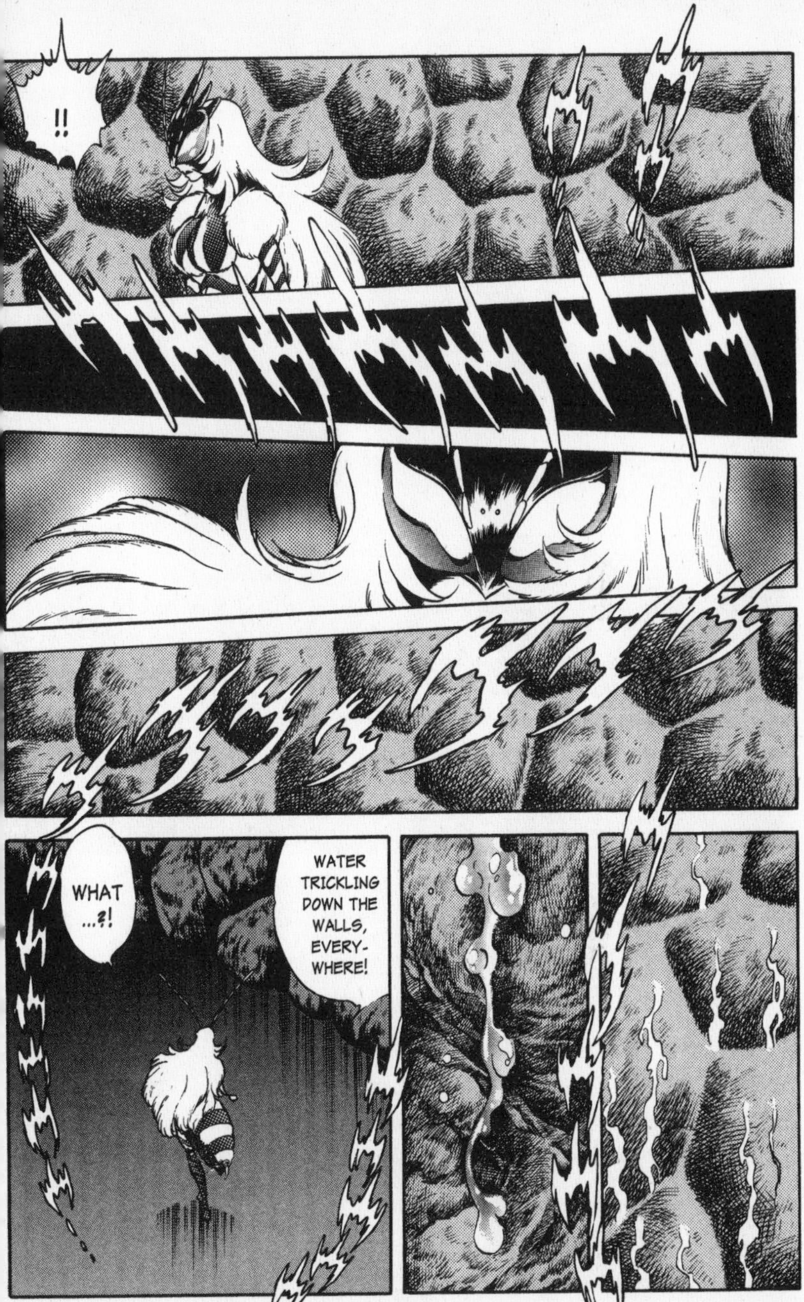
!!
WATER TRICKLING DOWN THE WALLS, EVERY-WHERE!
WHAT ...?!

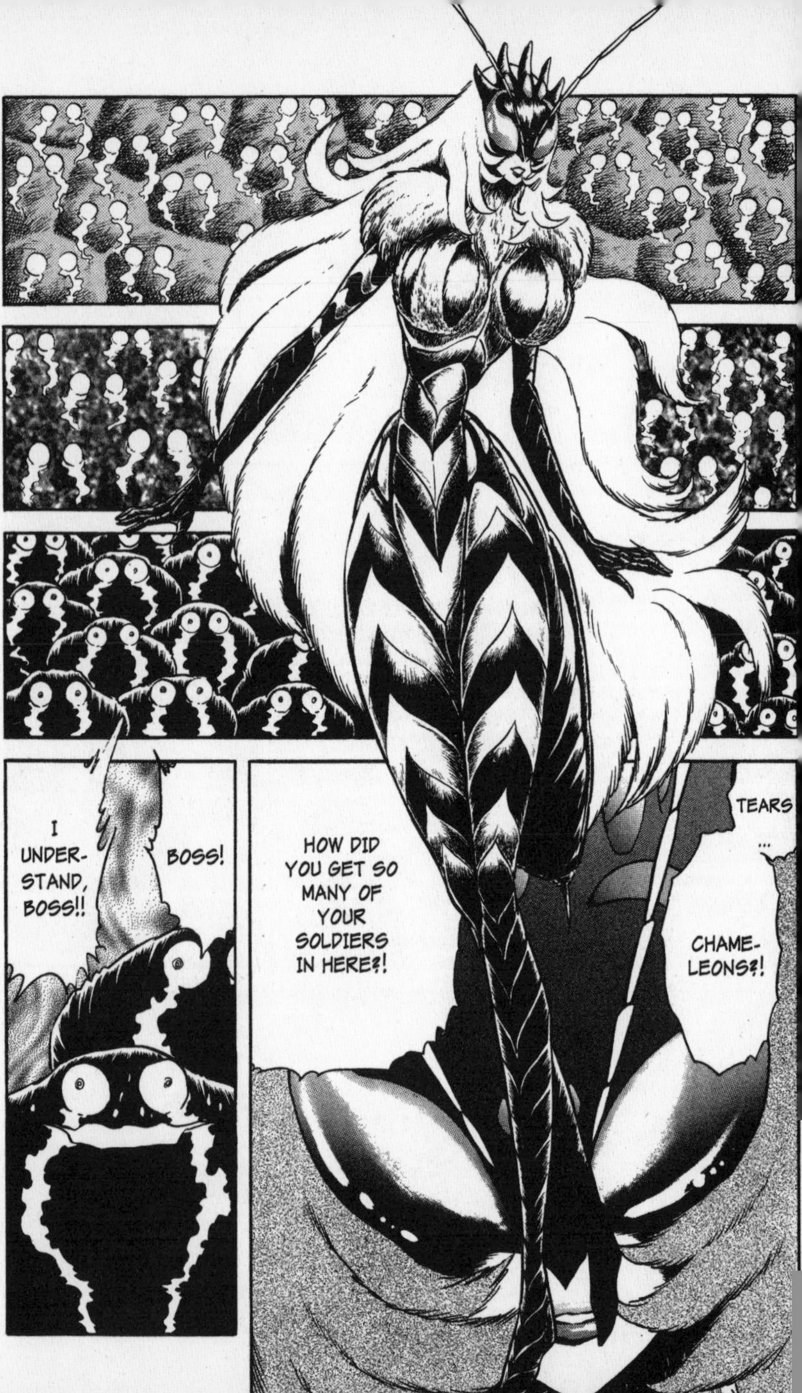
TEARS ... CHAMELEONS?!
HOW DID YOU GET SO MANY OF YOUR SOLDIERS IN HERE?!
BOSS!
I UNDERSTAND, BOSS!!

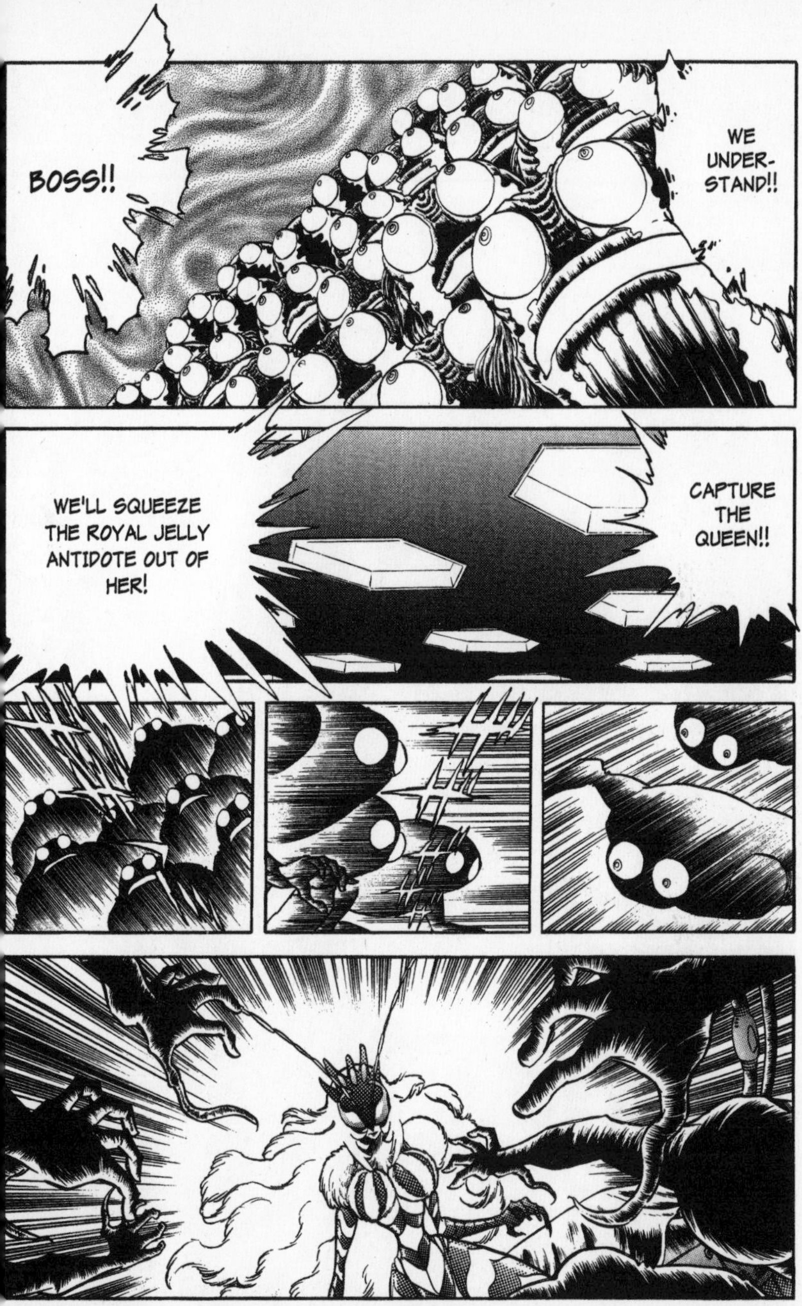
WE UNDER-STAND!!
BOSS!!
CAPTURE THE QUEEN!!
WE'LL SQUEEZE THE ROYAL JELLY ANTIDOTE OUT OF HER!

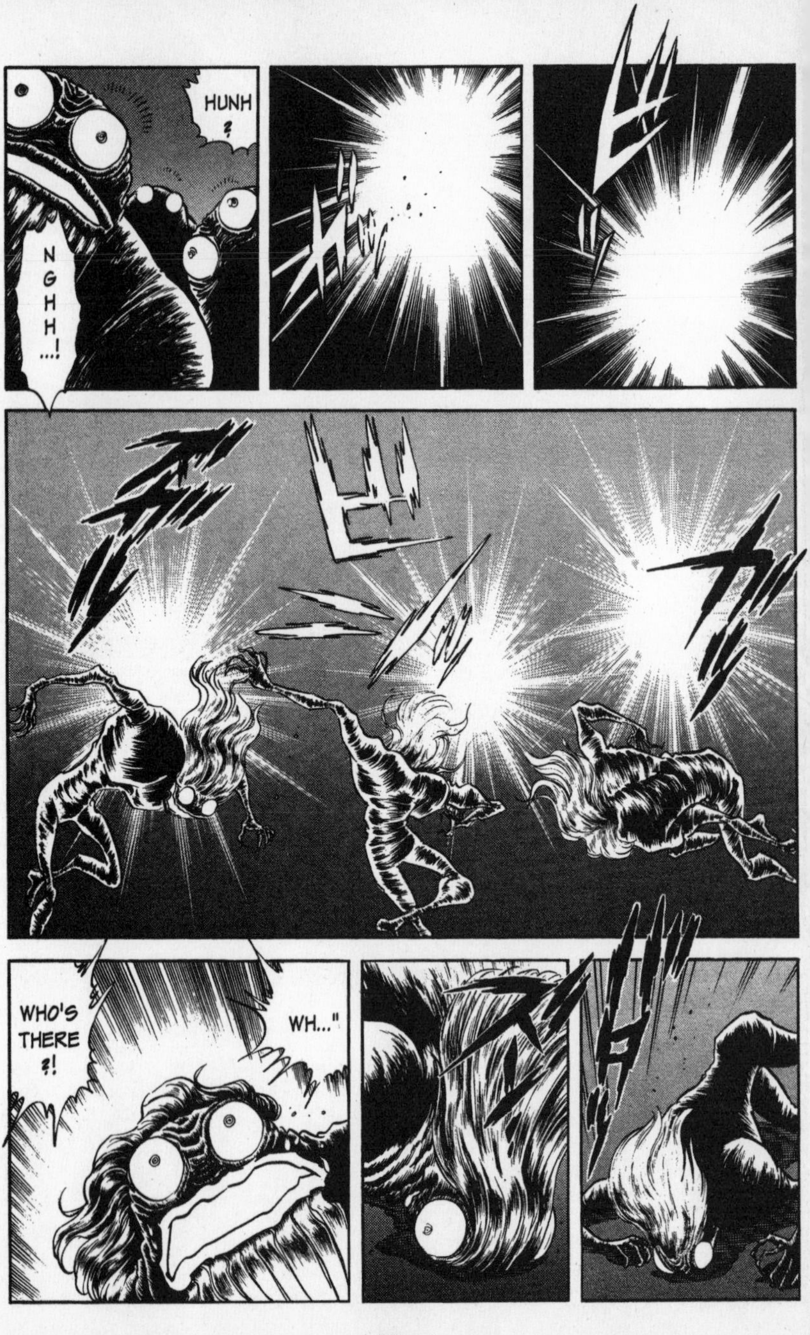
HUNH ?
NGHH ...!
WH..."
WHO'S THERE ?!

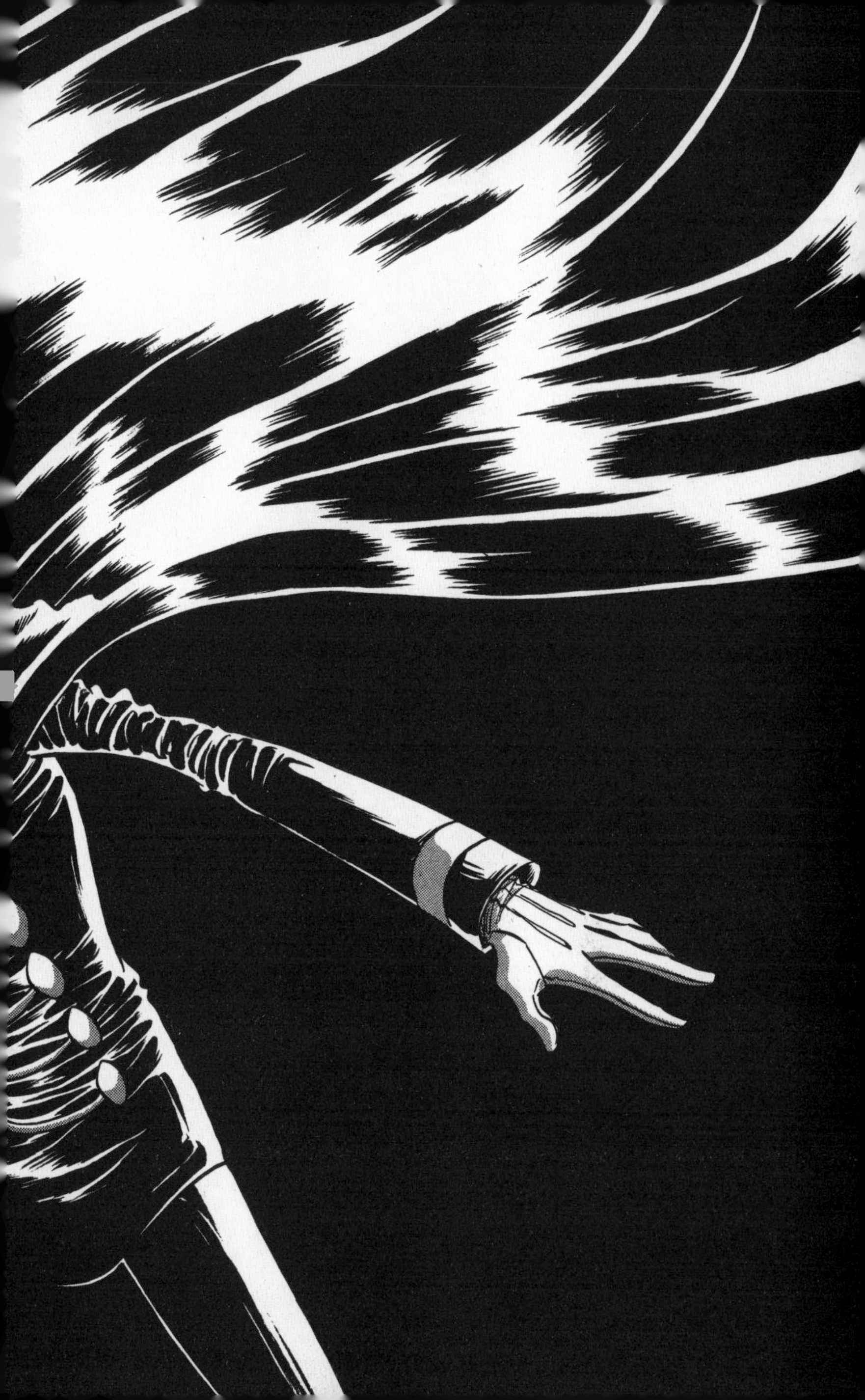

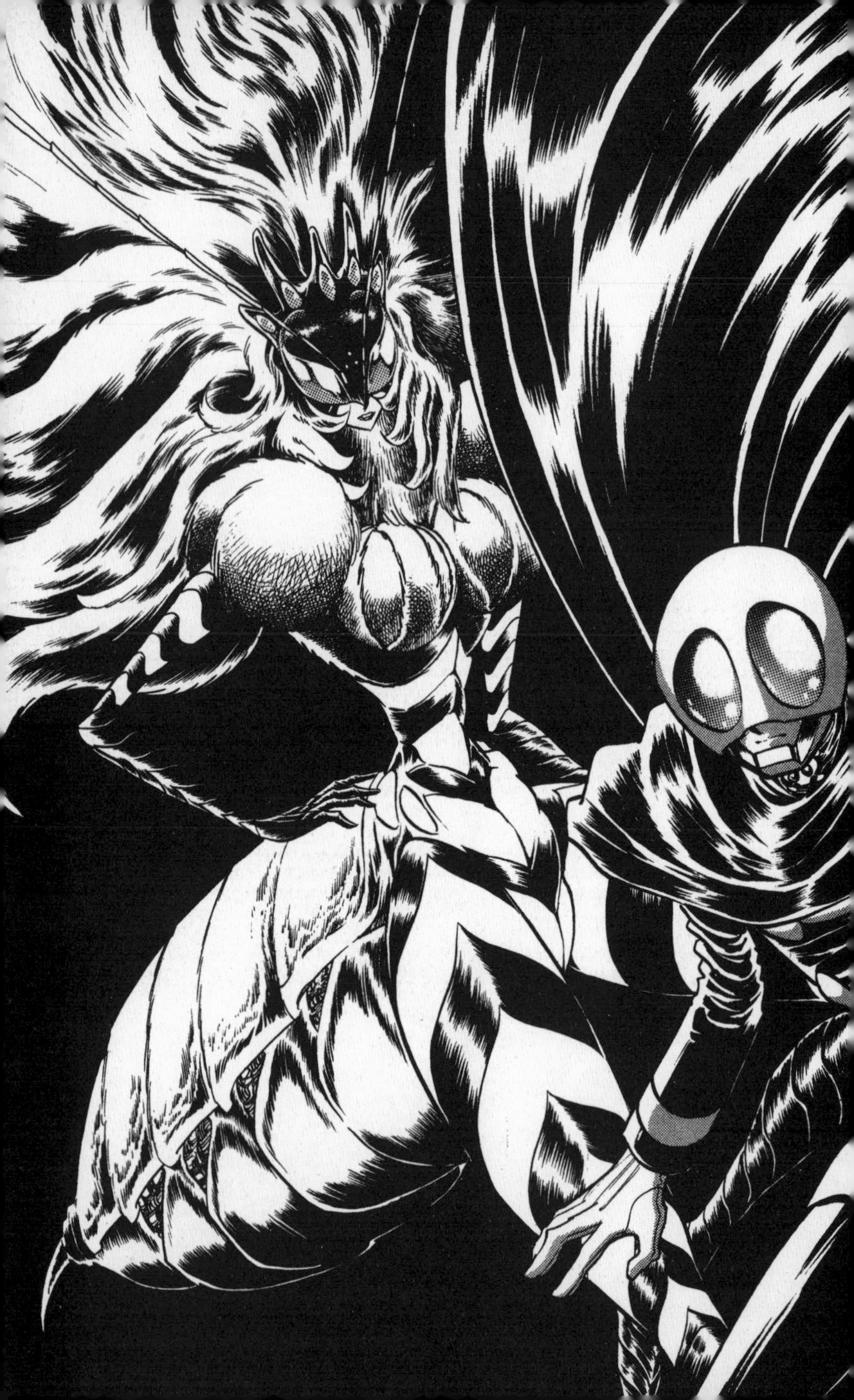

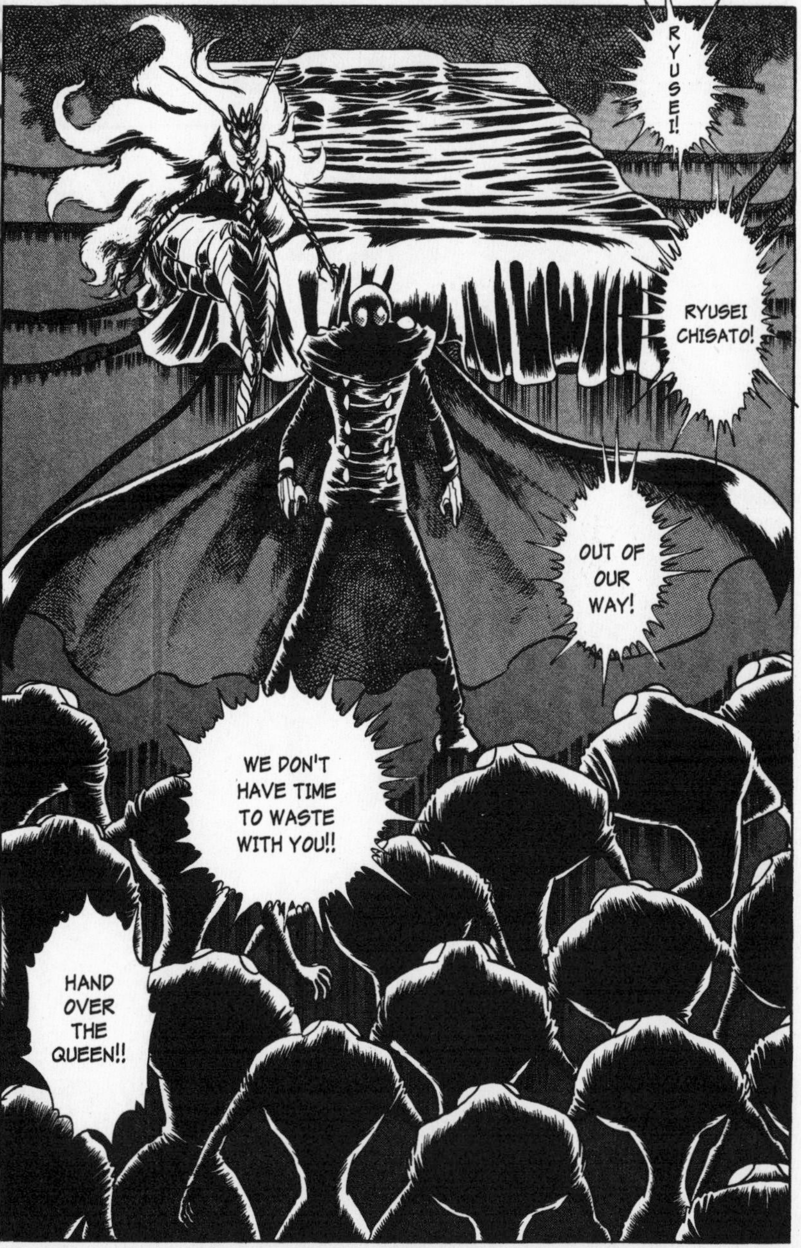
RYUSEI!!
RYUSEI CHISATO!
OUT OF OUR WAY!
WE DON'T HAVE TIME TO WASTE WITH YOU!!
HAND OVER THE QUEEN!!

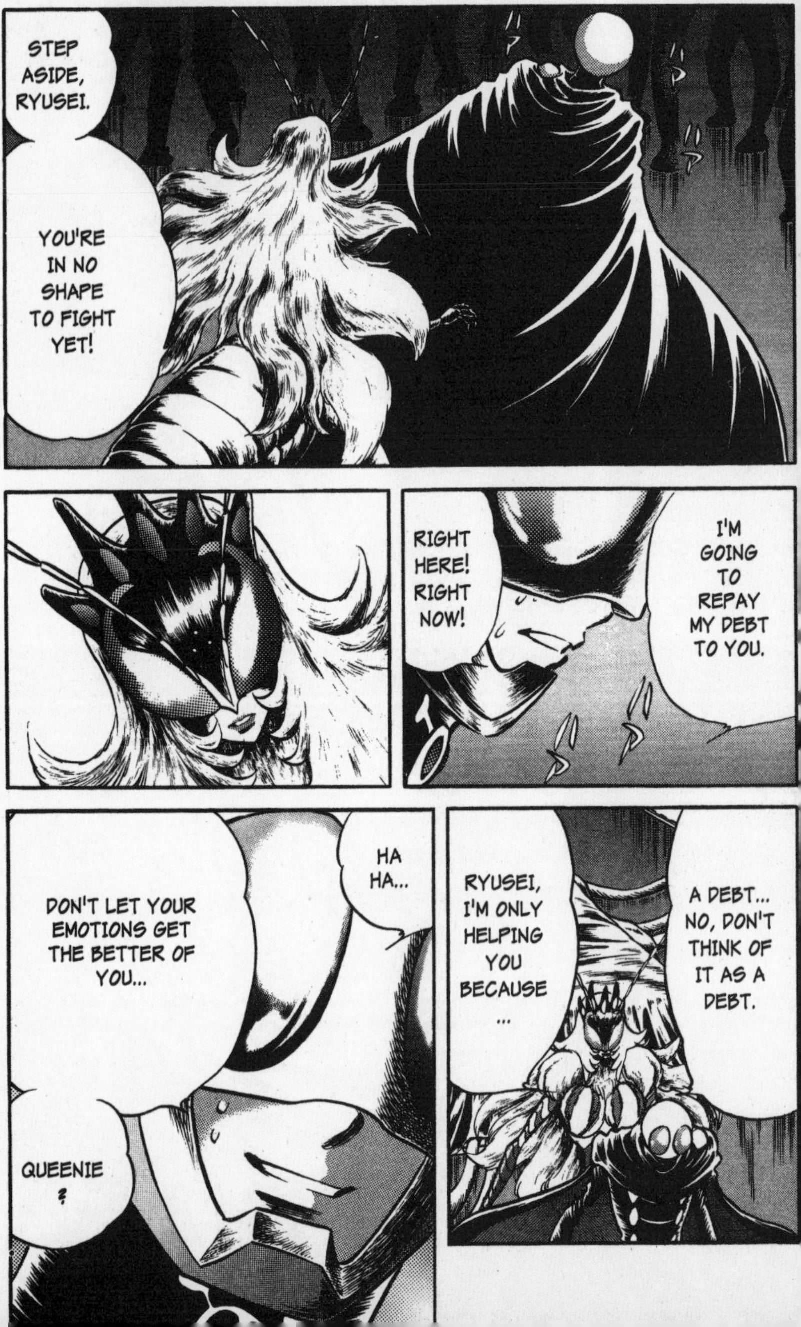
STEP ASIDE, RYUSEI.
YOU'RE IN NO SHAPE TO FIGHT YET!
I'M GOING TO REPAY MY DEBT TO YOU.
RIGHT HERE! RIGHT NOW!
A DEBT... NO, DON'T THINK OF IT AS A DEBT.
RYUSEI, I'M ONLY HELPING YOU BECAUSE ...
HA HA...
DON'T LET YOUR EMOTIONS GET THE BETTER OF YOU...
QUEENIE ?

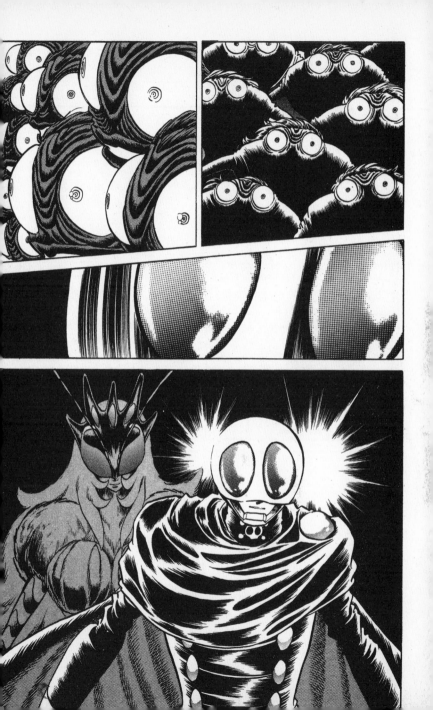

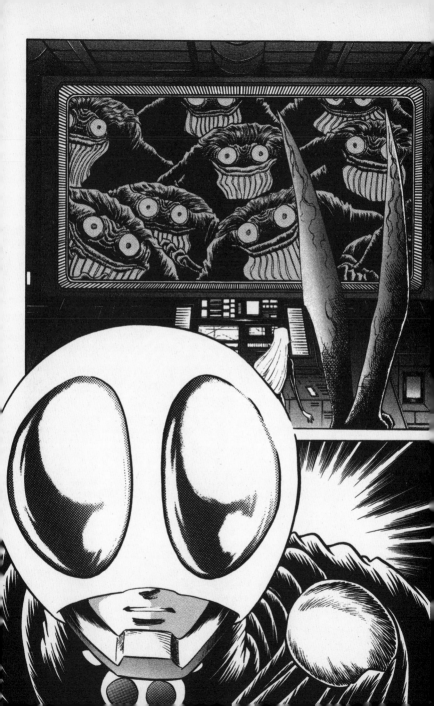

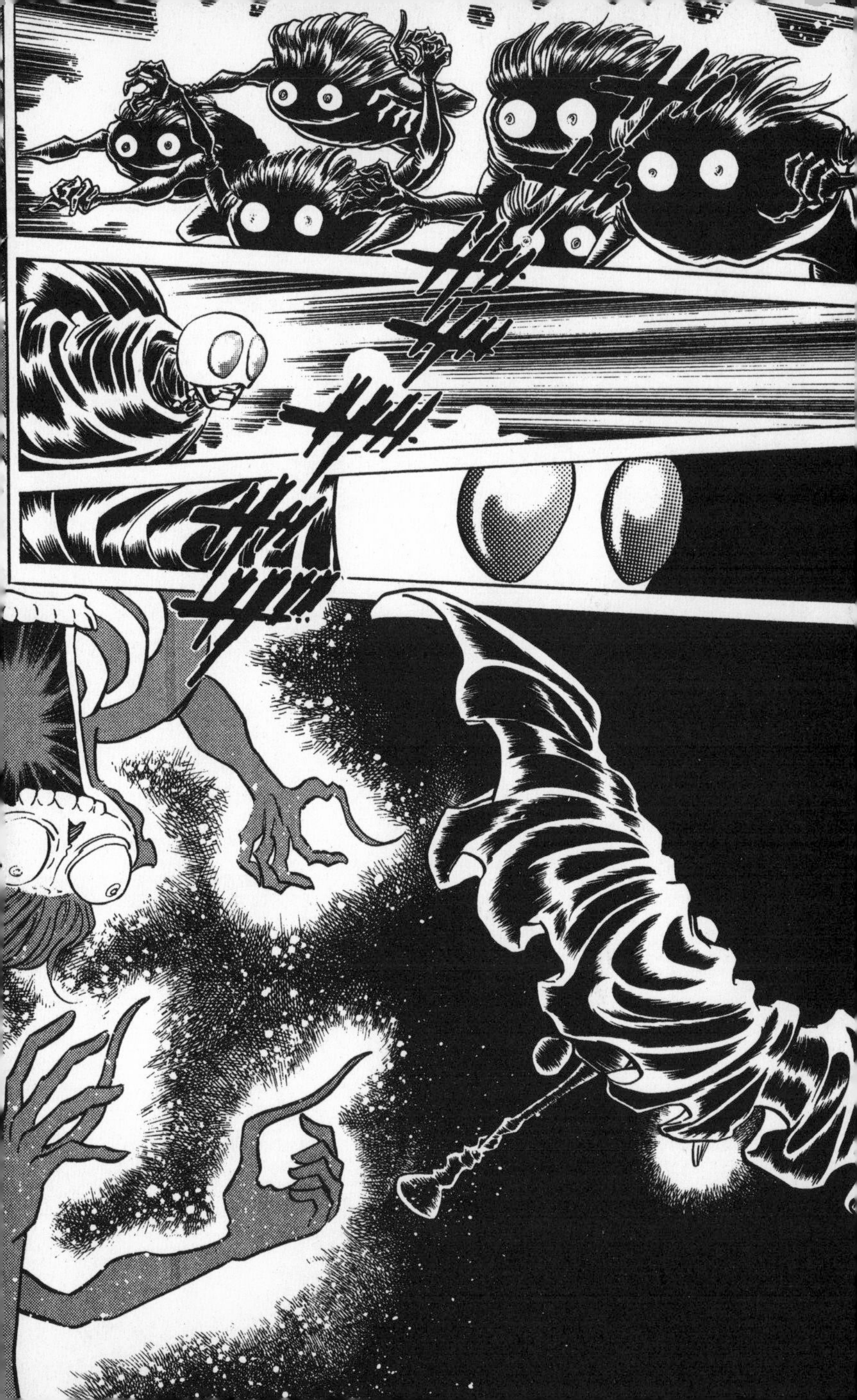

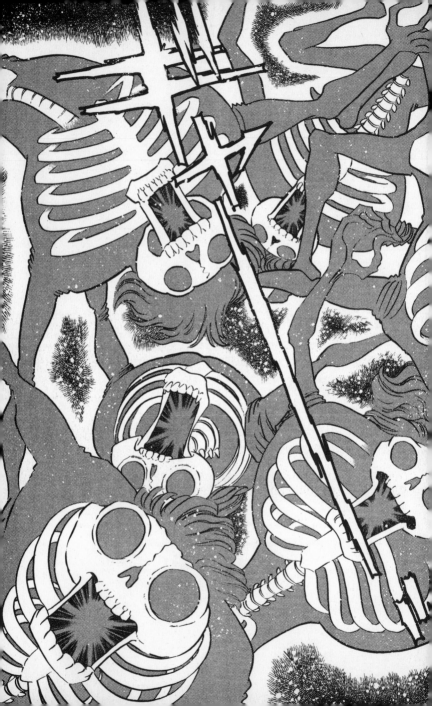

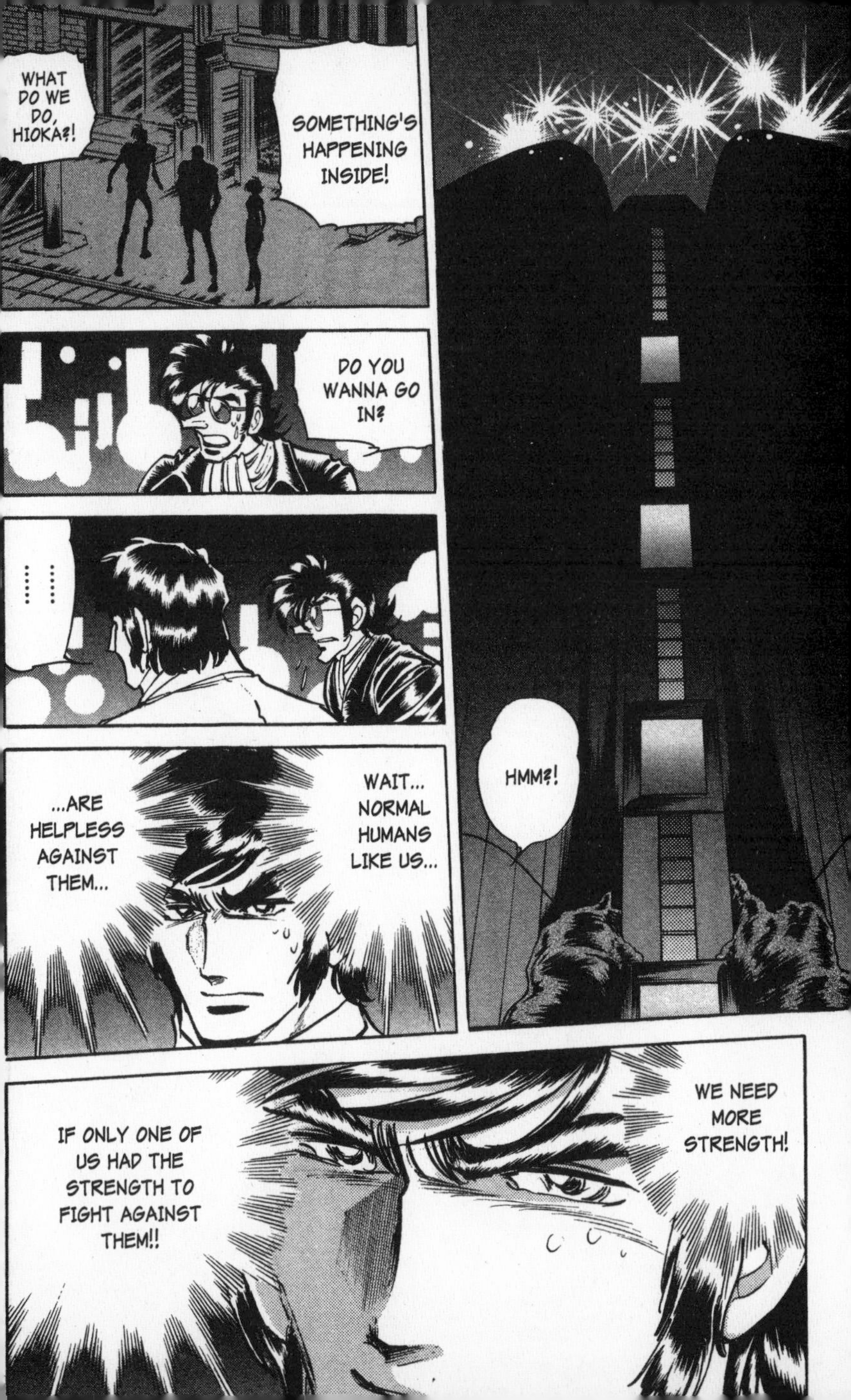
HMM?!
SOMETHING'S HAPPENING INSIDE!
WHAT DO WE DO, HIOKA?!
DO YOU WANNA GO IN?
......
WAIT... NORMAL HUMANS LIKE US...
...ARE HELPLESS AGAINST THEM...
WE NEED MORE STRENGTH!
IF ONLY ONE OF US HAD THE STRENGTH TO FIGHT AGAINST THEM!!

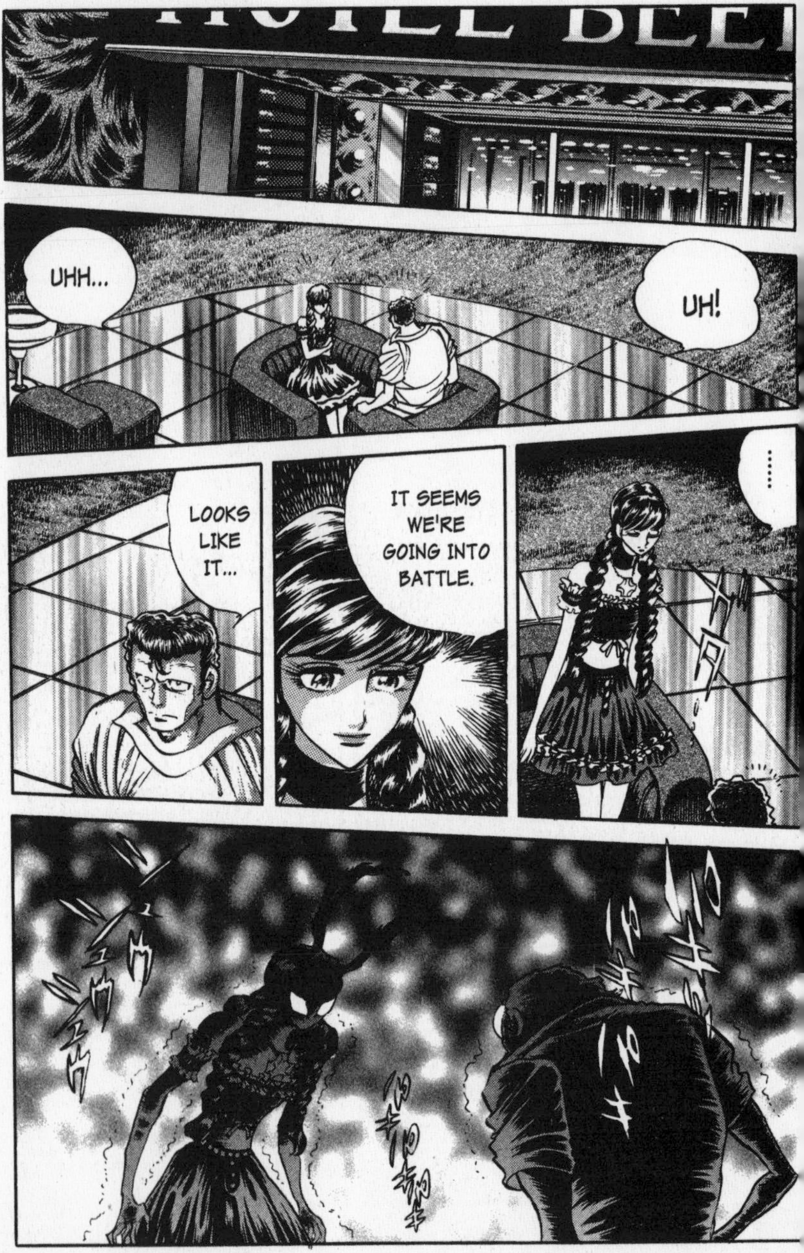
UH!
UHH...
......
IT SEEMS WE'RE GOING INTO BATTLE.
LOOKS LIKE IT...

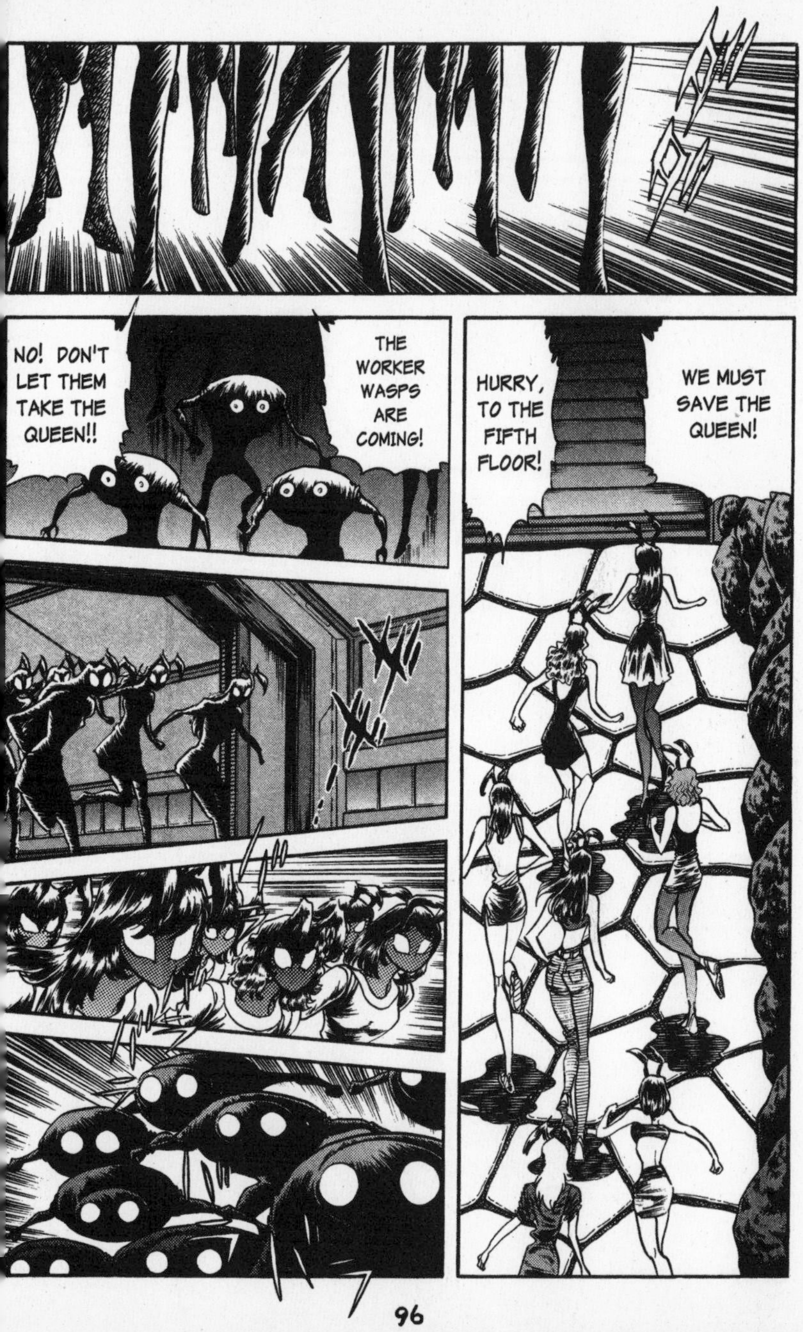
WE MUST SAVE THE QUEEN!
HURRY, TO THE FIFTH FLOOR!
THE WORKER WASPS ARE COMING!
NO! DON'T LET THEM TAKE THE QUEEN!!

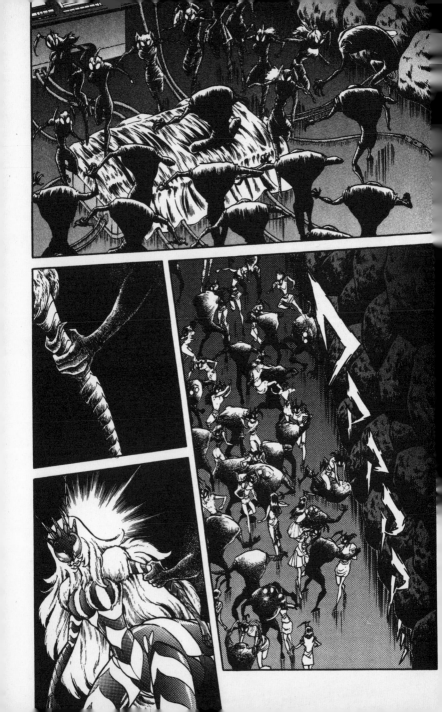

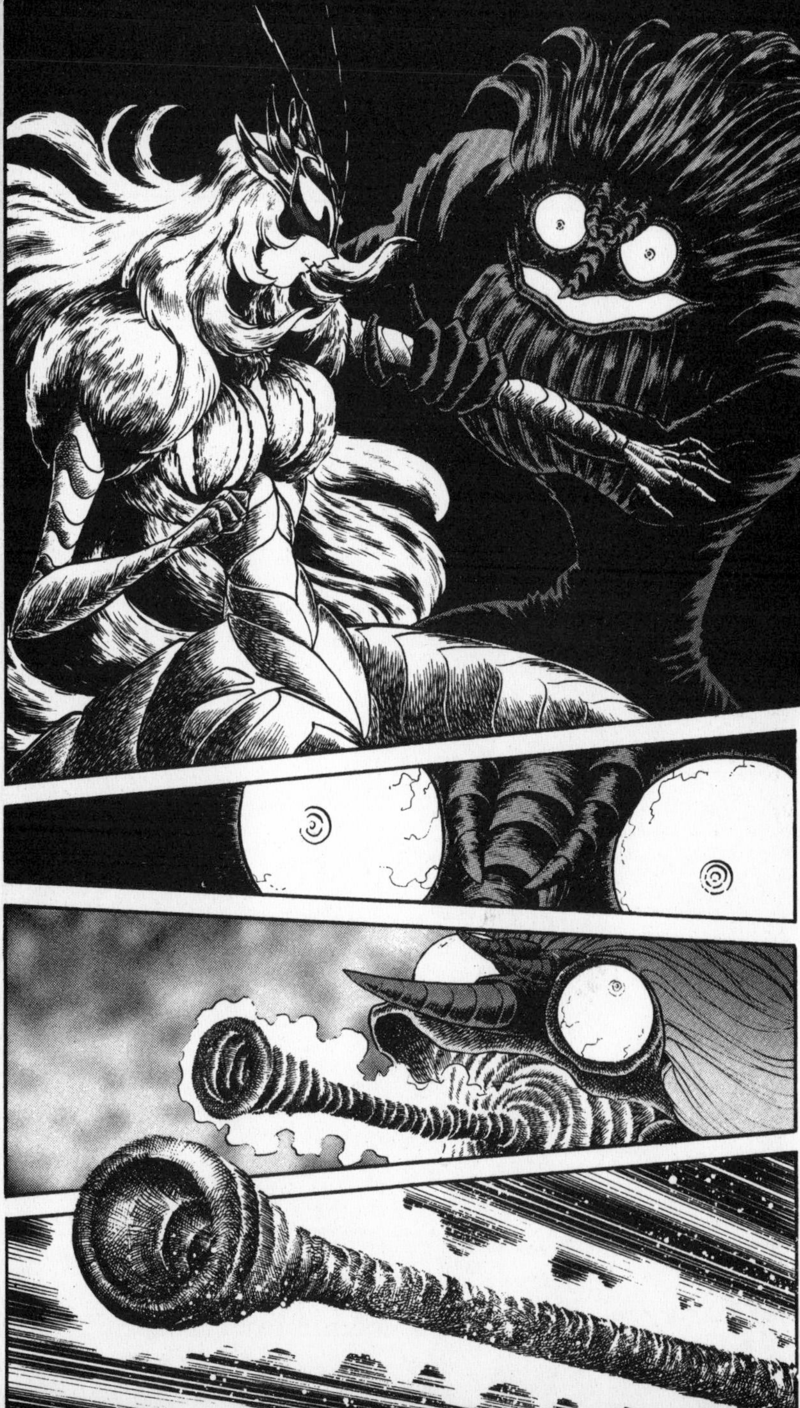

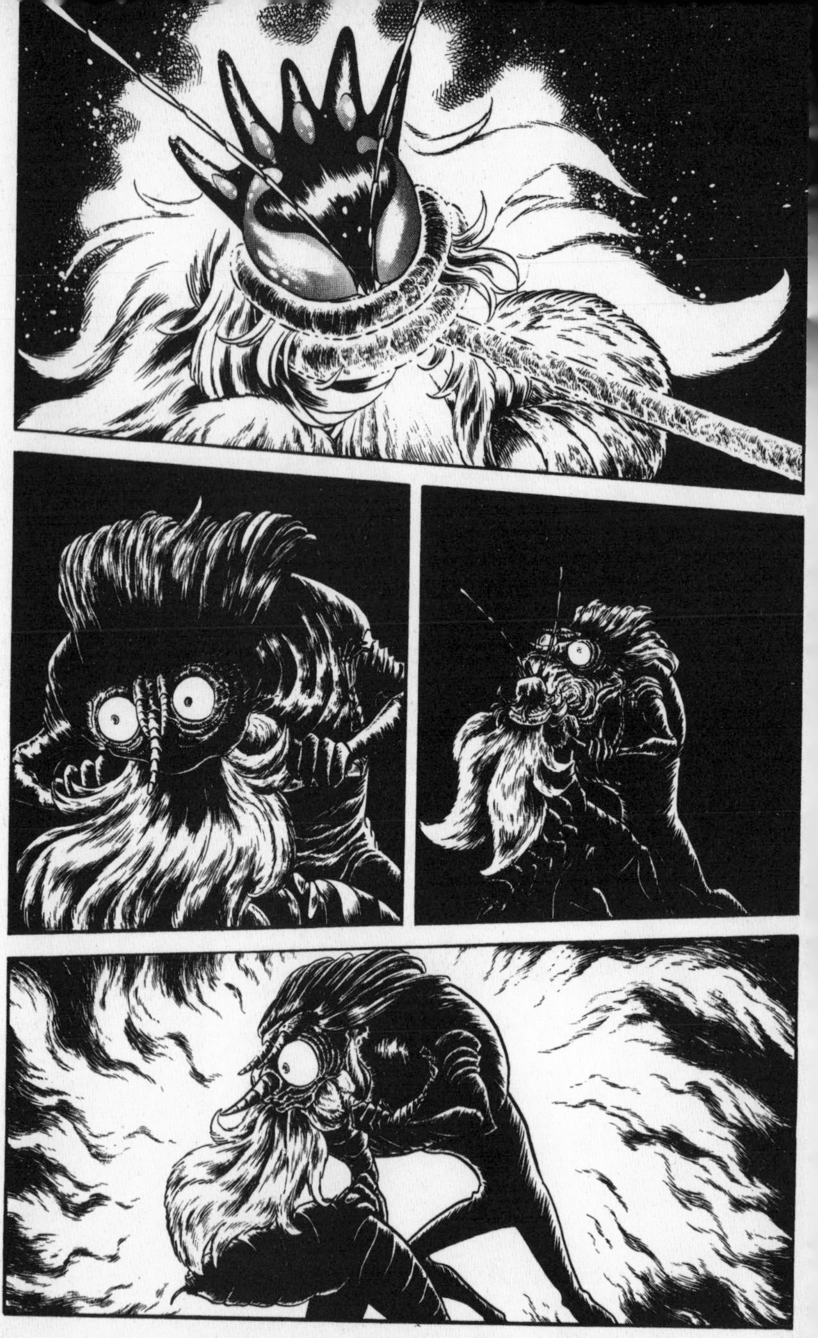

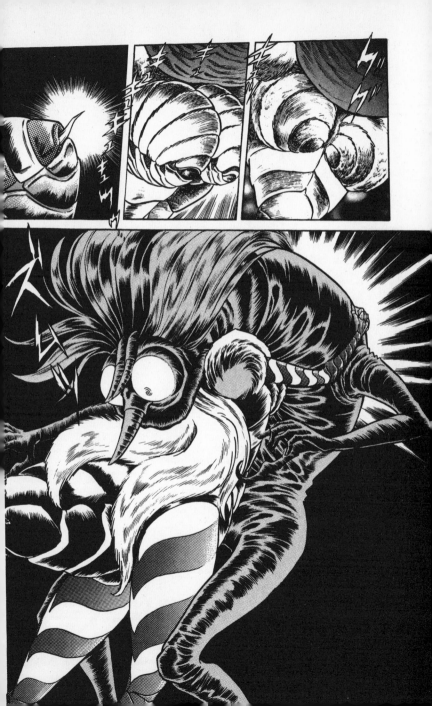

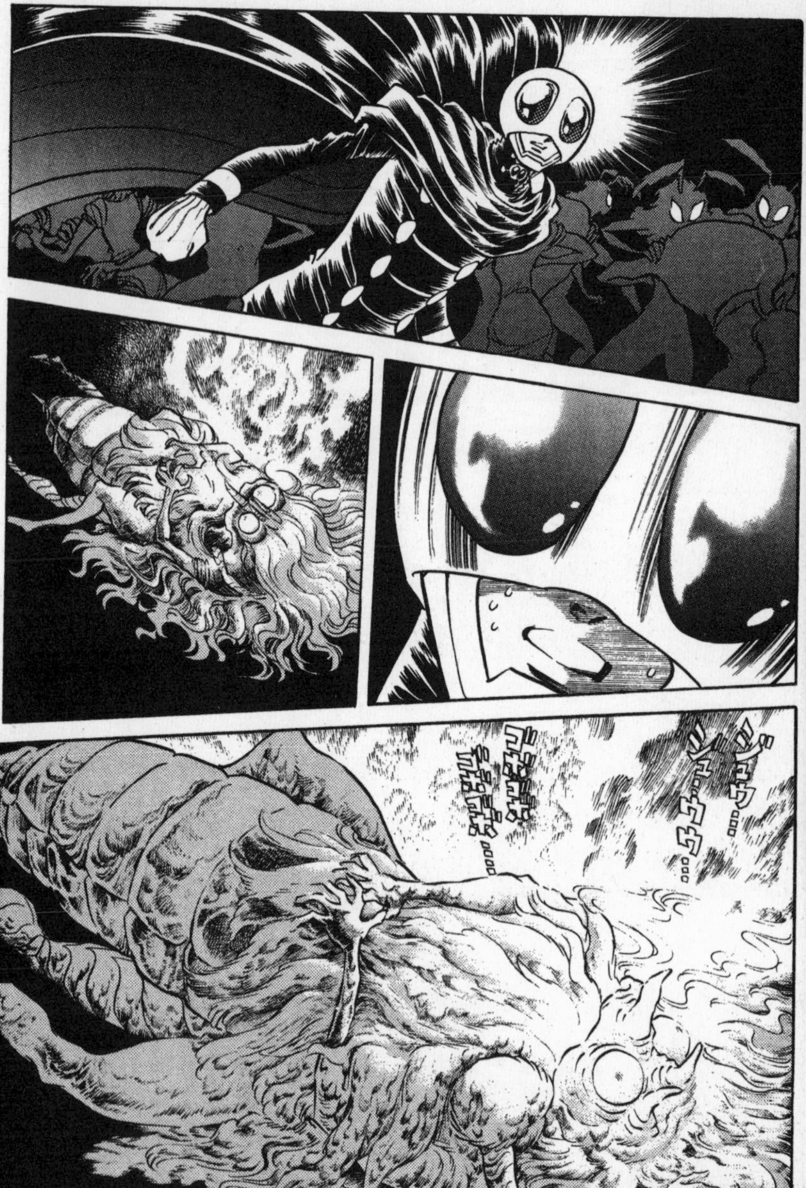
ジュウ……
ジュウウウ……
ゴボゴボ
ゴボゴボ……

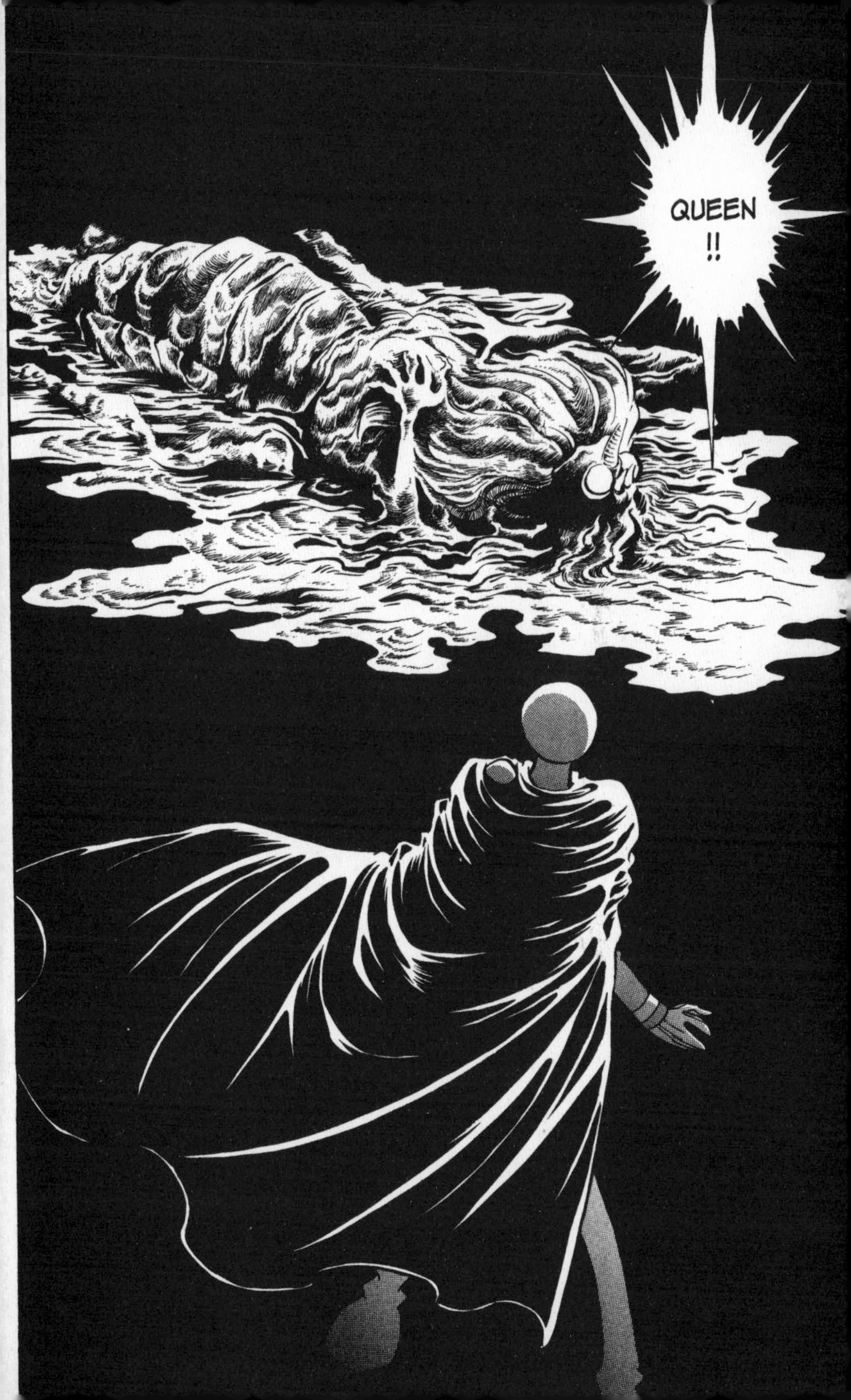
QUEEN !!

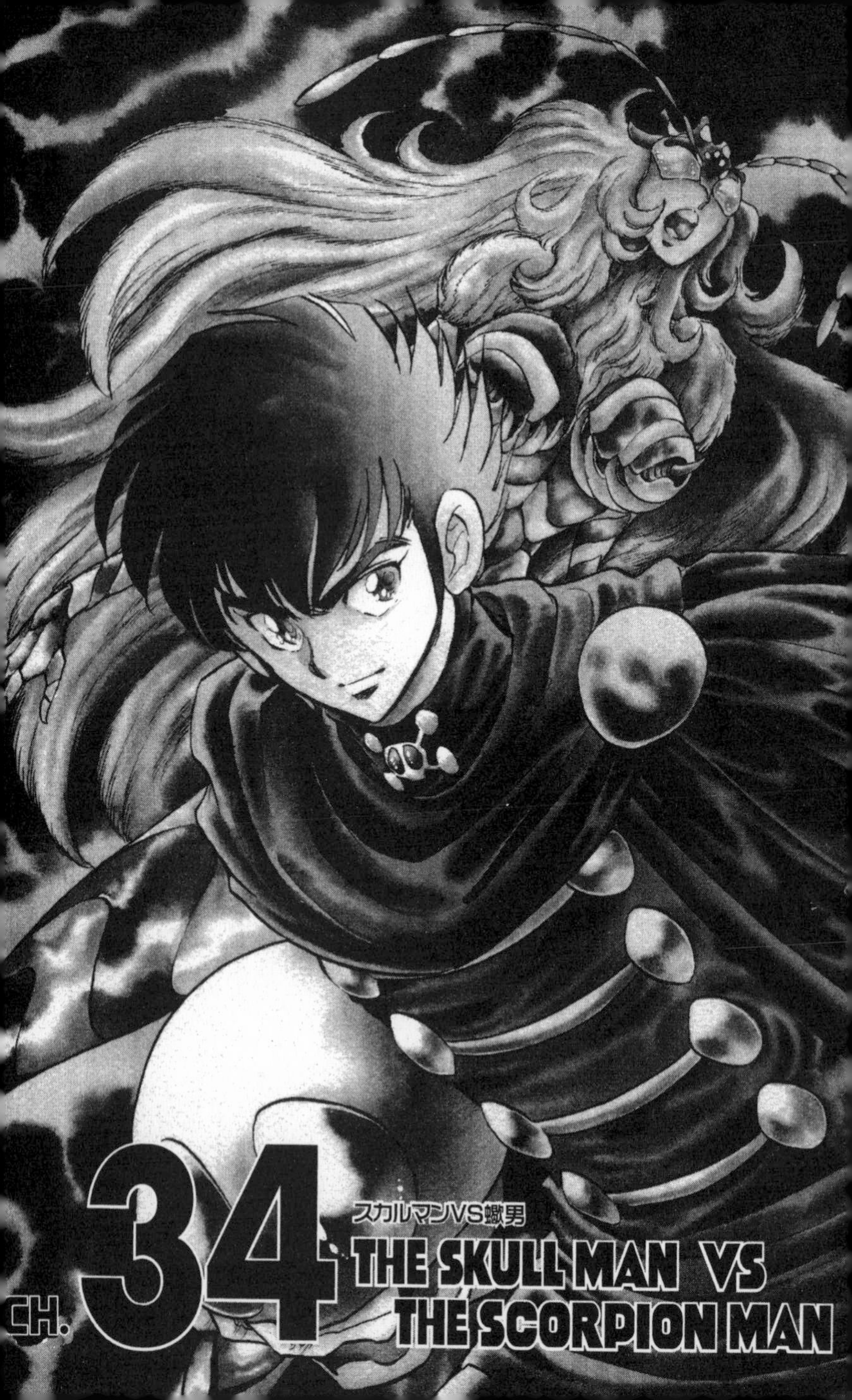
CH. 34
スカルマンVS蠍男
THE SKULL MAN VS THE SCORPION MAN

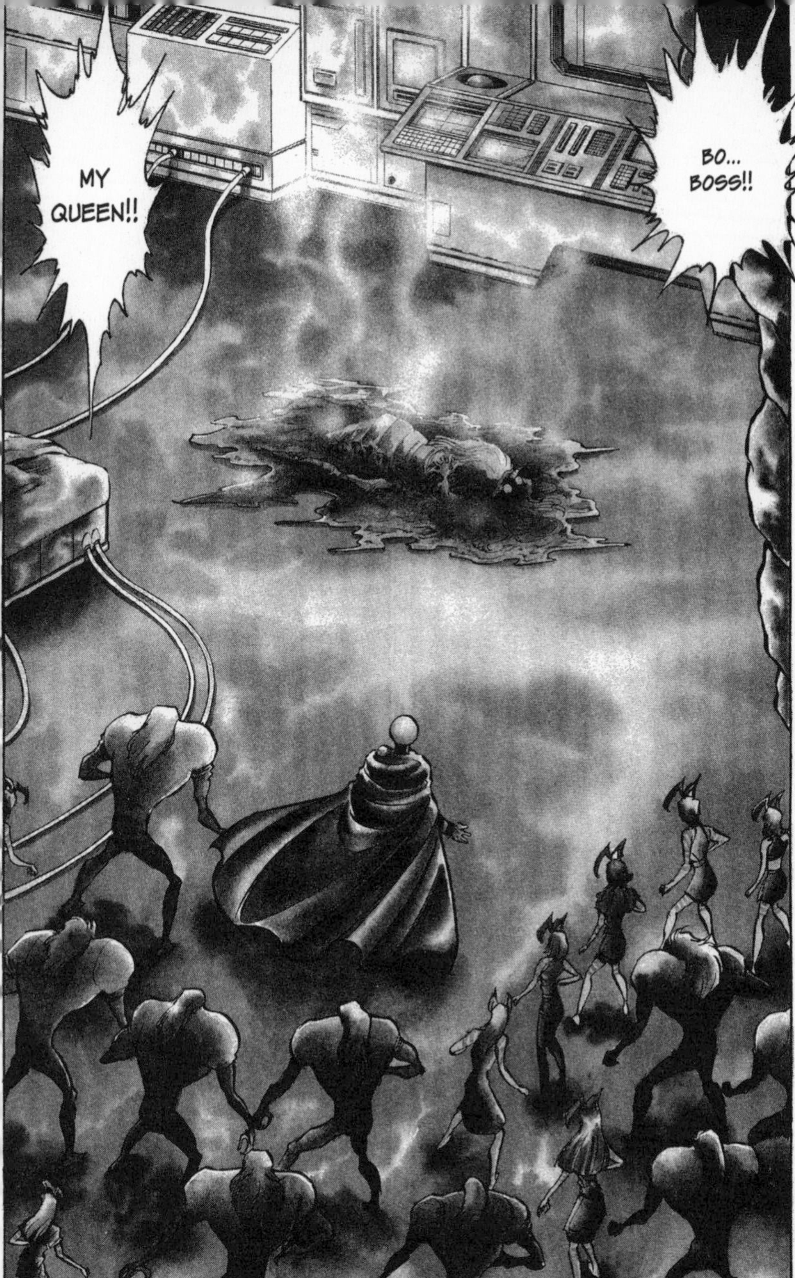
BO... BOSS!!
MY QUEEN!!

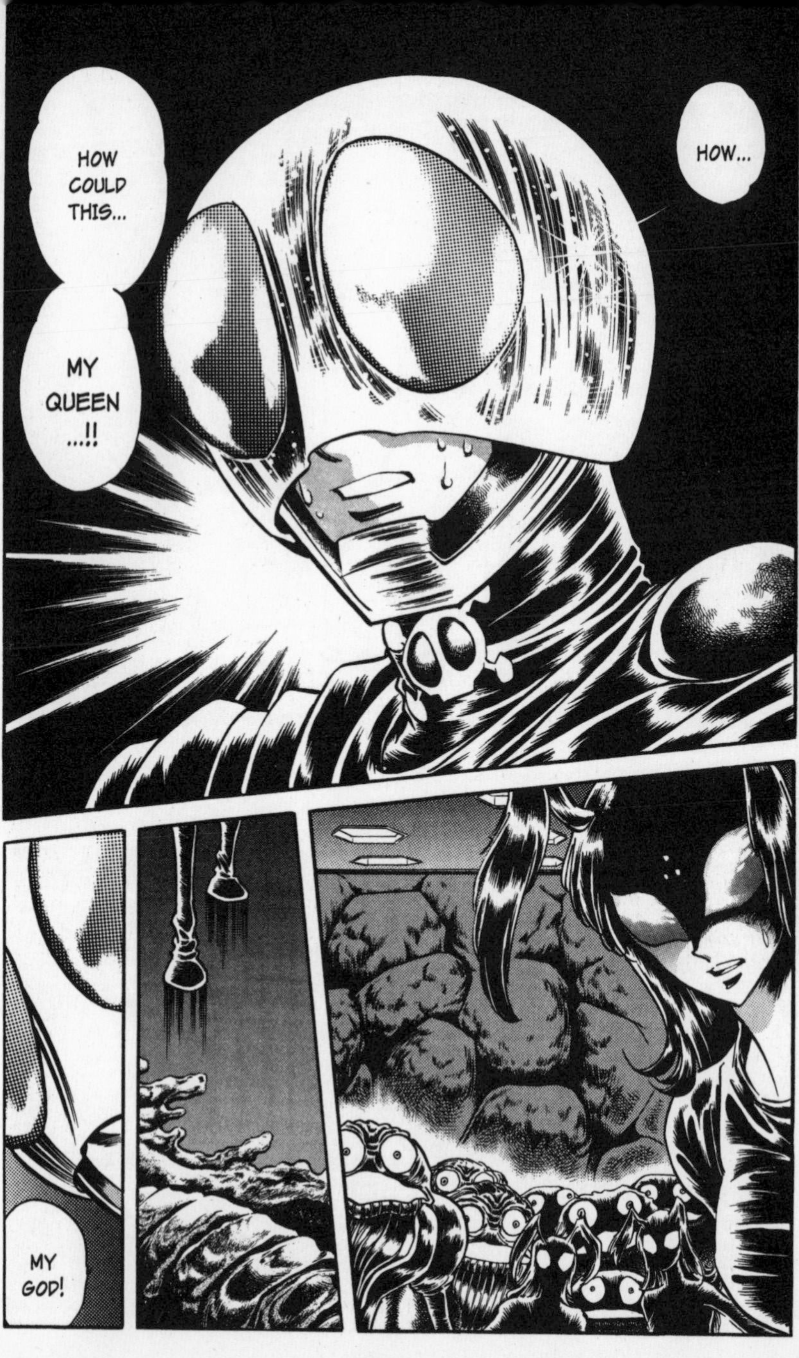
HOW...
HOW COULD THIS...
MY QUEEN ...!!
MY GOD!

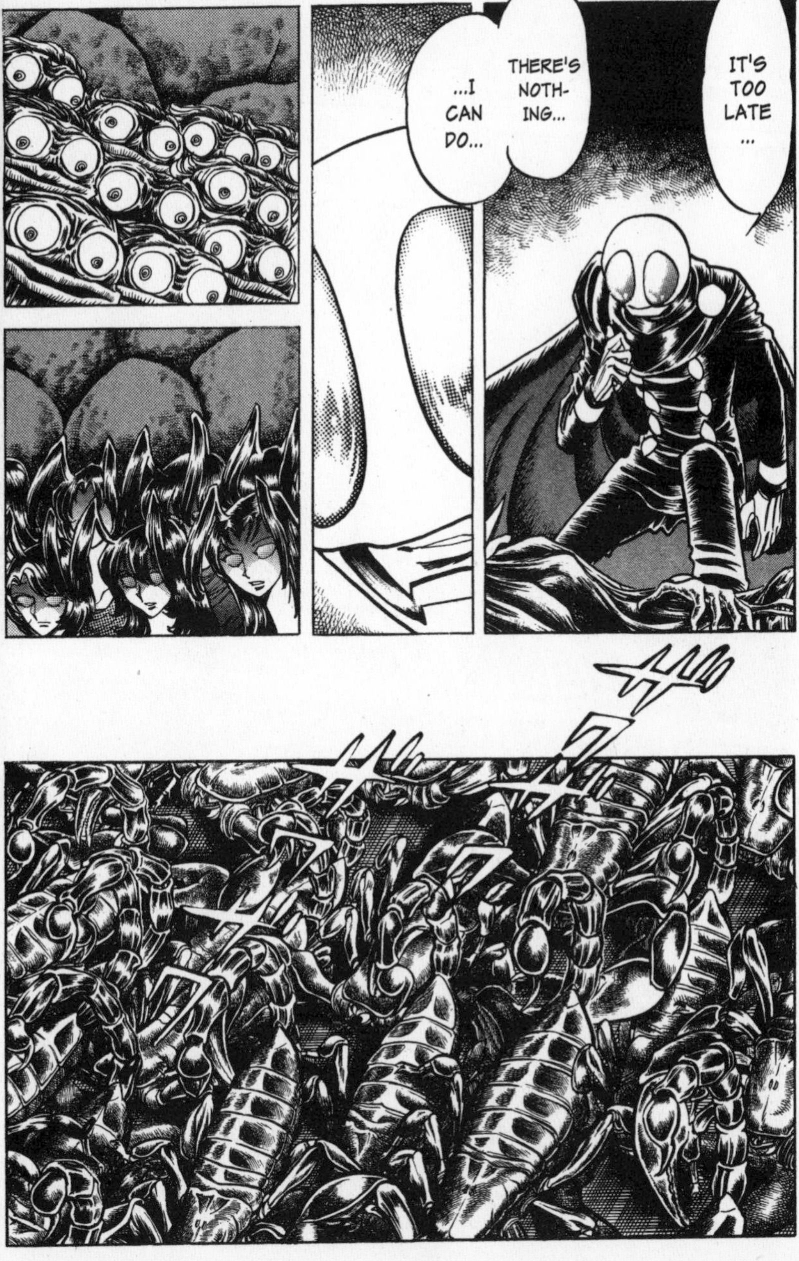
IT'S TOO LATE ...
THERE'S NOTHING...
...I CAN DO...

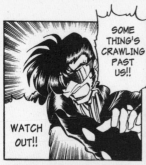

SOME THING'S CRAWLING PAST US!!

WATCH OUT!!

WHAT ?!

WHOA ?!

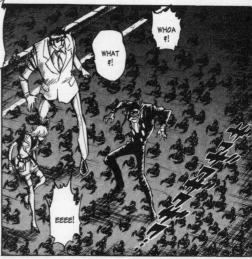

EEEE!

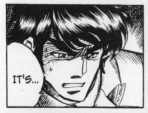

IT'S...

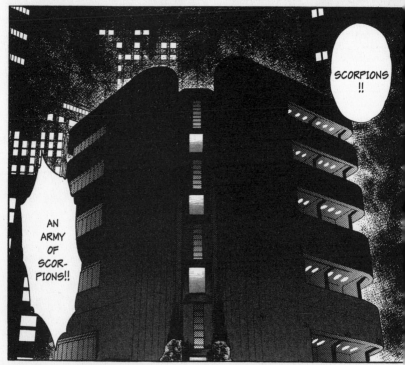

AN ARMY OF SCOR- PIONS!!

SCORPIONS !!

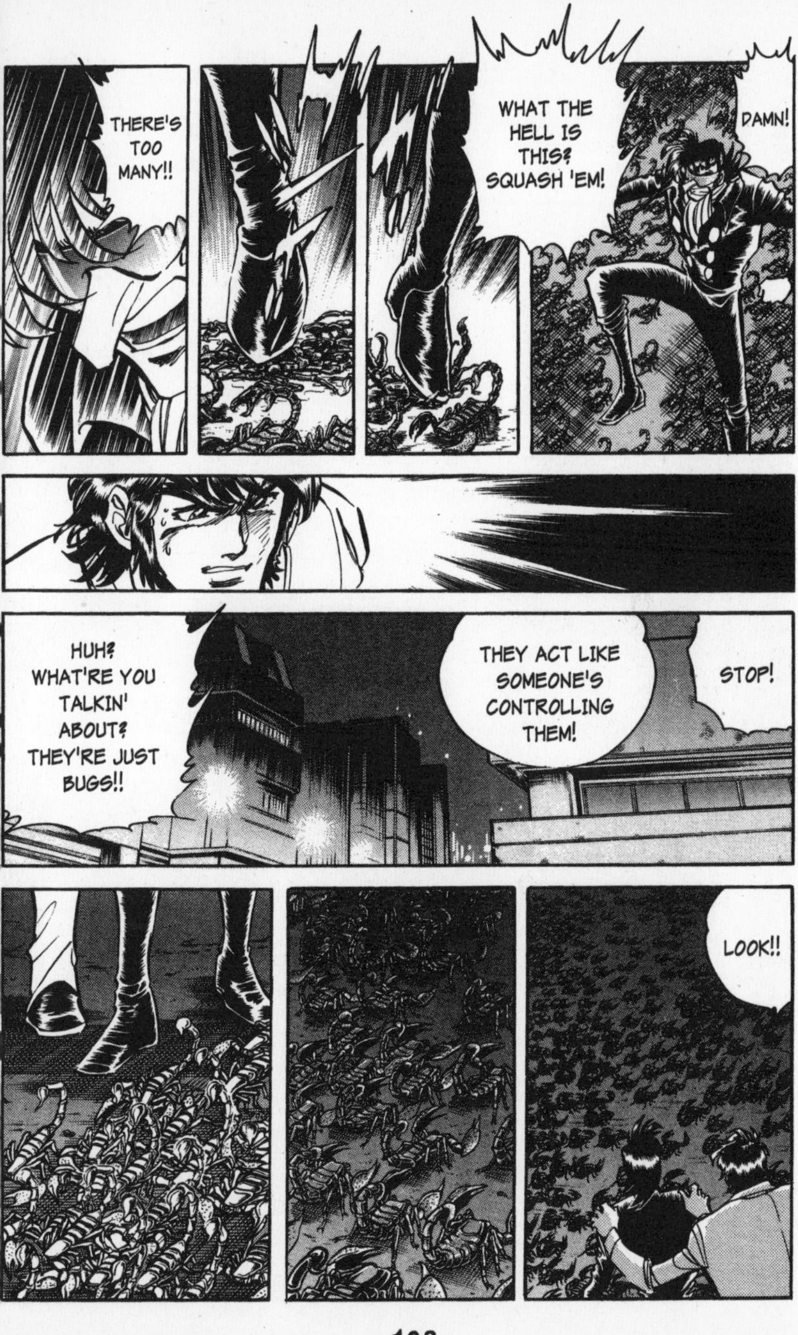
DAMN!
WHAT THE HELL IS THIS? SQUASH 'EM!
THERE'S TOO MANY!!
STOP!
THEY ACT LIKE SOMEONE'S CONTROLLING THEM!
HUH? WHAT'RE YOU TALKIN' ABOUT? THEY'RE JUST BUGS!!
LOOK!!

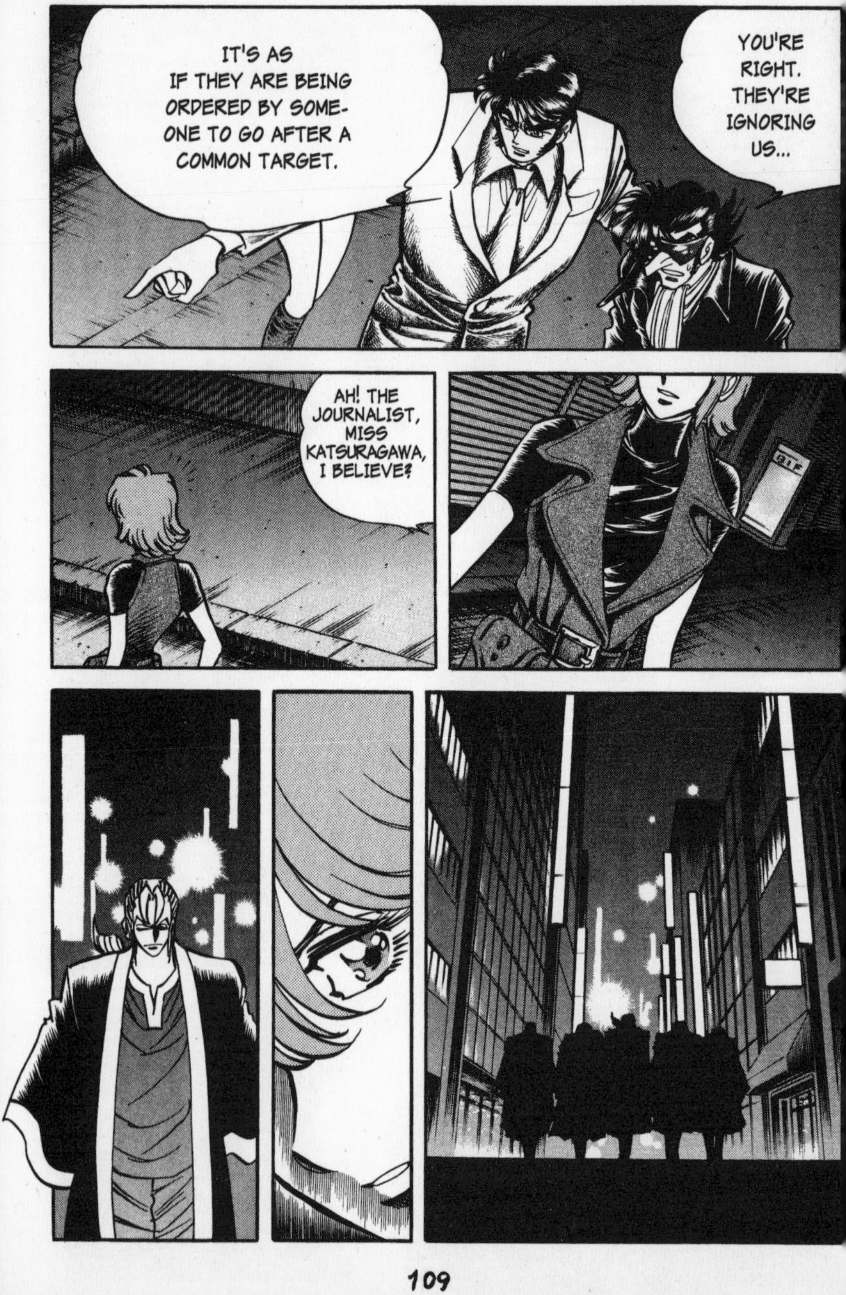
YOU'RE RIGHT. THEY'RE IGNORING US...
IT'S AS IF THEY ARE BEING ORDERED BY SOME-ONE TO GO AFTER A COMMON TARGET.
AH! THE JOURNALIST, MISS KATSURAGAWA, I BELIEVE?

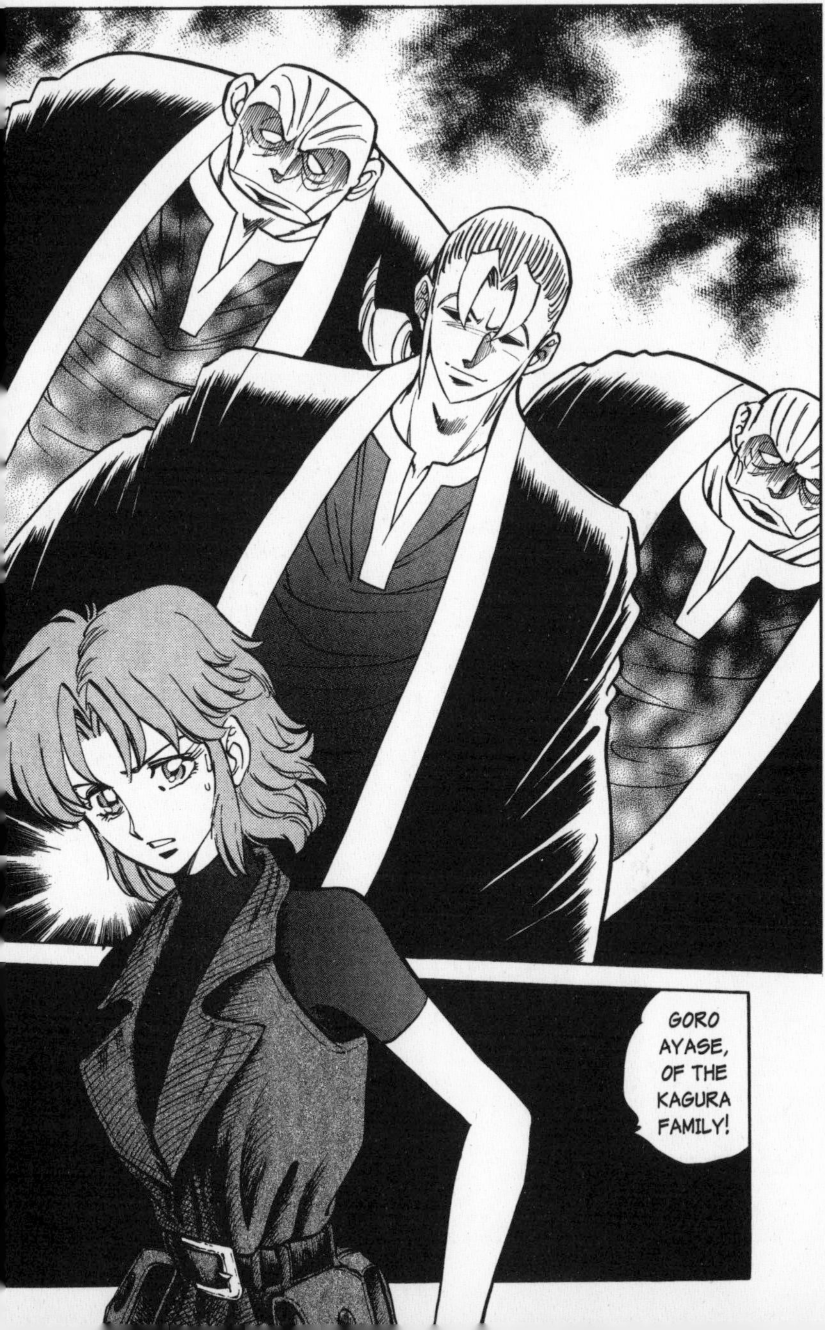
GORO AYASE, OF THE KAGURA FAMILY!

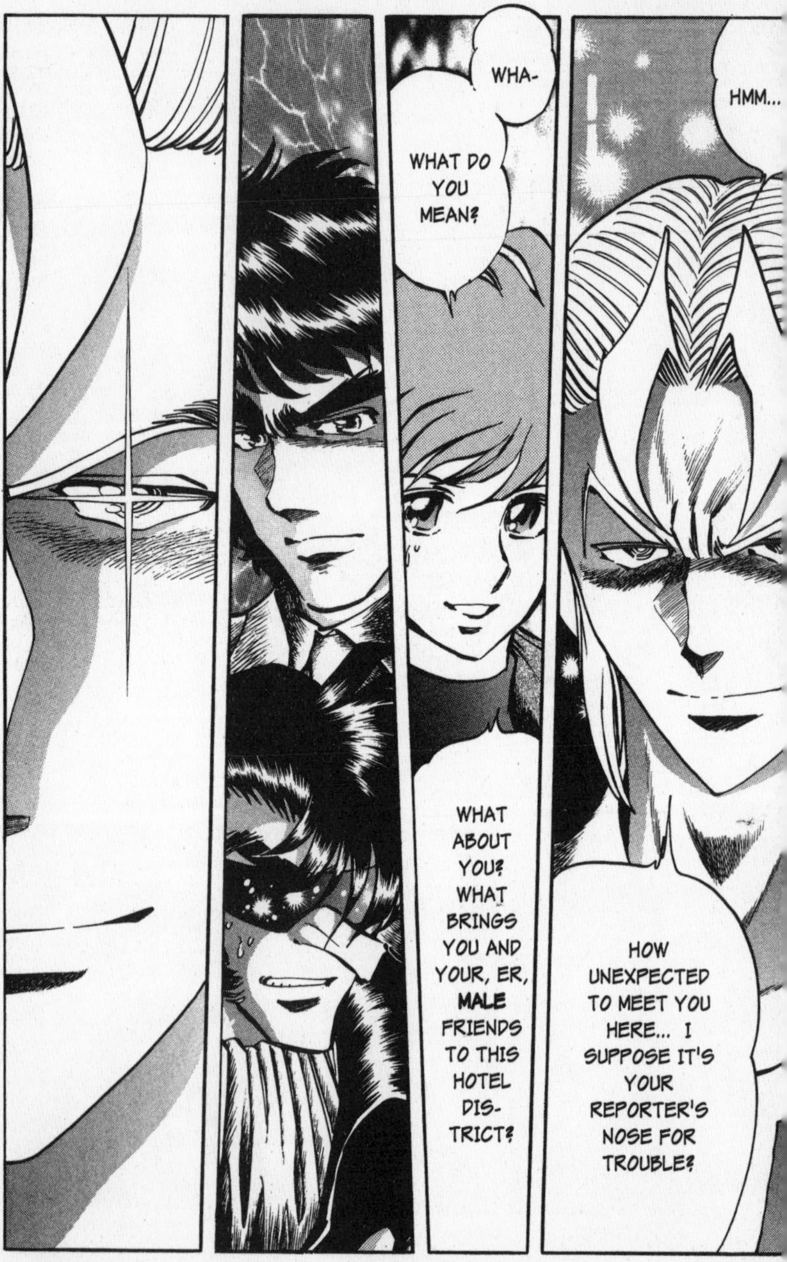
HMM...
HOW UNEXPECTED TO MEET YOU HERE... I SUPPOSE IT'S YOUR REPORTER'S NOSE FOR TROUBLE?
WHA-
WHAT DO YOU MEAN?
WHAT ABOUT YOU? WHAT BRINGS YOU AND YOUR, ER, **MALE** FRIENDS TO THIS HOTEL DIS-TRICT?

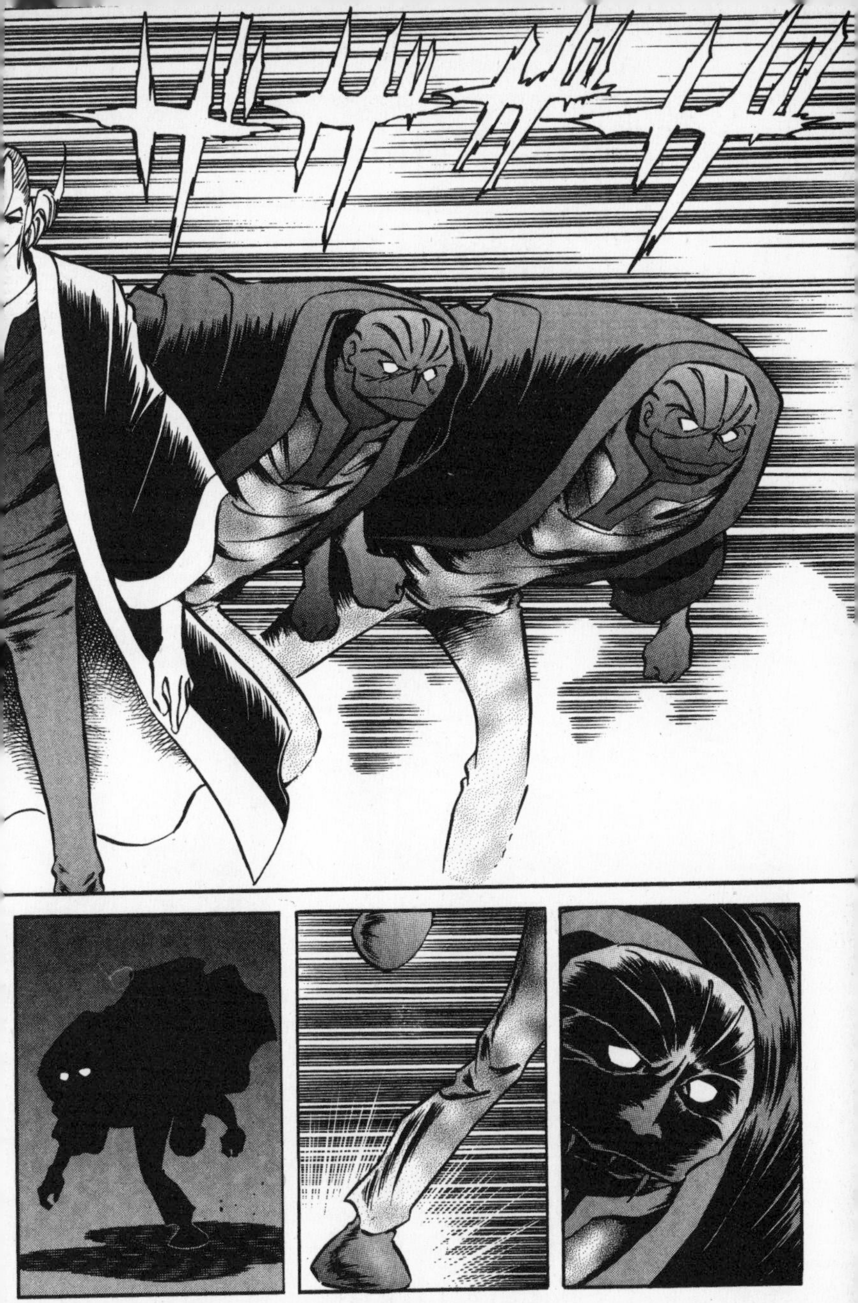

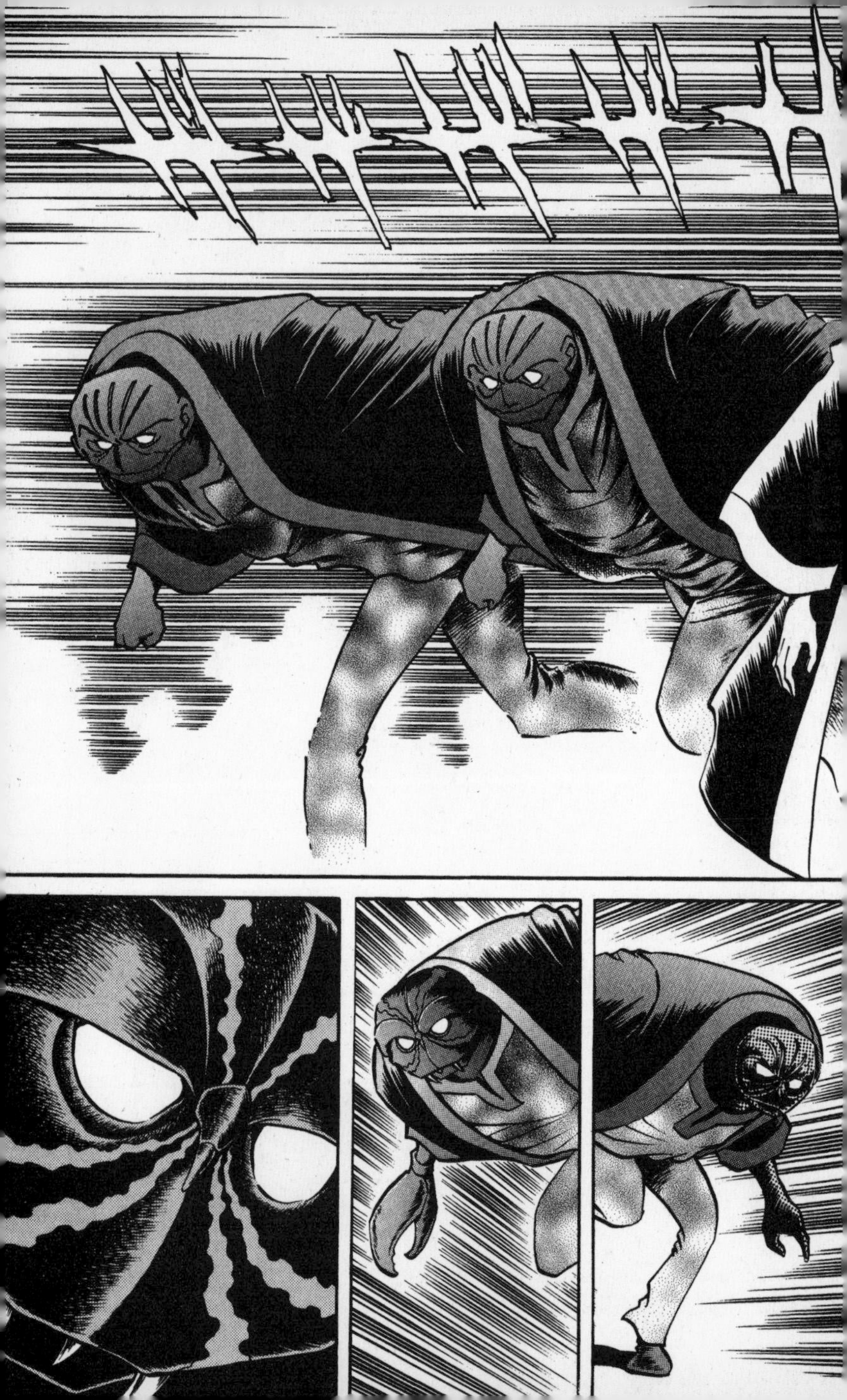

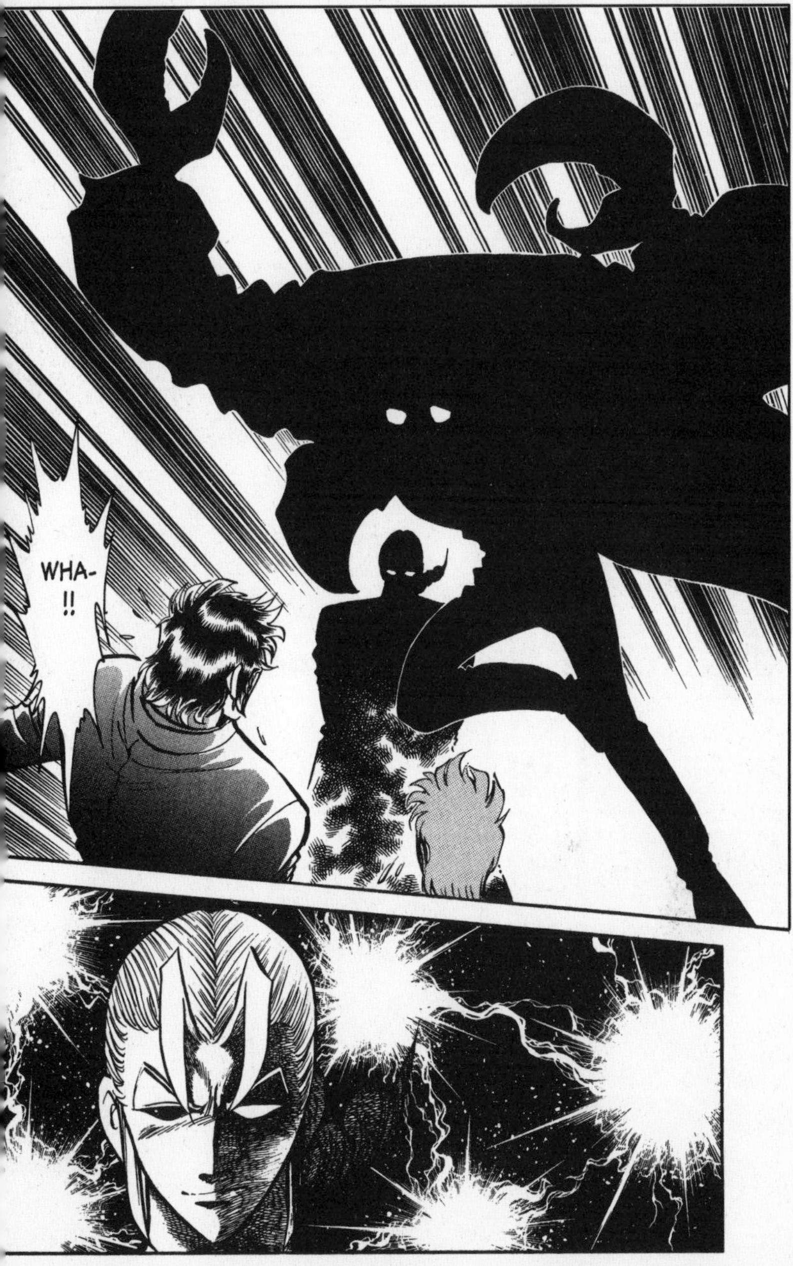
WHA-
!!

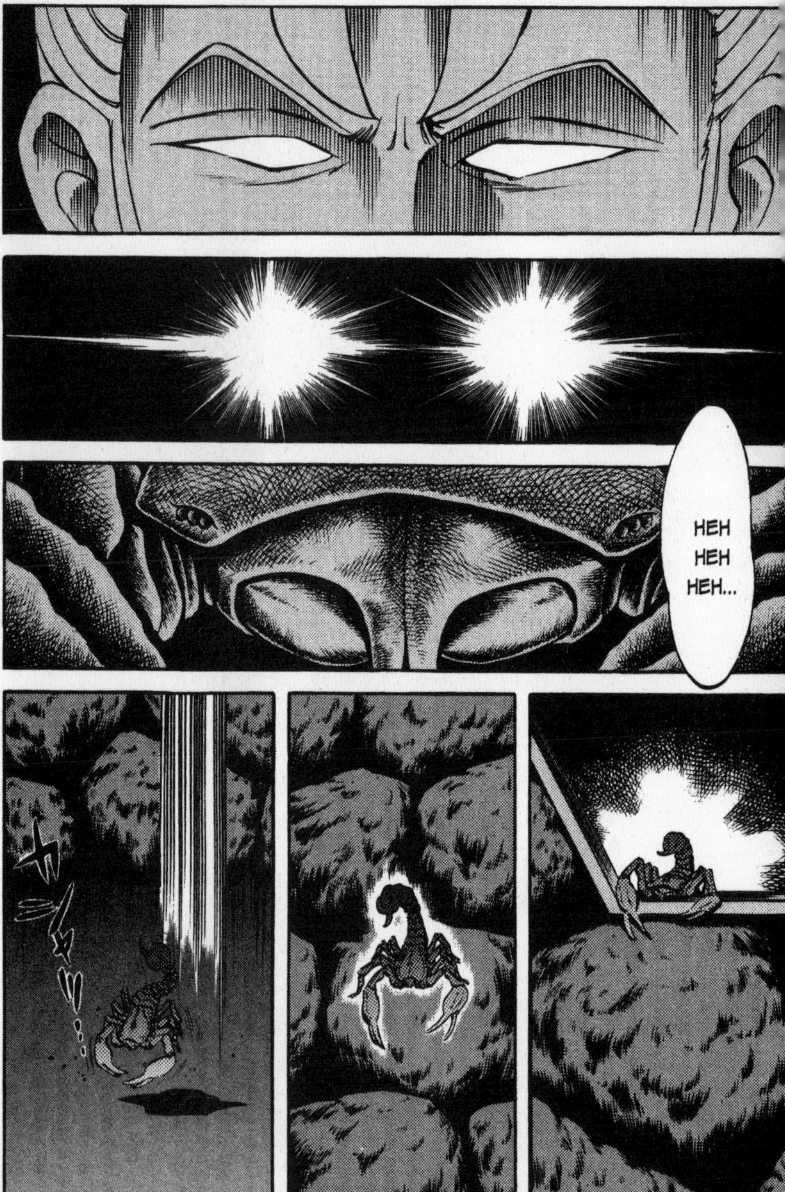
HEH
HEH
HEH...

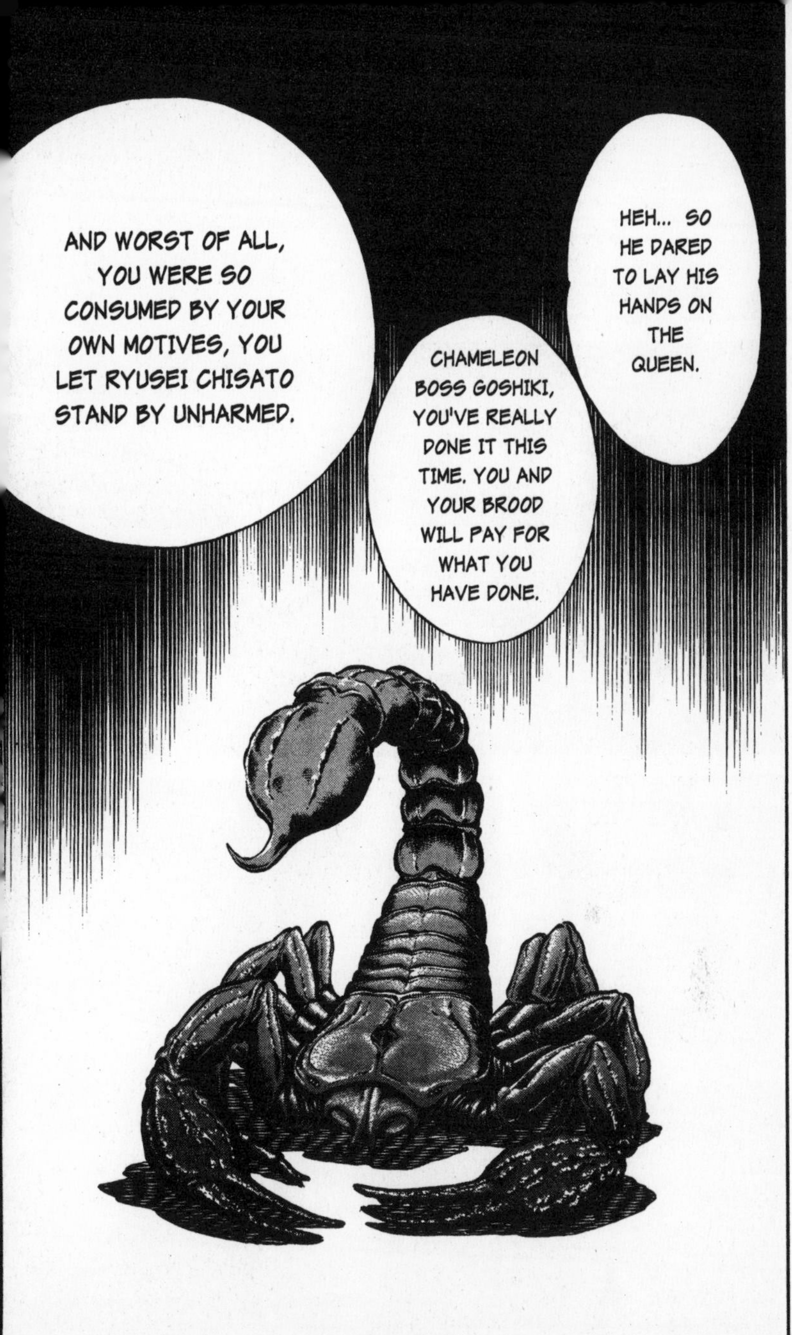
HEH... SO HE DARED TO LAY HIS HANDS ON THE QUEEN.
CHAMELEON BOSS GOSHIKI, YOU'VE REALLY DONE IT THIS TIME. YOU AND YOUR BROOD WILL PAY FOR WHAT YOU HAVE DONE.
AND WORST OF ALL, YOU WERE SO CONSUMED BY YOUR OWN MOTIVES, YOU LET RYUSEI CHISATO STAND BY UNHARMED.

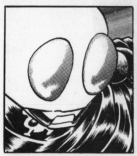
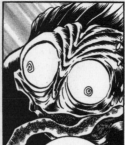
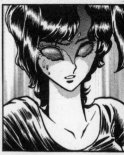

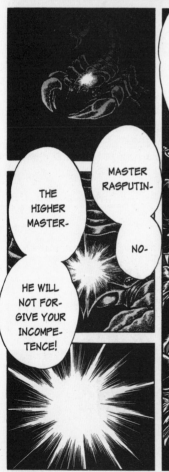

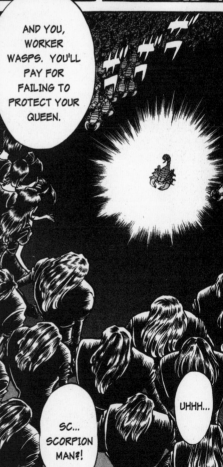

AND YOU, WORKER WASPS. YOU'LL PAY FOR FAILING TO PROTECT YOUR QUEEN.

MASTER RASPUTIN-

NO-

THE HIGHER MASTER-

HE WILL NOT FORGIVE YOUR INCOMPETENCE!

SC... SCORPION MAN?!

UHHH...

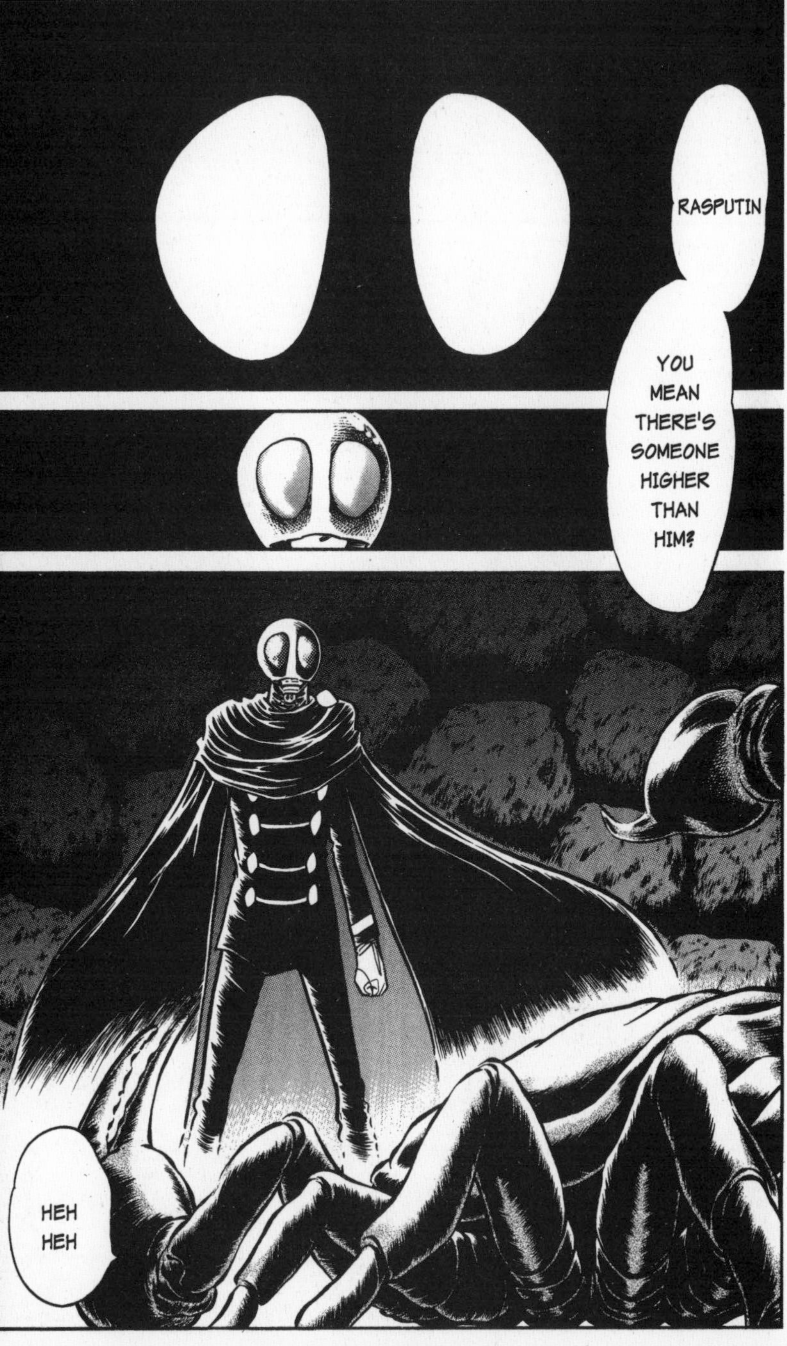
RASPUTIN
YOU MEAN THERE'S SOMEONE HIGHER THAN HIM?
HEH HEH

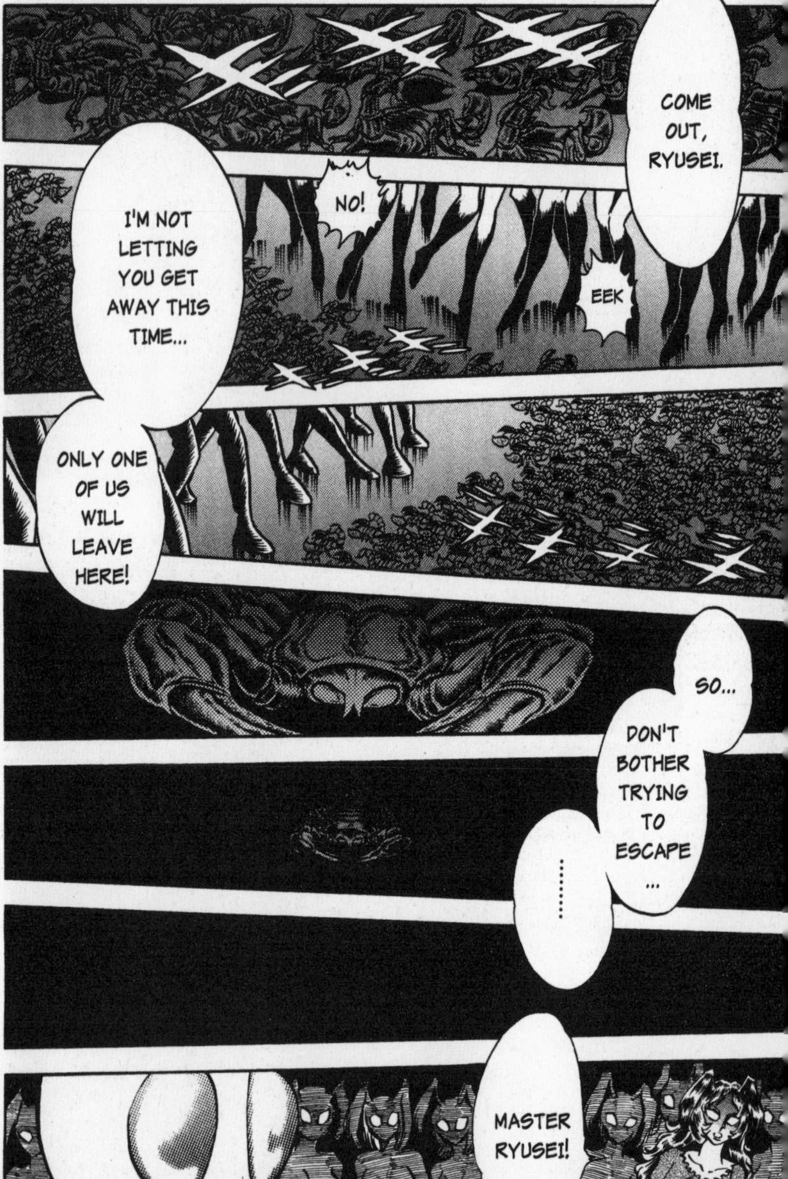
COME OUT, RYUSEI.
NO!
EEK
I'M NOT LETTING YOU GET AWAY THIS TIME...
ONLY ONE OF US WILL LEAVE HERE!
SO...
DON'T BOTHER TRYING TO ESCAPE ...
......
MASTER RYUSEI!

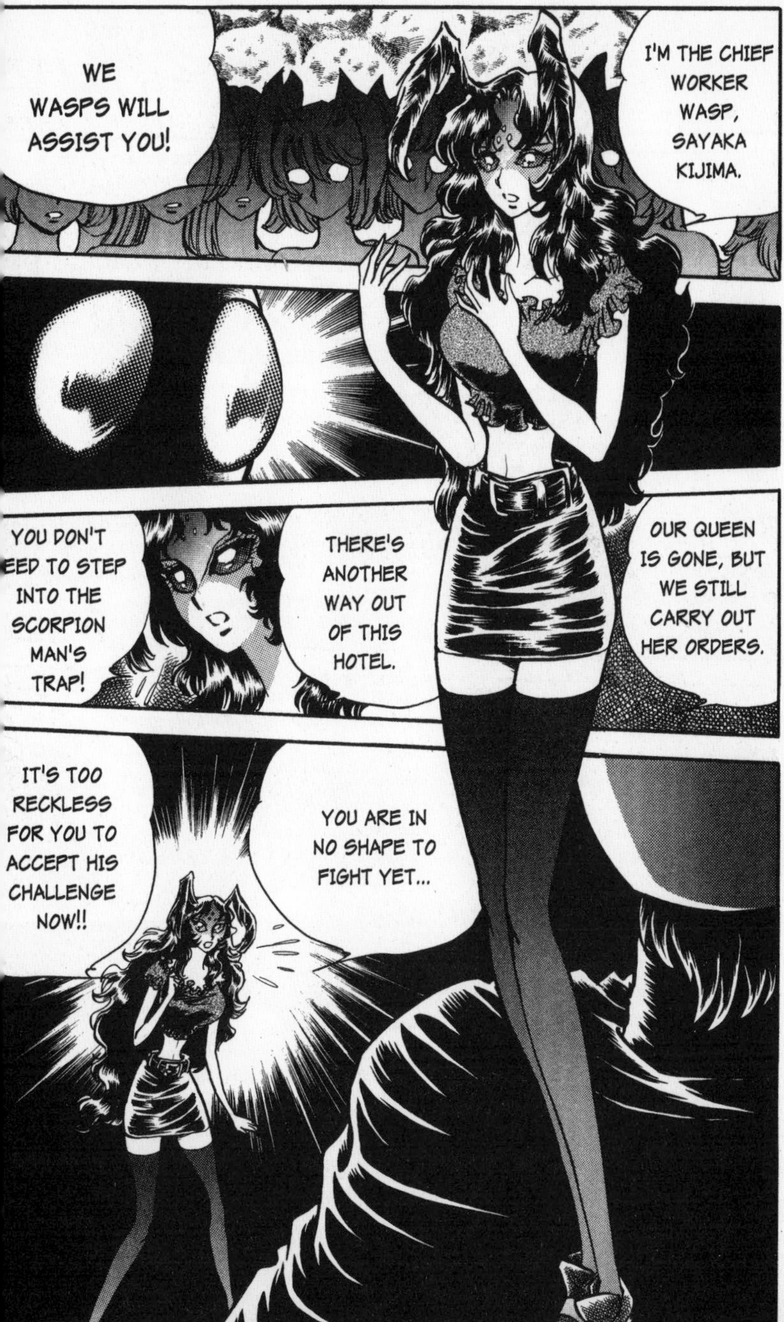
I'M THE CHIEF WORKER WASP, SAYAKA KIJIMA.
WE WASPS WILL ASSIST YOU!
OUR QUEEN IS GONE, BUT WE STILL CARRY OUT HER ORDERS.
THERE'S ANOTHER WAY OUT OF THIS HOTEL.
YOU DON'T EED TO STEP INTO THE SCORPION MAN'S TRAP!
YOU ARE IN NO SHAPE TO FIGHT YET...
IT'S TOO RECKLESS FOR YOU TO ACCEPT HIS CHALLENGE NOW!!

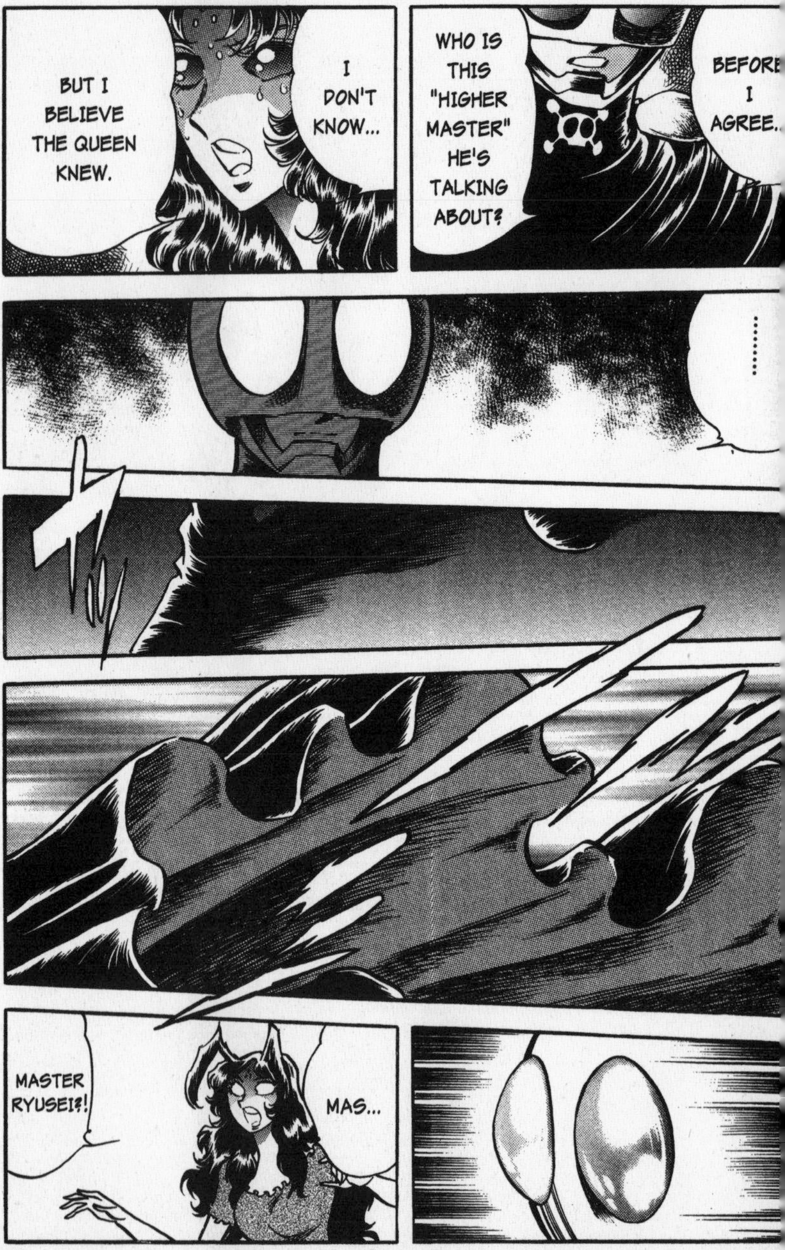
BEFORE I AGREE...
WHO IS THIS "HIGHER MASTER" HE'S TALKING ABOUT?
I DON'T KNOW...
BUT I BELIEVE THE QUEEN KNEW.
......
MAS...
MASTER RYUSEI?!

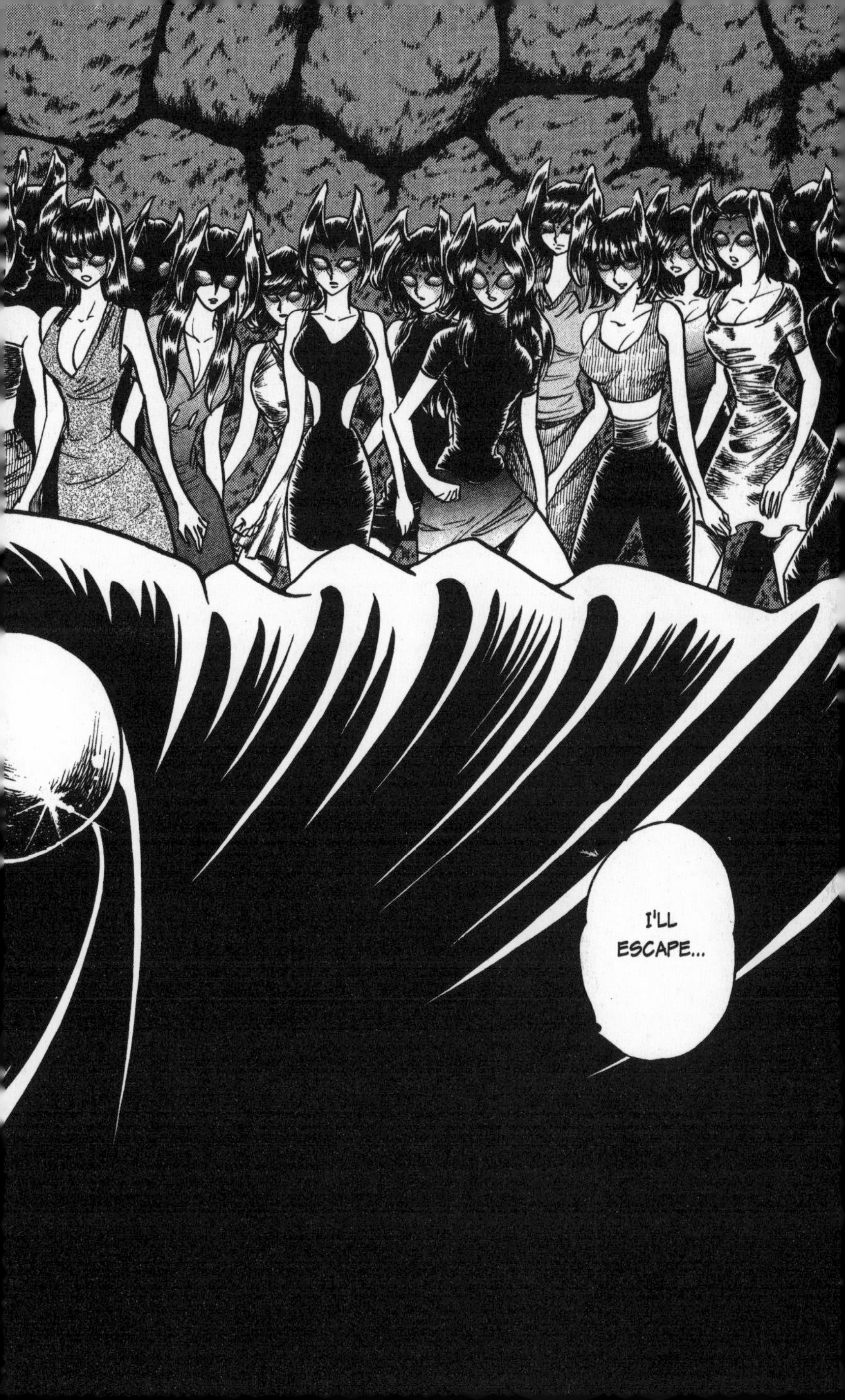
I'LL ESCAPE...

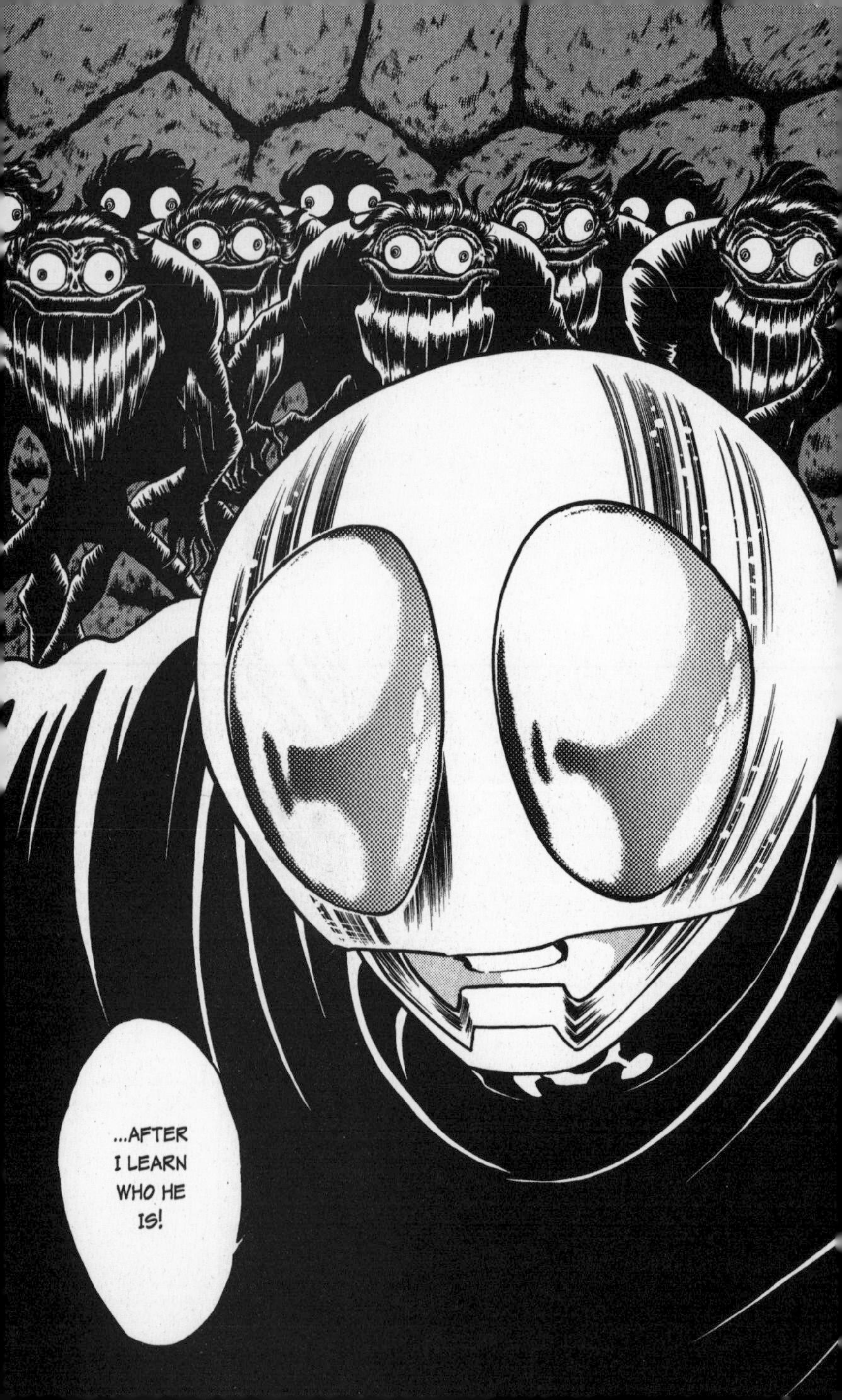
...AFTER I LEARN WHO HE IS!

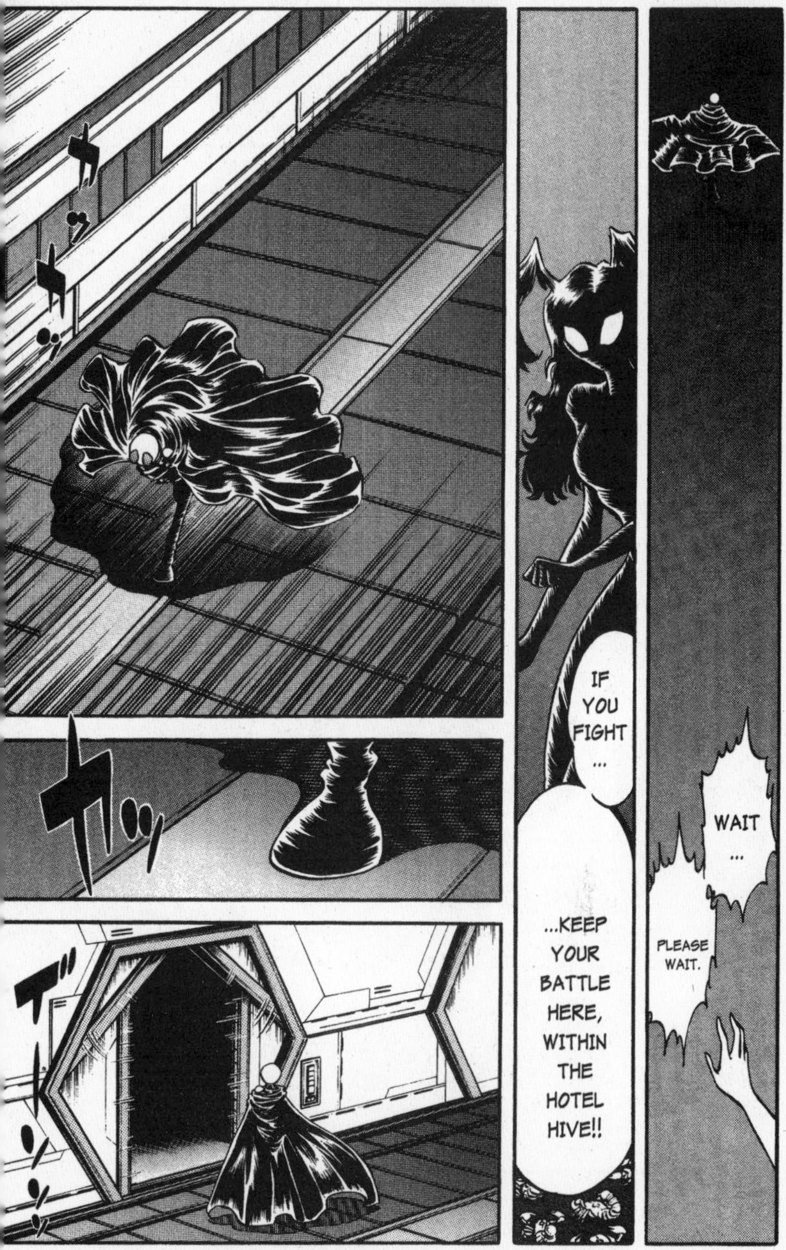
WAIT ...
PLEASE WAIT.
IF YOU FIGHT ...
...KEEP YOUR BATTLE HERE, WITHIN THE HOTEL HIVE!!

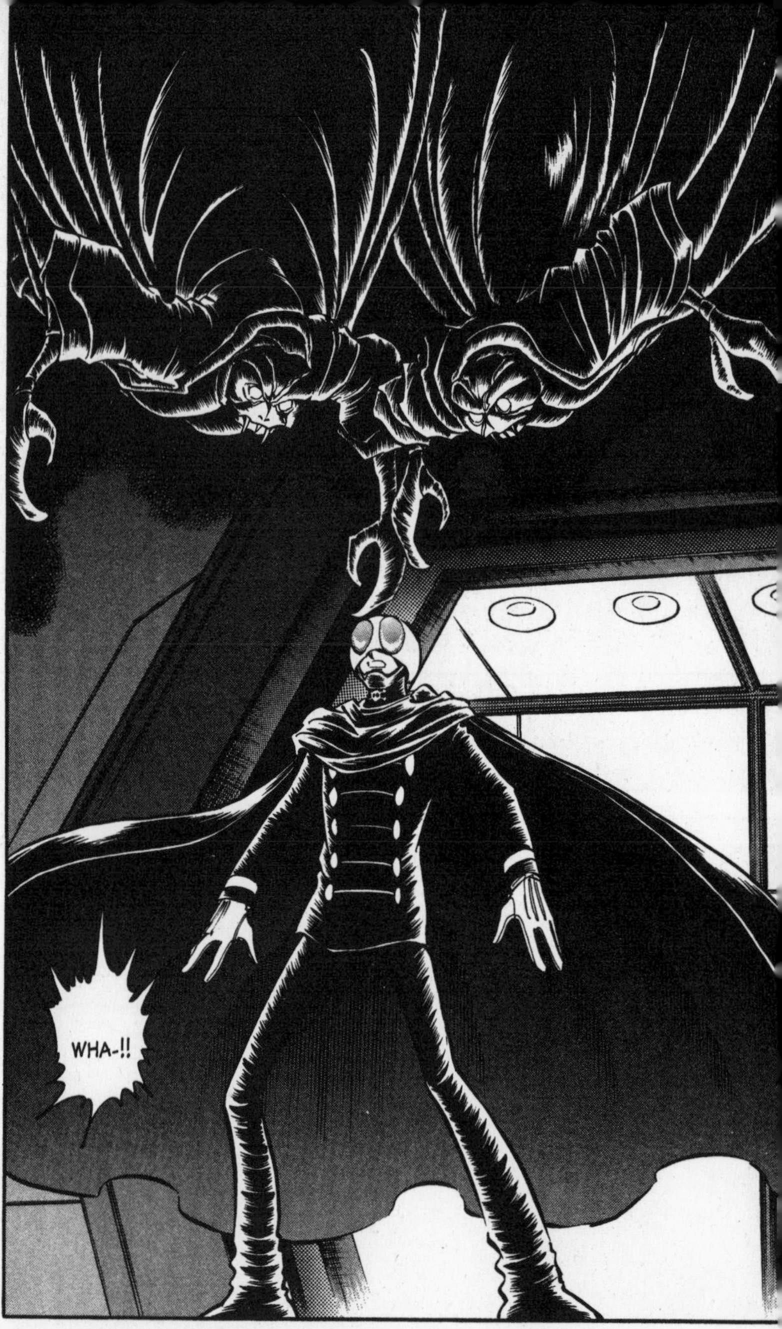
WHA-!!

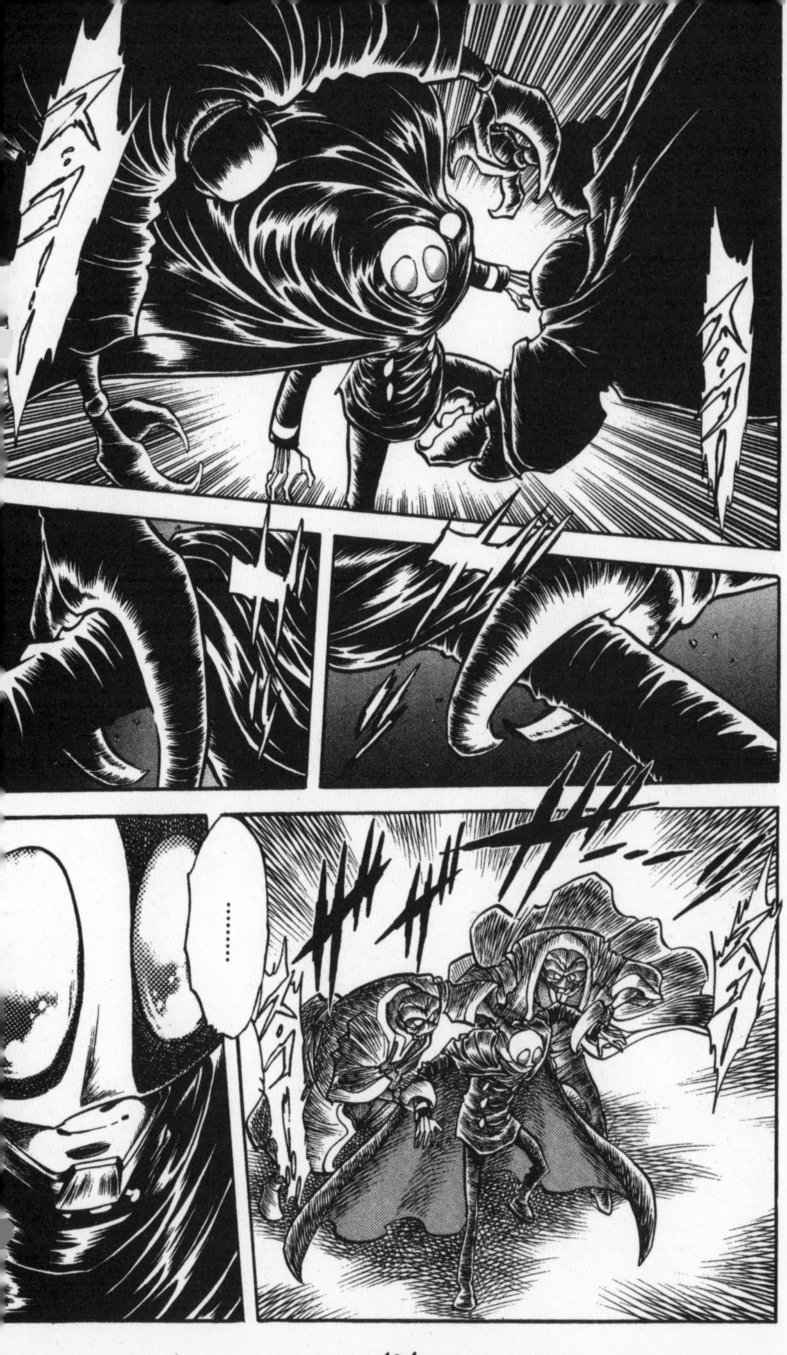
....

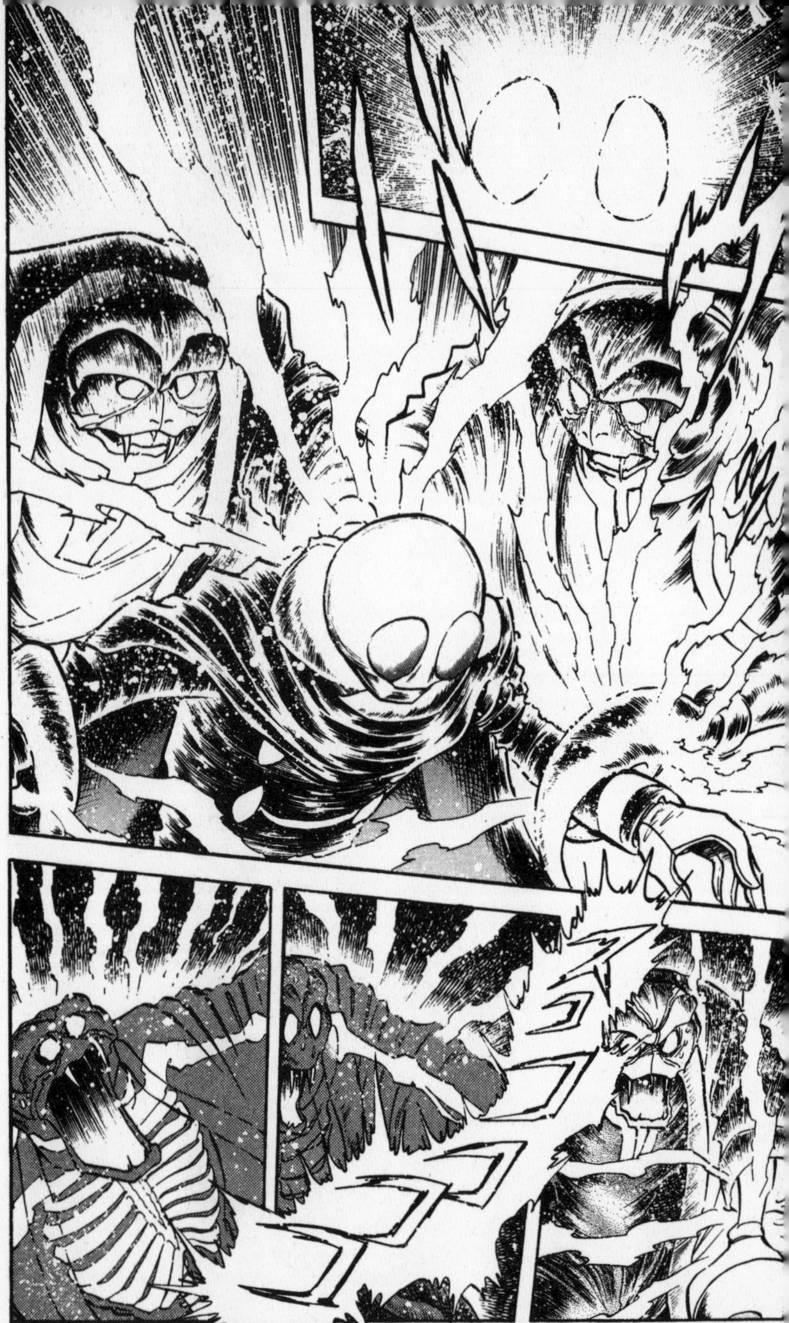

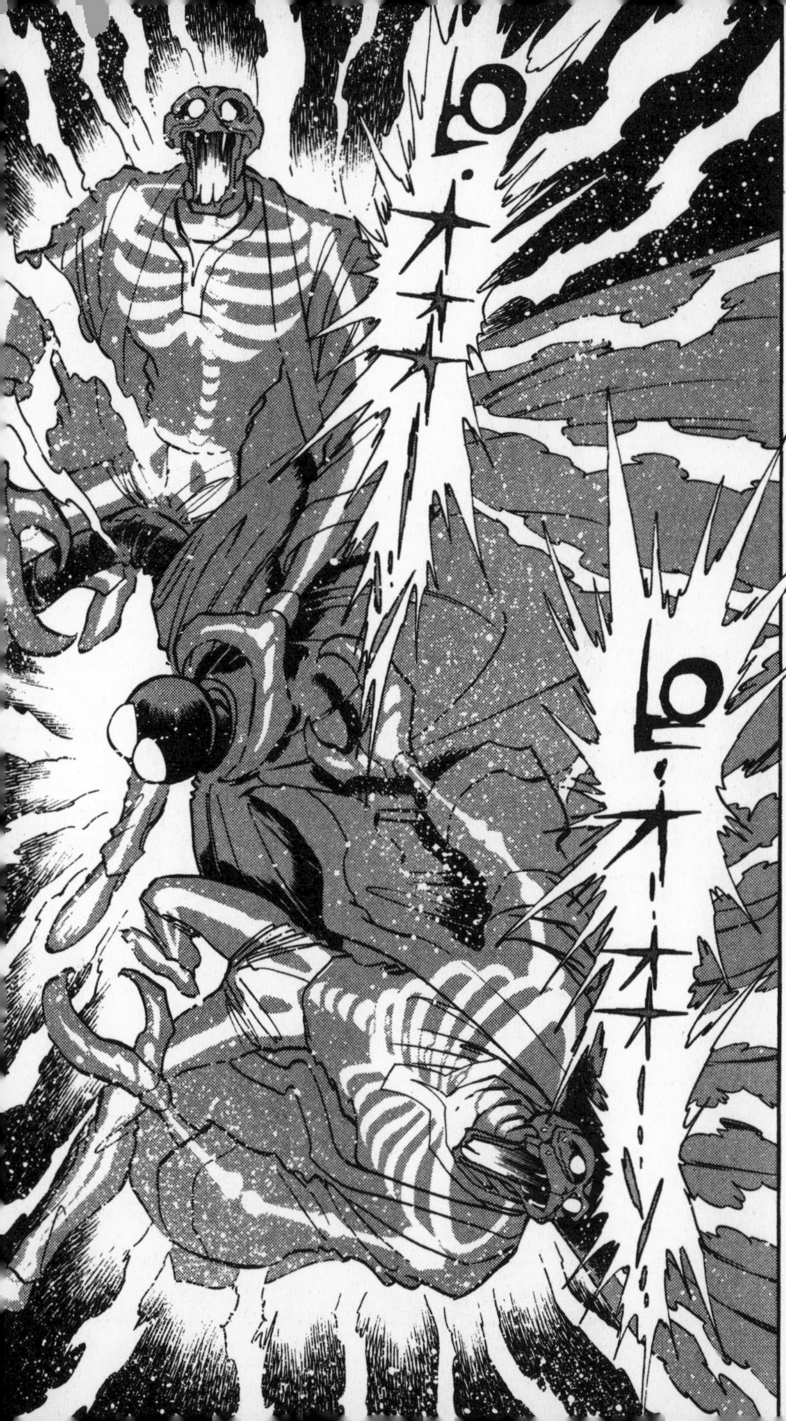

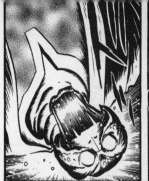

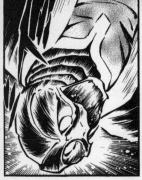

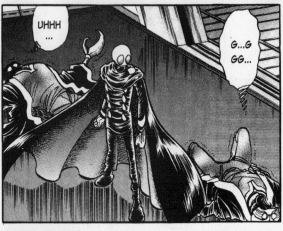

G...G
GG...
UHHH
...
DON'T WORRY. THAT WAS JUST A FRACTION OF MY POWER.
YOU WON'T DIE.
BUT IF YOU WANT TO WALK AGAIN, YOU'LL HAVE TO SUFFER THROUGH WORSE PAIN THAN THIS.

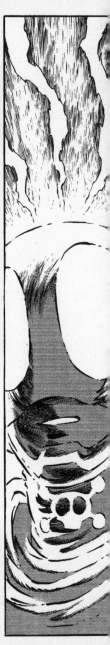

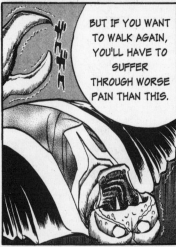

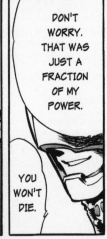

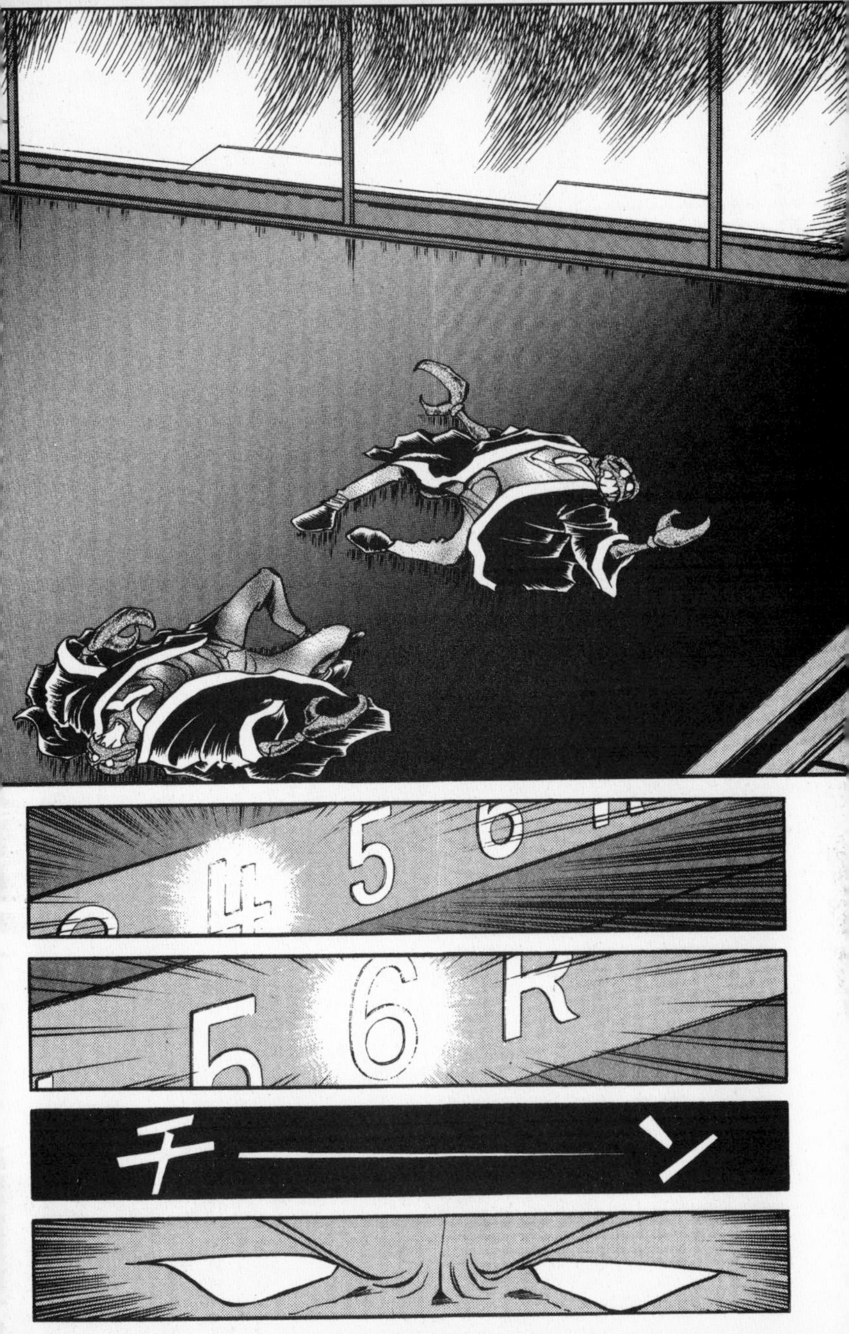
4 5 6
5 6 R
チーーーン

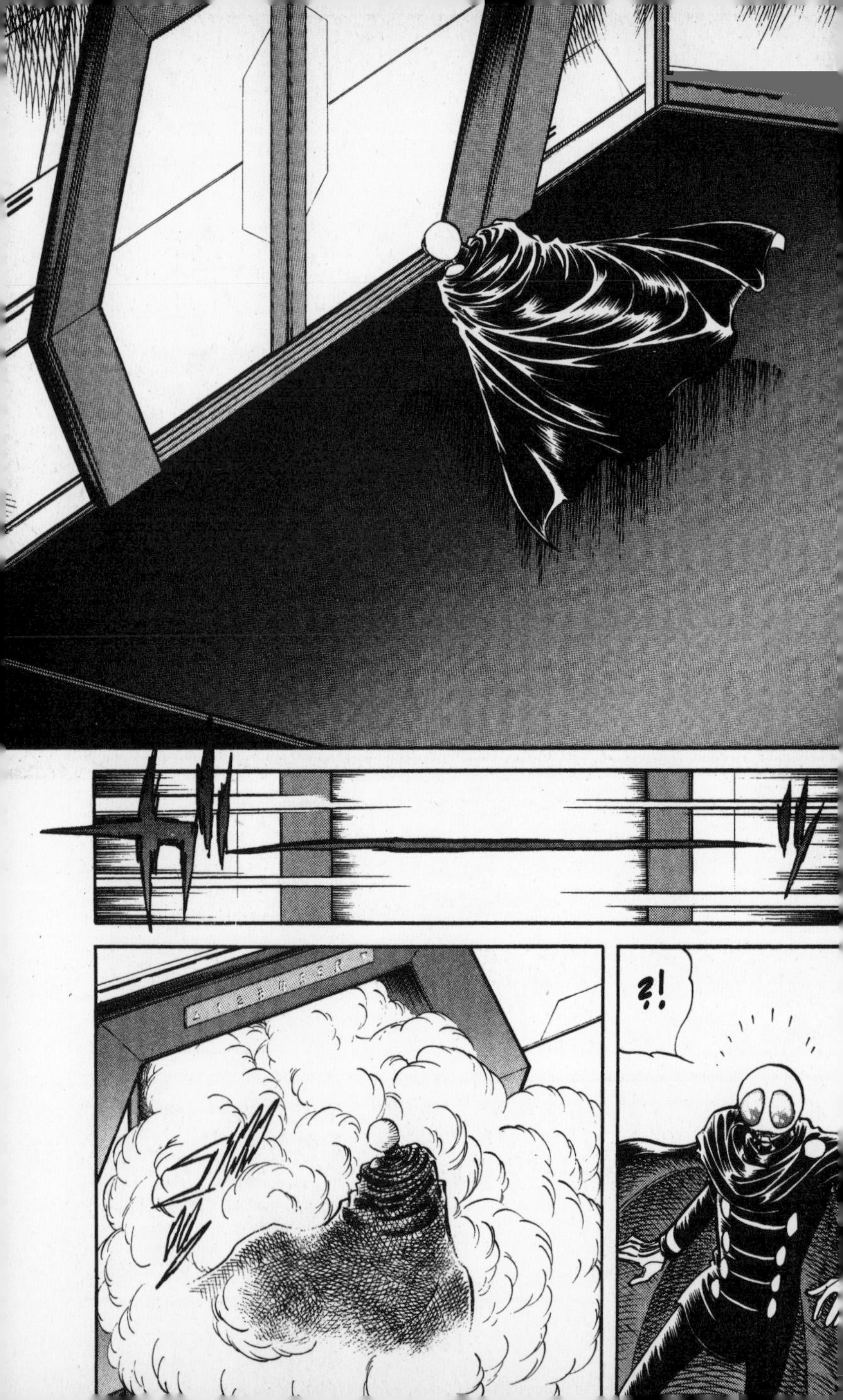
?!

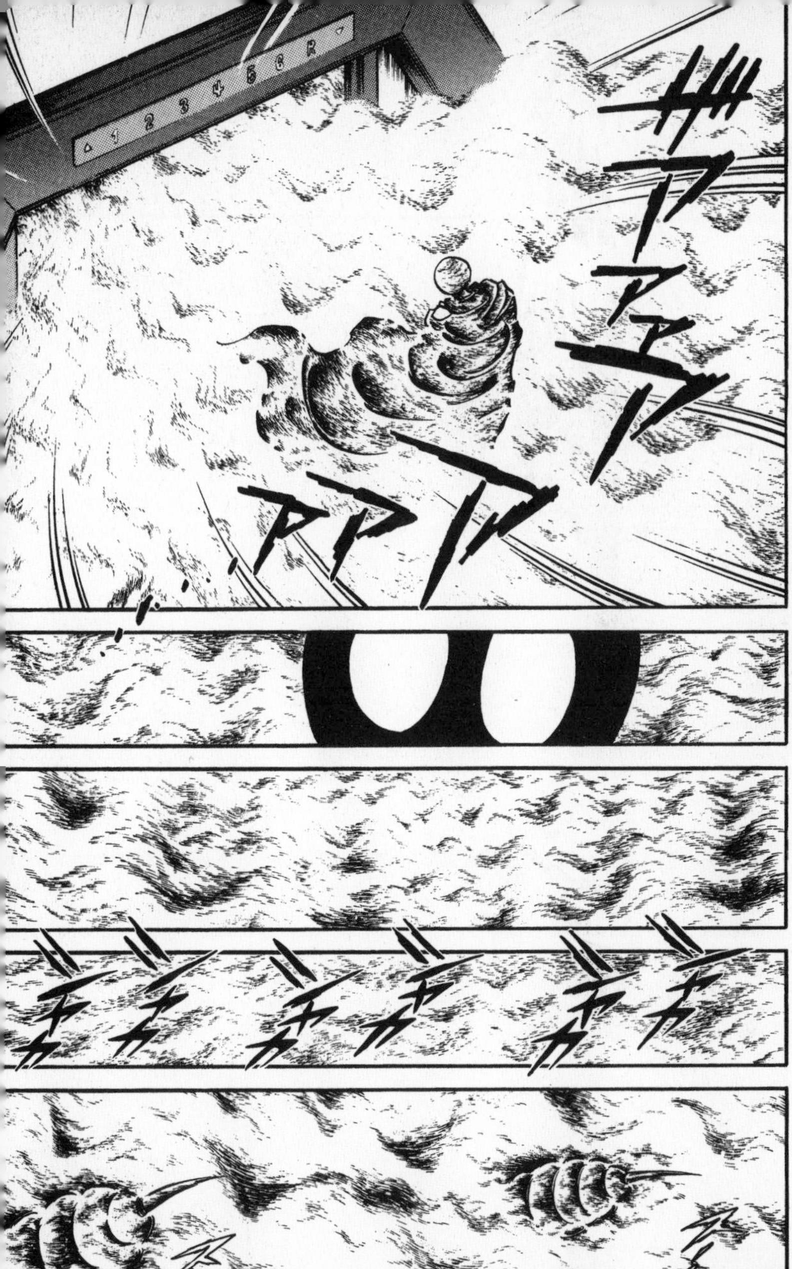
1 2 3 4 5 6 R

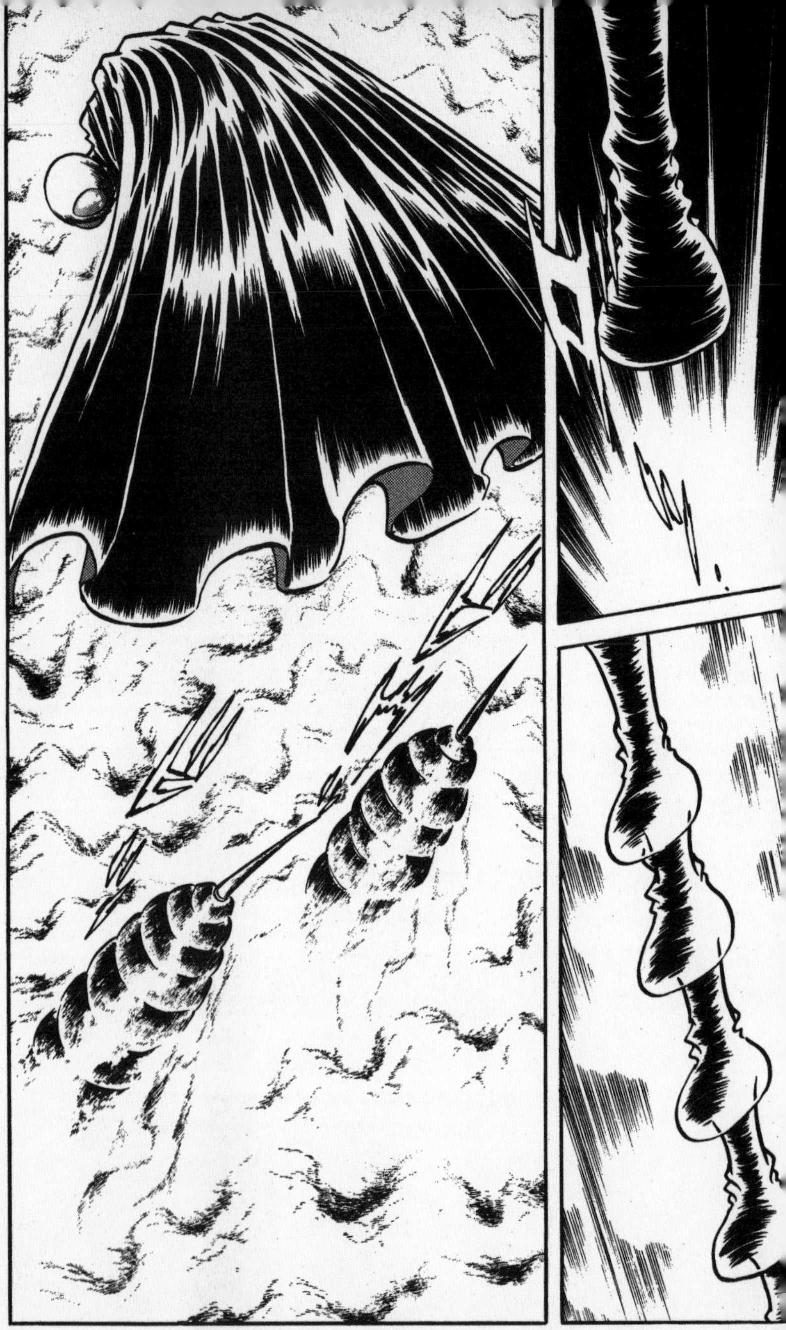

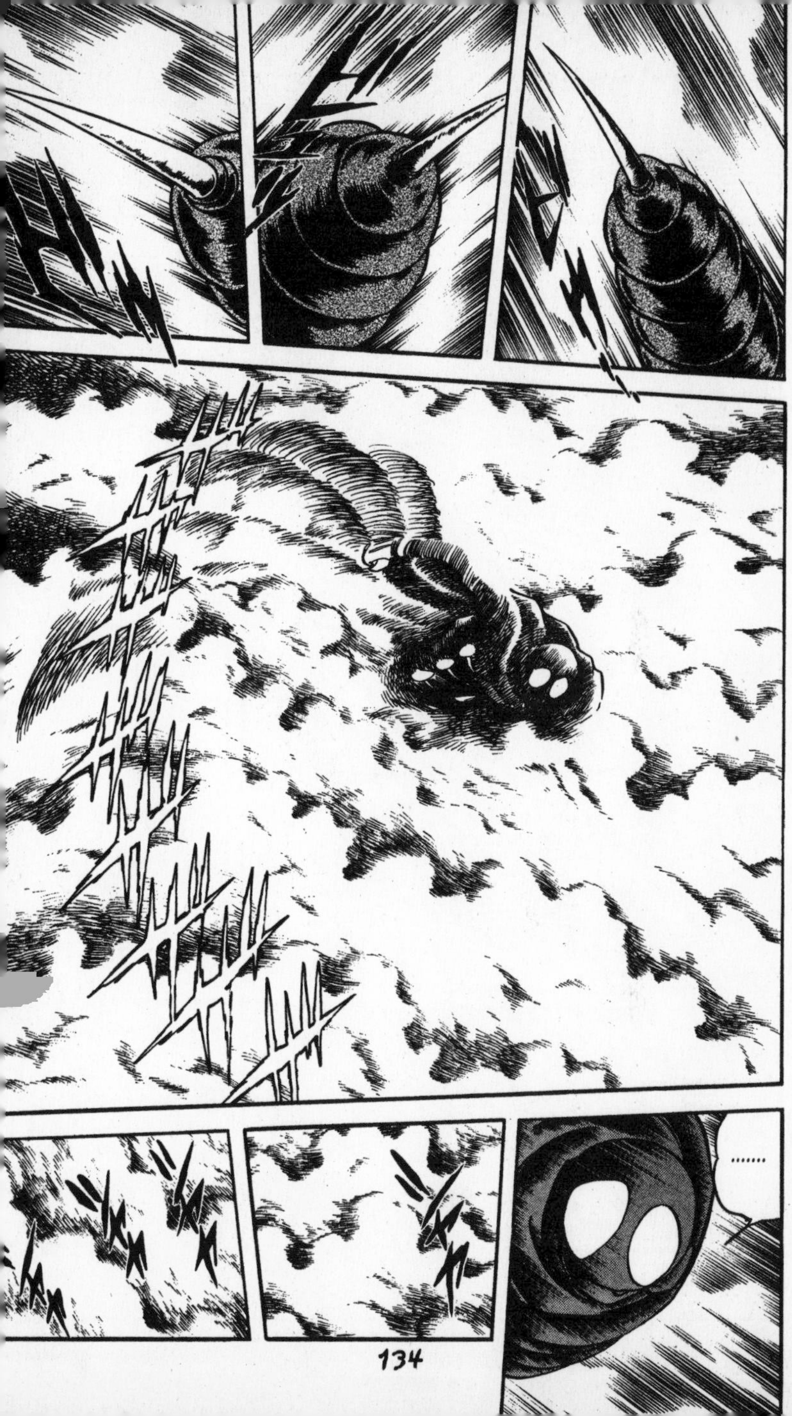
......

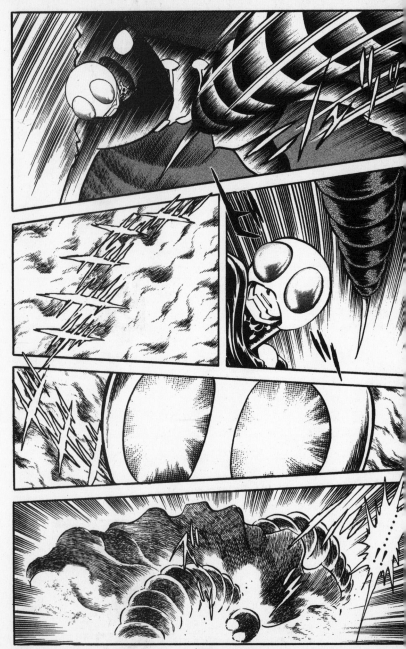

135

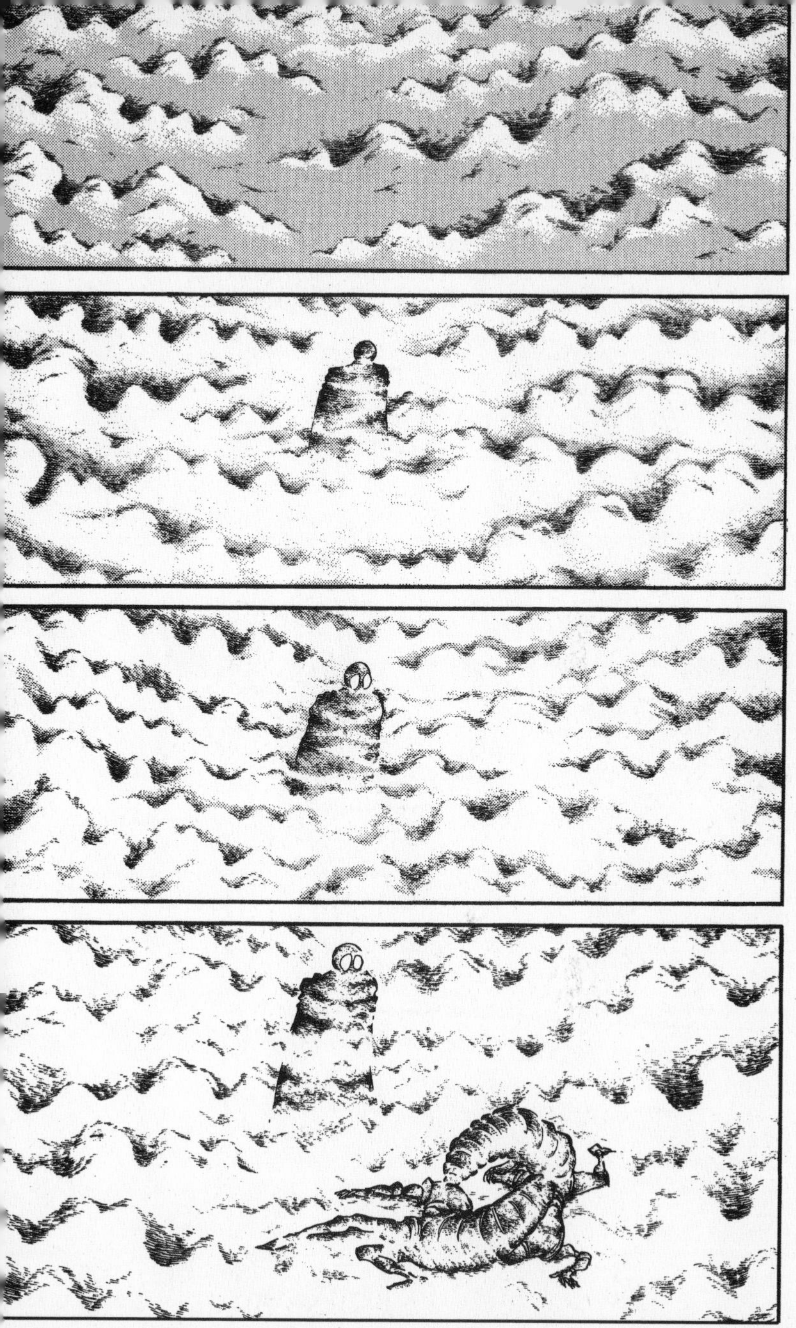

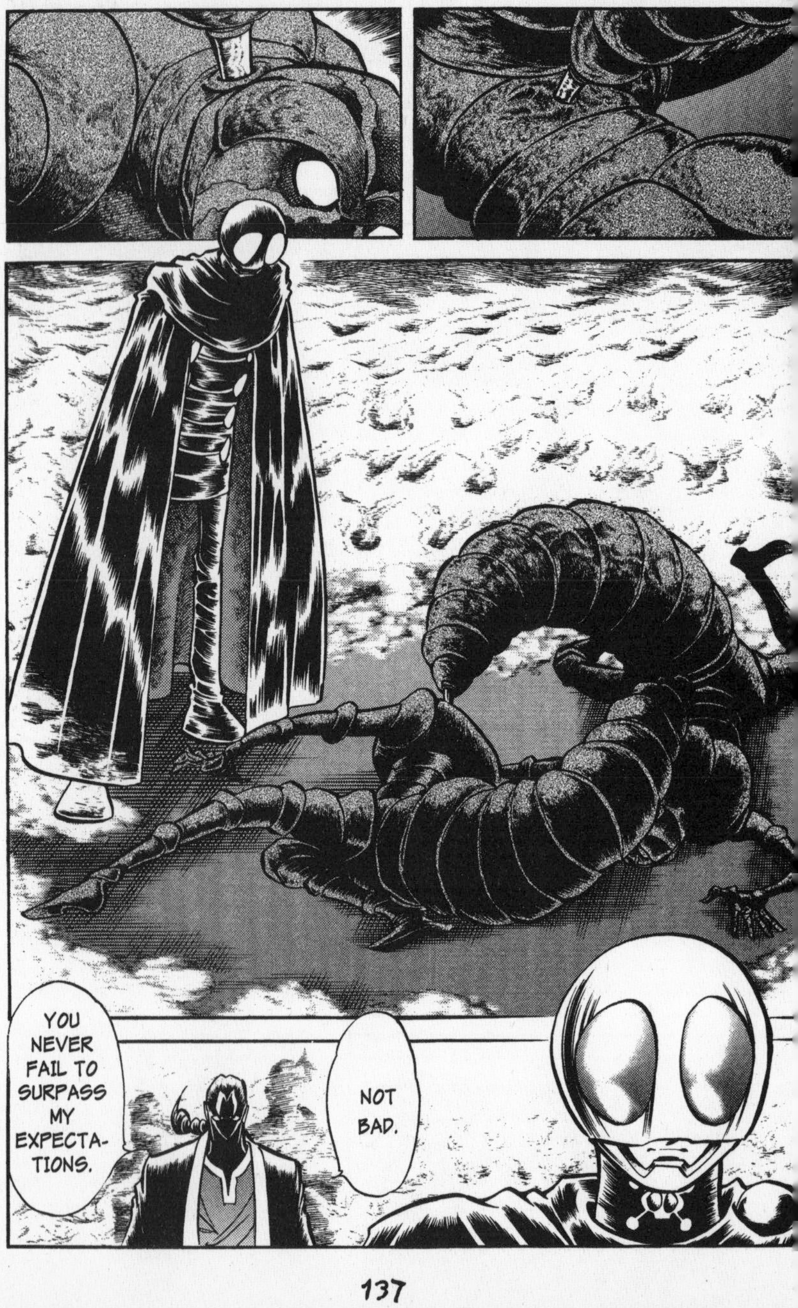
NOT BAD.
YOU NEVER FAIL TO SURPASS MY EXPECTA-TIONS.

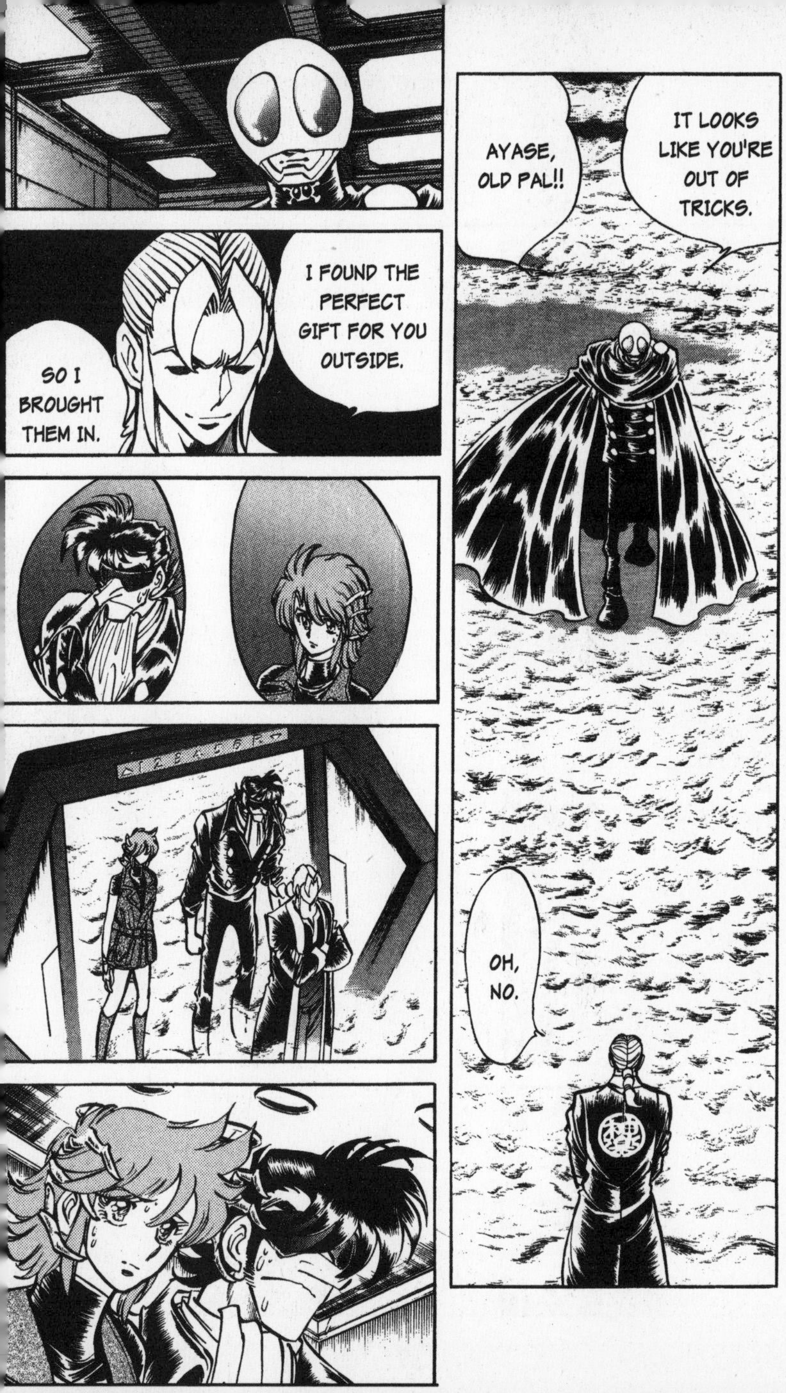
IT LOOKS LIKE YOU'RE OUT OF TRICKS.
AYASE, OLD PAL!!
OH, NO.
I FOUND THE PERFECT GIFT FOR YOU OUTSIDE.
SO I BROUGHT THEM IN.

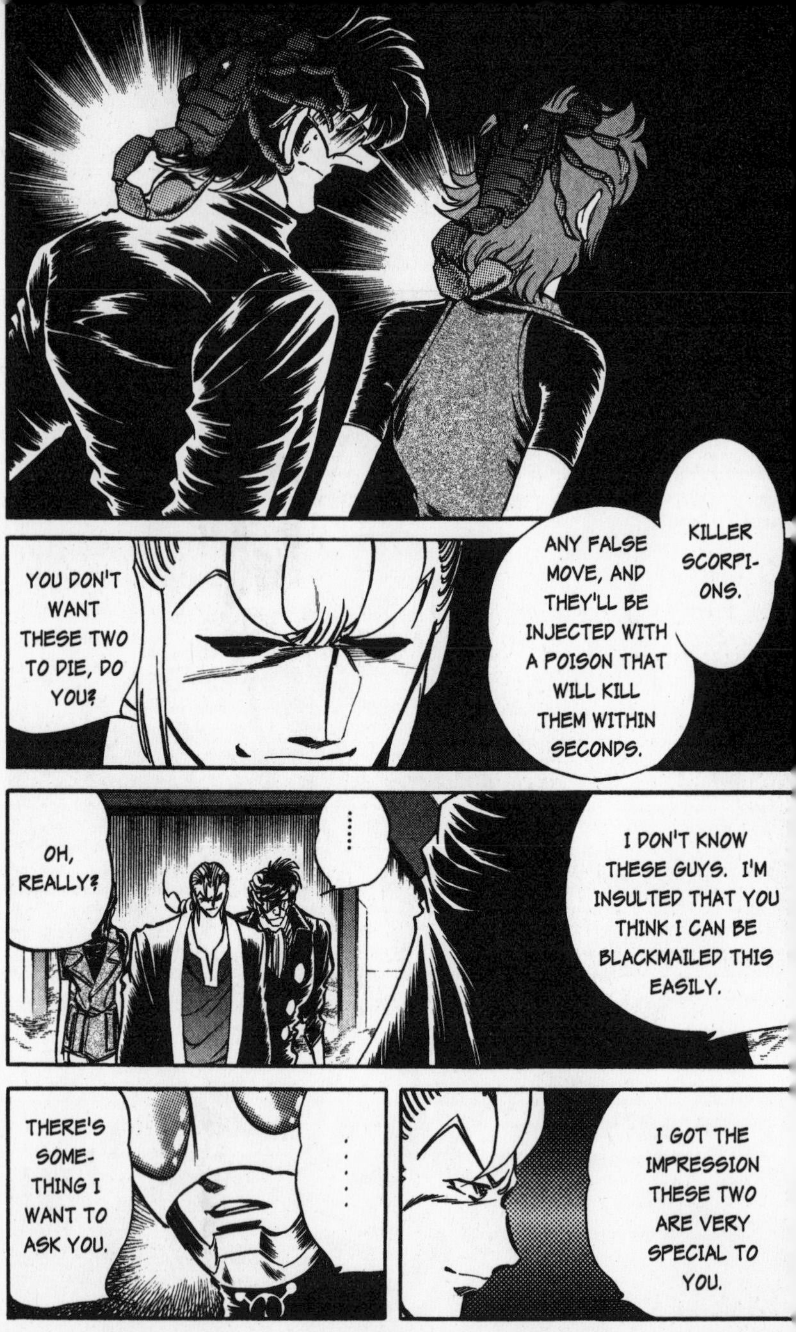
KILLER SCORPI- ONS.
ANY FALSE MOVE, AND THEY'LL BE INJECTED WITH A POISON THAT WILL KILL THEM WITHIN SECONDS.
YOU DON'T WANT THESE TWO TO DIE, DO YOU?
I DON'T KNOW THESE GUYS. I'M INSULTED THAT YOU THINK I CAN BE BLACKMAILED THIS EASILY.
......
OH, REALLY?
I GOT THE IMPRESSION THESE TWO ARE VERY SPECIAL TO YOU.
.....
THERE'S SOME- THING I WANT TO ASK YOU.

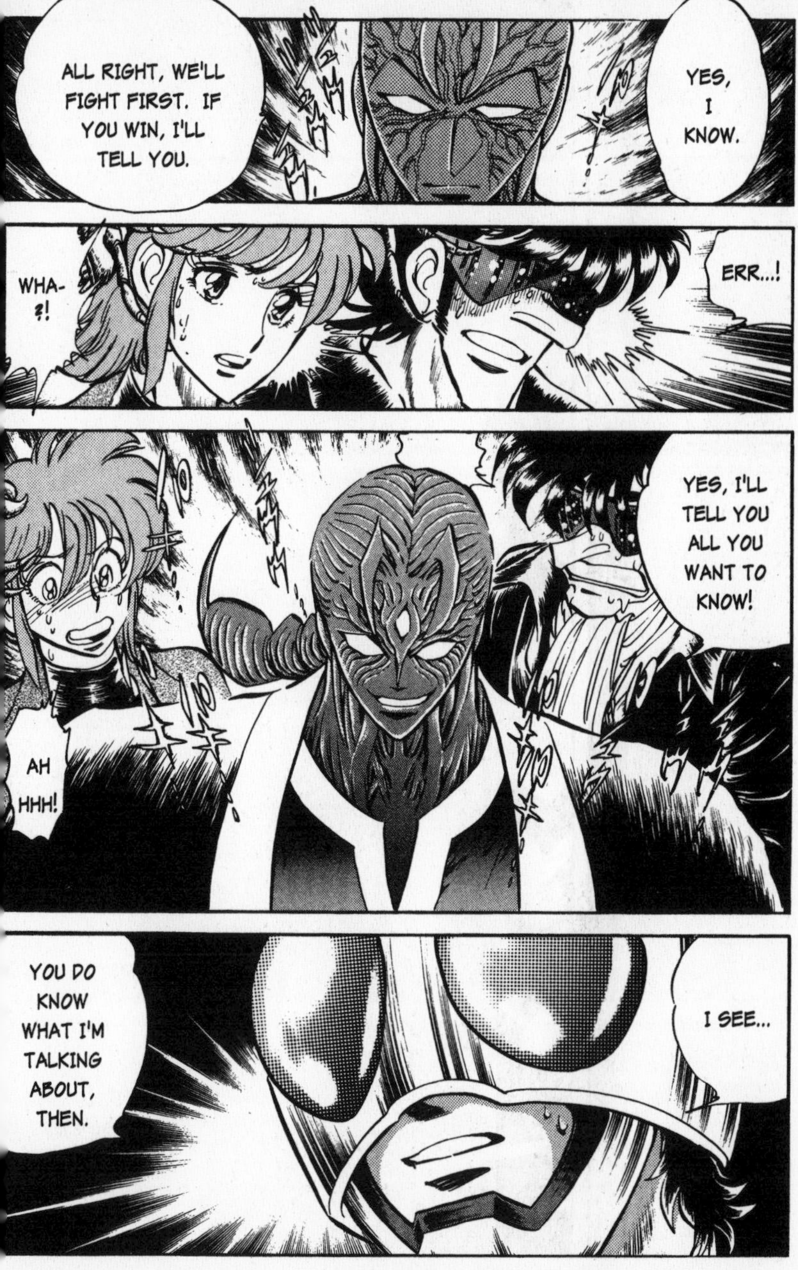
YES, I KNOW.
ALL RIGHT, WE'LL FIGHT FIRST. IF YOU WIN, I'LL TELL YOU.
ERR...!
WHA-?!
YES, I'LL TELL YOU ALL YOU WANT TO KNOW!
AH HHH!
I SEE...
YOU DO KNOW WHAT I'M TALKING ABOUT, THEN.

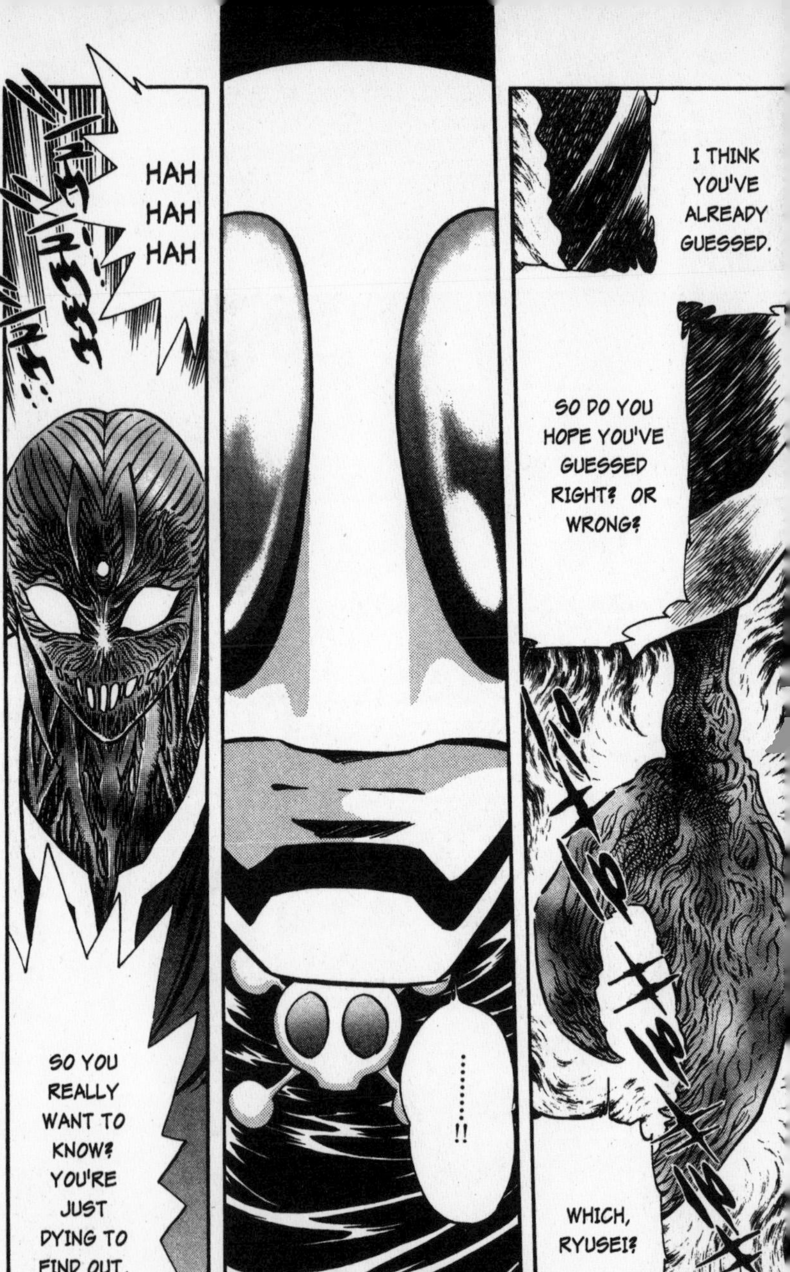
I THINK YOU'VE ALREADY GUESSED.
SO DO YOU HOPE YOU'VE GUESSED RIGHT? OR WRONG?
WHICH, RYUSEI?
......!!
HAH HAH HAH
SO YOU REALLY WANT TO KNOW? YOU'RE JUST DYING TO FIND OUT, EH?

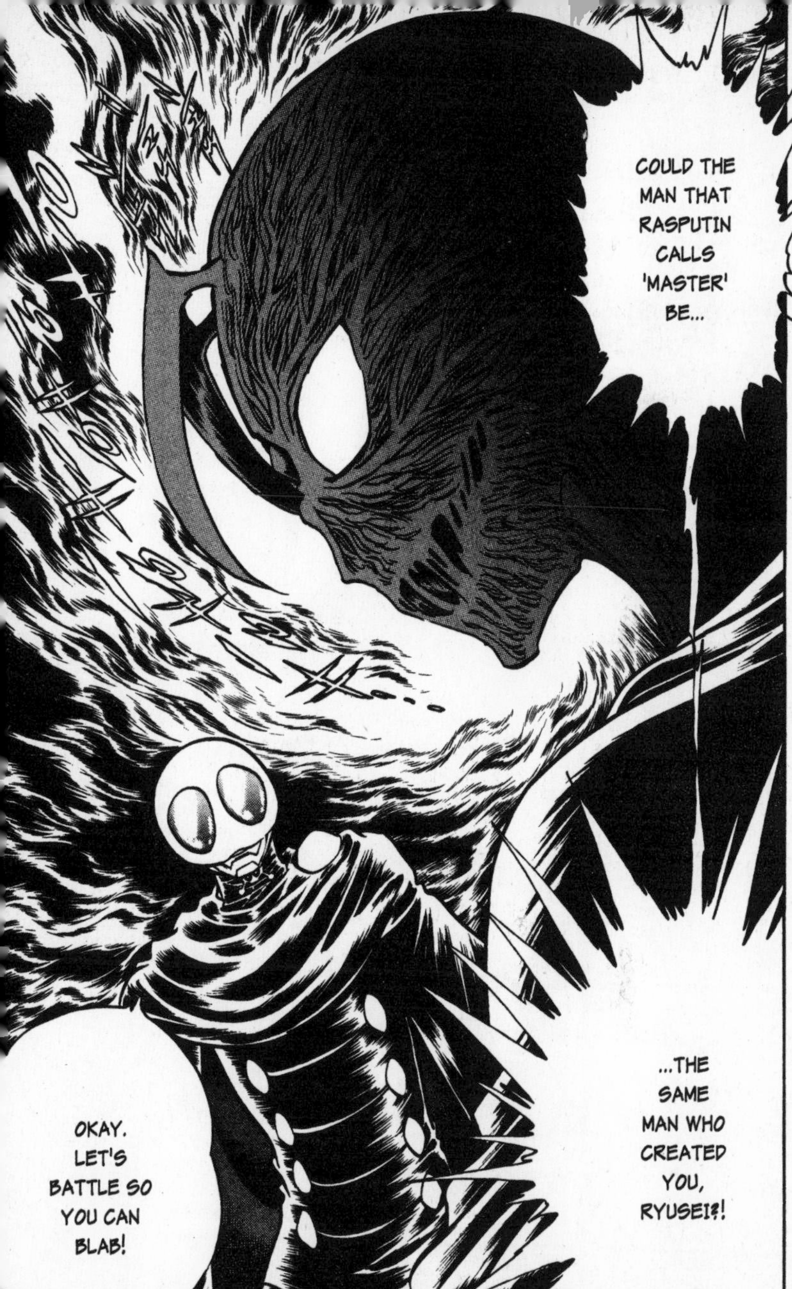
COULD THE MAN THAT RASPUTIN CALLS 'MASTER' BE...
...THE SAME MAN WHO CREATED YOU, RYUSEI!?!
OKAY. LET'S BATTLE SO YOU CAN BLAB!

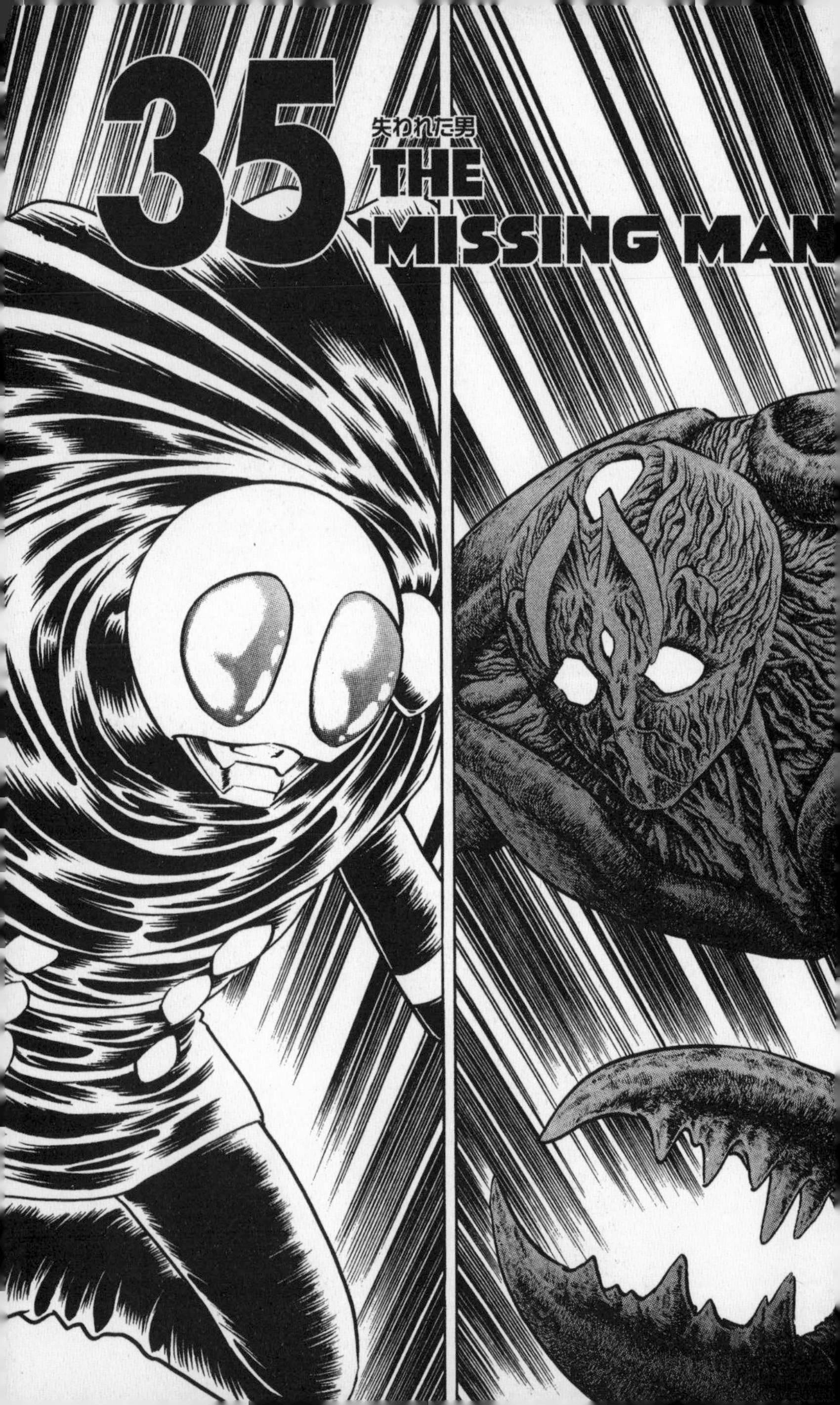

35
失われた男
THE MISSING MAN

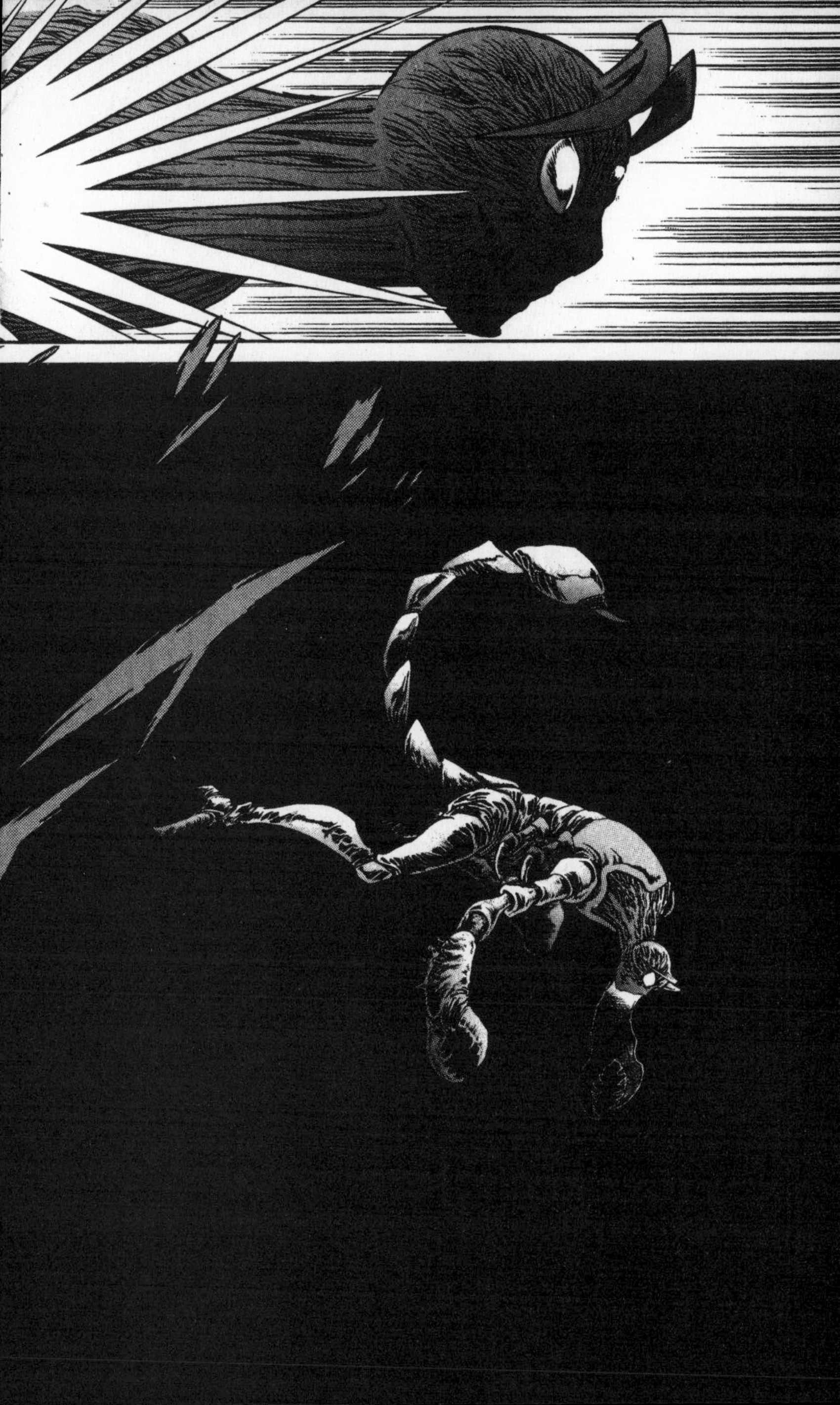

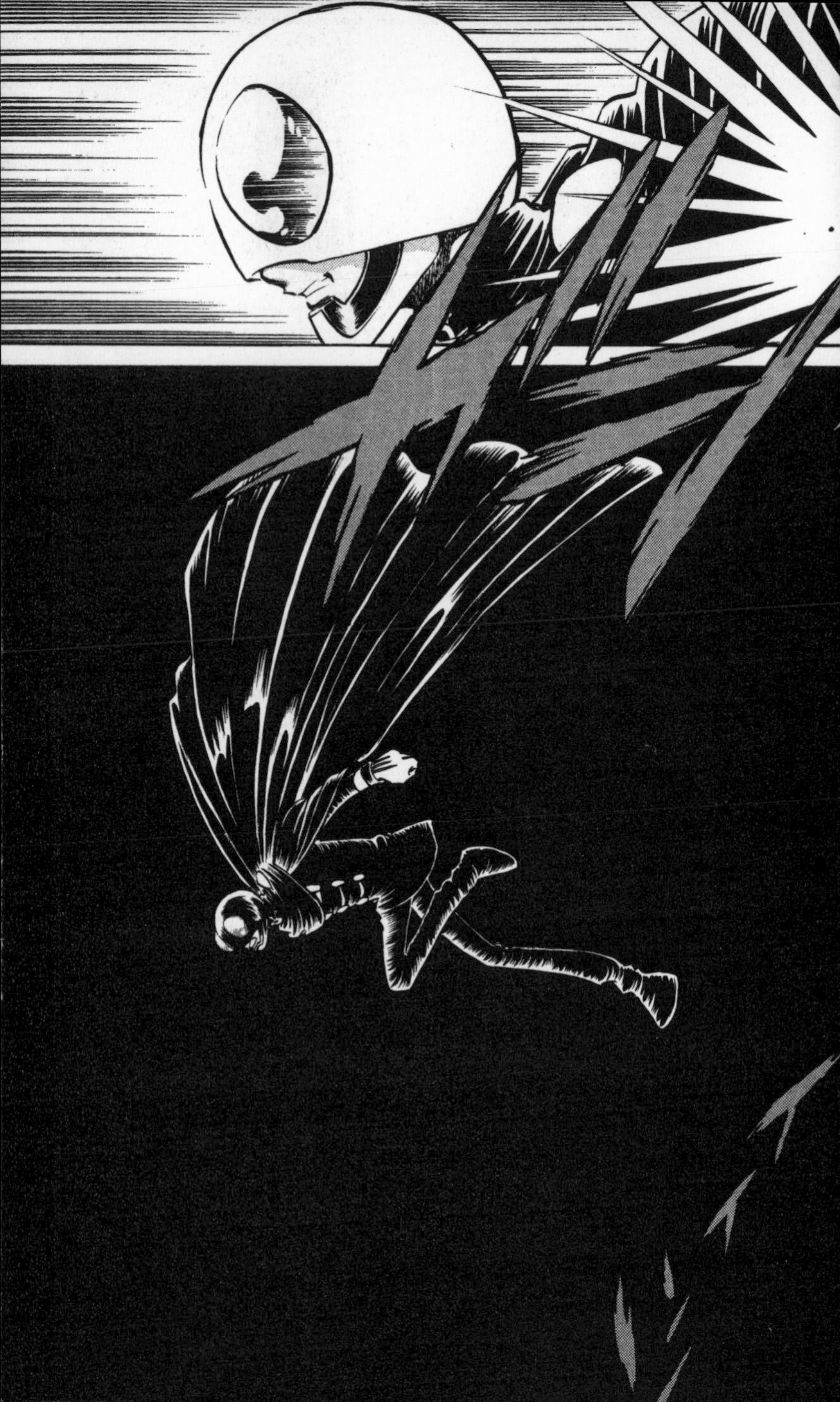

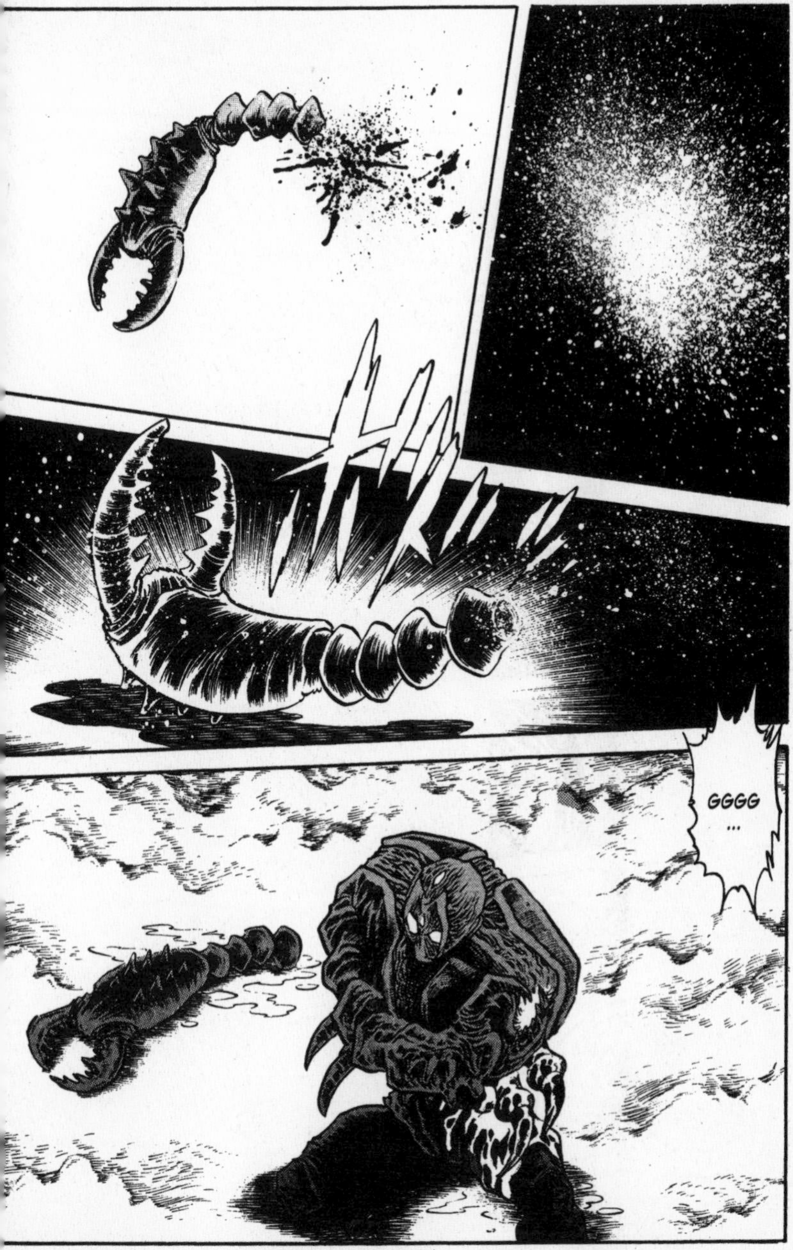
GGGG
...

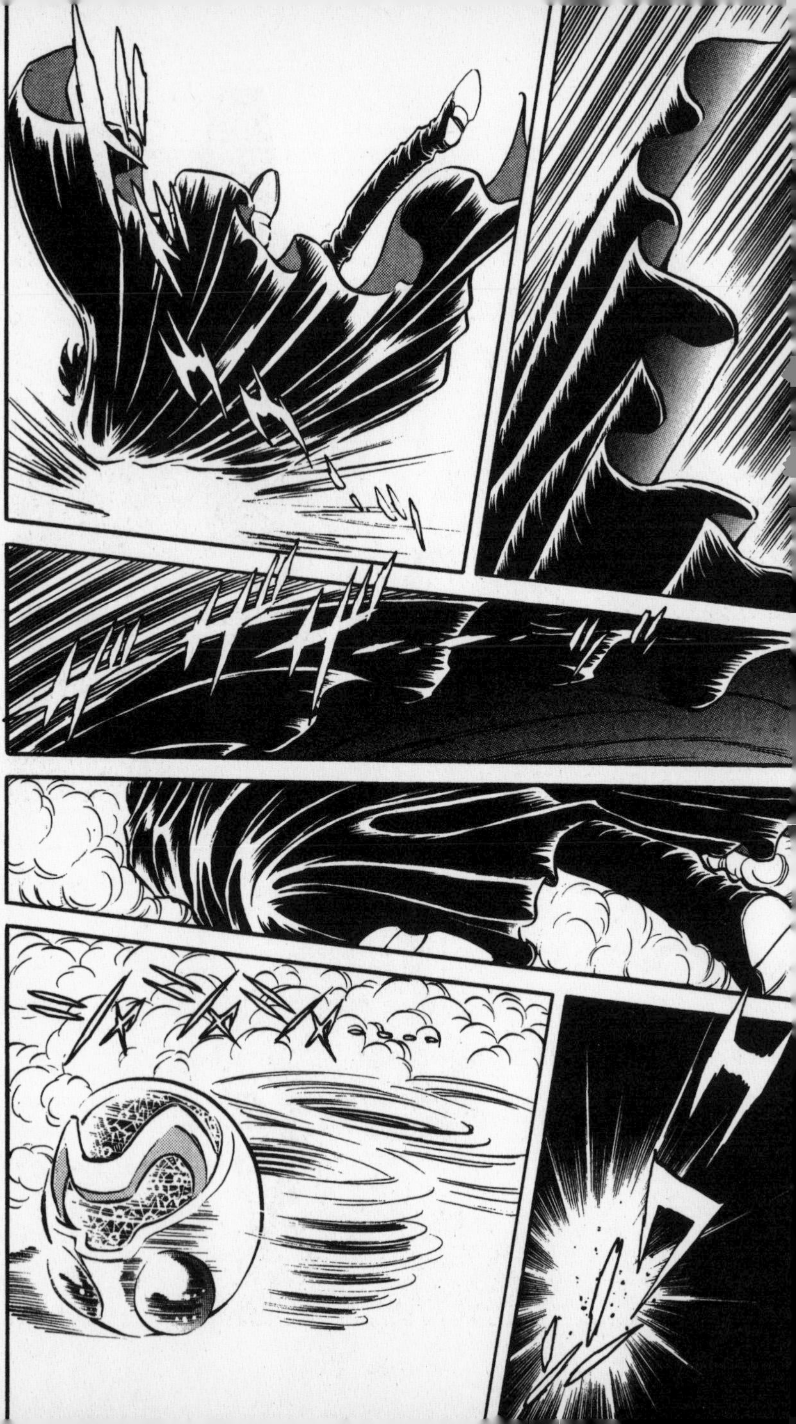

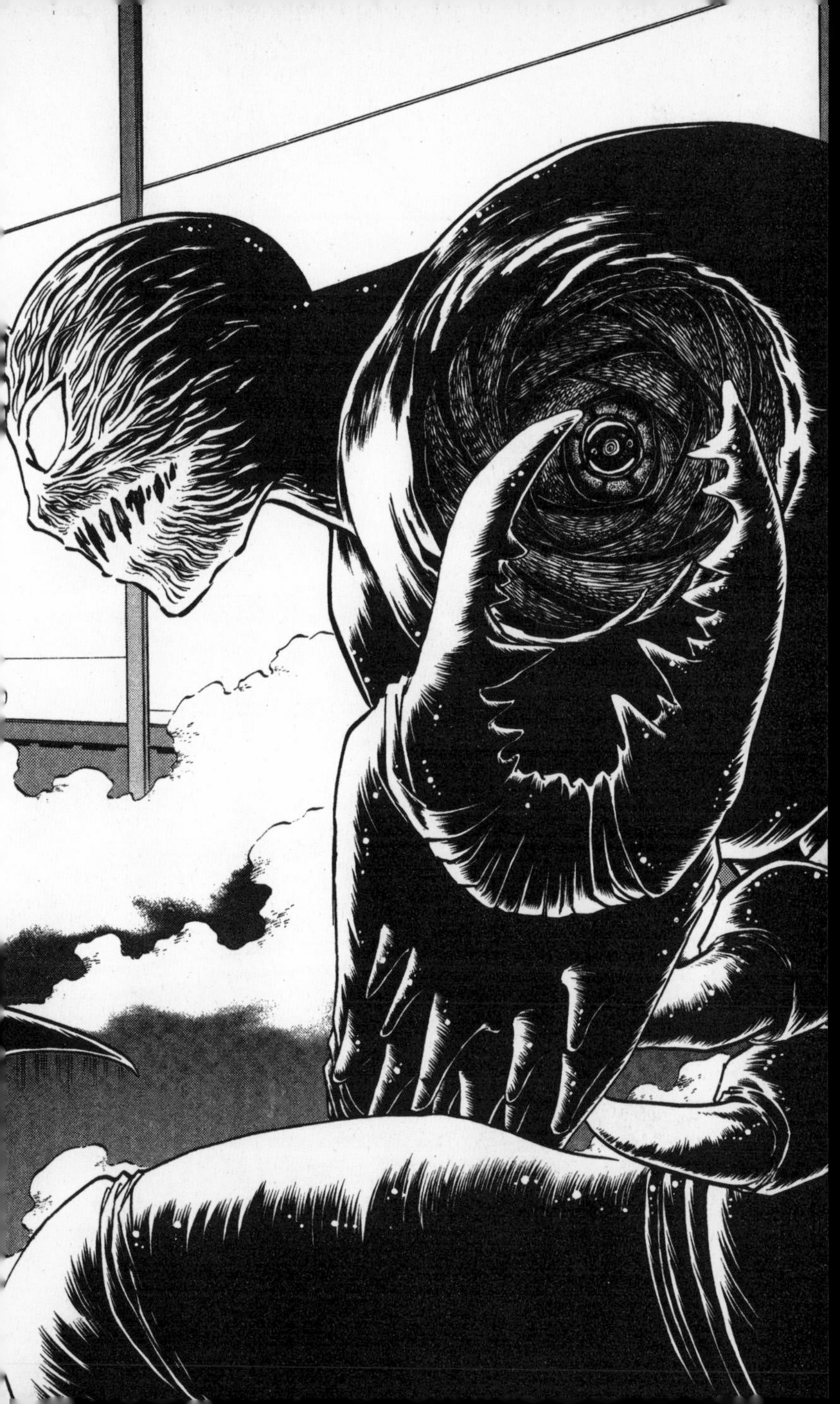

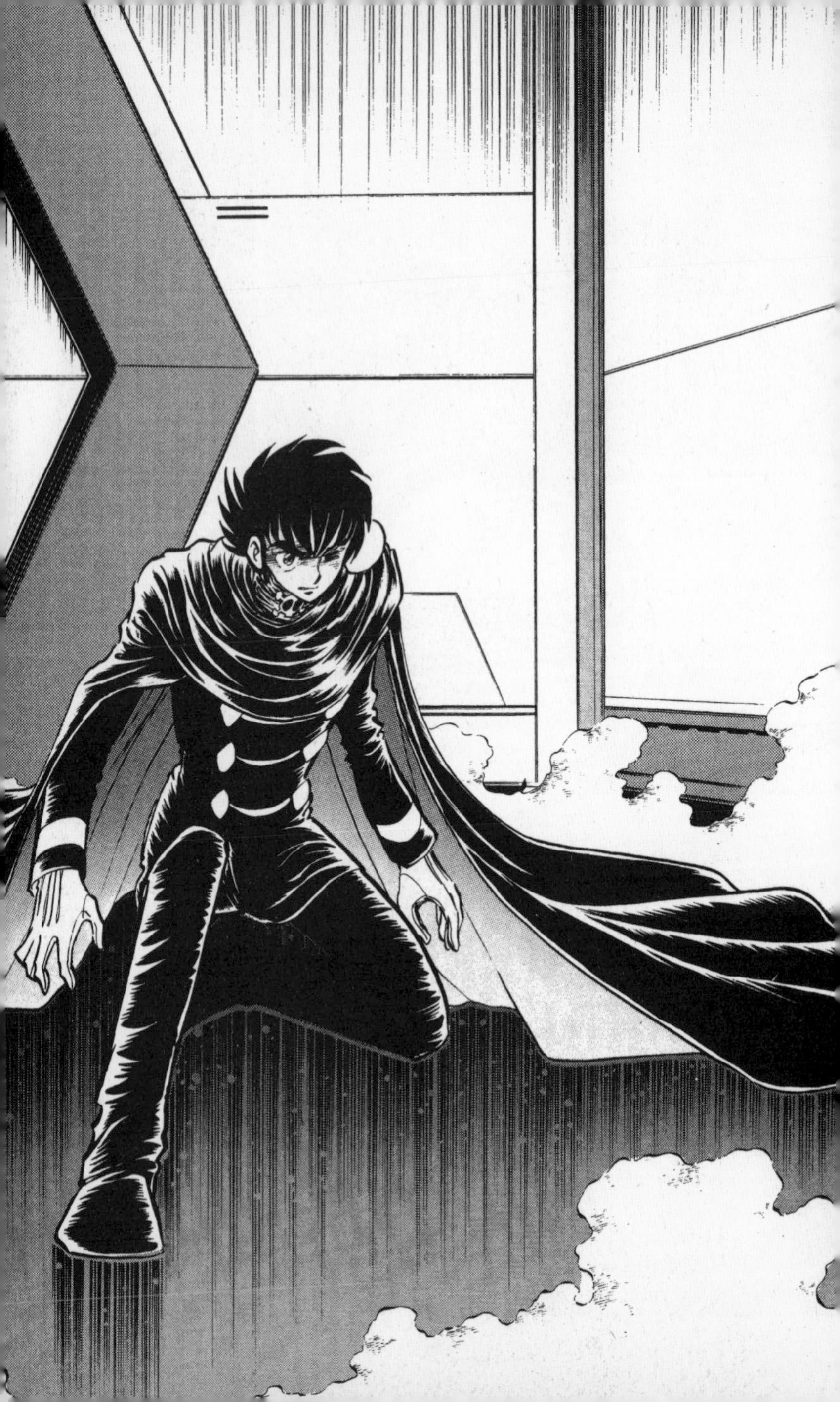

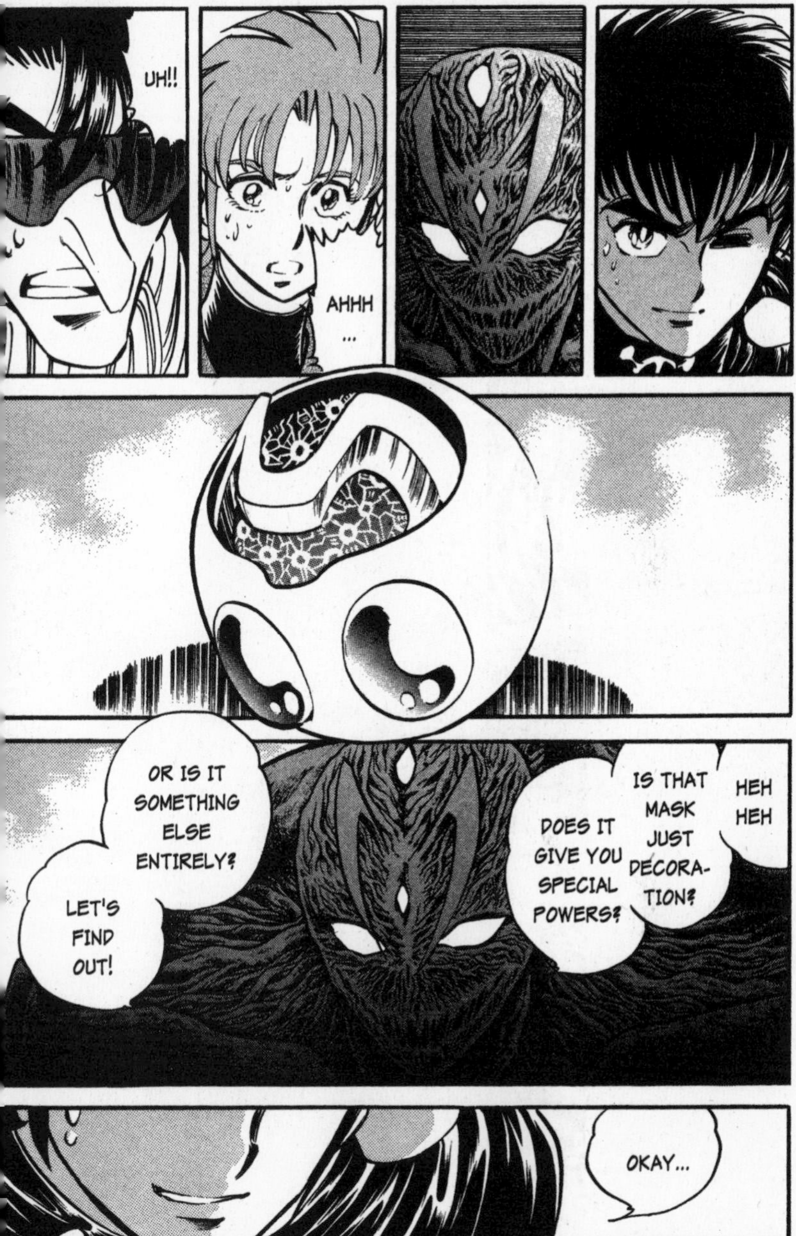
AHHH ...
UH!!
HEH HEH
IS THAT MASK JUST DECORA-TION?
DOES IT GIVE YOU SPECIAL POWERS?
OR IS IT SOMETHING ELSE ENTIRELY?
LET'S FIND OUT!
OKAY...

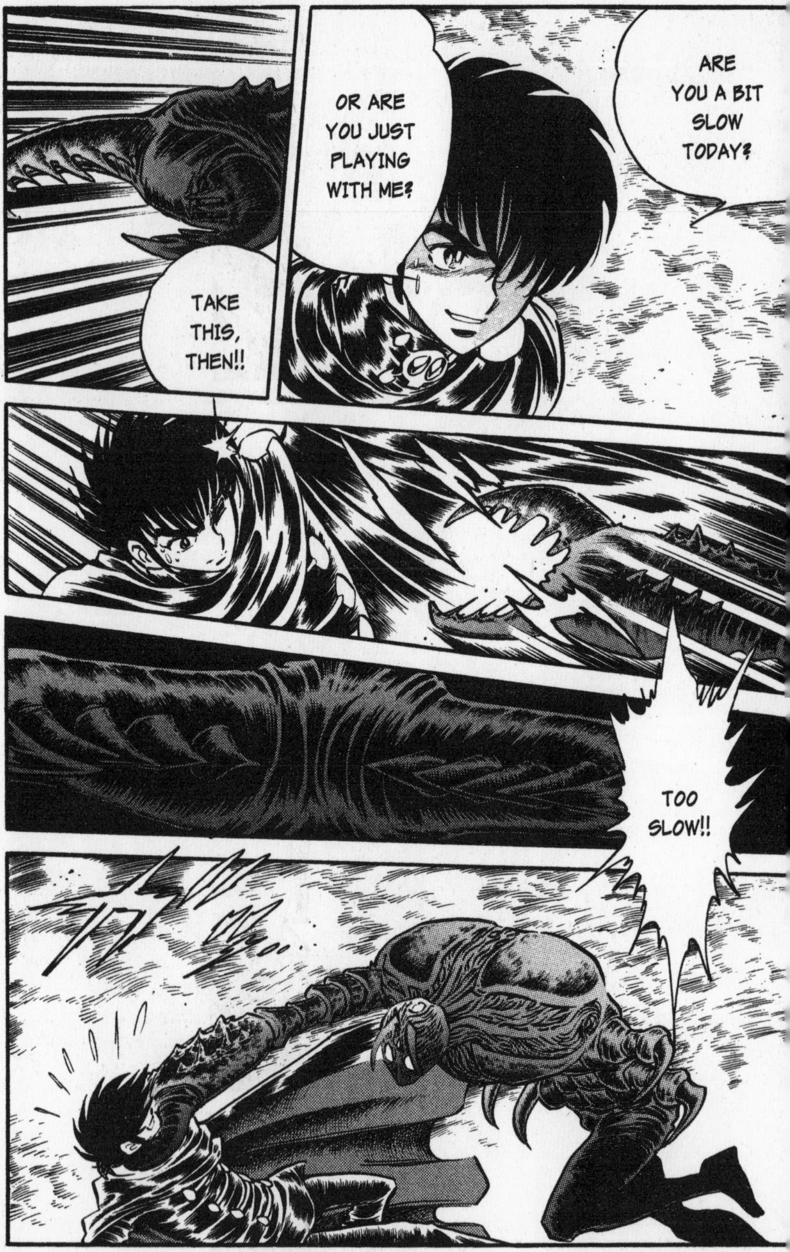
ARE YOU A BIT SLOW TODAY?
OR ARE YOU JUST PLAYING WITH ME?
TAKE THIS, THEN!!
TOO SLOW!!

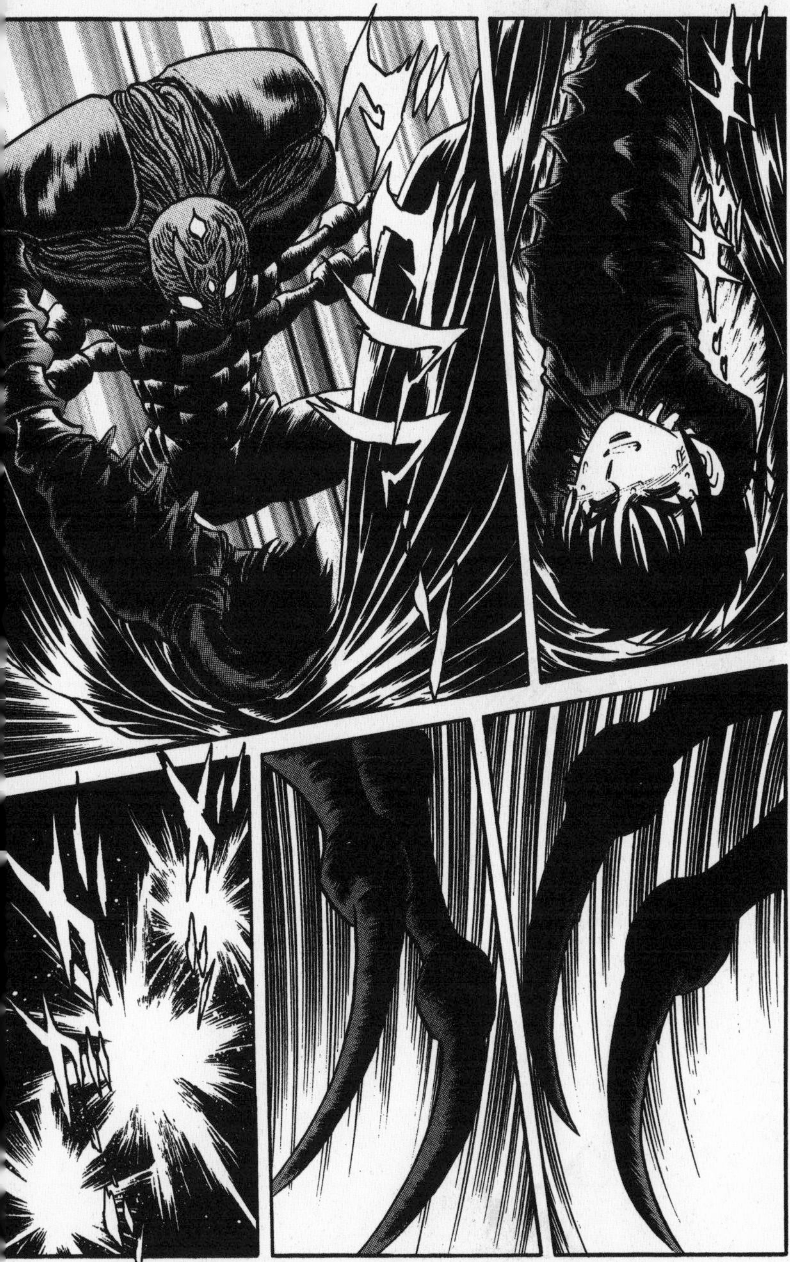

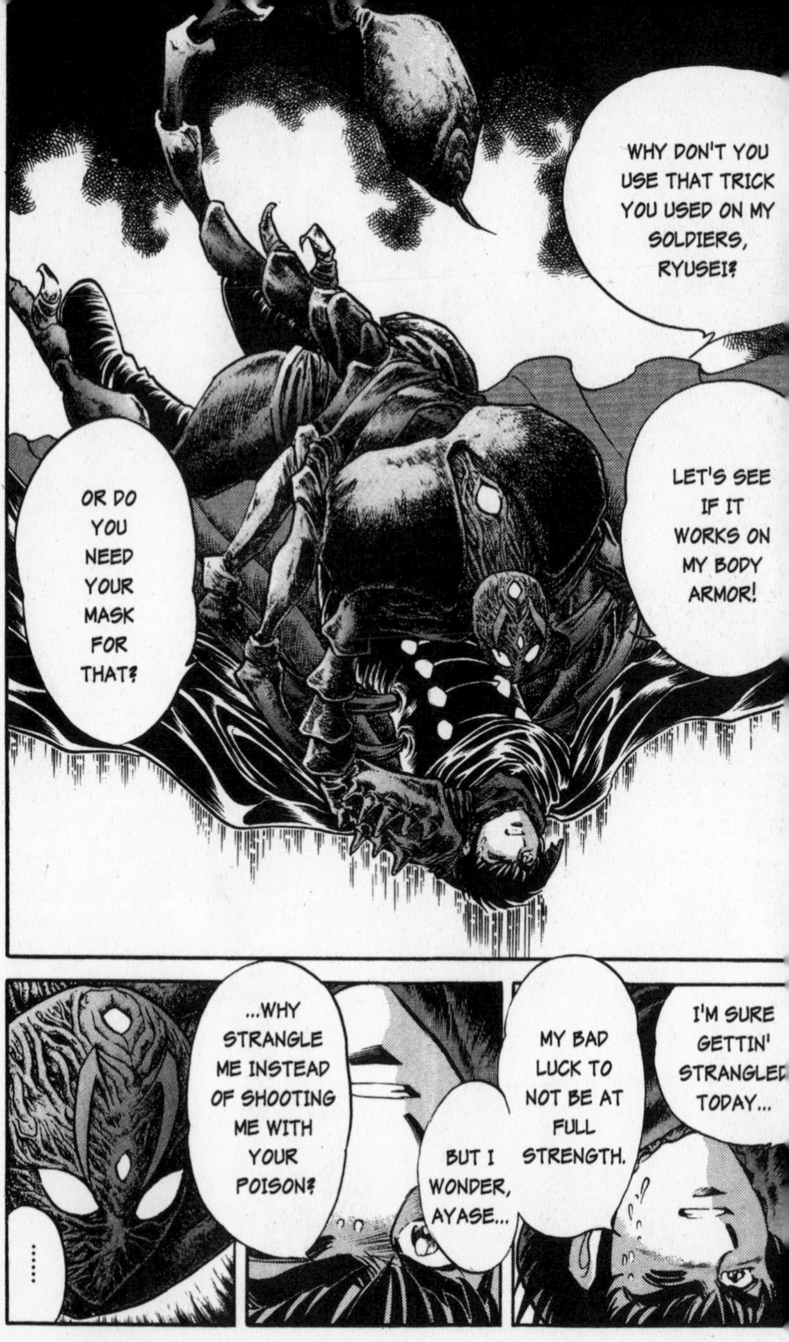
WHY DON'T YOU USE THAT TRICK YOU USED ON MY SOLDIERS, RYUSEI?
LET'S SEE IF IT WORKS ON MY BODY ARMOR!
OR DO YOU NEED YOUR MASK FOR THAT?
I'M SURE GETTIN' STRANGLED TODAY...
MY BAD LUCK TO NOT BE AT FULL STRENGTH.
BUT I WONDER, AYASE...
...WHY STRANGLE ME INSTEAD OF SHOOTING ME WITH YOUR POISON?
......

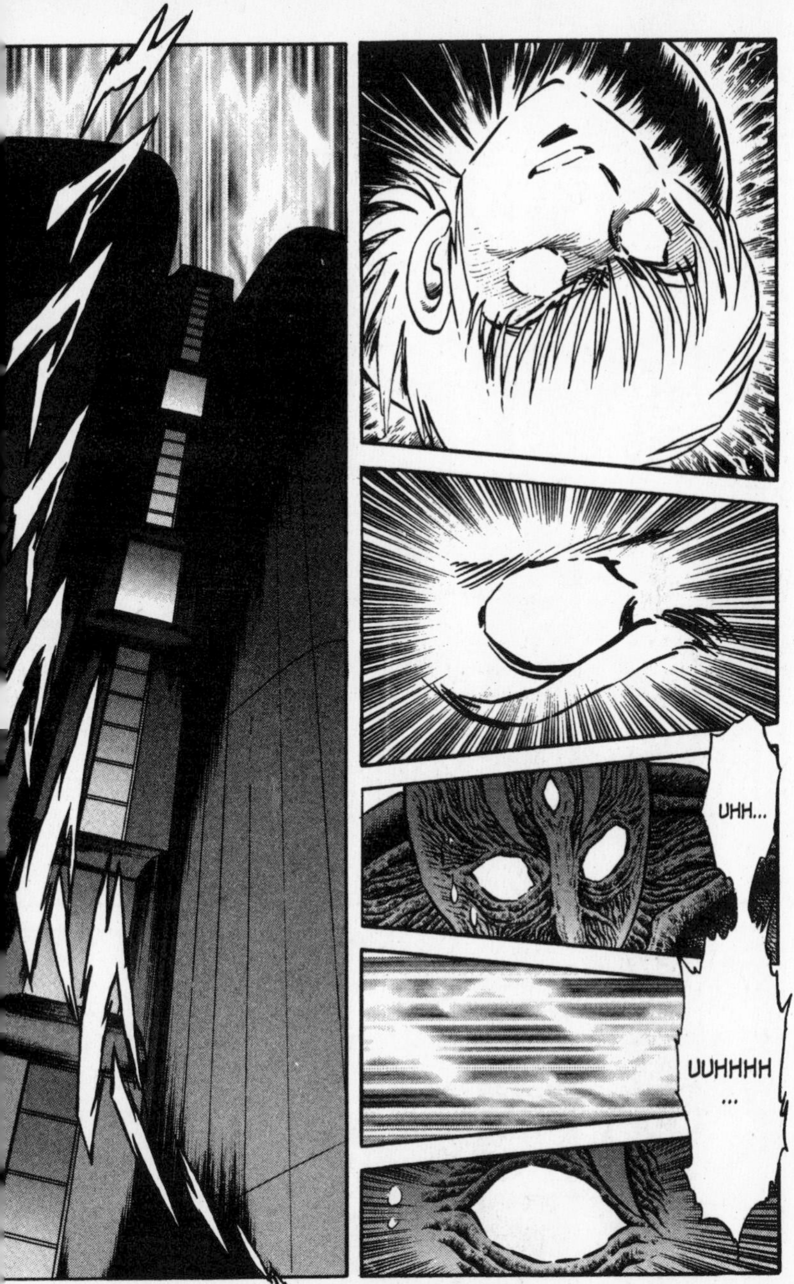
UHH...
UUHHHH
...

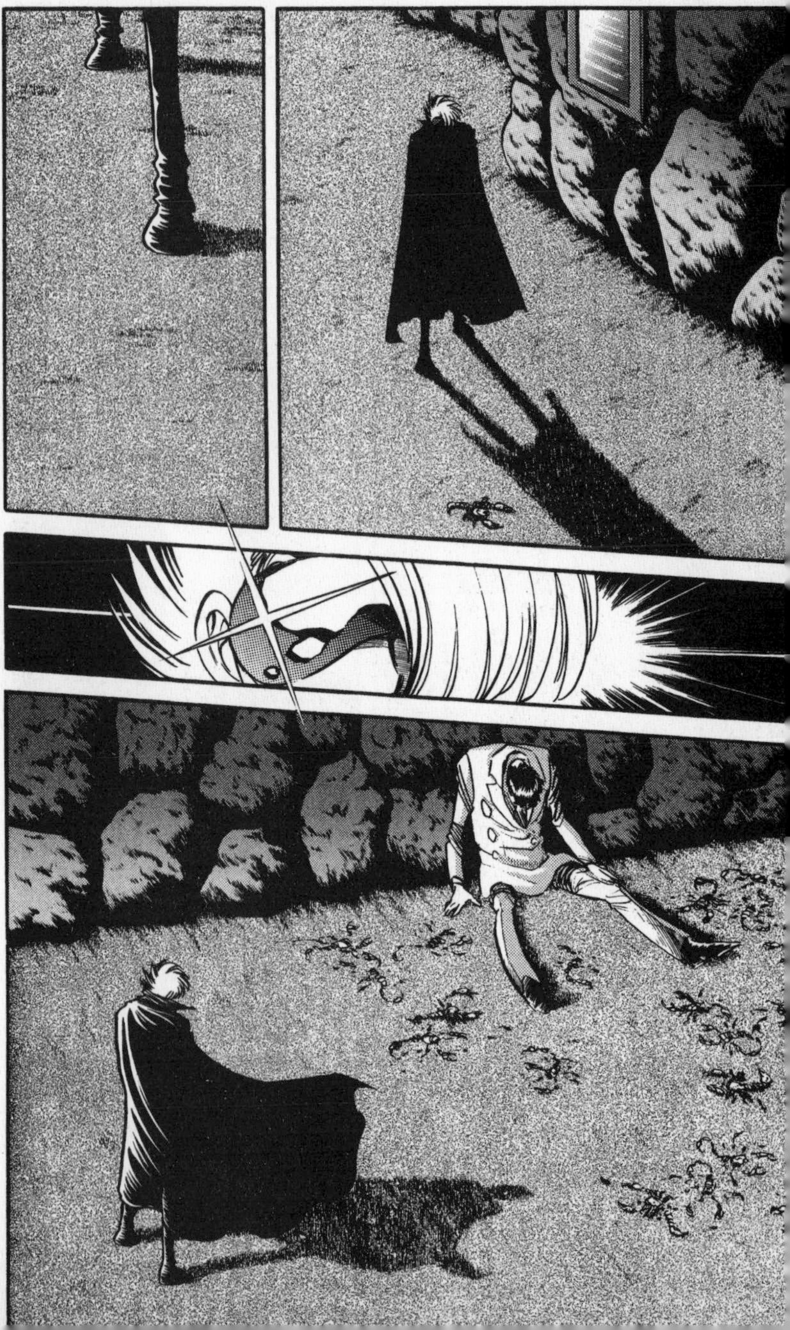

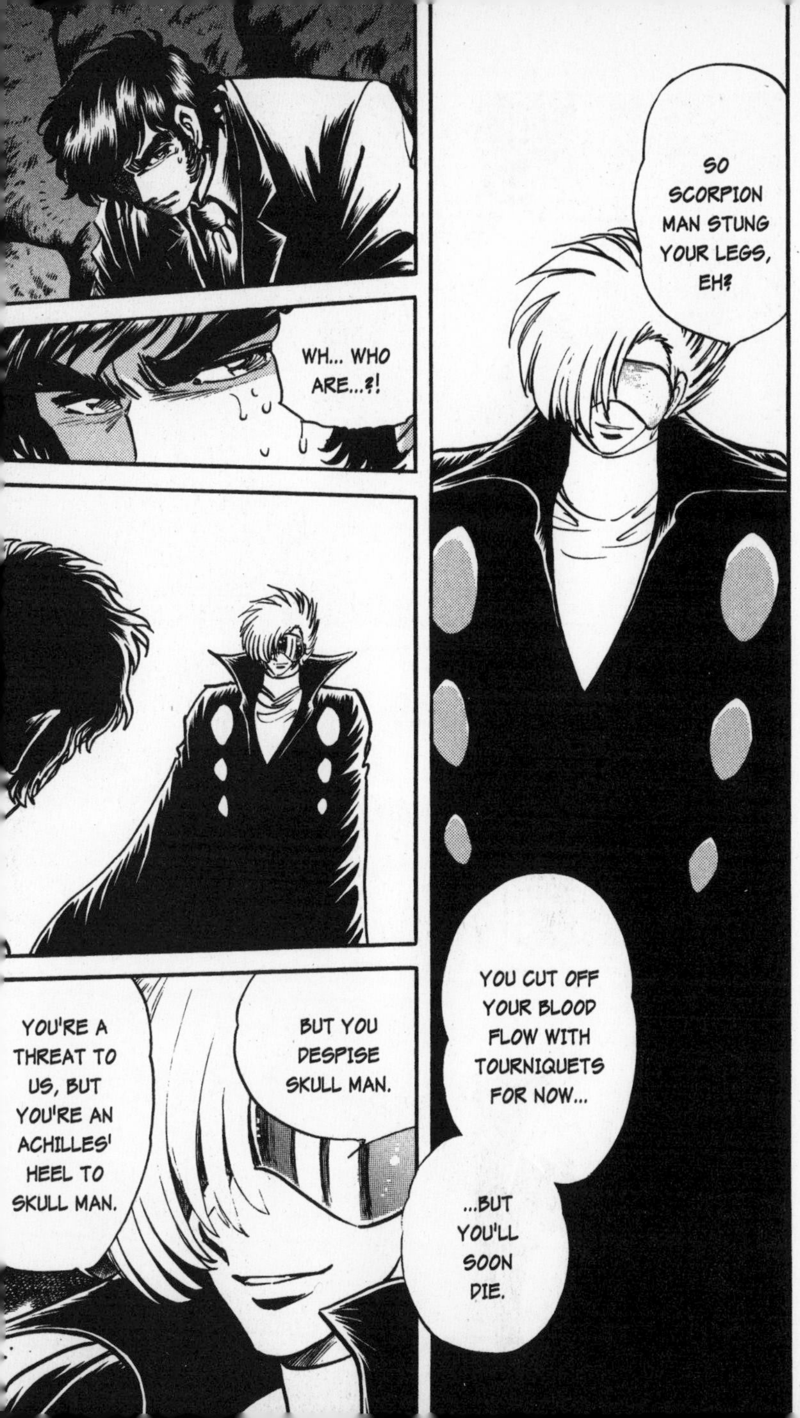
SO SCORPION MAN STUNG YOUR LEGS, EH?
YOU CUT OFF YOUR BLOOD FLOW WITH TOURNIQUETS FOR NOW...
...BUT YOU'LL SOON DIE.
WH... WHO ARE...?!
BUT YOU DESPISE SKULL MAN.
YOU'RE A THREAT TO US, BUT YOU'RE AN ACHILLES' HEEL TO SKULL MAN.

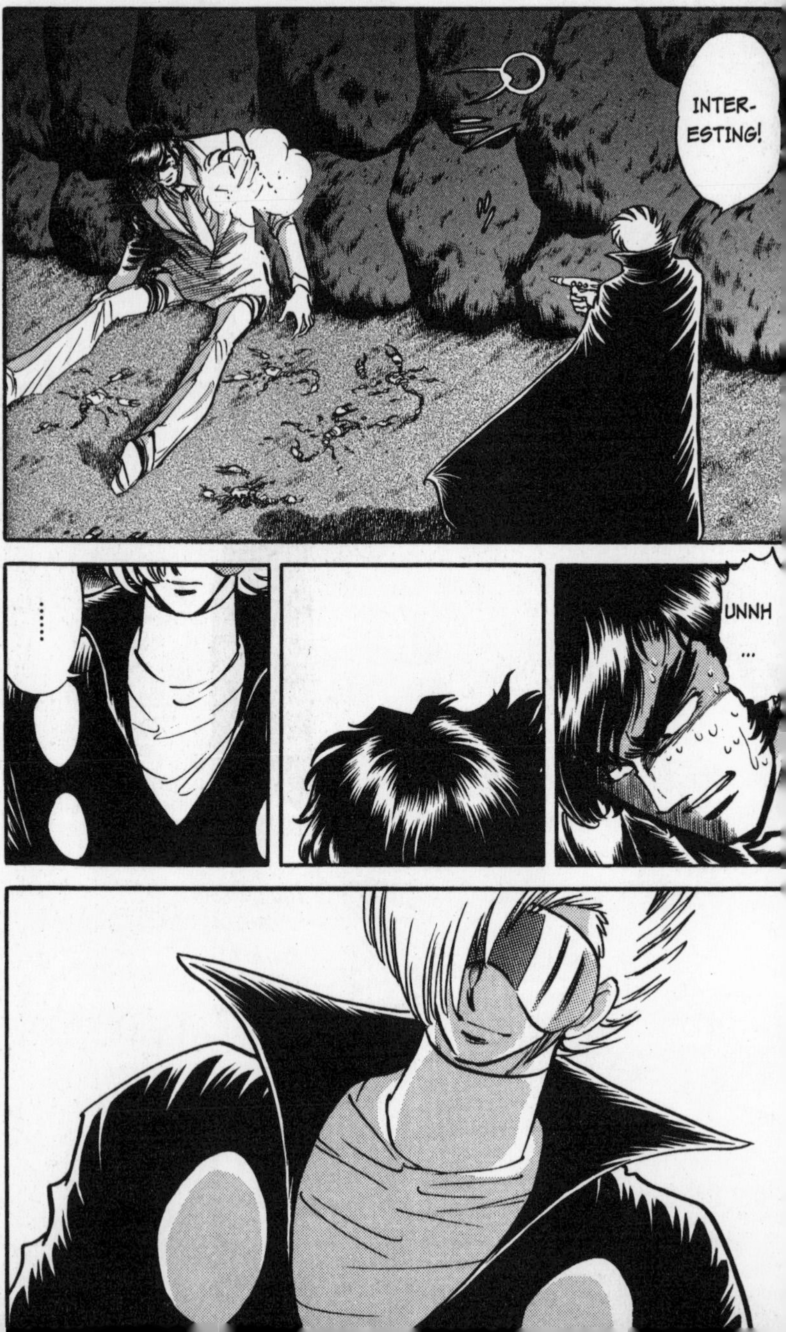
INTER-
ESTING!
UNNH
...
......

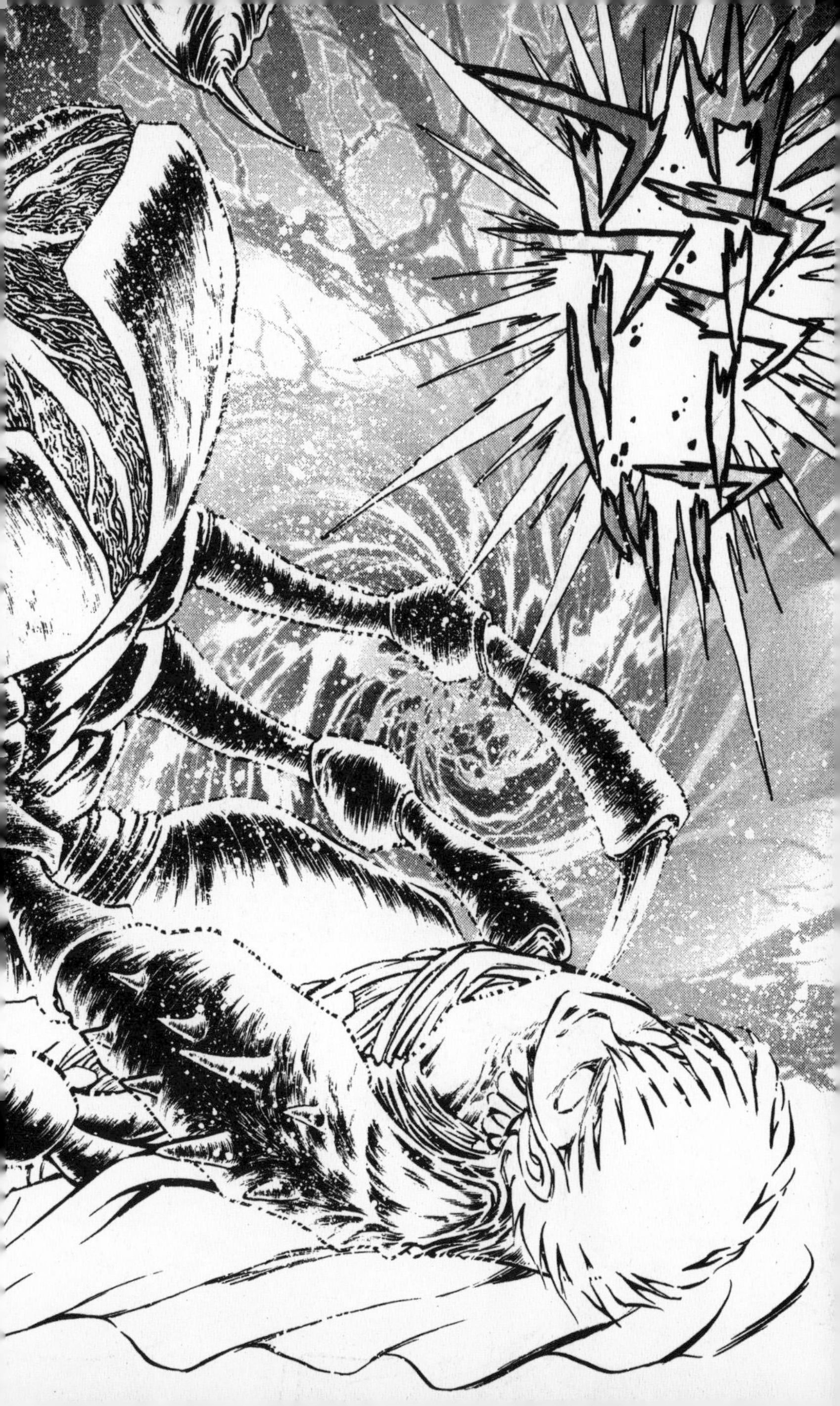

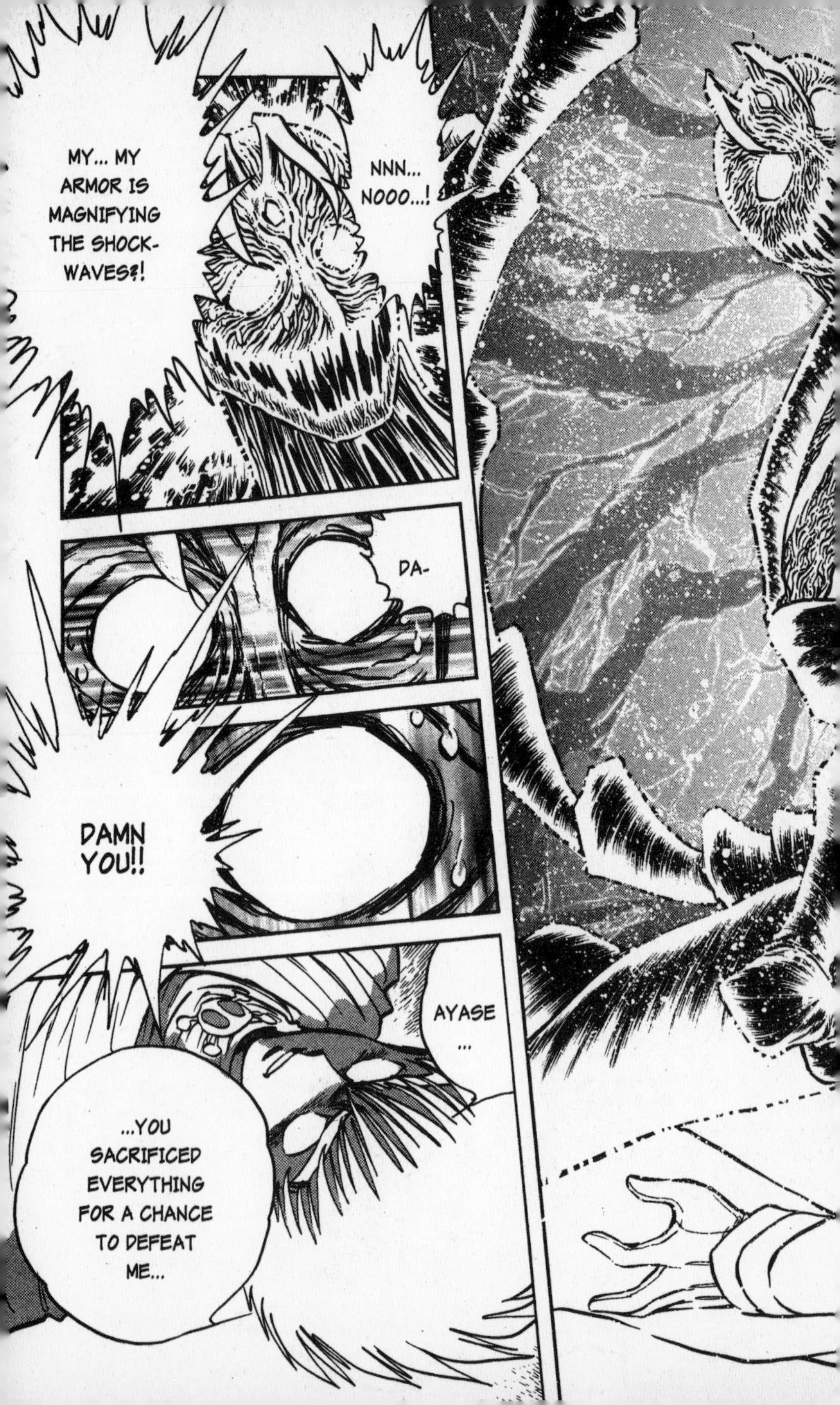
NNN... NOOO...!
MY... MY ARMOR IS MAGNIFYING THE SHOCK-WAVES?!
DA-
DAMN YOU!!
AYASE ...
...YOU SACRIFICED EVERYTHING FOR A CHANCE TO DEFEAT ME...

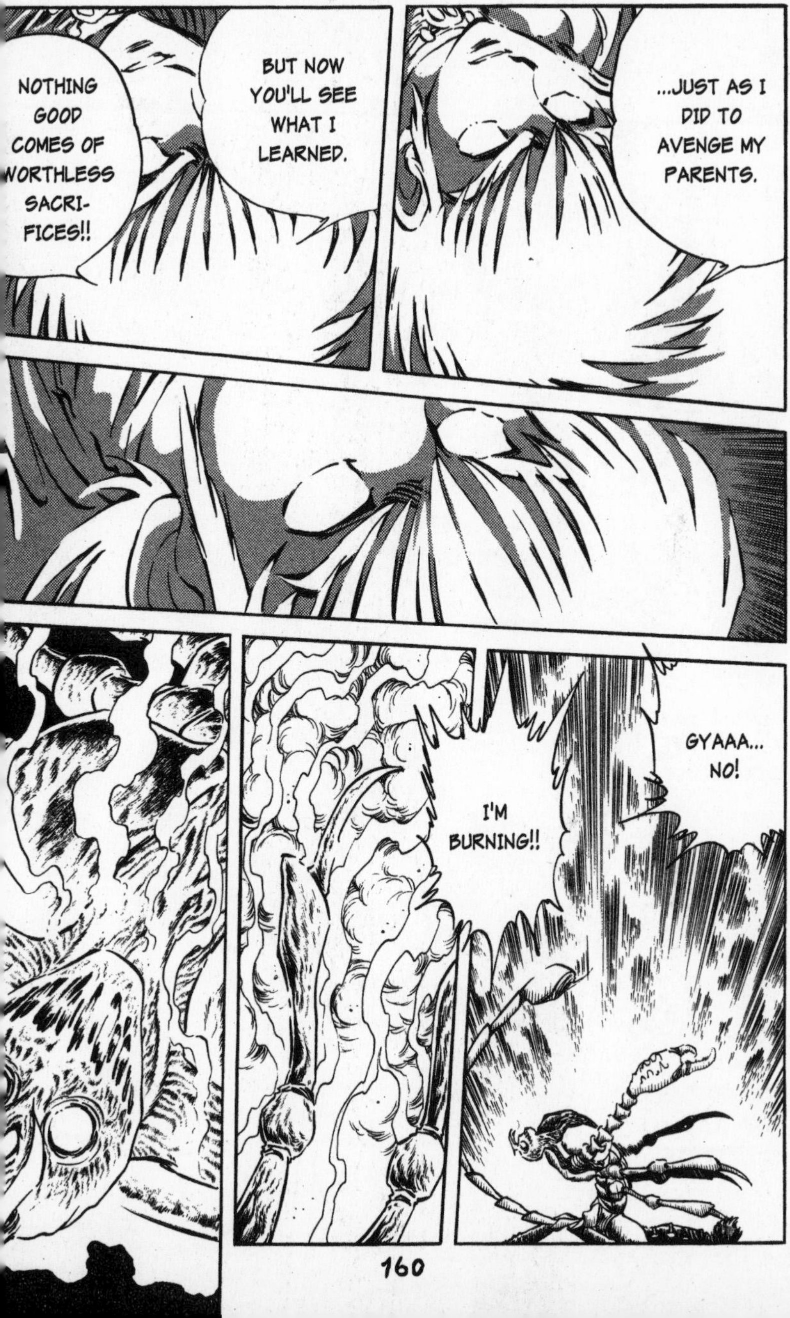
NOTHING GOOD COMES OF WORTHLESS SACRI-FICES!!
BUT NOW YOU'LL SEE WHAT I LEARNED.
...JUST AS I DID TO AVENGE MY PARENTS.
I'M BURNING!!
GYAAA... NO!

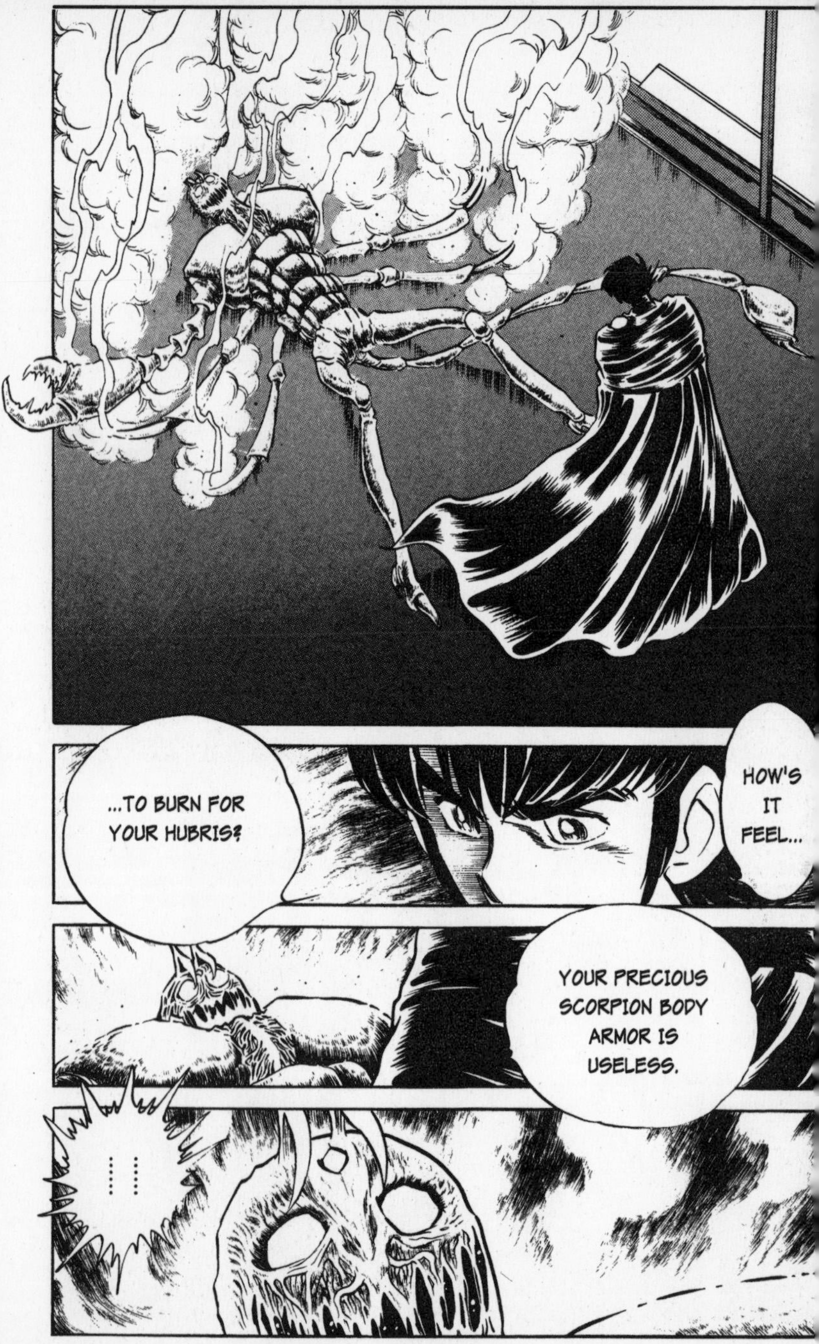
HOW'S IT FEEL...
...TO BURN FOR YOUR HUBRIS?
YOUR PRECIOUS SCORPION BODY ARMOR IS USELESS.
......

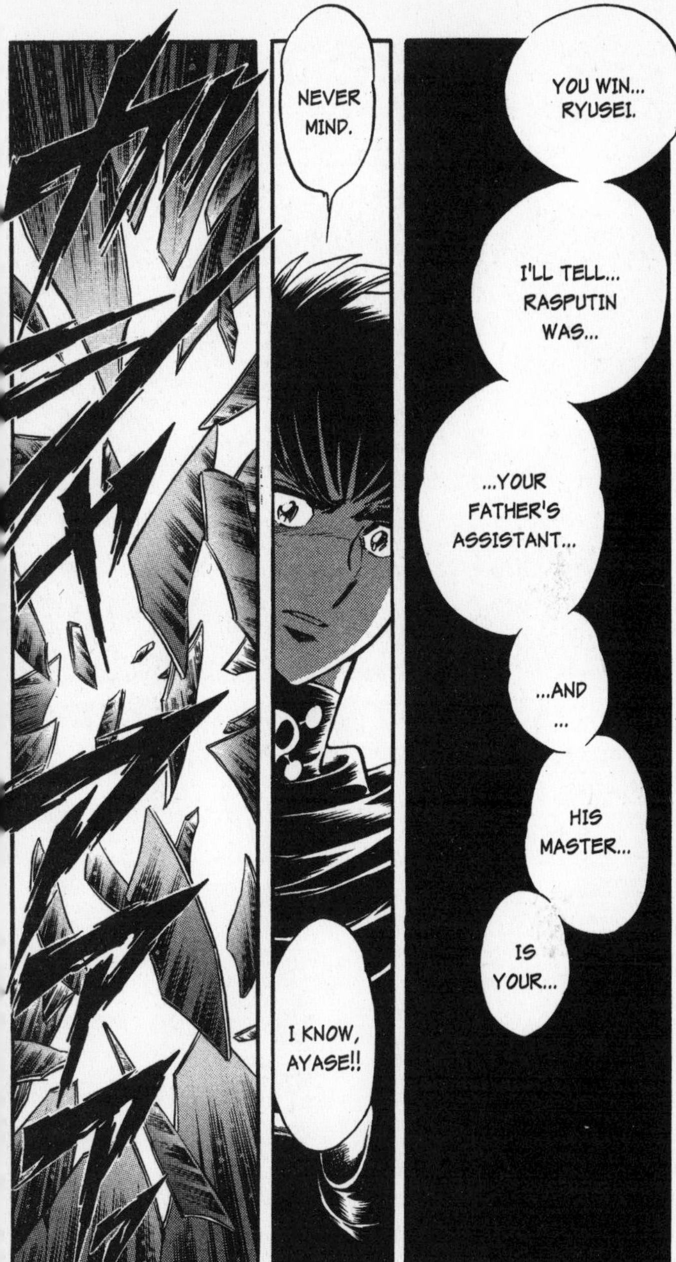
YOU WIN... RYUSEI.
I'LL TELL... RASPUTIN WAS...
...YOUR FATHER'S ASSISTANT...
...AND ...
HIS MASTER...
IS YOUR...
NEVER MIND.
I KNOW, AYASE!!

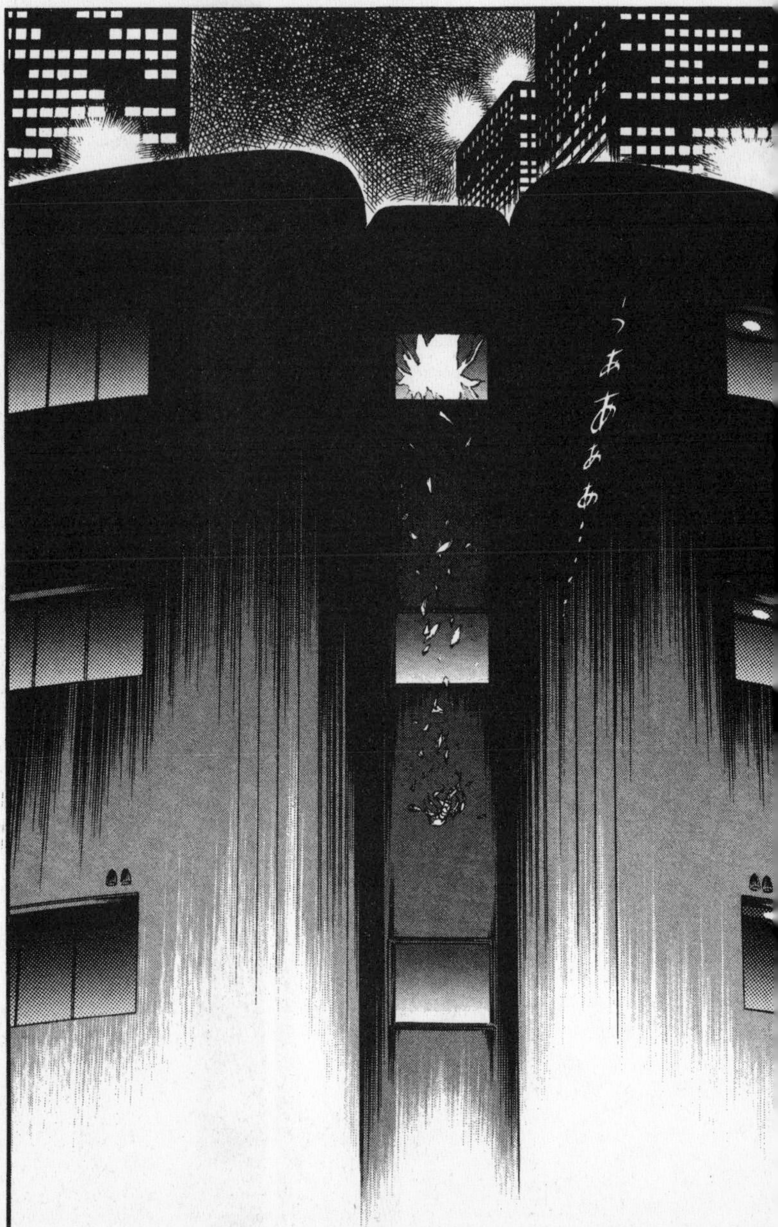
っあああぁ……

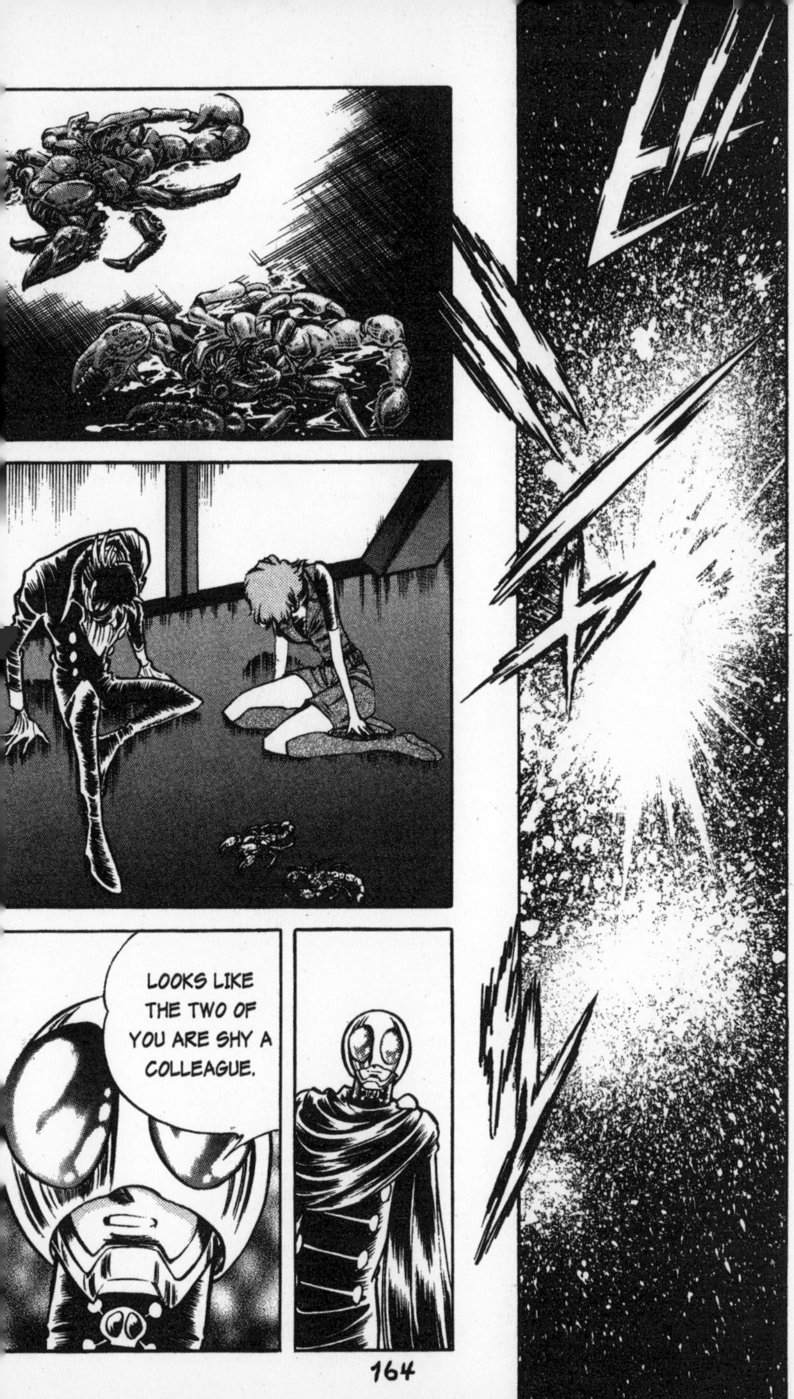
LOOKS LIKE THE TWO OF YOU ARE SHY A COLLEAGUE.

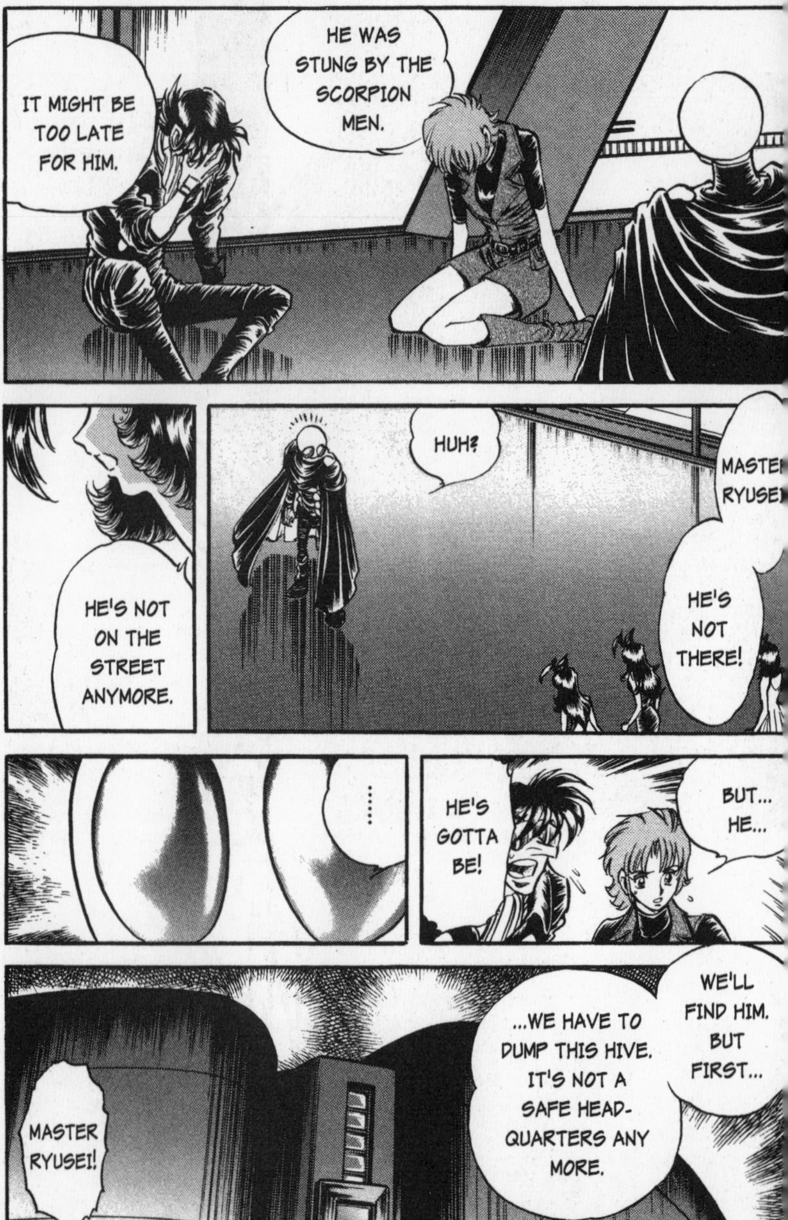
HE WAS STUNG BY THE SCORPION MEN.
IT MIGHT BE TOO LATE FOR HIM.
MASTE RYUSE
HE'S NOT THERE!
HUH?
HE'S NOT ON THE STREET ANYMORE.
BUT... HE...
HE'S GOTTA BE!
......
WE'LL FIND HIM. BUT FIRST...
...WE HAVE TO DUMP THIS HIVE. IT'S NOT A SAFE HEAD-QUARTERS ANY MORE.
MASTER RYUSEI!

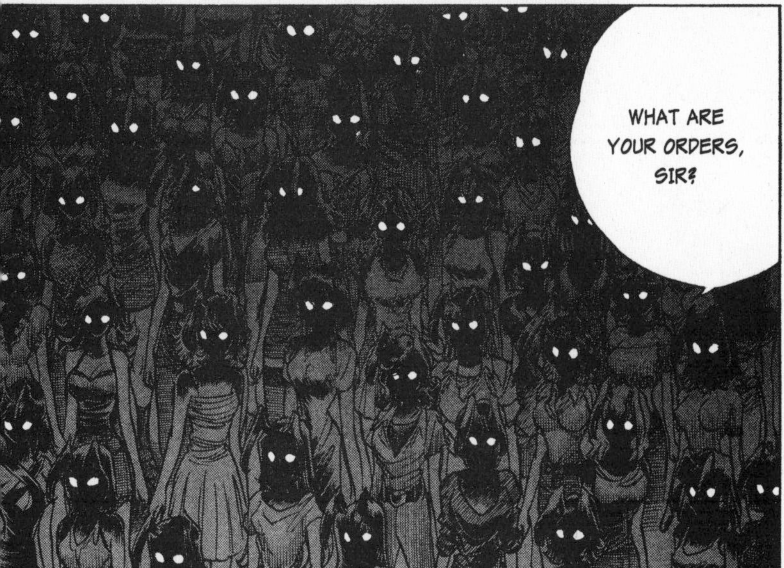
WHAT ARE YOUR ORDERS, SIR?

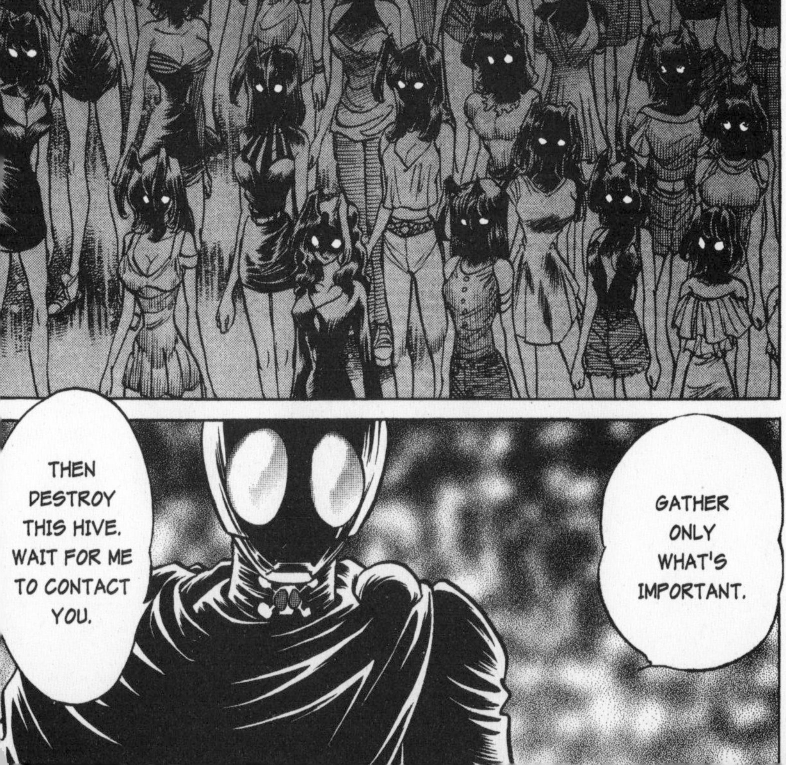
GATHER ONLY WHAT'S IMPORTANT.
THEN DESTROY THIS HIVE. WAIT FOR ME TO CONTACT YOU.

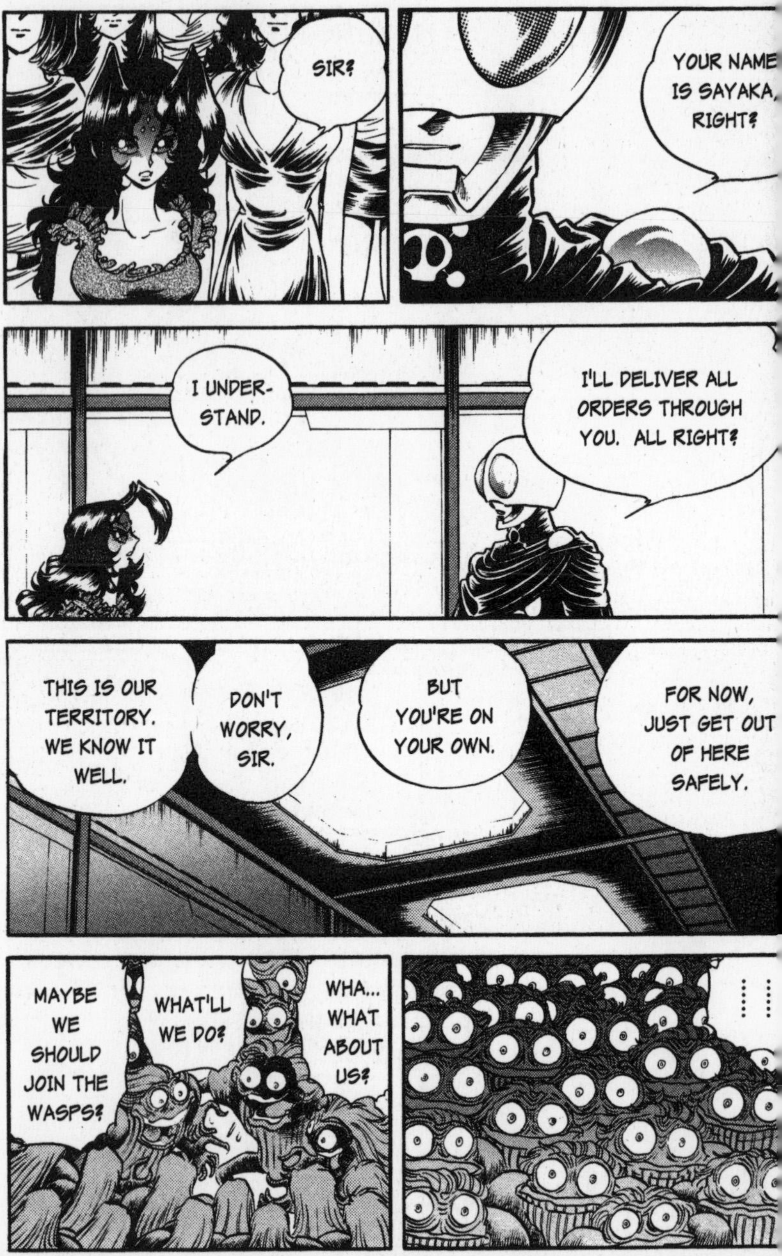
YOUR NAME IS SAYAKA, RIGHT?
SIR?
I'LL DELIVER ALL ORDERS THROUGH YOU. ALL RIGHT?
I UNDER-STAND.
FOR NOW, JUST GET OUT OF HERE SAFELY.
BUT YOU'RE ON YOUR OWN.
DON'T WORRY, SIR.
THIS IS OUR TERRITORY. WE KNOW IT WELL.
......
WHA... WHAT ABOUT US?
WHAT'LL WE DO?
MAYBE WE SHOULD JOIN THE WASPS?

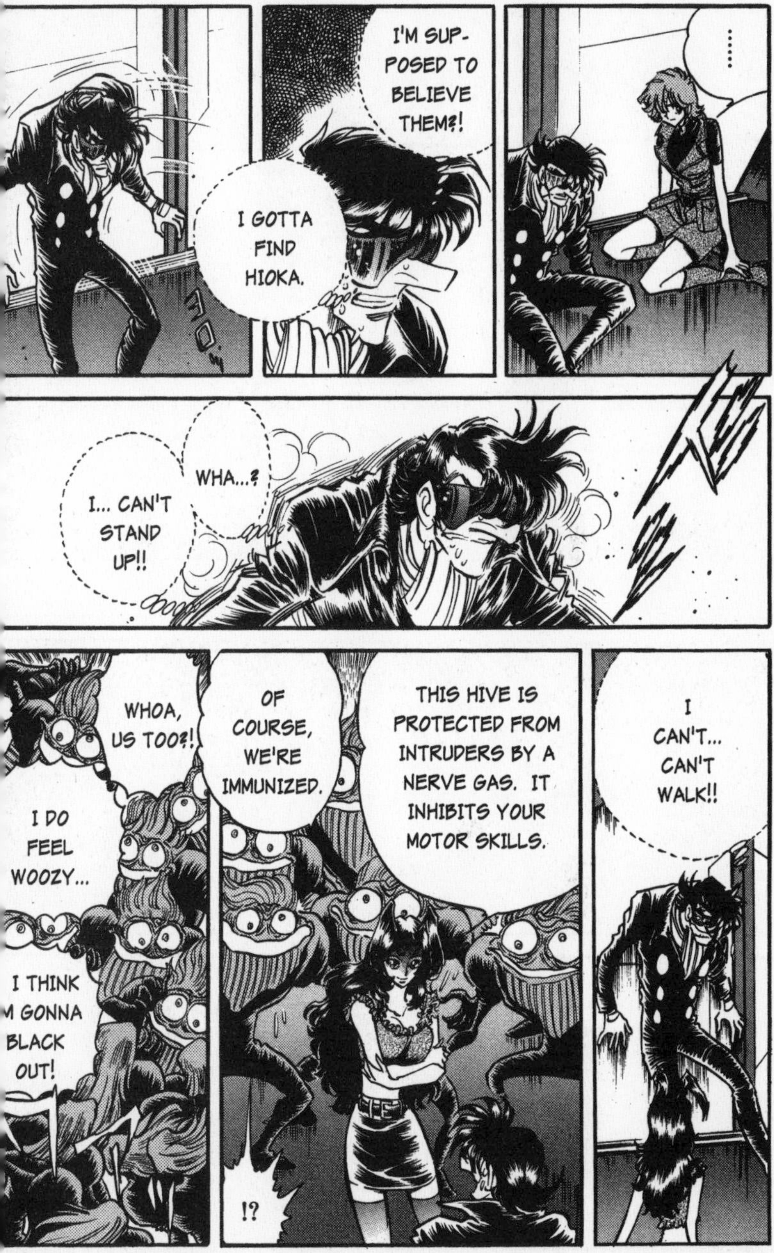

......
I'M SUP-POSED TO BELIEVE THEM?!
I GOTTA FIND HIOKA.
WHA...?
I... CAN'T STAND UP!!
I CAN'T... CAN'T WALK!!
THIS HIVE IS PROTECTED FROM INTRUDERS BY A NERVE GAS. IT INHIBITS YOUR MOTOR SKILLS.
OF COURSE, WE'RE IMMUNIZED.
!?
WHOA, US TOO?!
I DO FEEL WOOZY...
I THINK M GONNA BLACK OUT!

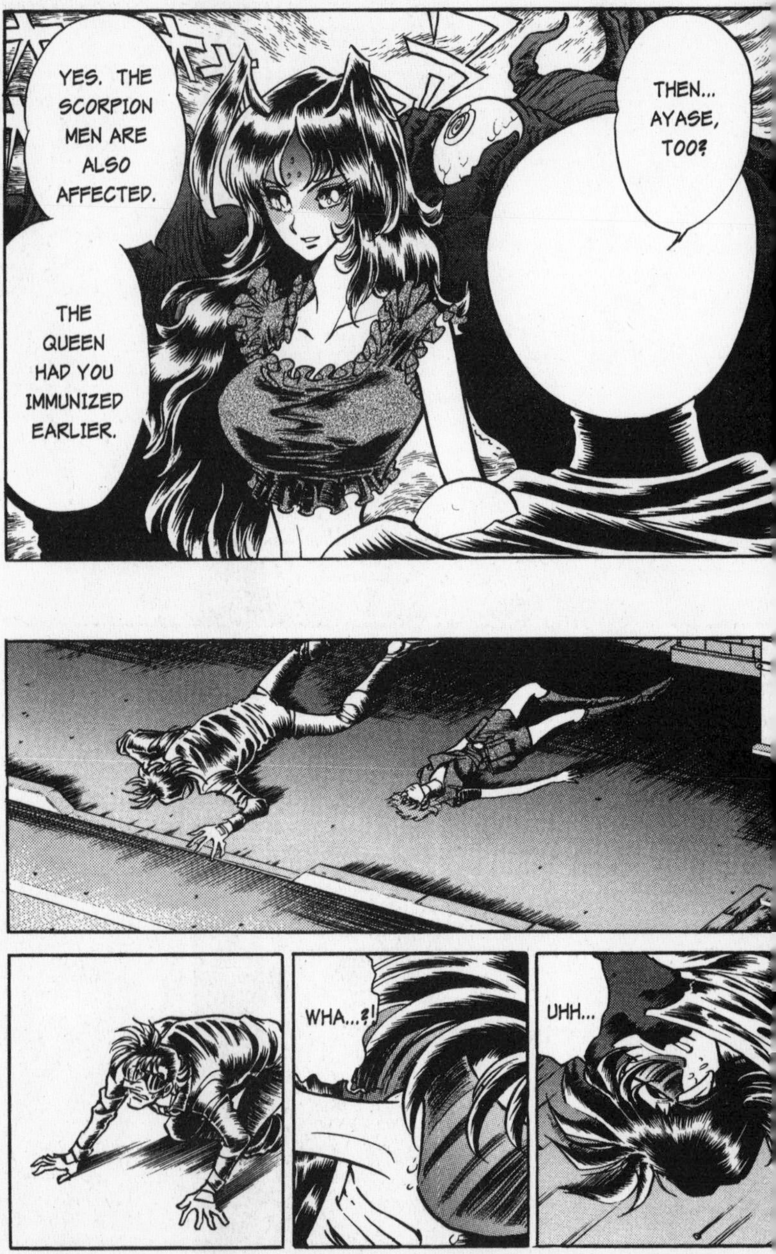
THEN... AYASE, TOO?
YES. THE SCORPION MEN ARE ALSO AFFECTED.
THE QUEEN HAD YOU IMMUNIZED EARLIER.
UHH...
WHA...?!

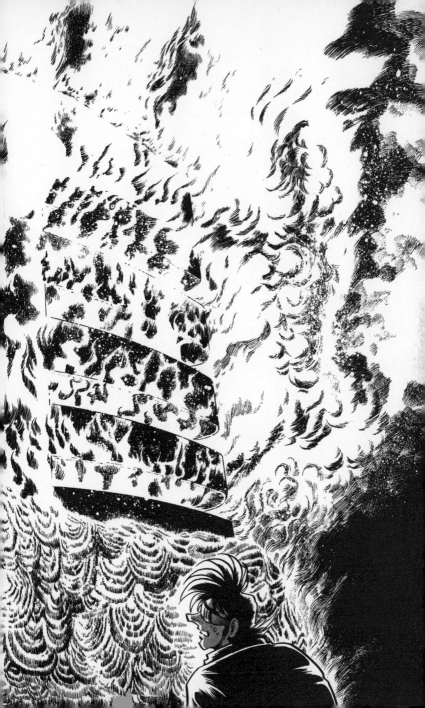

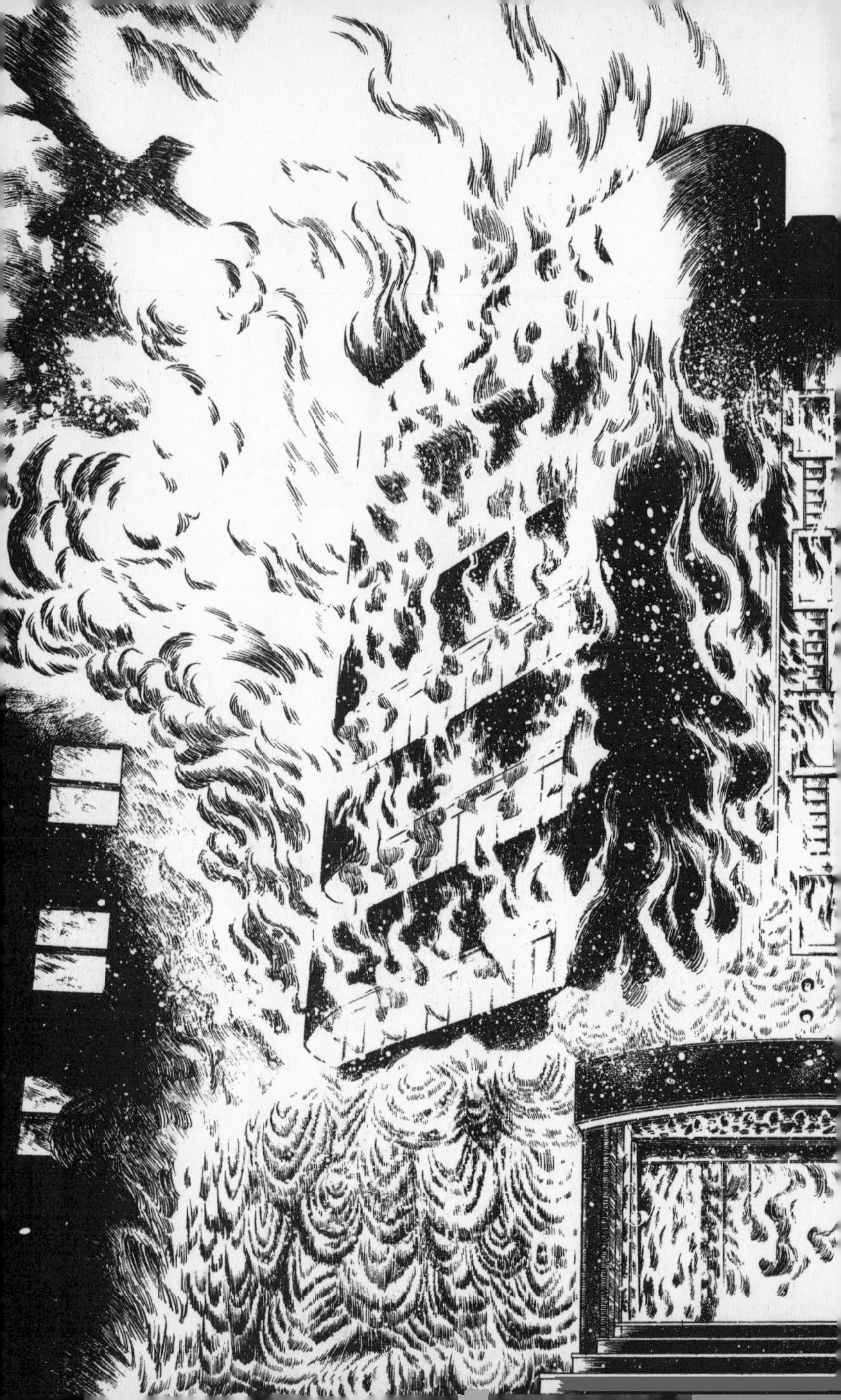

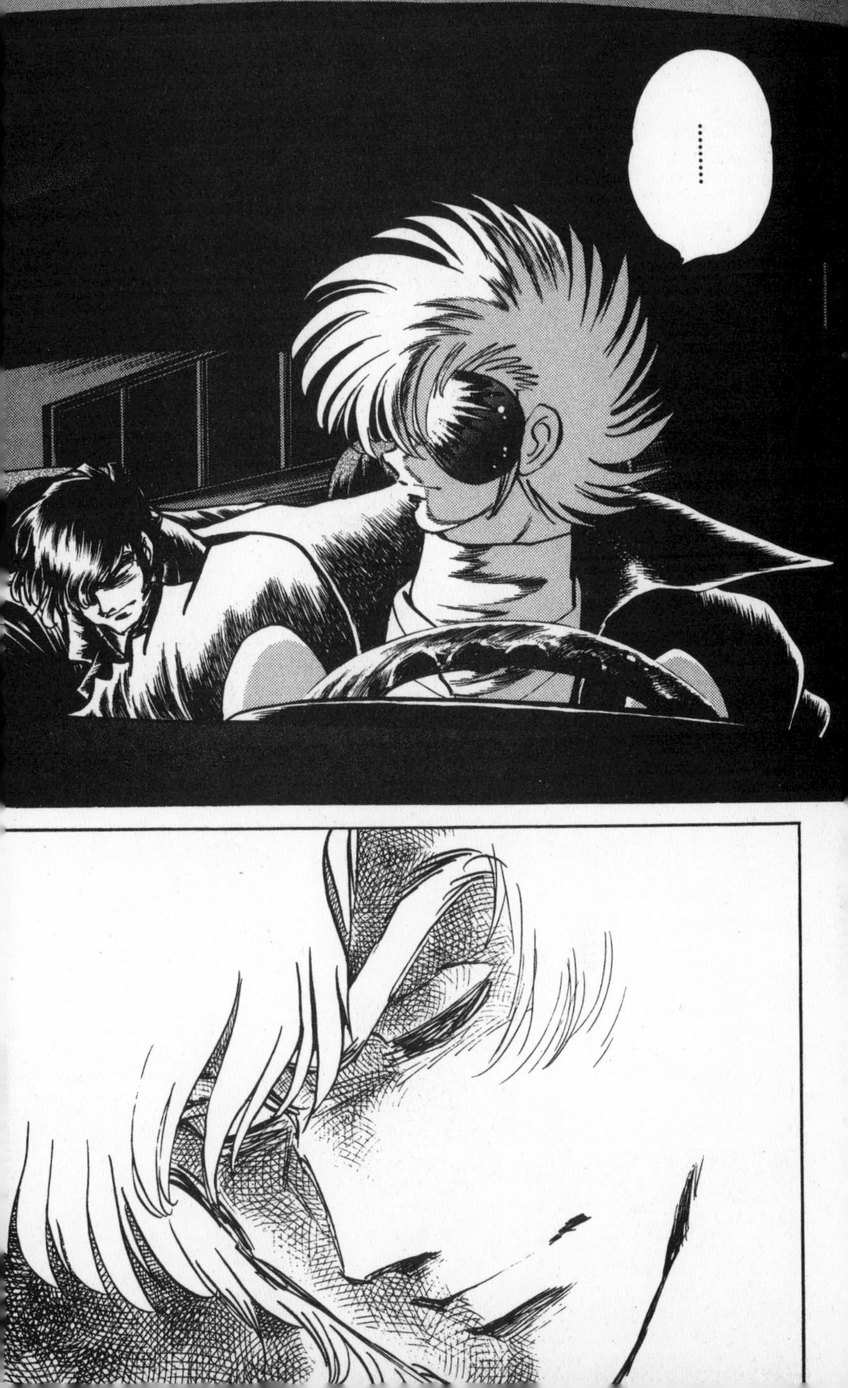
……

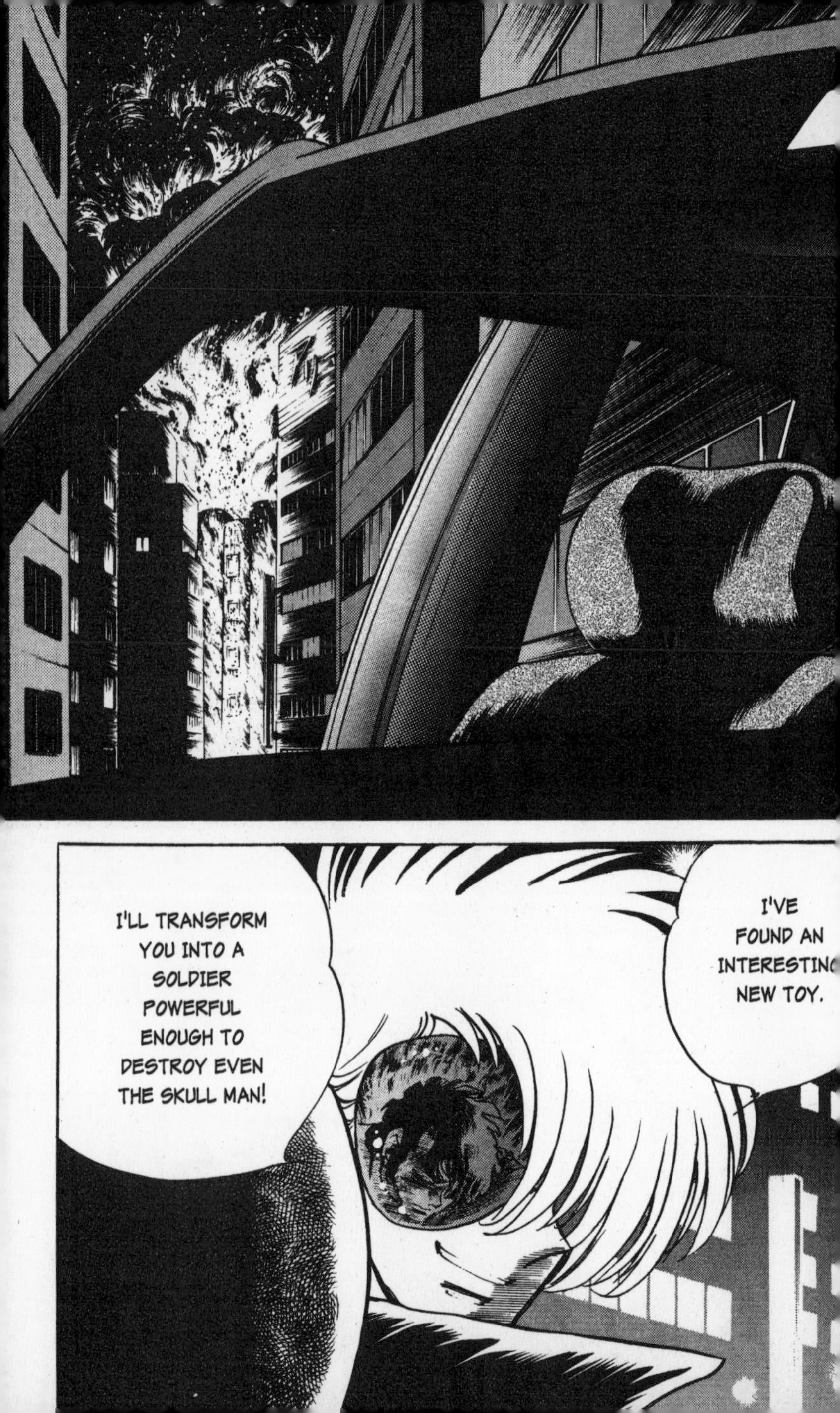
I'VE FOUND AN INTERESTING NEW TOY.
I'LL TRANSFORM YOU INTO A SOLDIER POWERFUL ENOUGH TO DESTROY EVEN THE SKULL MAN!

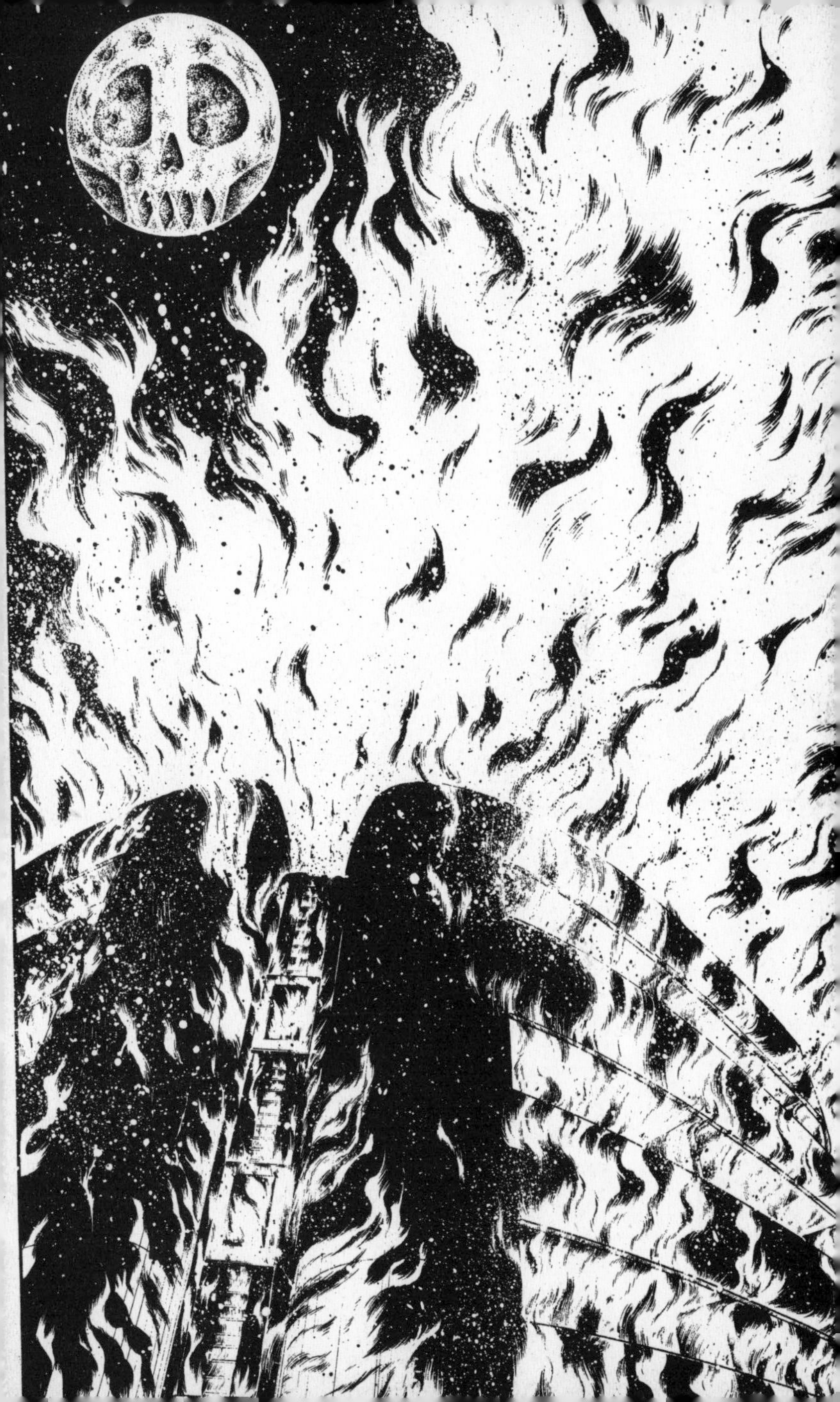

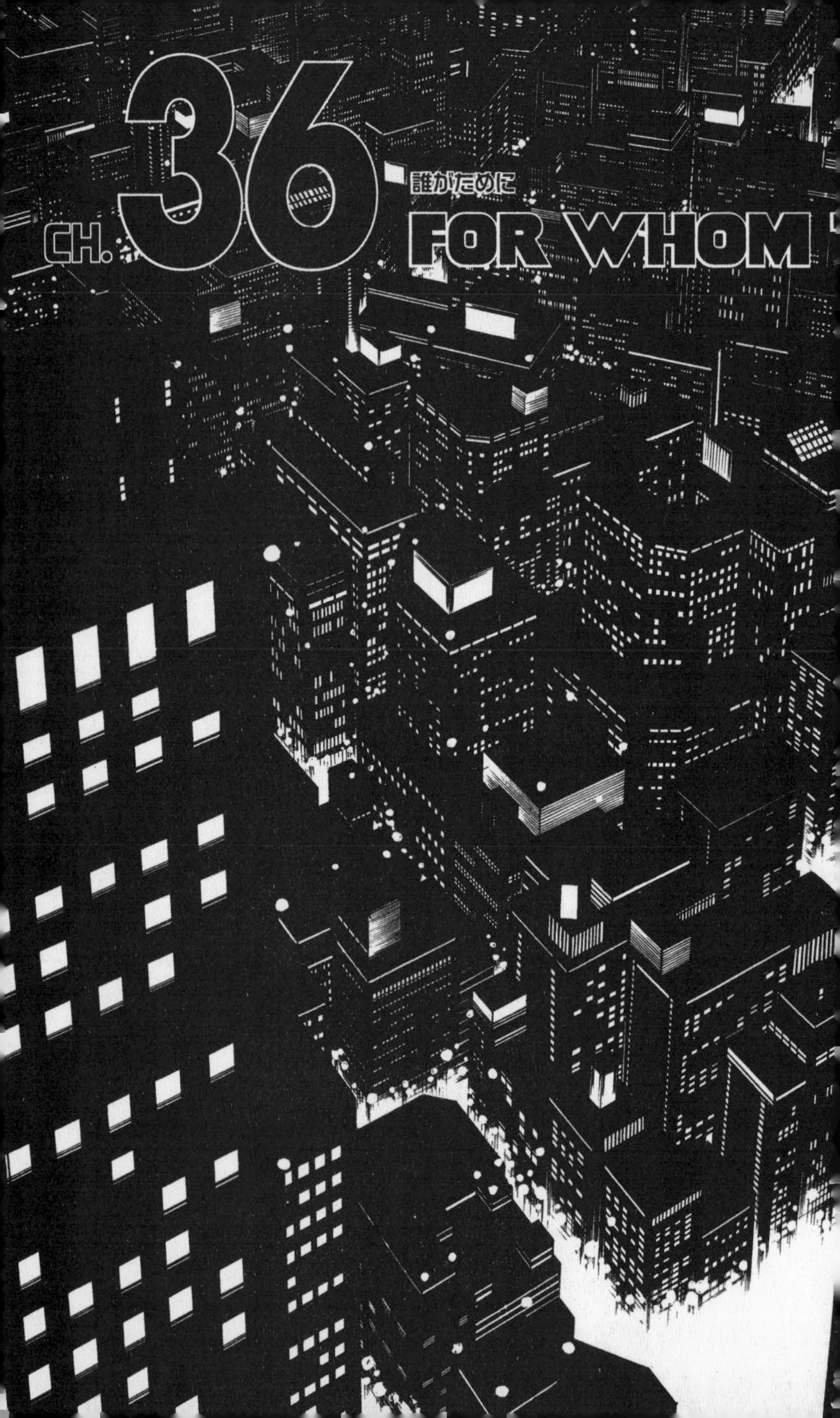
CH. 36
誰がために
FOR WHOM

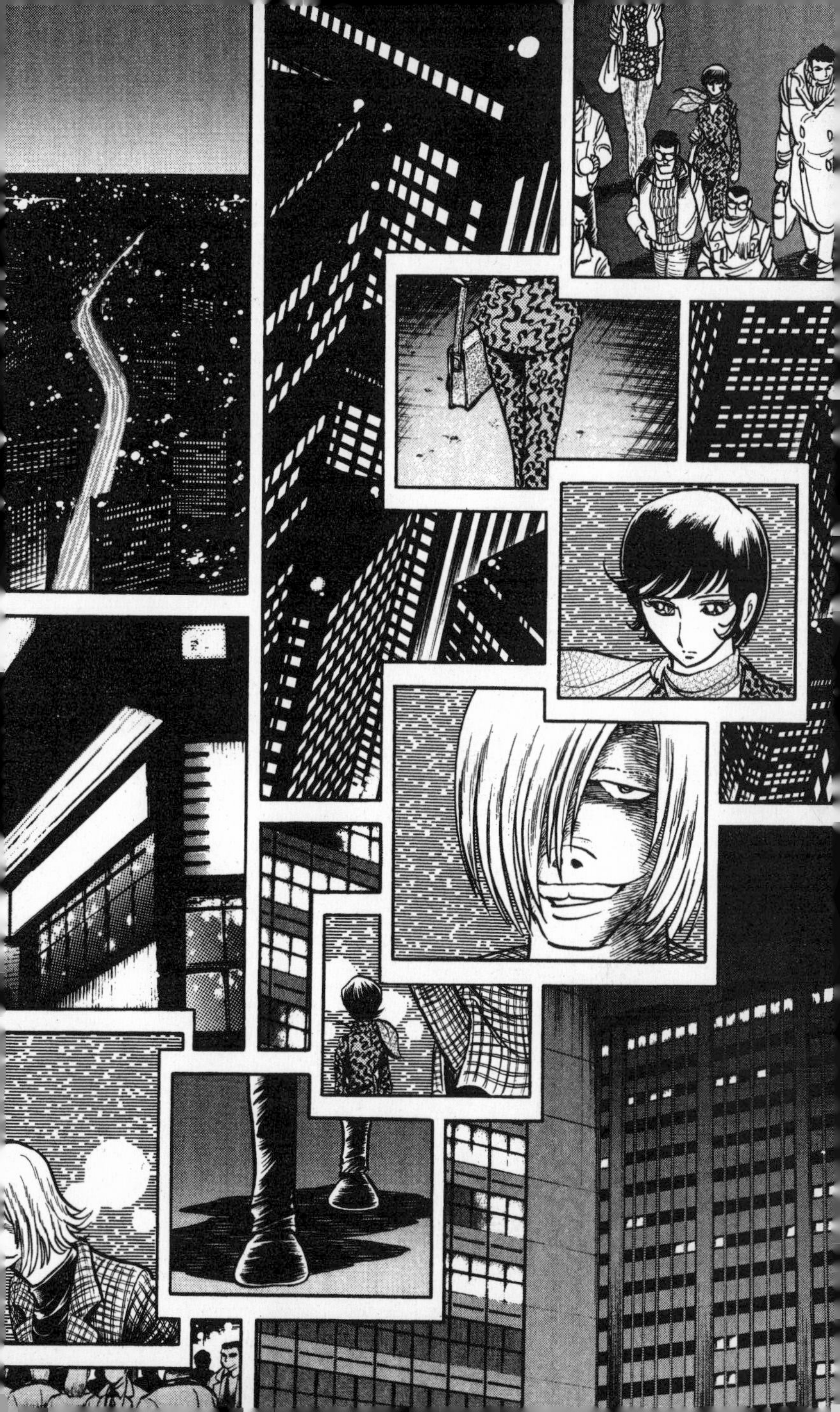

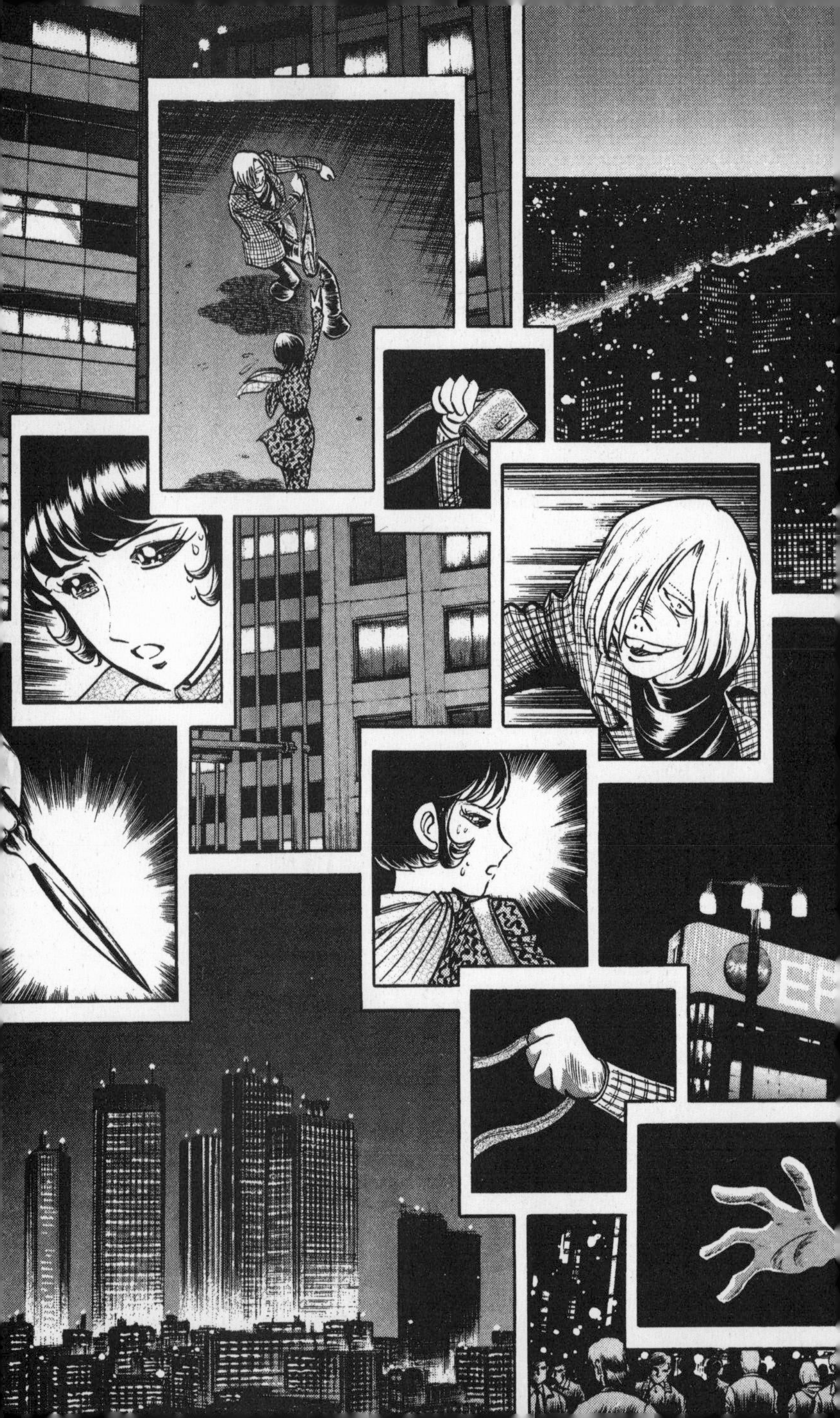

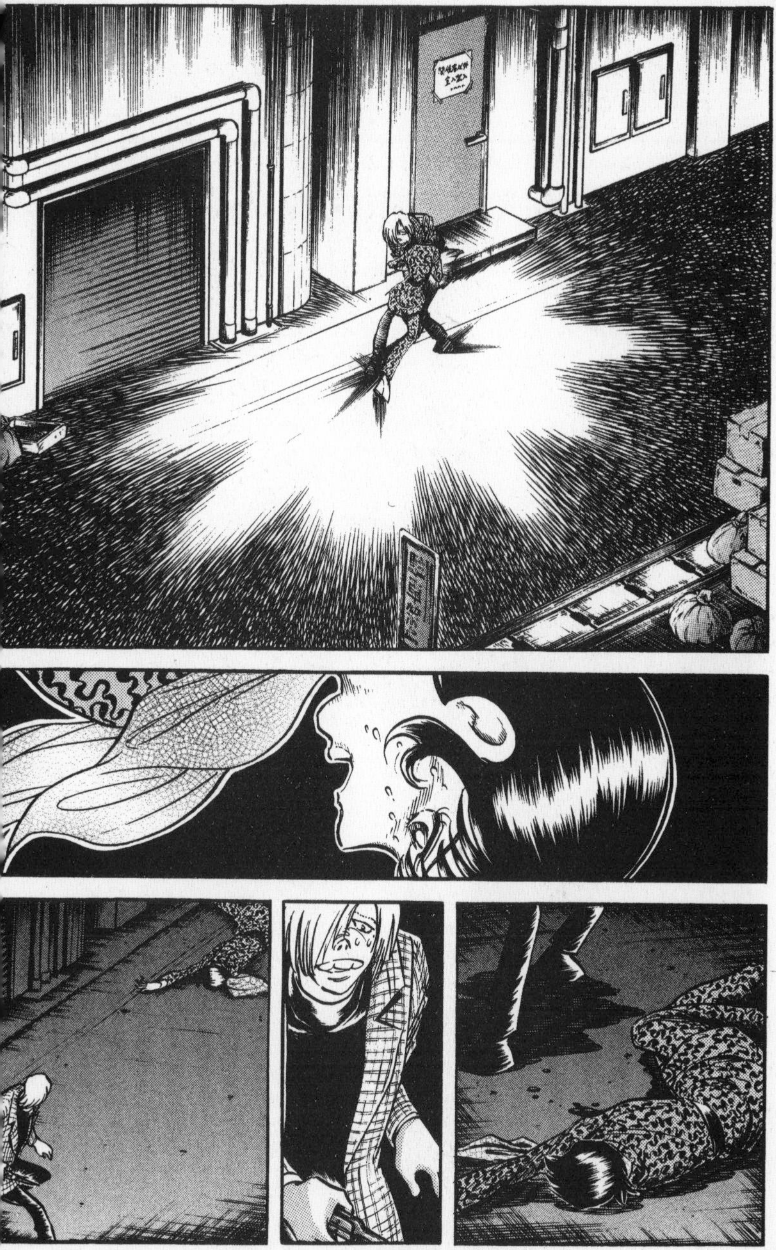

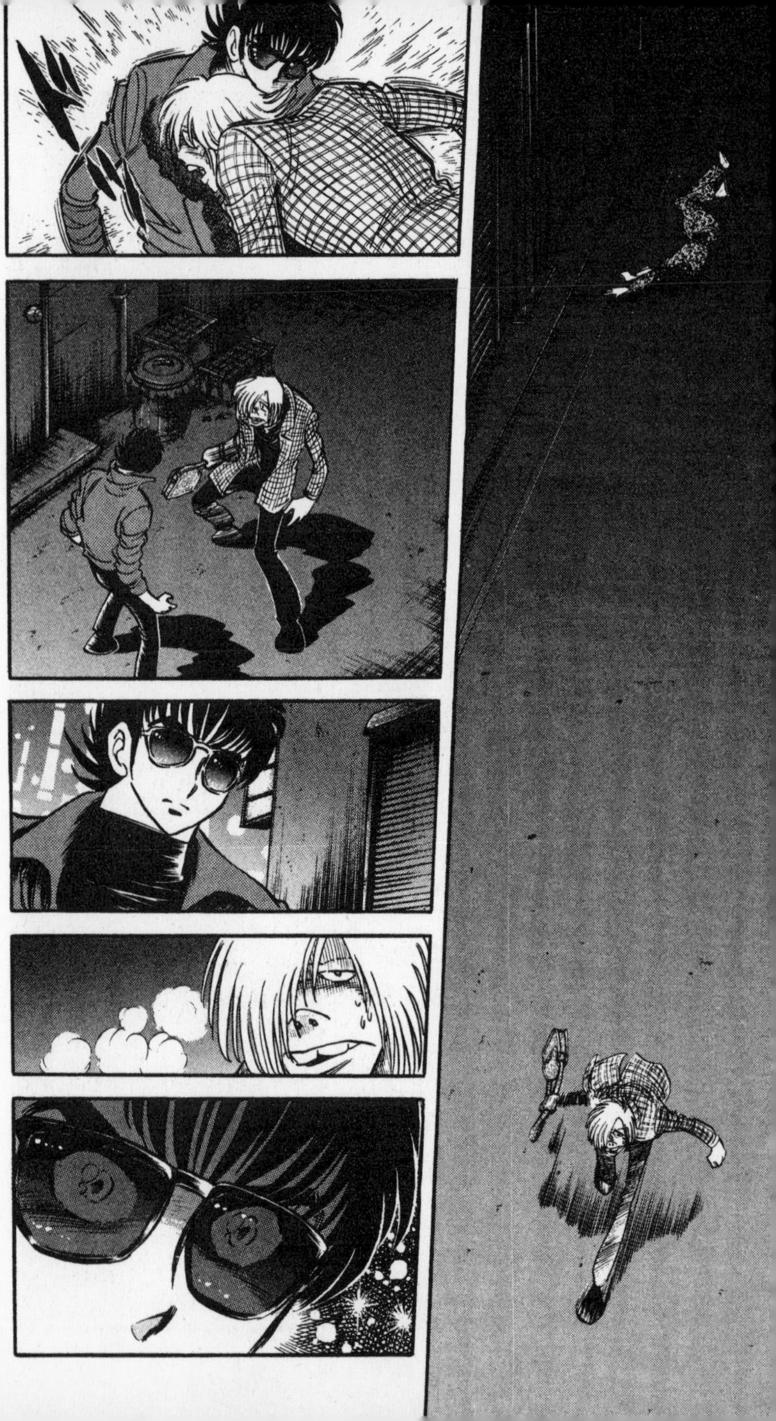

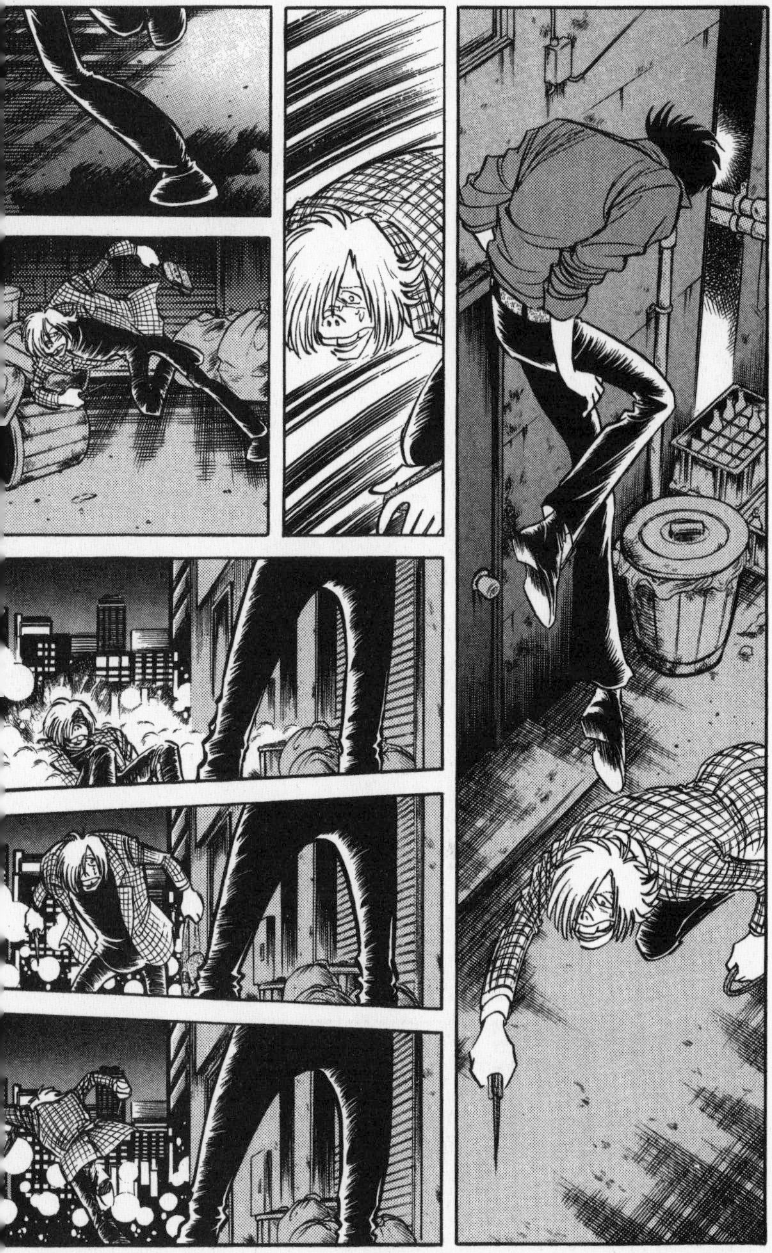

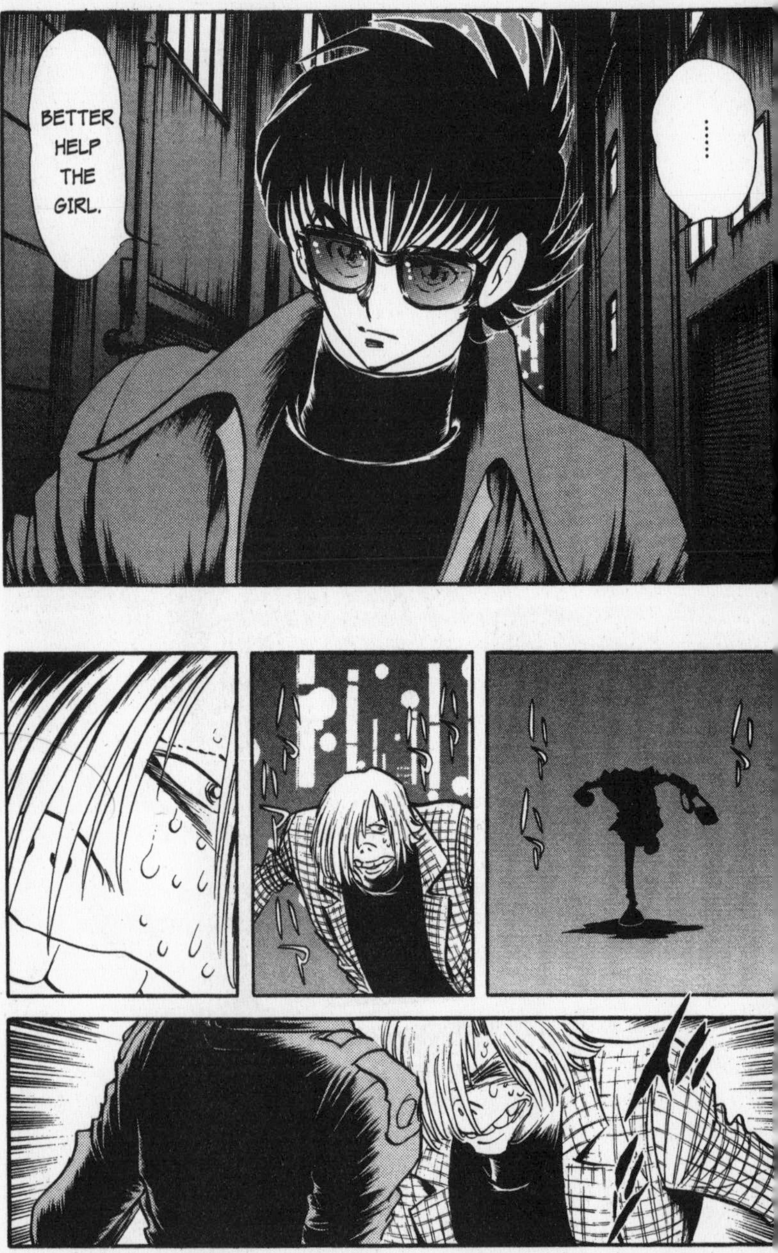
......
BETTER HELP THE GIRL.

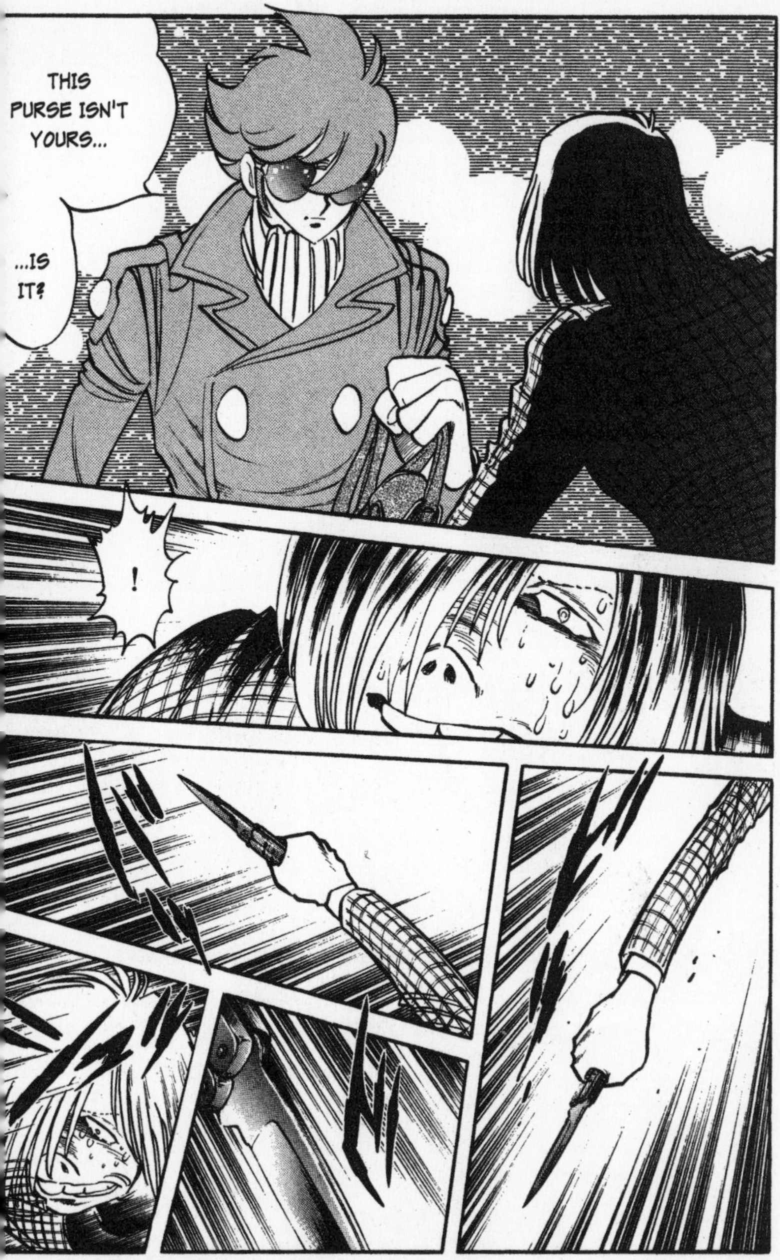
THIS PURSE ISN'T YOURS...
...IS IT?
!

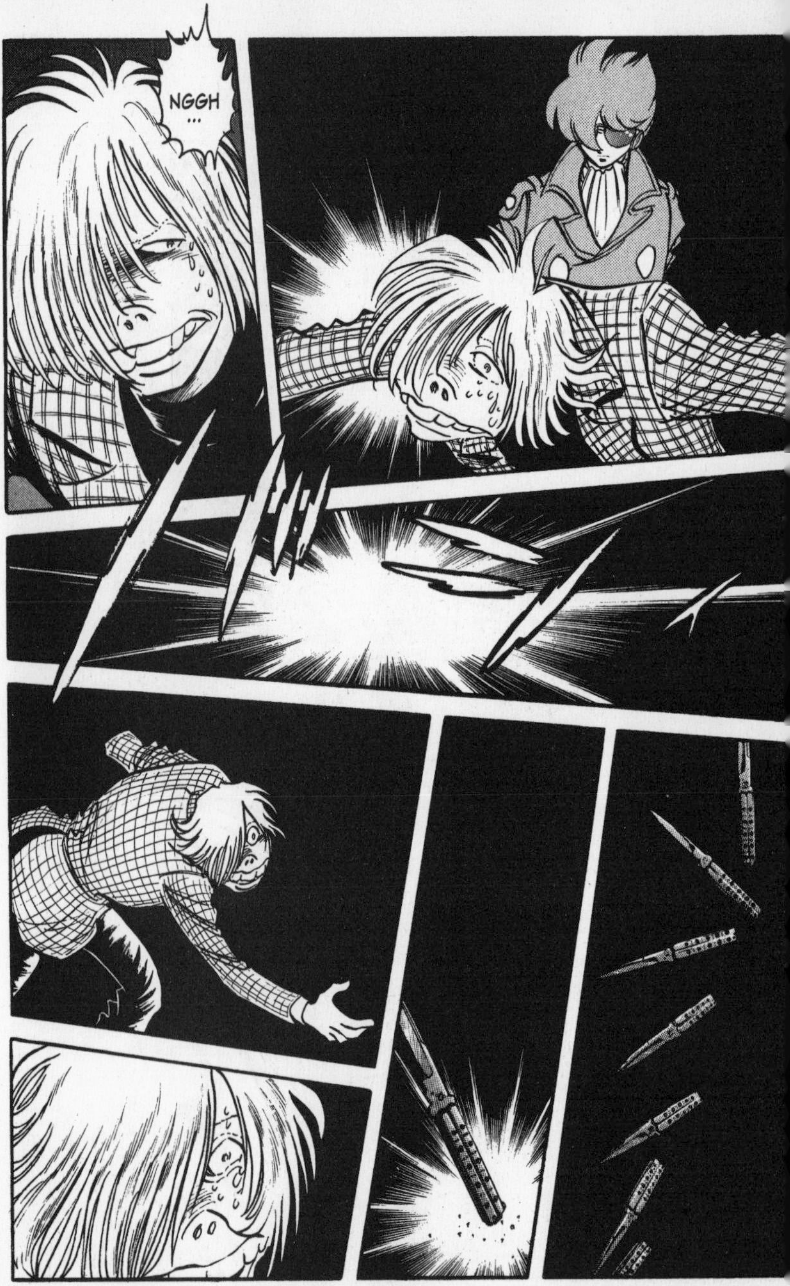
NGGH
...

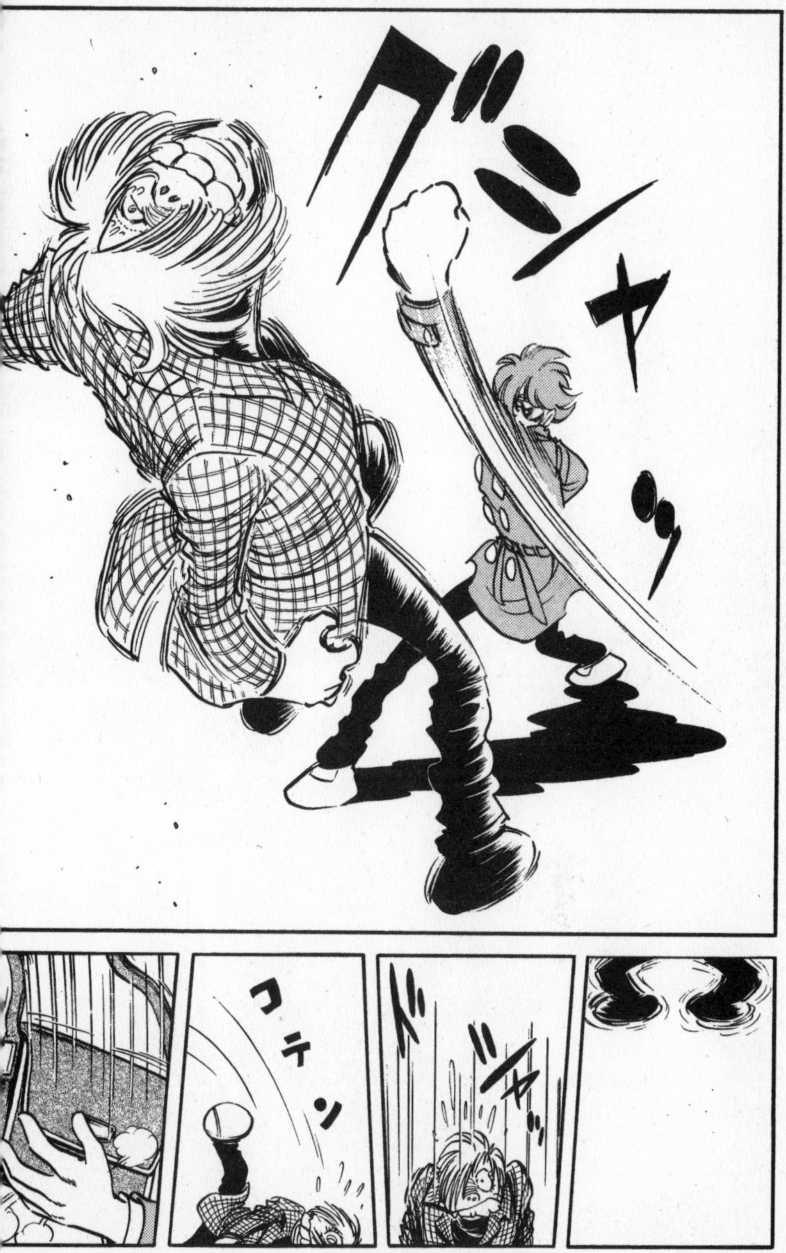
グシャッ
ドシャッ
コテン

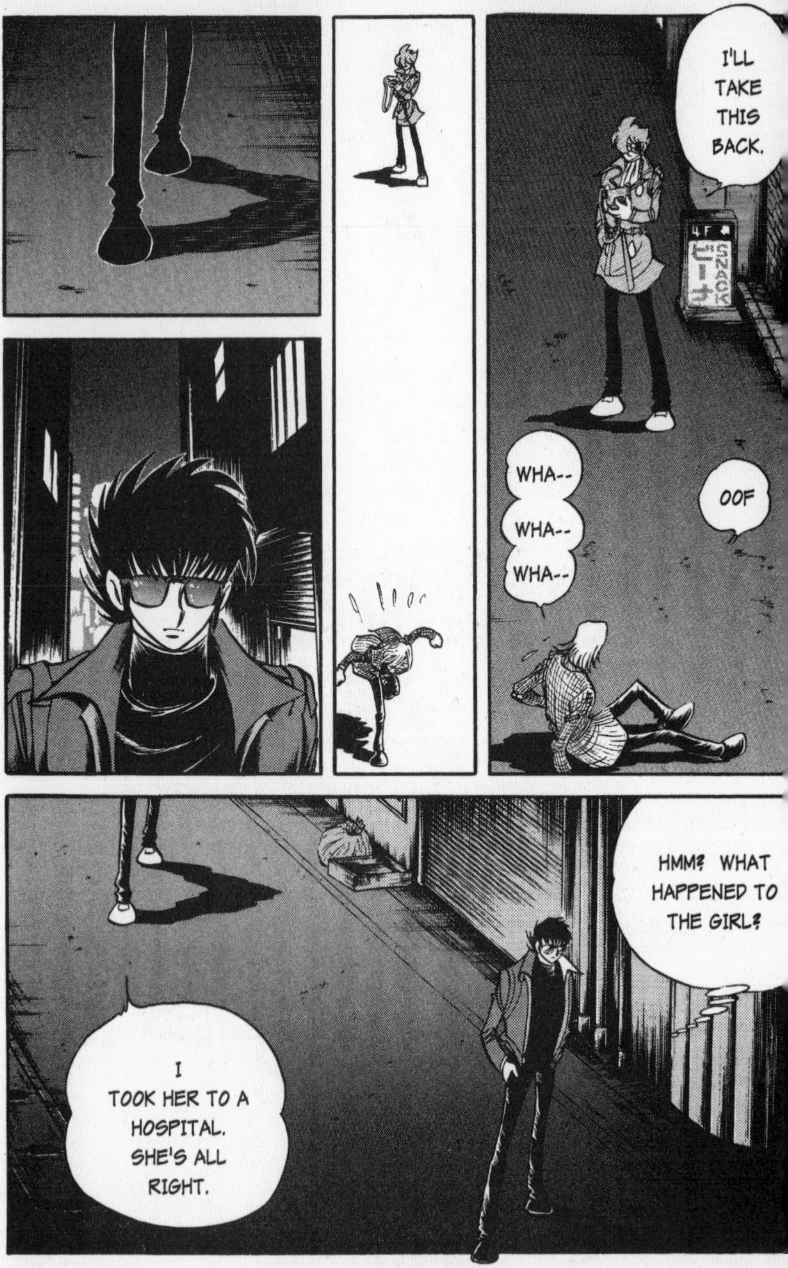
I'LL TAKE THIS BACK.
4F
SNACK
OOF
WHA--
WHA--
WHA--
HMM? WHAT HAPPENED TO THE GIRL?
I TOOK HER TO A HOSPITAL. SHE'S ALL RIGHT.

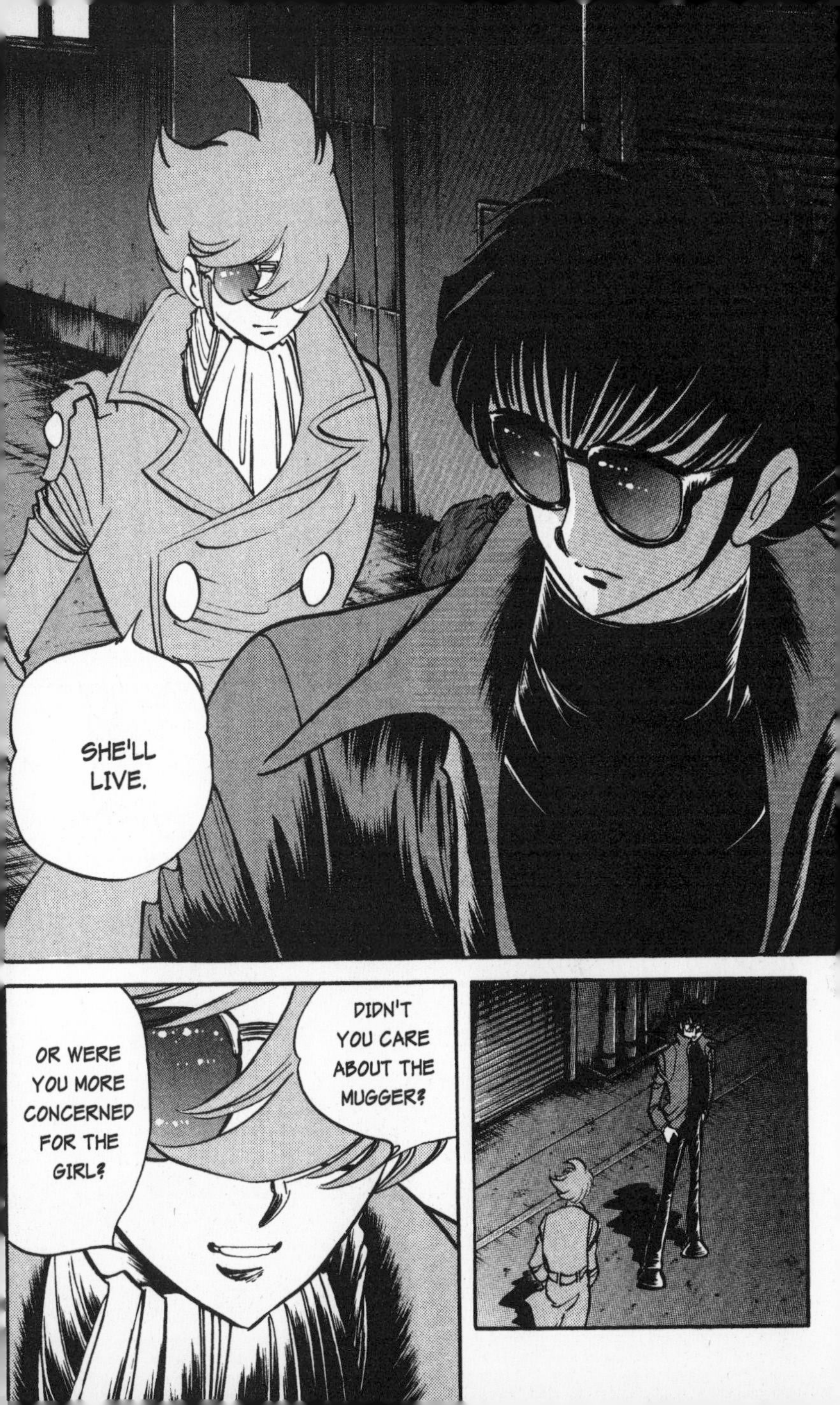
SHE'LL LIVE.
DIDN'T YOU CARE ABOUT THE MUGGER?
OR WERE YOU MORE CONCERNED FOR THE GIRL?

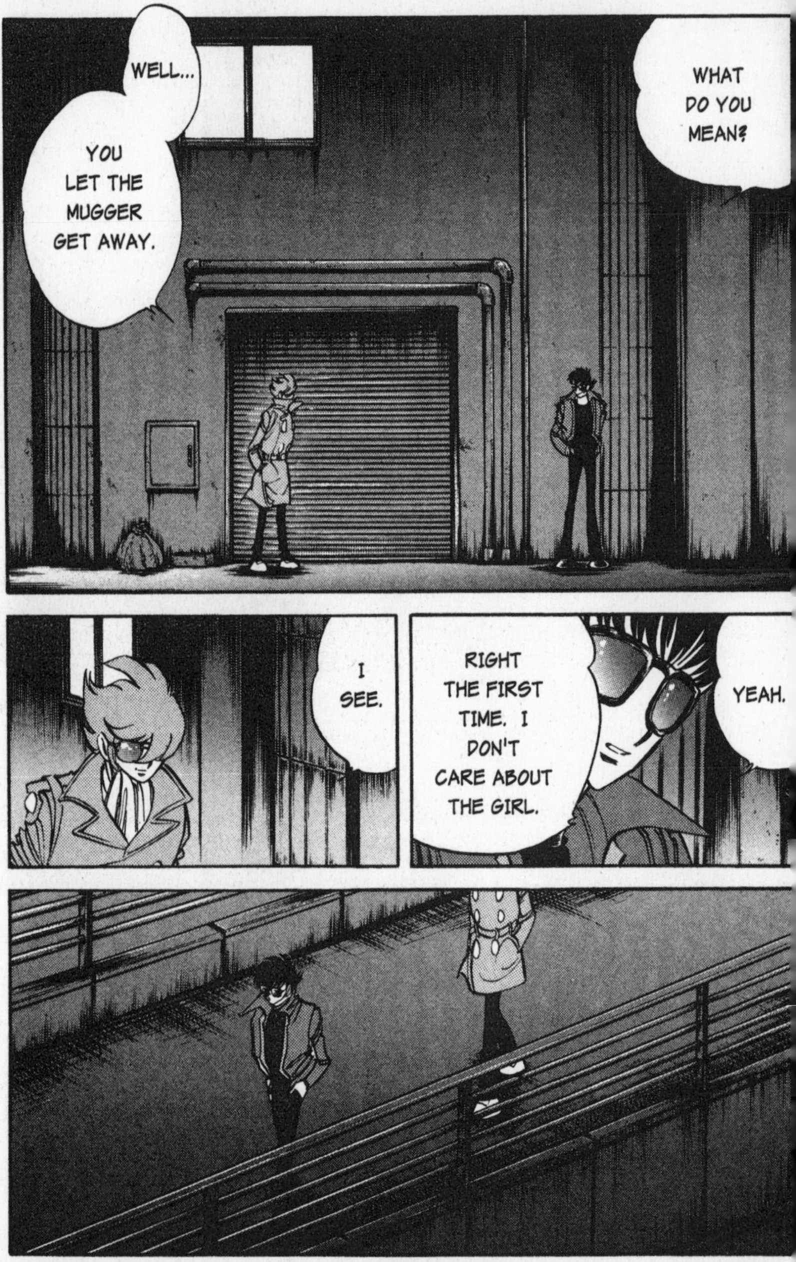
WHAT DO YOU MEAN?
WELL...
YOU LET THE MUGGER GET AWAY.
YEAH.
RIGHT THE FIRST TIME. I DON'T CARE ABOUT THE GIRL.
I SEE.

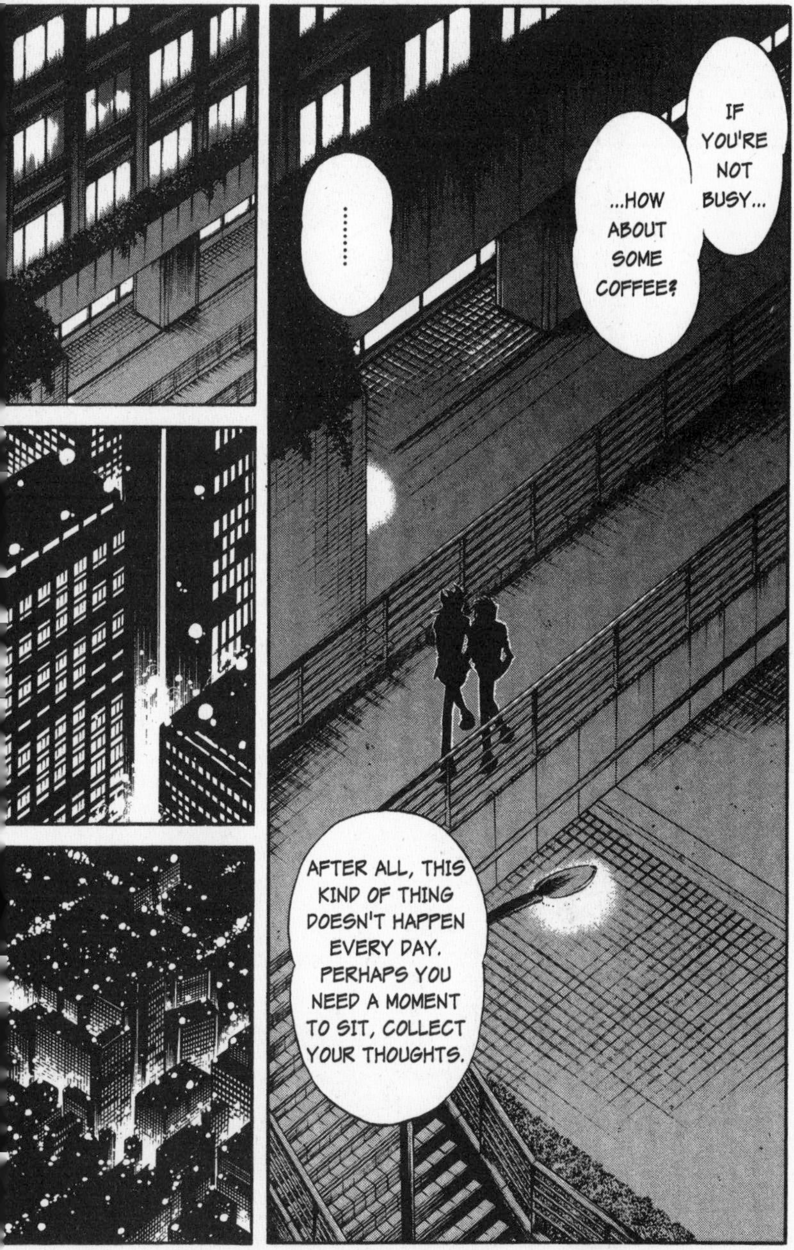
IF YOU'RE NOT BUSY...
...HOW ABOUT SOME COFFEE?
....
AFTER ALL, THIS KIND OF THING DOESN'T HAPPEN EVERY DAY. PERHAPS YOU NEED A MOMENT TO SIT, COLLECT YOUR THOUGHTS.

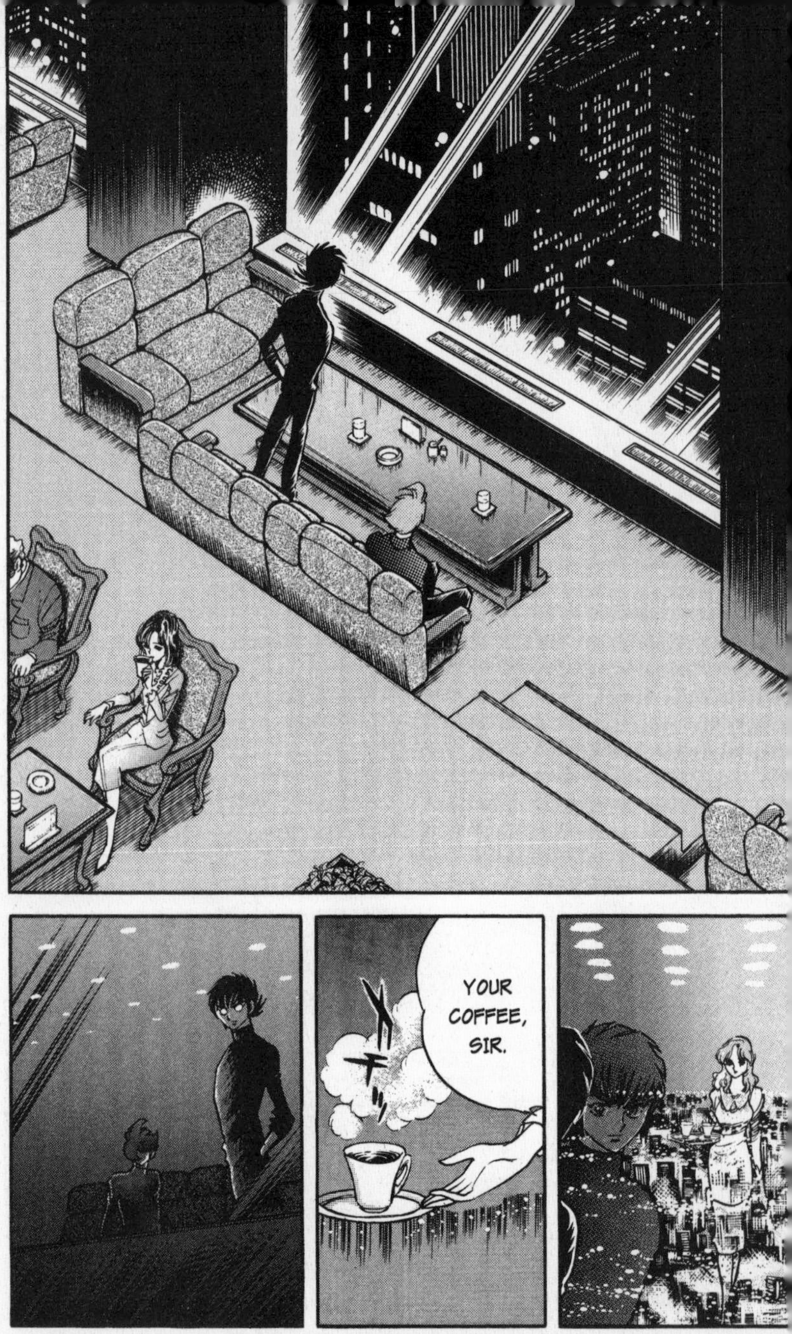
YOUR COFFEE, SIR.

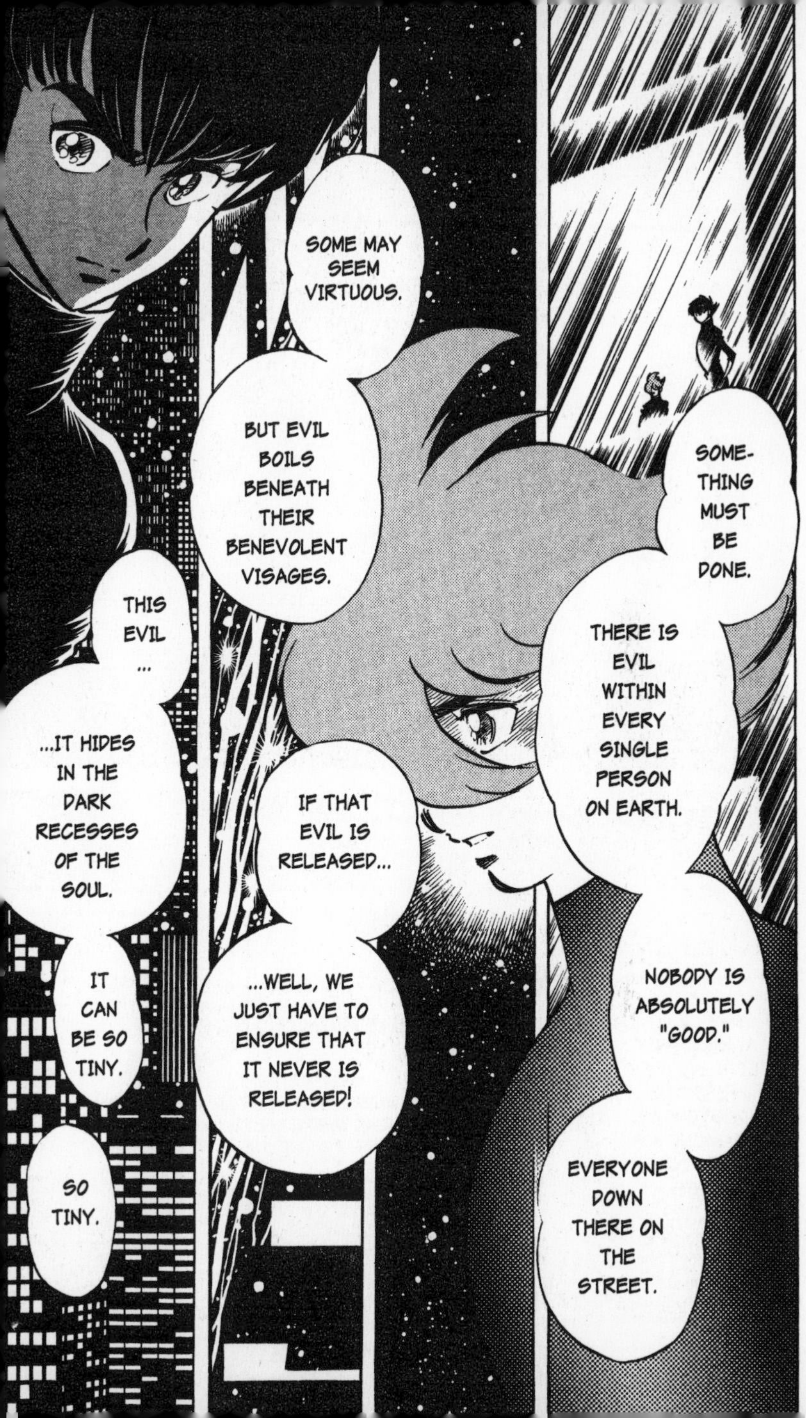
SOME-THING MUST BE DONE.
THERE IS EVIL WITHIN EVERY SINGLE PERSON ON EARTH.
NOBODY IS ABSOLUTELY "GOOD."
EVERYONE DOWN THERE ON THE STREET.
SOME MAY SEEM VIRTUOUS.
BUT EVIL BOILS BENEATH THEIR BENEVOLENT VISAGES.
IF THAT EVIL IS RELEASED...
...WELL, WE JUST HAVE TO ENSURE THAT IT NEVER IS RELEASED!
THIS EVIL ...
...IT HIDES IN THE DARK RECESSES OF THE SOUL.
IT CAN BE SO TINY.
SO TINY.

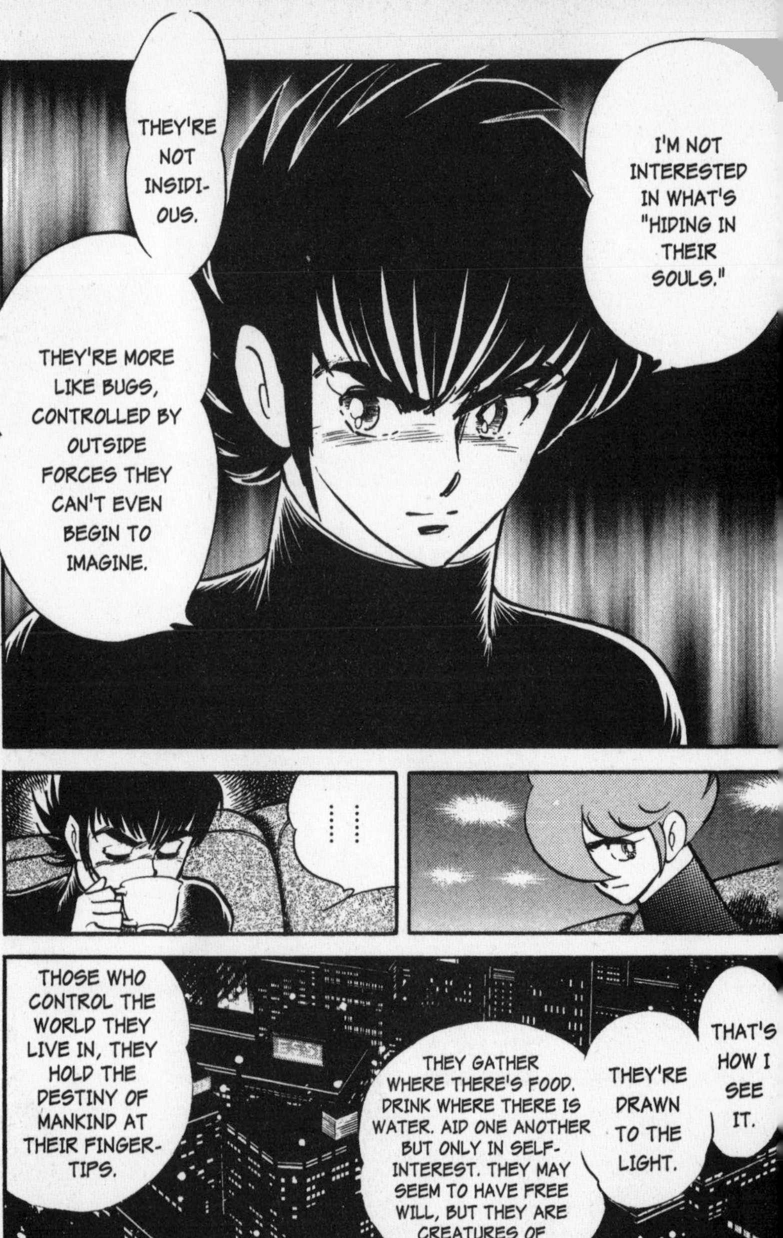
I'M NOT INTERESTED IN WHAT'S "HIDING IN THEIR SOULS."
THEY'RE NOT INSIDI-OUS.
THEY'RE MORE LIKE BUGS, CONTROLLED BY OUTSIDE FORCES THEY CAN'T EVEN BEGIN TO IMAGINE.
......
THAT'S HOW I SEE IT.
THEY'RE DRAWN TO THE LIGHT.
THEY GATHER WHERE THERE'S FOOD. DRINK WHERE THERE IS WATER. AID ONE ANOTHER BUT ONLY IN SELF-INTEREST. THEY MAY SEEM TO HAVE FREE WILL, BUT THEY ARE CREATURES OF INSTINCT.
THOSE WHO CONTROL THE WORLD THEY LIVE IN, THEY HOLD THE DESTINY OF MANKIND AT THEIR FINGER-TIPS.

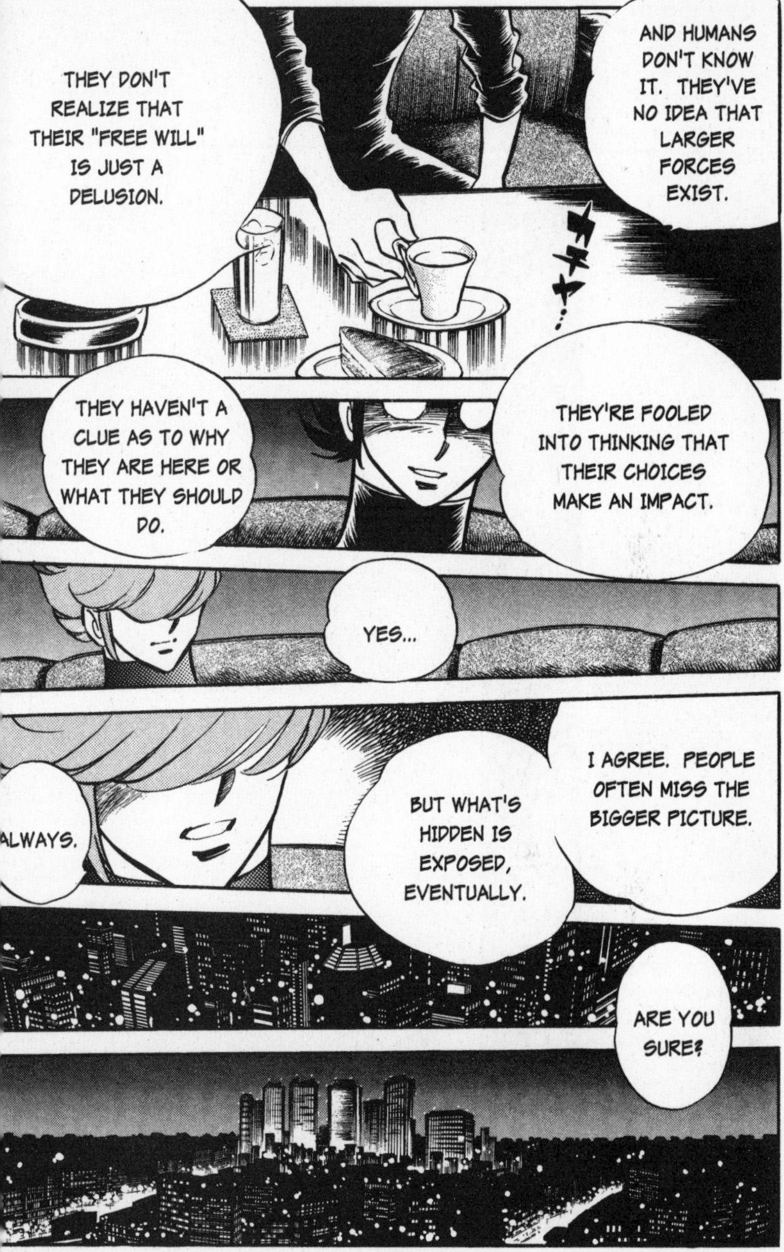
AND HUMANS DON'T KNOW IT. THEY'VE NO IDEA THAT LARGER FORCES EXIST.
THEY DON'T REALIZE THAT THEIR "FREE WILL" IS JUST A DELUSION.
THEY'RE FOOLED INTO THINKING THAT THEIR CHOICES MAKE AN IMPACT.
THEY HAVEN'T A CLUE AS TO WHY THEY ARE HERE OR WHAT THEY SHOULD DO.
YES...
I AGREE. PEOPLE OFTEN MISS THE BIGGER PICTURE.
BUT WHAT'S HIDDEN IS EXPOSED, EVENTUALLY.
ALWAYS.
ARE YOU SURE?

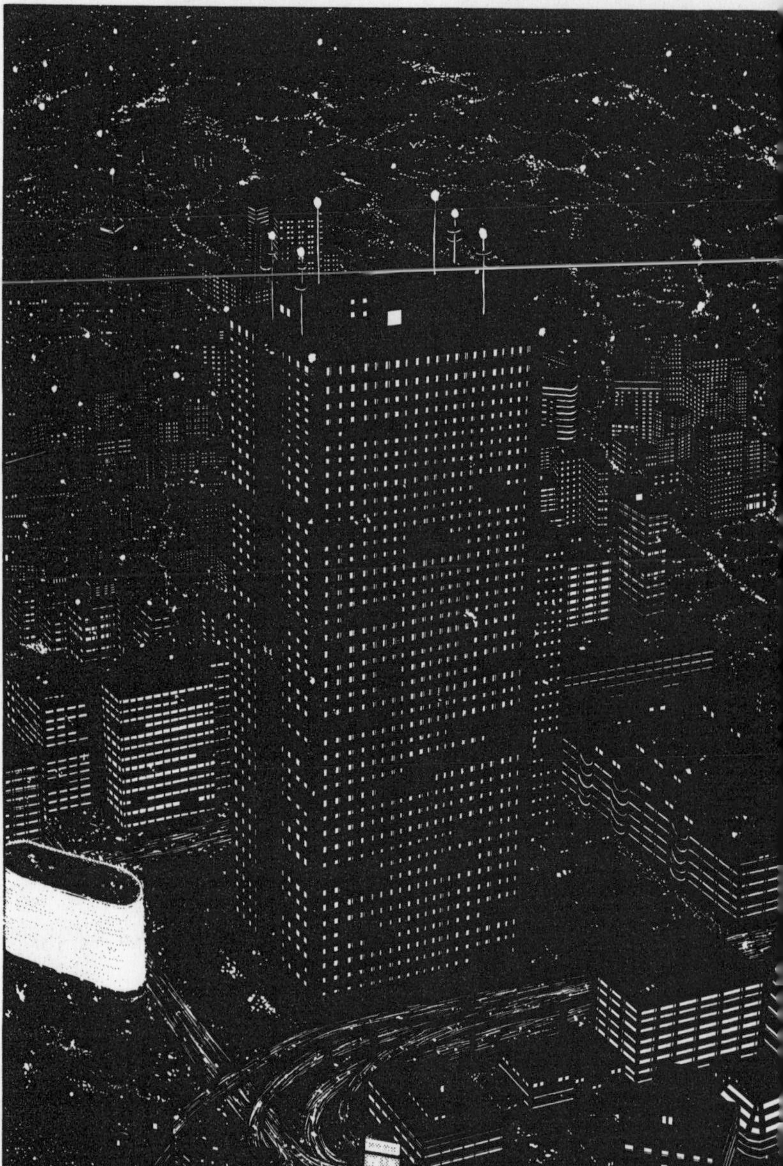

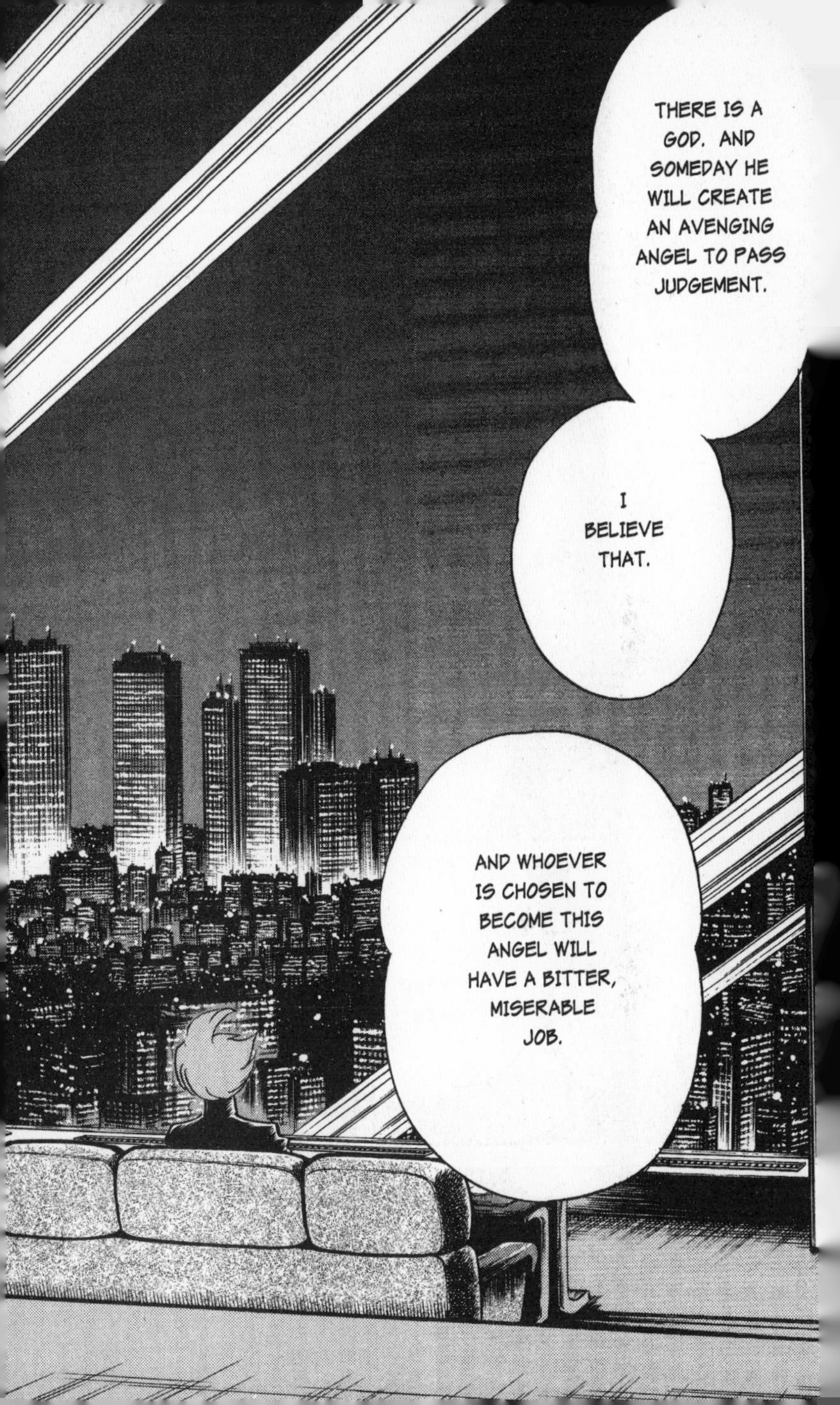
THERE IS A GOD. AND SOMEDAY HE WILL CREATE AN AVENGING ANGEL TO PASS JUDGEMENT.
I BELIEVE THAT.
AND WHOEVER IS CHOSEN TO BECOME THIS ANGEL WILL HAVE A BITTER, MISERABLE JOB.

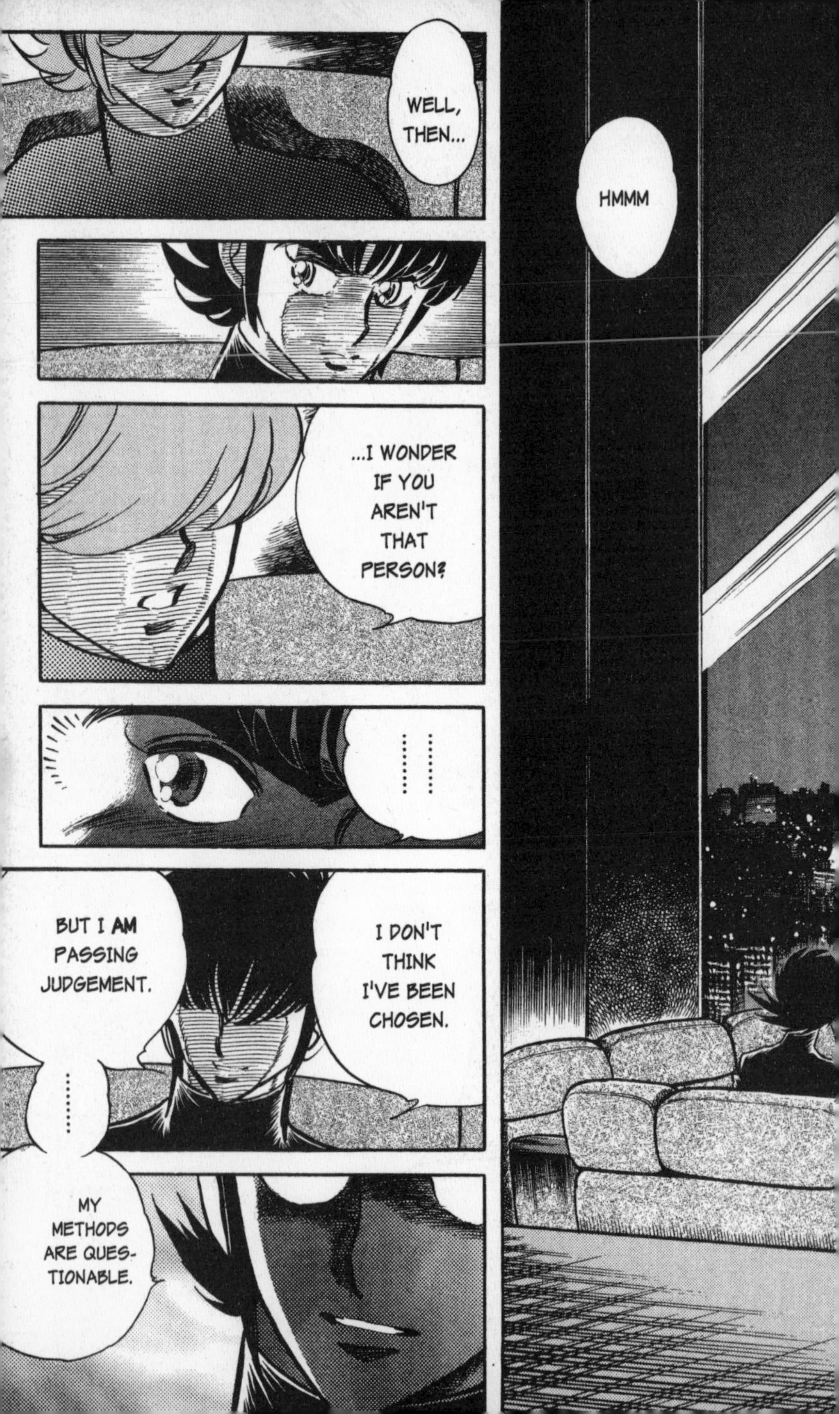
HMMM
WELL, THEN...
...I WONDER IF YOU AREN'T THAT PERSON?
......
I DON'T THINK I'VE BEEN CHOSEN.
BUT I AM PASSING JUDGEMENT.
......
MY METHODS ARE QUES-TIONABLE.

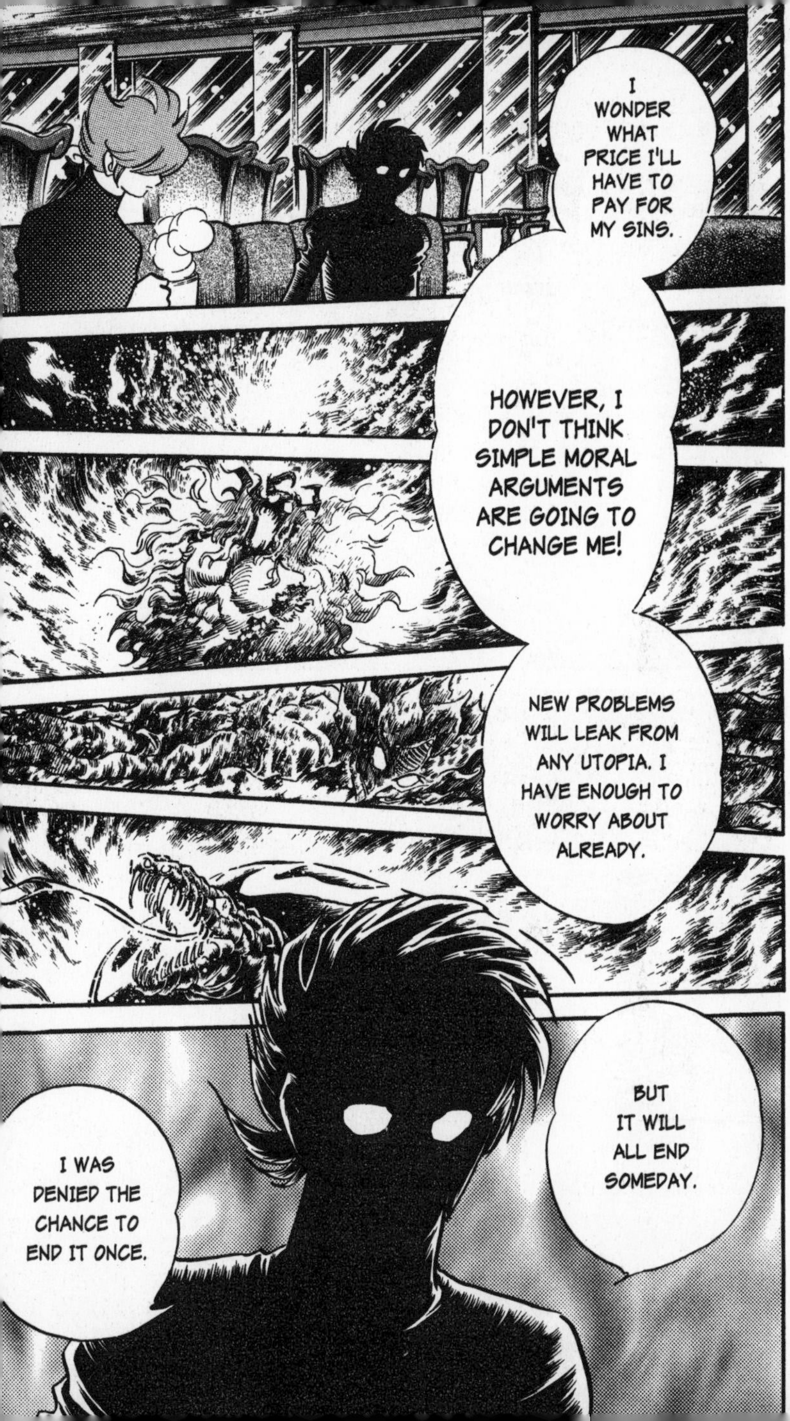
I WONDER WHAT PRICE I'LL HAVE TO PAY FOR MY SINS.
HOWEVER, I DON'T THINK SIMPLE MORAL ARGUMENTS ARE GOING TO CHANGE ME!
NEW PROBLEMS WILL LEAK FROM ANY UTOPIA. I HAVE ENOUGH TO WORRY ABOUT ALREADY.
BUT IT WILL ALL END SOMEDAY.
I WAS DENIED THE CHANCE TO END IT ONCE.

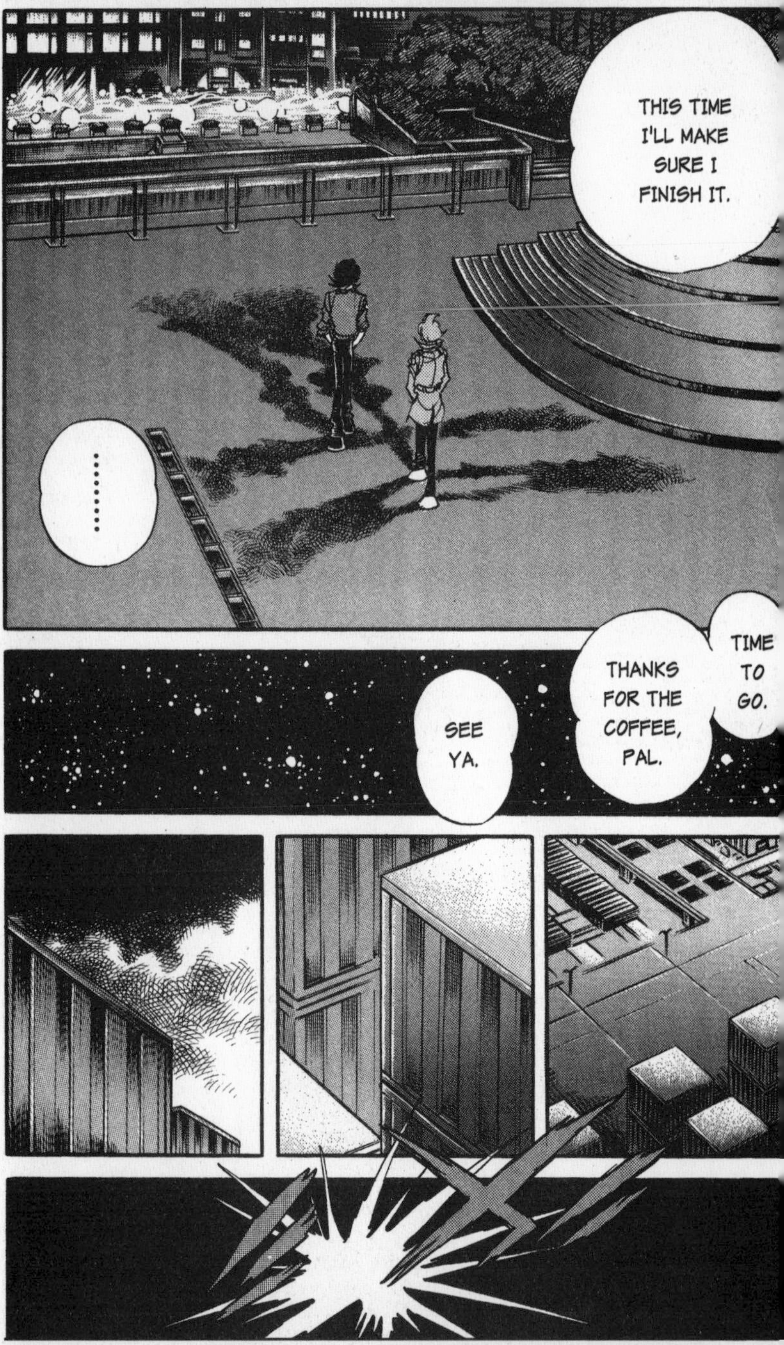
THIS TIME I'LL MAKE SURE I FINISH IT.
....
TIME TO GO.
THANKS FOR THE COFFEE, PAL.
SEE YA.

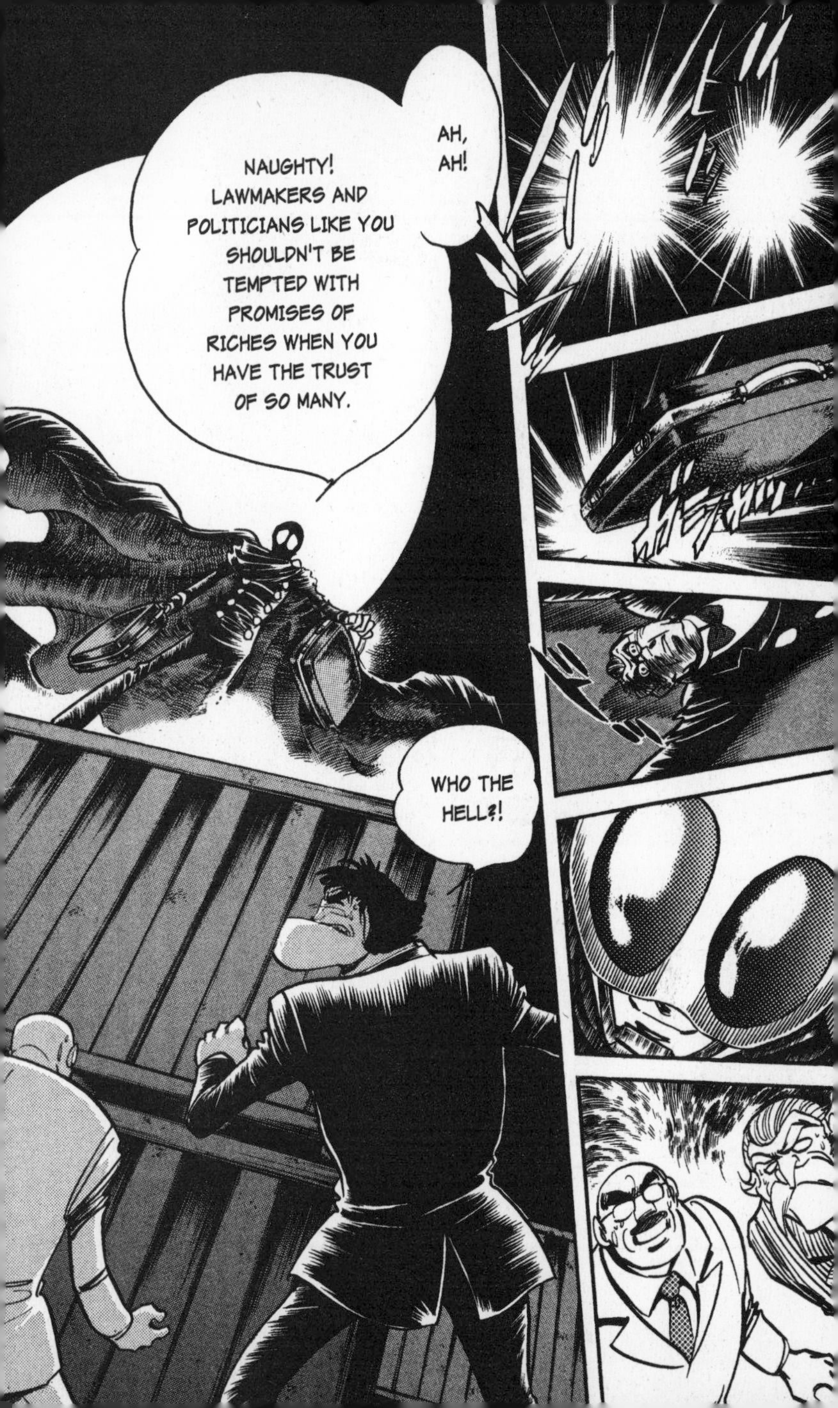
AH, AH!
NAUGHTY! LAWMAKERS AND POLITICIANS LIKE YOU SHOULDN'T BE TEMPTED WITH PROMISES OF RICHES WHEN YOU HAVE THE TRUST OF SO MANY.
WHO THE HELL?!

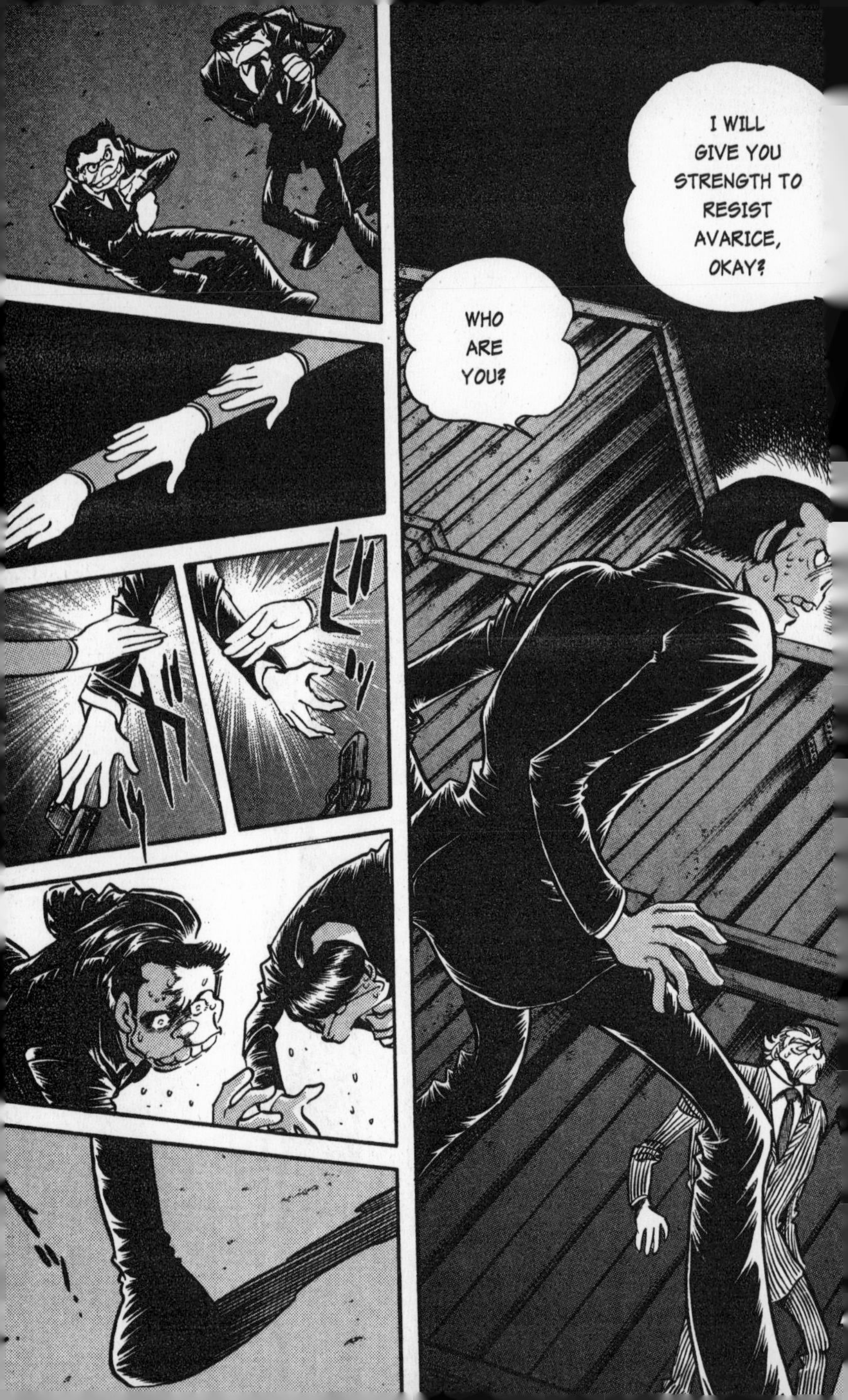
I WILL GIVE YOU STRENGTH TO RESIST AVARICE, OKAY?
WHO ARE YOU?

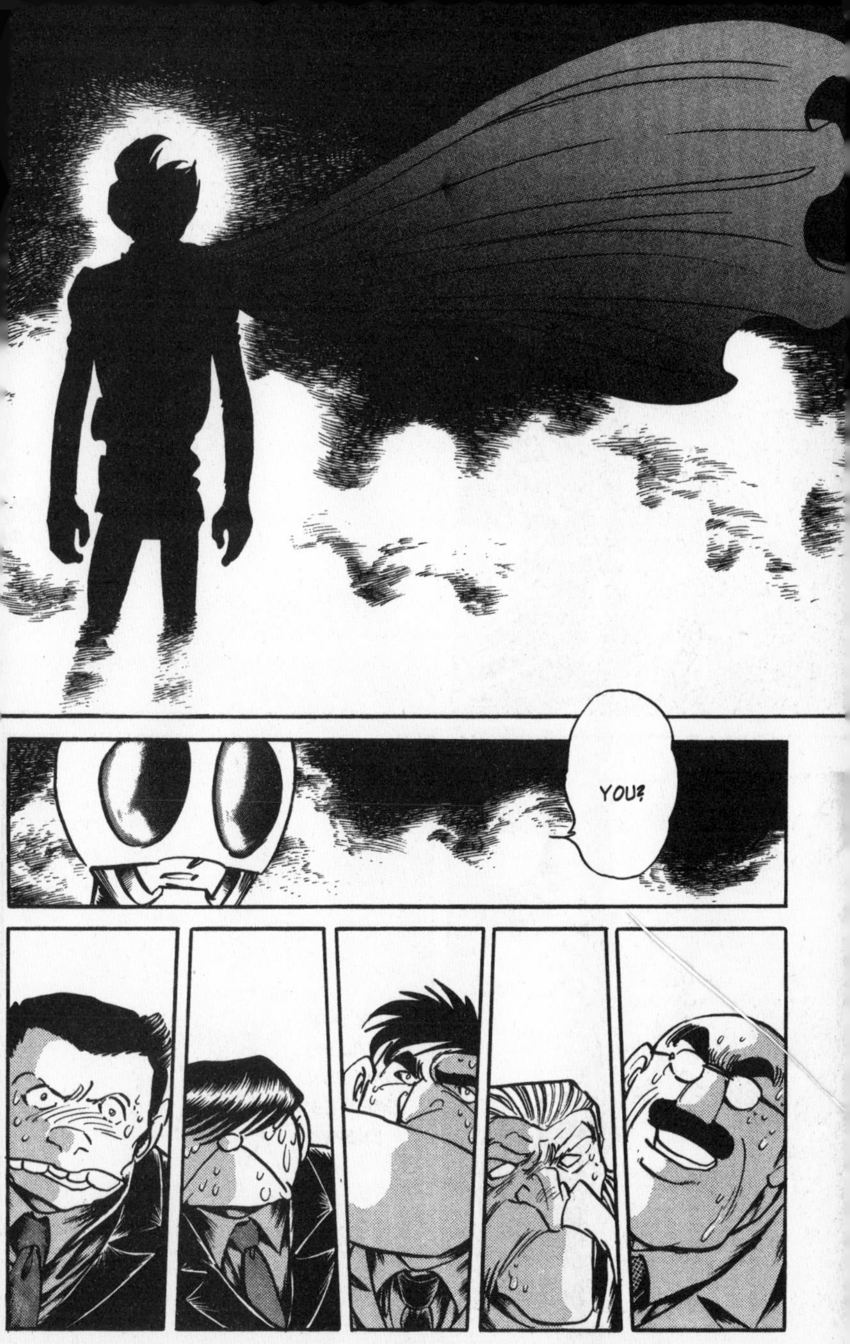
YOU?

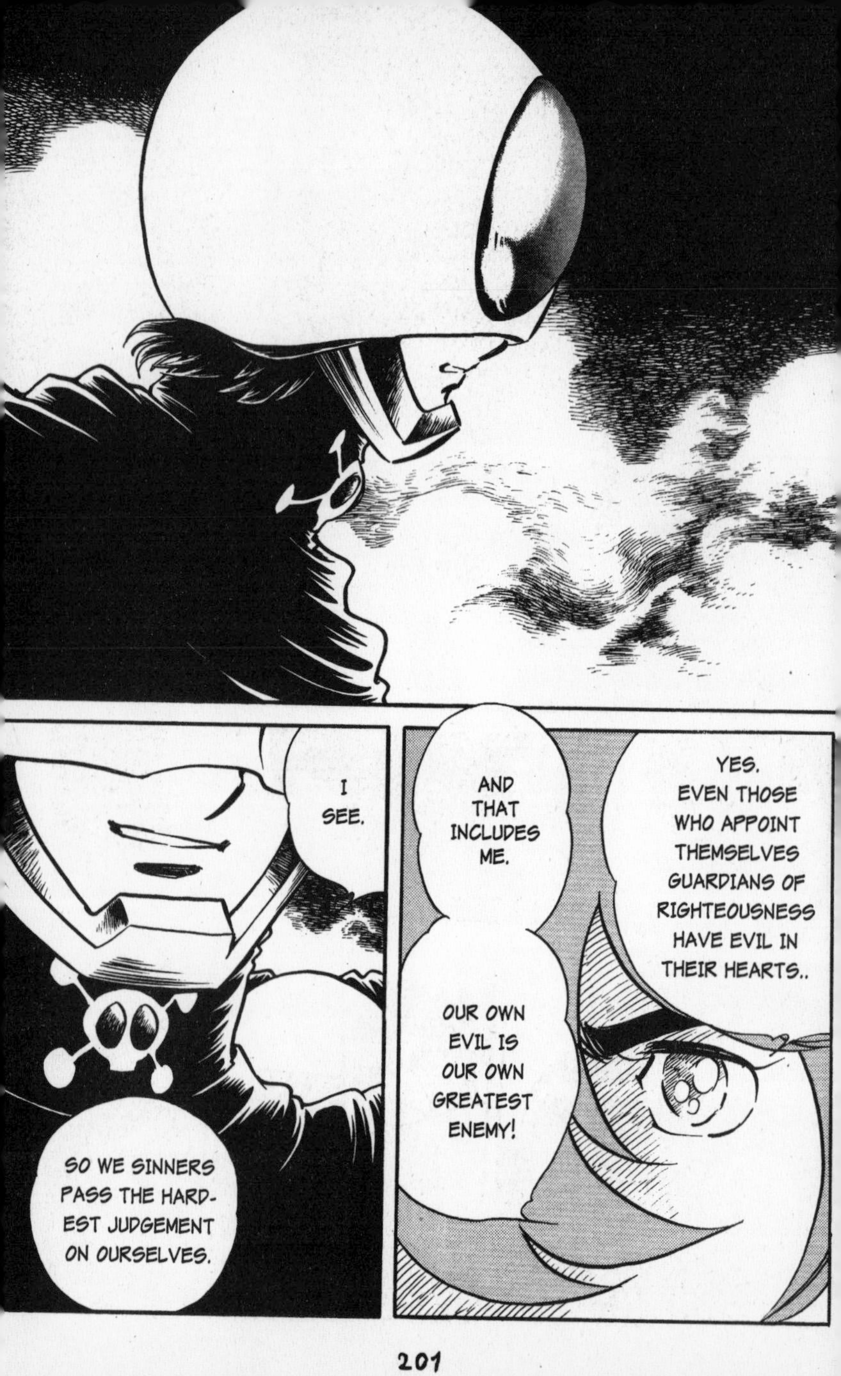
YES. EVEN THOSE WHO APPOINT THEMSELVES GUARDIANS OF RIGHTEOUSNESS HAVE EVIL IN THEIR HEARTS..
AND THAT INCLUDES ME.
OUR OWN EVIL IS OUR OWN GREATEST ENEMY!
I SEE.
SO WE SINNERS PASS THE HARD-EST JUDGEMENT ON OURSELVES.

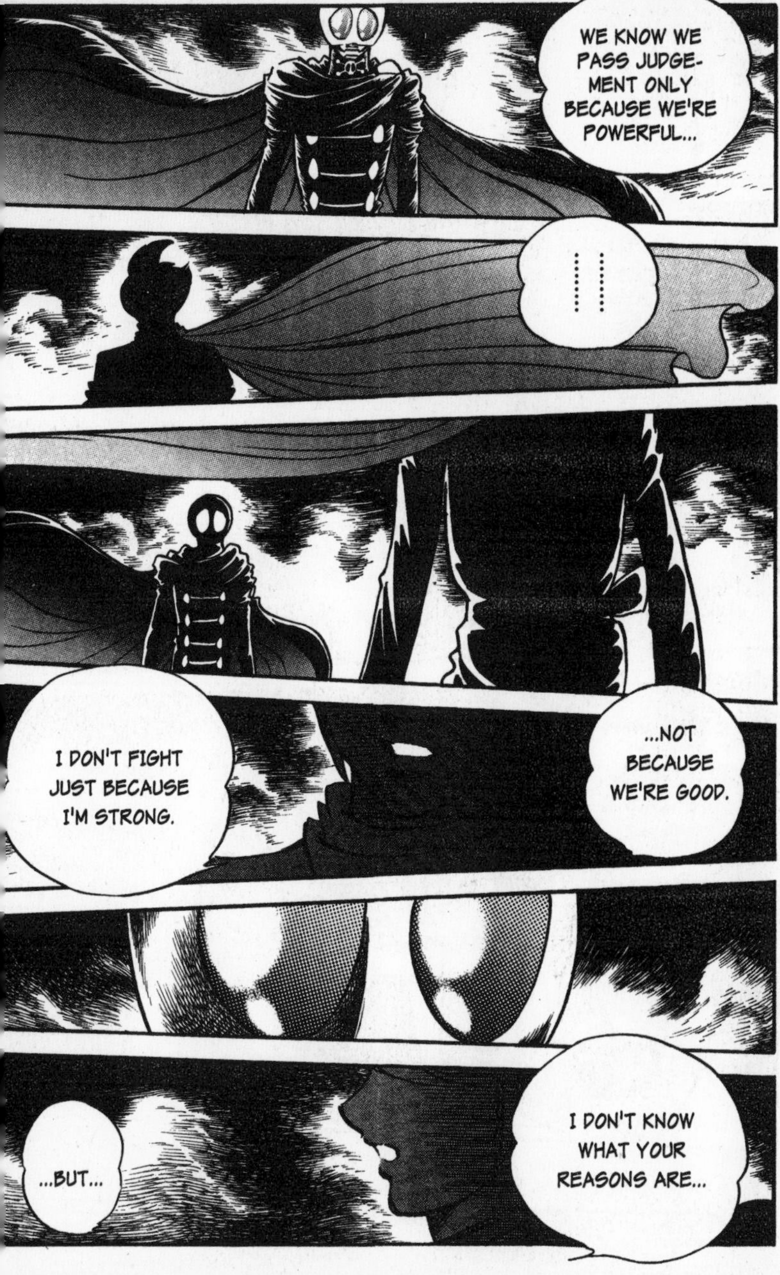
WE KNOW WE PASS JUDGEMENT ONLY BECAUSE WE'RE POWERFUL...
......
...NOT BECAUSE WE'RE GOOD.
I DON'T FIGHT JUST BECAUSE I'M STRONG.
I DON'T KNOW WHAT YOUR REASONS ARE...
...BUT...

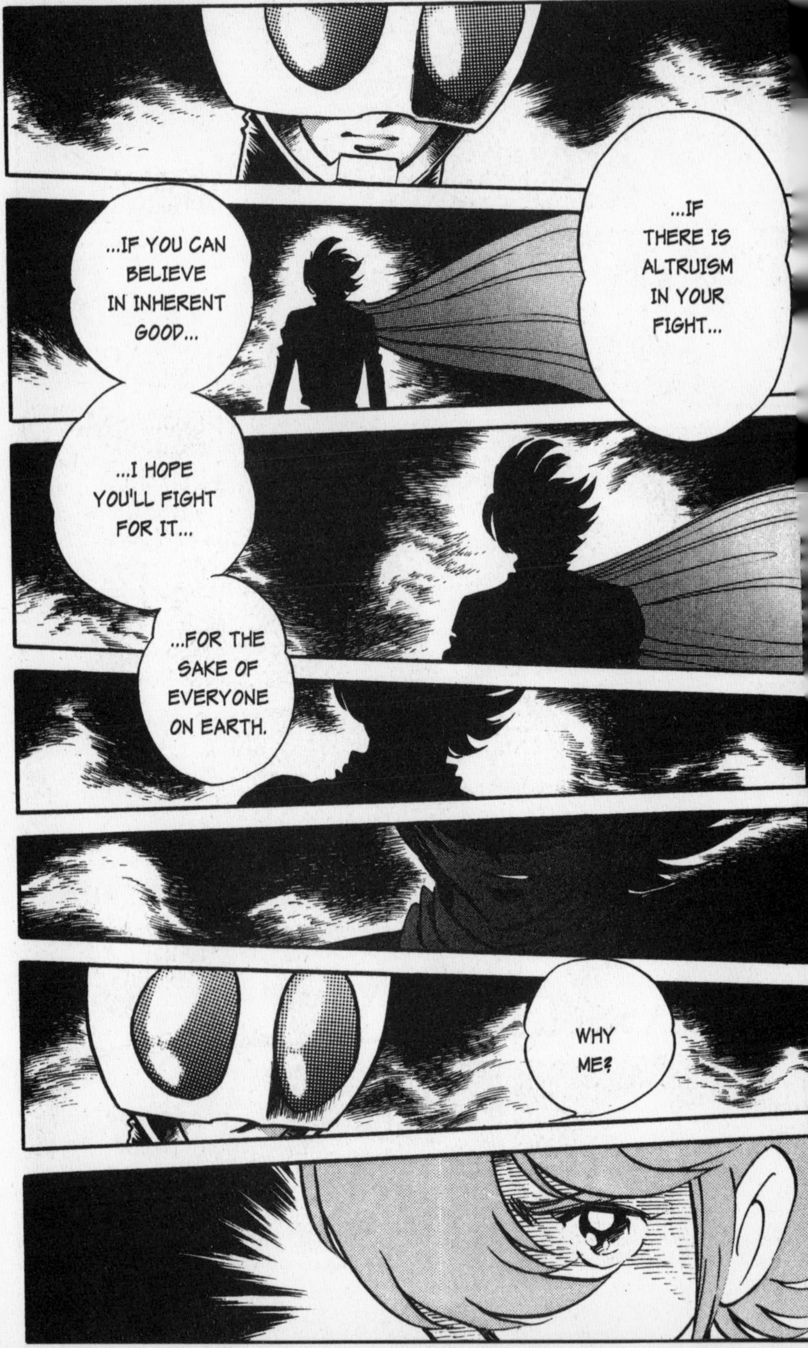
...IF THERE IS ALTRUISM IN YOUR FIGHT...
...IF YOU CAN BELIEVE IN INHERENT GOOD...
...I HOPE YOU'LL FIGHT FOR IT...
...FOR THE SAKE OF EVERYONE ON EARTH.
WHY ME?

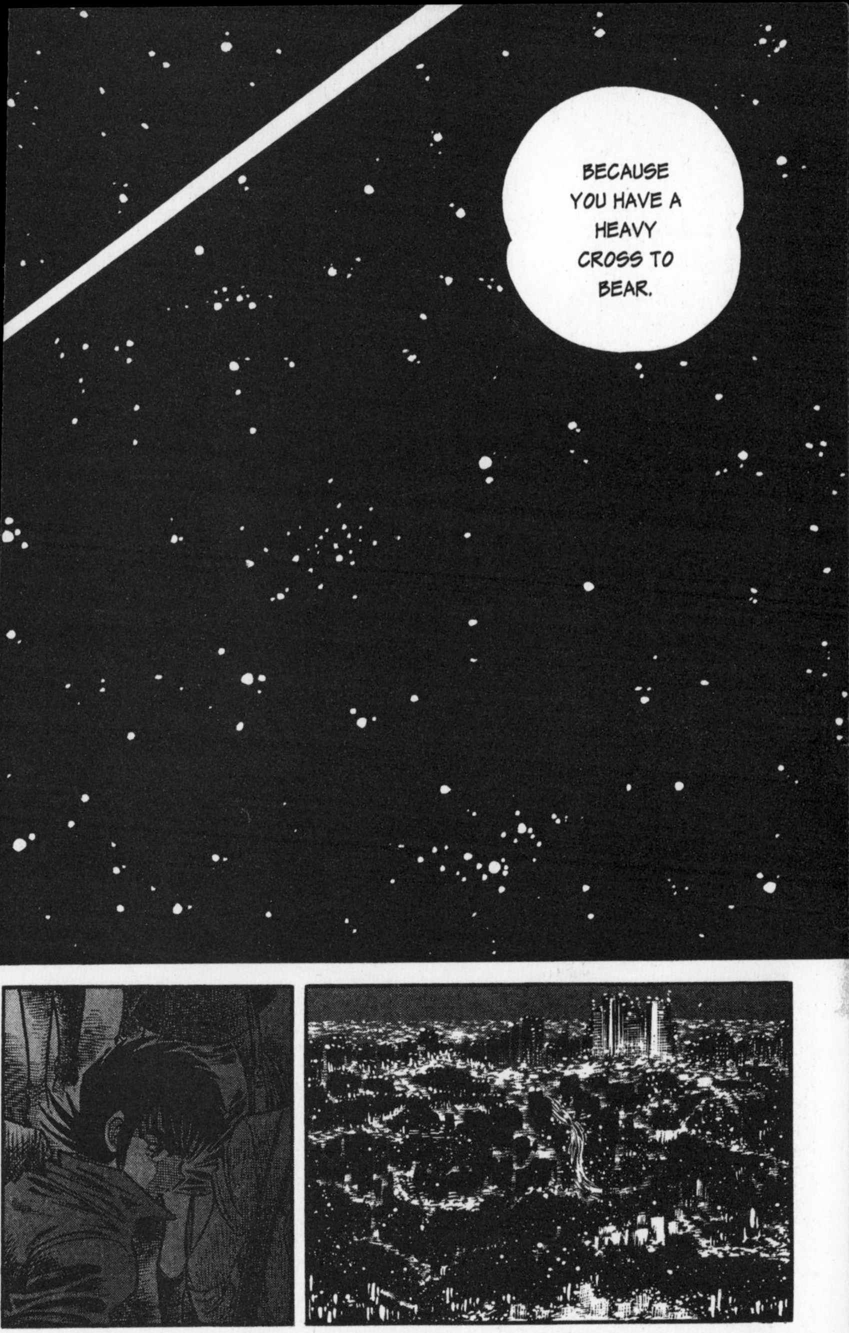
BECAUSE YOU HAVE A HEAVY CROSS TO BEAR.

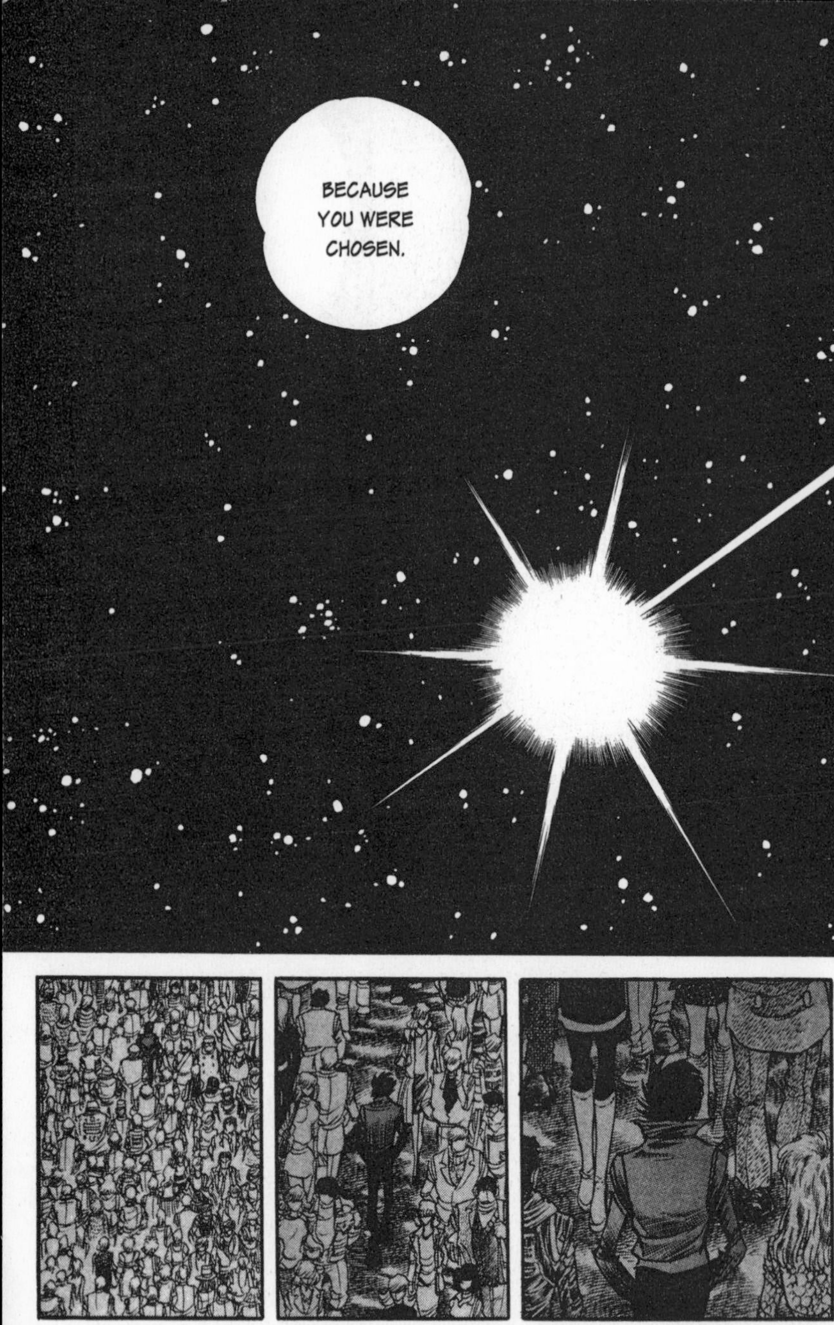
BECAUSE YOU WERE CHOSEN.

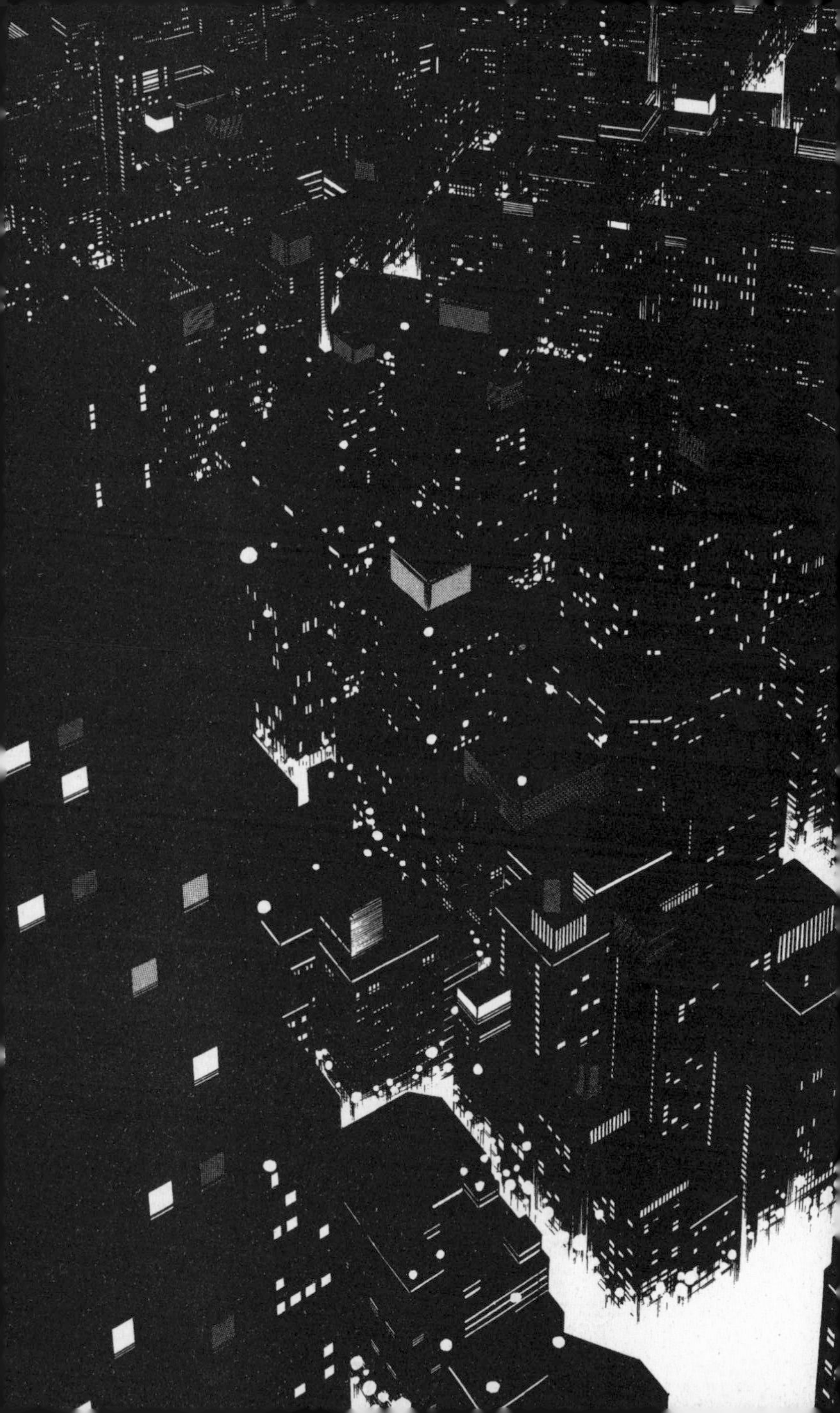

Preview for Skull Man
Volume 6

Despite losing the loyalty of the Wasp
and Chameleon armies, Rasputin, still
has the upper hand. He has captured
both Detective Hioka, a man still dis-
trustful of the Skull Man, and Maria,
the agent who has rebelled against his
organization, and taken them to an
undersea fortress. There he attempts
to turn Hioka into a warrior-slave and
forces Maria to reveal the Skull Man's
secrets. Only their true moral character can save them, but what might
Rasputin's efforts reveal about their
true moral character? Back in Tokyo,
the Skull Man faces yet another of
Rasputin's mutagenic flock, the Vulture
Man.

STOP!

This is the back of the book.
You wouldn't want to spoil a great ending!

This book is printed "manga-style," in the authentic Japanese right-to-left format. Since none of the artwork has been flipped or altered, readers get to experience the story just as the creator intended. You've been asking for it, so TOKYOPOP® delivered: authentic, hot-off-the-press, and far more fun!

DIRECTIONS

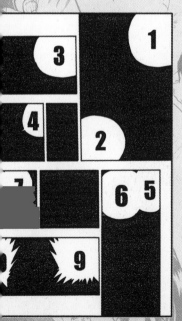

If this is your first time reading manga-style, here's a quick guide to help you understand how it works.

It's easy... just start in the top right panel and follow the numbers. Have fun, and look for more 100% authentic manga from TOKYOPOP®!

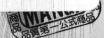

D1203039